Pubs and Inns Guide 2005
The Road to Good Food

Les Routiers is an association of mainly owner-managed establishements. However, membership is not automatic. Many applications are refused because every establishment displaying Les Routiers' symbol must satisfy our rigorous quality criteria.
All opinions included in the Guide entries are based upon the findings of external assessors.

Published 2004 by:
Routiers Limited
190 Earl's Court Road
London SW5 9QG
Tel: 020 7370 5113
Fax: 020 7370 4528
E-mail: info@routiers.co.uk

Book trade distribution:
Portfolio Books Ltd
Unit 5, Perivale Industrial Park
Horsenden Lane South
Greenford, Middlesex
UB6 7RL

ISBN 0-900057-20-3
Copyright © 2004 Routiers Limited

Maps © Routiers Limited 2004
Great Britain Digital Database and
Greater London Digital Data
© Cosmographics Limited.
Maps designed and produced by Cosmographics.
Reproduced by kind permission of Ordnance
Survey. Crown Copyright NC/01/365".
Including mapping content © Automobile
Association Developments Limited 2001 and
© Bartholomew Digital Database.
Greater London Map based on information
derived from satellite imagery and an original
ground survey by Cosmographics. Satellite data
provided by USGS and Infoterra Ltd.

British Library Cataloguing in Publication Data.
A catalogue record for this book is available from
the British Library.

Editor:
David Hancock
Production and Design Editor:
Holly Hall
Design:
Oliver Carter

Editorial Contributors:
Ted Bruning
Alex Chambers
Nicholas Stanley

Location Photographers:
Annie Hanson
Rebecca Harris
Nicholas Stanley
www.britainonview.com

Pub Walks
Chris Bagshaw
Nick Channer
Neil Coates
David Hancock

Maps:
Cosmographics Limited, Watford

Printed in Great Britain by:
London Print and Design plc,
Warwick

Thanks to:
Elgood's Brewery, Wisbech

For Les Routiers:
Director:
Nicholas Stanley
Operations Director:
Imogen Clist
Marketing Manager:
Victoria Borrows

www.routiers.co.uk

The King and I

Les Routiers
Pubs and Inns Guide 2005

Contents

How to Use this Guide	page 6
Les Routiers Awards 2005	page 10
Coast-to-Coast Walk	page 18
Brewing Process	page 28
London	page 34
England	page 46
Scotland	page 226
Wales	page 246

Food Maps

Alma Tavern, London SW18	page 40
Ivy House, Chalfont St Giles, Buckinghamshire	page 54
Brackenrigg Inn, Ullswater, Cumbria	page 80
Bell at Sapperton, Sapperton, Gloucestershire	page 100
Wyndham Arms, Clearwell, Gloucestershire	page 104
The Cabinet, Reed, Hertfordshire	page 118
White Horse Inn, Bridge, Kent	page 124
Red Lion, Stodmarsh, Kent	page 128
Red Cat, St Helens, Merseyside	page 136
Red Lion, Strathern, Leicestershire	page 140
Lord Nelson, Burnham Thorpe, Norfolk	page 144
Kings Head Inn, Bledington, Oxfordshire	page 158
Crooked Billet, Stoke Row, Oxfordshire	page 168
Holly Bush, Stafford, Staffordshire	page 178
Ship Inn, Ipswich, Suffolk	page 186
Fountain Inn, Tenbury Wells, Worcestershire	page 206
Friars Head at Akebar, Leyburn, North Yorkshire	page 214
Appletree Country Inn, Marton, North Yorkshire	page 220
Unicorn Inn, Kincardine, Fife	page 234
Plockton Hotel, Plockton, Highland	page 240
Greyhound Inn, Usk, Powys	page 254
Felin Fach Griffin, Brecon, Powys	page 260

Pub Walks

Five Arrows Hotel, Waddesdon, Buckinghamshire — page 266
Pheasant Inn, Chester, Cheshire — page 268
Oddfellows Arms, Mellor, Cheshire — page 270
Rose and Crown, Romaldkirk, Co. Durham — page 272
Dukes Head, Armathwaite, Cumbria — page 274
Burnmoor Inn, Eskdale, Cumbria — page 276
Red Lion Inn, Ashbourne, Derbyshire — page 278
Fox Inn, Corscombe, Dorset — page 280
Plough at Kelmscott, Kelmscott, Gloucestershire — page 282
White Hart Inn, Winchcombe, Gloucestershire — page 284
Wykeham Arms, Winchester, Hampshire — page 286
Stagg Inn, Titley, Herefordshire — page 288
Alford Arms, Frithsden, Hertfordshire — page 290
Inn at Whitewell, Whitewell, Lancashire — page 292
Victoria at Holkham, Holkham, Norfolk — page 294
Walpole Arms, Itteringham, Norfolk — page 296
Pheasant Inn, Kielder Water, Northumberland — page 298
Martins Arms, Colston Bassett, Nottinghamshire — page 300
Bull Inn, Charlbury, Oxfordshire — page 302
Perch & Pike Inn, South Stoke, Oxfordshire — page 304
Old White Hart Inn, Lyddington, Rutland — page 306
The Crown, Exford, Somerset — page 308
Crown and Castle, Orford, Suffolk — page 310
White Swan, Pickering, North Yorkshire — page 312
Clachaig Inn, Glencoe, Highland — page 314
Bell at Skenfrith, Skenfrith, Monmouthshire — page 316

Maps — page 319
A-Z Index — page 333
Report Forms — page 339
Wine Vouchers — page 347

How to use this Guide

Finding an establishment

Les Routiers Pubs and Inns Guide 2005 is sectioned into London, England, Scotland and Wales. London is ordered alphabetically into Central, East, North, South and West. The countries are listed alphabetically by county, listing town and then establishment name. There are four ways to track down an establishment or establishments.

1. If you are seeking a place in a particular area, first go to the maps at the back of the book. County boundaries are marked in lilac and each establishment has a relevant marker alongside their listing town shown in bold. Once you know the locality, go to the relevant section in the book to find the entry for the pub or inn.

2. Page borders are colour coded for each country and also have the appropriate county at the top of each page so you can flick through the book and find the correct area with ease.

3. Turn to the index on page 333 where both establishment names and listing towns appear in alphabetical order.

4. To find a country turn to contents on page 4.

How to read a guide entry

A sample entry is set out on the facing page. At the top of the entry you will find the establishment's name, address, and telephone number and, if it has them, an e-mail and website address. Also, any symbols that may apply to the establishment; an explanation of what these symbols stand for appears beside the sample entry. The middle part of the entry describes accommodation, atmosphere, food, wines and so on, while the final section gives additional statistical information and the map reference number.

Miscellaneous information

Disabled: As disabilities (and needs) vary considerably, Les Routiers has taken the decision not to note whether a place is suitable for the disabled. A more satisfactory course for all concerned is to telephone the hotel or restaurant of your choice and discuss your needs with the manager or proprietor.

Vegetarians: Most restaurants now offer some vegetarian choice. Where there is greater imaginative choice, or none at all, it is mentioned in the main body of the entry.

Listing Town and County: Because many of our establishments are in the countryside, their Listing Towns may be a town several miles away. If you are unsure of the county look the town up in the index and it will refer you to the correct page.

Telephone: Two numbers are included here, an 0870 number and normal telephone number, both reach the same destination. We encourage you to use the first 0870 number charged at national rate.

Numbers include the international code for dialling the UK from abroad. To dial from within the UK start the number with the 0 in brackets (0); from outside the UK dial all numbers except the 0 in brackets (0).

Last orders: Times to order by are given for the bar and food where applicable. For each a lunch and dinner last order is given. Where there is only an evening time given, the establishment serves throughout the day.

Closed: Where 'Never' is stated the establishment is open throughout the year. Where 'Rarely' is stated the establishment is open throughout the year bar important holidays (Christmas, New Year). Otherwise dates and days closed are stated.

Other Points:
Credit cards - Very few places fail to take credit cards; those that don't are stated here.

Children - Although we indicate whether children are welcome in the establishment, we do not list facilities for guests with babies; we advise telephoning beforehand to sort out any particular requirements.

Dogs - It is specified whether dogs are allowed in the public bar and/or overnight accommodation of the establishment. However, please mention this when booking.

Listing Town

Name

Address
Telephone: +44(0)870 000000
+44(0)1888 000000
excellentpub@hotmail.com

This quirky 15th-century pub stands on a narrow country road in a sleepy village.........

Rooms: **3, not en suite. Double room from £60.**
Prices: **Bar main course from £9.95.**
House wine £10.95.
Last orders: **Bar 23.00. Food: lunch 14.00; dinner 21.30.**
Closed: **Rarely.**
Food: **Traditional British using local produce.**
Real Ale: **Greene King Old Speckled Hen, Abbot Ale & IPA.**
Other points: **Children welcome. Dogs welcome in the bar. Garden. Car park.**
Directions: **A257 east from Canterbury, follow signs left to Stodmarsh. (Map 6, C7)**

Directions: These have been supplied by the proprietor of the establishment. The map reference at the end refers to the map section at the back of the Guide.

Symbols:

◈ Accommodation
▶ Range of Real Ale
▮ Set Menu
★ Award Winner 2003
☆ Award Winner 2004
▼ Free glass of wine

(turn to page 347)

We do not have a food or good wine symbol as it is part of our requirements for membership that all Les Routiers establishments serve good food and wine at reasonable prices.

Rooms: For establishments offering overnight accommodation the number of rooms is given, along with the lowest price for a double and single room. Where this price is per person it is indicated. Prices usually include breakfast. Where the price includes bed, breakfast and dinner it is indicated.

Prices: Set meals usually consist of three courses but can include more. If a set meal has fewer or more than three courses, this is stated. Where no set lunch or dinner is offered, we give the price of the cheapest main course on the menu. House wine prices are by the bottle. Prices are meant as a guideline to the cost of a meal only. All prices include Value Added Tax (VAT).

About the Guide

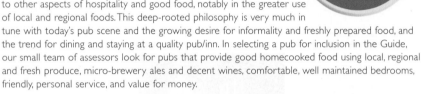

Since it was first seen in Paris in 1935, the distinctive blue-and-red Les Routiers sign has traditionally identified hotels and restaurants of individual character, often managed by the owner, offering good food, warm hospitality and excellent value for money. These continue to be our guiding principles but we are now also strongly committed to other aspects of hospitality and good food, notably in the greater use of local and regional foods. This deep-rooted philosophy is very much in tune with today's pub scene and the growing desire for informality and freshly prepared food, and the trend for dining and staying at a quality pub/inn. In selecting a pub for inclusion in the Guide, our small team of assessors look for pubs that provide good homecooked food using local, regional and fresh produce, micro-brewery ales and decent wines, comfortable, well maintained bedrooms, friendly, personal service, and value for money.

Local Foods

Within these pages some of England's top gastropubs rub shoulders with traditional country locals and upmarket inns, the principle factor linking them all being a passion for sourcing and utilising fresh local produce. New for this edition are 22 Food Maps which identify our 'Champions of Local Foods' and highlight how 'local' their key suppliers are, be it a micro-brewery, a farm rearing rare breed pigs or growing first-class asparagus, a smallholding that delivers organic fruits and vegetables to the pub door, or a local fishing boat that lands fresh fish and crab along the quay.

Making Beer

In our headline feature 'Brewing Process', Ted Bruning, editor of What's Brewing, the national newspaper of the Campaign for Real Ale, guides us through the complex process of brewing beer. Winemakers have it easy, Ted informs us, so find out why and learn more about the malts and hops and the role of yeast in producing the huge range of cask conditioned beers by Britain's 400-plus brewers.

Country Escapes

An increasing number of pubs and inns now successfully combine a relaxing, informal atmosphere with good food and smart en suite accommodation. They provide the discerning pub-goer with a quality alternative to a budget Travel Inn or a large, impersonal and often pricey country hotel. Perfect for a long weekend, or a mid-week break in the country, 25 of our top inns feature on a full-page entry. To aid your rest and relaxation we have included useful information on where to shop, local sporting activities and the top attractions to visit in the area.

Pubs and Walking

To the walker, beer, pubs and beautiful countryside go hand in hand, providing the essential ingredients for a great day's ramble. Few things in life are as pleasurable as running a finger along the red dotted line of a map until it arrives at those magical initials, PH, in search of your lunchtime refuelling stop or a cosy refuge at the end of your walk. Having stimulated a healthy appetite and a parched throat, the sight of a welcoming country pub will quicken the steps of even the weariest of walking legs. Our Pub Walks pages feature 12 new exciting walks across the country. Most start from the front door of cosy inns with comfortable accommodation, so take your walking boots with you for the weekend and explore the surrounding countryside. More adventurous walkers should read our headline feature, Coast-to-Coast, which traces Nicholas Stanley's, Les Routiers Director, epic 11-day walk from St Bee's Head in Cumbria to Robin Hood's Bay in North Yorkshire.

Les Routiers
Pubs and Inns Awards 2004

Les Routiers pubs and Inns have been carefully selected for their warmth of welcome, quality of food and accommodation, and value for money. Les Routiers Awards are given to those establishments who surpass these high entry standards and excel in one of the following categories.

Inn of the Year 2004

Here we highlight some of Britain's great inns - the country's new breed of country hotels and restaurants. Our winners successfully combine a relaxing, informal atmosphere with superlative food, genuine warm hospitality, individuality and comfortable accommodation.

Regional Winners

London and South East - The Royal Oak, Chichester, West Sussex
South West - Wild Duck Inn, Cirencester, Gloucestershire
Central and East Anglia - The Cricketers, Clavering, Essex
The North - Nags Head Inn, Pickhill, North Yorkshire
Scotland - Loch Tummel Inn, Pitlochry, Perthshire
Wales and the Welsh Borders - Bell at Skenfrith, Monmouthshire

National Winner

Bell at Skenfrith, Monmouthshire

Dining Pub of the Year 2004

In recent years we have seen welcome improvements in the style and quality of pub food. Innovation, imagination and use of local, regional and fresh produce are the key ingredients in judging this award. All our winners offer first-class modern British cooking.

Regional Winners

London and South East - Red Lion, Stodmarsh, Kent
South West - White Horse, Frampton Mansell, Gloucestershire
Central and East Anglia - Holly Bush, Salt, Staffordshire
The North - The Highland Drove Inn, Penrith, Cumbria
Scotland - Royal Hotel, Comrie, Perth and Kinross
Wales and the Welsh Borders - Hundred House Hotel, Telford, Shropshire

National Winner

White Horse, Frampton Mansell, Gloucestershire

Real Ale Pub of the Year 2004

This award applauds those enthusiastic, even fanatical, landlords whose passion for beer extends beyond their quest to offer a tip-top pint at every pull to only featuring local micro and regional brewery beers.

Regional Winners

London and South East - The Duke of Cumberland, Midhurst, West Sussex
South West - Tower Inn, Slapton, Devon
Central and East Anglia - The Wig and Pen, Norwich, Norfolk
The North - Wasdale Head Inn, Wasdale, Cumbria
Scotland - The Clachaig Inn, Glencoe, Highland
Wales and the Welsh Borders - The Fountain Inn, Tenbury Wells, Worcestershire

National Winner

The Clachaig Inn, Glencoe, Highland

Wine Pub of the Year 2004

For this award we look for passion and enthusiasm for wine, well chosen wine lists, value for money and an exceptional range of quality wines by the glass.

Regional Winners

London and South East - Five Arrows Hotel, Waddesdon, Buckinghamshire
South West - Vine Tree, Norton, Wiltshire
Central and East Anglia - The Crown, Southwold, Suffolk
The North - The Crown, Great Ouseburn, North Yorkshire
Scotland - Inn at Lathones, St Andrews, Fife

National Winner

The Crown, Southwold, Suffolk

'Locally Produced Food Supporters' Award 2004

Pubs winning this award are true champions of local produce, run by food-loving chefs or landlords who go out of their way to source, use and promote first-class food and drink from select suppliers in their immediate area.

Why do they do it? It brings things closer to you, fresher and better flavours, supports the community, gives an identity and makes a good reason for visitors to come to appreciate the local characteristic 'gout de terroir' which the French understand - cuts down on transport and promotes local crop and livestock breeds.

Regional Winners

London and South East - The Cabinet, Reed, Hertfordshire
South West - The Tradesmans Arms, Stokenham, Devon
Central and East Anglia - The Kings Head Inn, Bledington, Oxfordshire
The North - The Appletree Country Inn, Marton, North Yorkshire
Scotland - The Plockton Hotel, Plockton, Highland
Wales and the Welsh Borders - The Felin Fach Griffin, Brecon, Powys

COAST-TO-COAST
WALK

*England's Coast-to-Coast Walk -
192 Miles of some of the finest scenery
in Britain; wonderful local foods; the
warmest hospitality - and very sore feet!
Les Routiers Director Nicholas Stanley tells
the tale of 11 days on the trail - and he
took the photos too!*

Galvanised by Steve Madden, owner of award-winning
Routiers member Shepherds Arms at Ennerdale Bridge in
Cumbria, I set off on a glorious September morning, from
St Bees Head on the Cumbrian coast to walk the 192
miles, across three of Britain's most beautiful National Parks
(Lake District, Yorkshire Dales, Yorkshire Moors), to the
equally majestic cliffs of Robin Hood's Bay on the Yorkshire
coast.

Buoyed up by bright morning sunshine, the sea breeze and
'Day One' enthusiasm, I set off across the Cumbrian beach
towards the cliffs and St Bees Head lighthouse. An hour
later, and hundreds of steep wooden steps on, I had had
my first taste of what was in store! My 40lb rucksack was
rapidly becoming very heavy.

Fortified with the best of local Cumbrian home cooking
and local foods; and restored by some of the warmest
hospitality from B&B's and excellent Routiers member Inns
(the Shepherds Arms and Seatoller House were high spots
in the Lake District) - I spent the next three momentous
days, crossing the Lake District, clambering up fells, along
lake sides, clinging all the while to Alfred Wainwright's
meticulously precise route maps, and enjoying the most
dramatic scenery I've ever walked though in the British
Isles - all miraculously bathed in late September sunshine.

It is with a mixture of relief and regret that, after three days, you finally leave the stunning scenery of the Lake District behind and move onto the flatter, but still very scenic rolling hills that lead you towards Shap and the route across the Yorkshire Dales. After a long day's walk, and nursing very sore feet, it took no time at all to accept Paul Bonsall's kind offer of a lift in his car to take me to and from the approved route to his lovely Fat Lamb Inn. Local beer, a nice wine list, simple food done brilliantly, and the warmest welcome was the best restorative anybody could wish for.

Back to the trail and the halfway point creeps enticingly within reach. Up onto the Pennines, past the celebrated Nine Standards (ancient standing stones) and on towards the pretty stone-built villages of Thwaite and Keld. Then across some of the most beautiful moorland in the British Isles and (only yards away from this trail) past the tweed-suited guns and labradors intent on their rising quarry of grouse on the world famous moors of Gunnerside and Reeth. A first-rate pint of local beer at the Charles Bathurst Inn marked the end of an afternoon walking through pretty Swaledale, with its enchanting waterfalls. The attractive market village of Reeth offers fine food and the best of simpler local food, and boasts one of the nicest small family-owned hotels I have stayed in a long time (The Arkleside).

A short day's walk to the Georgian market town of Richmond gave me the opportunity to stay with friend and distinguished Yorkshire wine merchant Simon Wrightson, where I was spoilt with locally shot grouse; fine wine from my host's cellar; freshly washed clothes; and Mr. Fortune's Whitby kippers for breakfast to set me on my way.

"Steaming hot baths were swiftly followed by mugs of strong tea and Yorkshire 'toasties'."

By now I was confident that I knew reliably how to read and interpret Wainwright's idiosyncratic and very precise hand-drawn route maps. However, after a day's walk up onto the Cleveland Hills and the first section of the Yorkshire Moors, I found myself staying somewhere quite different (and 2 miles away) from my fellow walkers. When, unable to thumb a lift, I finally arrive up the long climbing slope at Osmotherley, I decide that I am happy to be there. A handsome village, endowed with celebrated old pubs, and slightly surprisingly, an outstanding new wave inn (Three Tuns) of contemporary design and concept, in this traditional hub of Yorkshire Moors walkers.

After 7 or 8 days of more or less uninterrupted sunshine, the weather finally broke and we found ourselves slipping and sliding in torrential rain along treacherous moor-top stone paths, soaked to the skin, and two and a half miles from our scheduled overnight stop, once again the warmth of hospitality in Northern England surpassed itself - not daunted by quantities of soaking wet clothes and rucksacks, the delightful owner of the local B&B drove over to collect us. Steaming hot baths were swiftly followed by mugs of strong tea and Yorkshire 'toasties'.

More sunshine followed heavy rain, as hazardous moorland paths gave way to the beautiful undulating hills of Glaisdale. With rucksacks full of good home produced pork pies from Glaisdale's family butcher, it's all set for the final trek towards the coast and Robin Hood's Bay.

The last day of my adventure turns out to be the most frustrating. Early on in the day you can clearly see Whitby (with its famous Abbey), and the coast. But as if to tease, Wainwright's route meanders through more enchanting countryside and picture-book villages, including Grosmont with its heritage railway. It was late teatime when, having struggled around innumerable coastal bays and cliff-top paths, I finally strode through the Victorian outskirts of Robin Hood's Bay, down to the formal end of the walk at the waterside Bay Hotel.

If you can spare 11-14 days; enjoy good food, warm and friendly hospitality and sensational scenery - I commend the 192 miles of the Coast-to-Coast Walk to you as a thrilling and truly memorable experience. And may you be as lucky with the weather as I was.

Coast-to-Coast Walk - Fact File

Since the late Alfred Wainwright, writer and fellsman extraordinary, devised this challenging walk it has outstripped many of the official trails in popularity. It crosses England from the Irish Sea to the North Sea, traversing three National Parks in magnificent upland scenery. You have some wonderful walking across the Lake District mountains, over the Pennines and down into Swaledale, with the North York Moors your final challenge. A great cross-section of northern heritage and culture too.

Distance: 192 miles/306km
Duration: 11-14 days
Start/Finish: St Bees Head, Cumbria to Robin Hood's Bay, North Yorkshire
Terrain: A mixture of paths across steep and rugged mountains, river valleys, rolling hills and moorland, with some forestry tracks and tarred roads. Remote in places.
Waymarked: Very good in some places, but much less so in others:
good maps or a trail guide are essential.
Information: For maps, guidebooks and accommodation call Tourist Information Centres at Kirkby Stephen (017683 71199) and Richmond (01748 850252).
Accommodation and baggage transfer services contact: www.coast2coast.co.uk

CATCH
THE BEST
OF BRITISH

There are so many fabulous fish and shellfish available in Britain, that we should be making the most of what's on offer, says Seafish.

In Britain, we could dine out on a different species of fish or shellfish caught from around the world almost every day of the year. But according to the Sea Fish Industry Authority (Seafish) the nation's favourite three choices remain virtually unchanged.

Cod, salmon and haddock, and in that order, remain Britain's top three fish. But says Seafish, there are around 100 varieties of fish caught around our coastline that are readily available to try at restaurants and buy from fishmongers and fish markets. We just need to become more adventurous when it comes to netting some winners.

Celebrity chef Rick Stein has long been leading the trend for local seafood at his Seafood Restaurant in Padstow. There, 95 per cent of the seafood on the menu is locally caught. And he is setting new standards of fish and chips at his new chippie in Padstow. There you can enjoy the delights of Cornish gurnard or megrim with chips. Les Routiers' members are also at the forefront of this trend for serving locally caught fish, which is very often line-caught and bought fresh off the boat.

Surprisingly 90 per cent of our cod is imported and we have excellent stocks of other seafood around to tempt us. In winter, try alternatives to cod such as pollack, gurnard and ling; in summer there's amazing flatfish such as lemon or Dover sole, turbot and brill, and in winter mackerel and sardines. All year-round, we can tuck into marvellous monkfish and in Scotland they have redfish, that is similar to red snapper. Just a few to look out for on menus and at fishmongers around the country.

Seafish was set up in 1981 and works to help consumers find out about all types of fish, convey the health benefits of eating fish regularly, as well as help all sectors of the industry raise their standards, improve efficiency and ensure fish stocks remain sustainable for the future.

A key date in the Seafish calendar is the annual Seafood Week, which in 2004 runs from 1-8 October. And the date is no coincidence, as it's this time of year when we have the best stocks of many different fish available. During the week, Seafish will be advising on buying and cooking fish and shellfish. It will be running special promotions with restaurants and retailers, including a selection of Les Routiers establishments. For information about events for Seafood Week and a wealth of related information check out the Seafish website at www.seafish.org.uk.

BREWING
PROCESS

Ted Bruning, editor of CAMRA's 'What's Brewing' on why winemakers have it easy.

They grow their grapes. They crush their grapes. They ferment the juice - voila! They've got wine.

Brewers, by contrast, have it hard. Nature isn't so kind to them: they don't get all their ingredients - fermentables, aromatics, and liquid - in one neat little package. For each of these they must go to a different source, and to achieve a balanced and harmonious whole, they need a delicacy of judgement, a capacity for taking pains, and a mastery of subjects from microbiology to engineering that no winemaker can boast.

What's more, the near-infinity of variables along the route from raw materials to end product means that there's a near-infinite variety of beer. Britain's 400-odd brewers produce everything from light, refreshing pale ale to rich, warming barley wine, taking in old ale, brown ale, light ale, dry stout, sweet stout, chocolate stout, light mild, dark mild, strong mild, bitter, best bitter, golden bitter and a galaxy of others along the way. Cross the Channel and you could literally drown in different beers - there are more than half-a-dozen styles of lager alone, and that's before you've started on wheat beer, smoked beer, Trappist beer, lambic beer, fruit beer, bière de garde, bière ambrée, bière blonde - need I go on?

Brewers are more than a little miffed that their product gets less respect than wine. They claim there's a beer for every occasion and a beer for every dish; that a fine beer is every bit as complex, as demanding, and indeed as rewarding as a fine wine; and that snobbery is the only reason that every national newspaper has a wine-critic but none has a beer-writer. And they're right. Beer deserves far more honour than it gets. To prove it, let me take you on a whirlwind tour of brewing, and by the time we reach the sampling-room, I think you'll agree.

The Water

Beer is 95 per cent water, and water, as anyone who has ever had to descale the kettle knows, is not just H_2O. The hard water from the wells of Burton-on-Trent contains gypsum that quickens the enzymes that convert barley's insoluble starch into fermentable sugar, and magnesium sulphate that nourishes the yeast and makes for a quick, fierce fermentation. Perfect for brewing British beer, in fact. Soft water, such as that which filters through the Alpine granite to feed the wells of Bohemia and Bavaria, is ideal for the long, slow maturation that lager needs.

The Malt

The malt sugar at the heart of the beer is the result of a trick played by man on nature. Soak barley in warm water until it thinks it must be spring and starts to germinate. Pile it up on a heated floor and turn it every now and then, or rotate it in a giant drum constantly fed with warm air, to activate the enzymes that begin the process of starch-to-sugar conversion or saccharification. Then grind the grain - which is now malt - into a coarse flour and mash it in hot water until all the sugar has leached out. The resulting syrup, or wort, is ready - almost! - to be turned into beer.

Mind you, malt needn't be made from barley. Wheat, oats, and rye can all be malted too, to produce very different beers. The wheat beers of Germany and Belgium are soft, rounded, floral, and often hazy. Their aromas and flavours can include banana, clove, and even bubblegum. Oats come wrapped in fibrous husks that sink slowly through the wort collecting impurities as they go, to create a smooth, satiny mouthfeel particularly prized in some stouts.

Then, of course, there's the question of how you dry your malt. As with so many things in life, you can do it long, cool, and gentle, or you can do it quick, hot, and fierce. There's pale malt, lager malt, smoked malt, brown malt, crystal malt, amber malt, chocolate malt, black malt, roasted malt and a few others beside, all with different tastes - the hint of biscuit that characterises Fuller's London Pride comes from crystal malt; while the burnt-wood tang of Guinness comes from roasted malt. And of course, the proportion of malt in your mash affects the final strength of the beer - the more malt you use, the more alcohol you get.

The Hops

After the mash comes the boil. The wort is strained off the spent malt (which goes to make cattle-cake) and boiled with hops, a climbing plant related to cannabis and nettles which contains bitter-tasting acids whose antibacterial properties are a great preservative. But hops also contain oils and resins, all with their own flavours. The Saaz, Hallertau, Herrsbrucker and Hallertau hops used by lager brewers are low in alpha acids but rich in floral, perfumy oils; so a perfect lager will smell like a bouquet of flowers but will have little bitter aftertaste; whereas the high-acid British types such as Fuggles, Goldings or Bramling Cross give more bitterness but less aroma. These, too, have their own flavours: Fuggles are earthy, Goldings are lemony, while Bramling Coss creates a hint of blackcurrant.

Now we've mashed our malt and hopped our wort. It's time to turn it into beer by pitching it with yeast. Simple? No such luck! Different strains of yeast work in different ways, and at different temperatures. British ale is made with top-fermenting yeast which forms a thick and volatile head on top of the liquid and works quickly - seven days is a long time for a British beer to ferment, and most take only one or two. This fast-working ferment often creates esters, which give British beer its fruitiness. Lager yeasts work far more slowly, and at much lower temperatures; after their first fermentation, lagers go into a maturing tank for a secondary fermentation that can - and should - last two months or more. The result is, or should be, a much cleaner, less fruity, beer.

The fermentation can be highly efficient, in which case most of the sugar turns to alcohol and the beer is strong and dry. Or it can be less so, leaving plenty of unfermented maltose for a richer, fuller flavour. Different shapes of fermenting vessel also create their own characters: the old-fashioned horizontal lagering tank - essentially a big barrel laid on its side - was not all that efficient; beers made in them were richer than modern lagers matured in giant upright cylinders. In Britain, fermenters are traditionally open; in many regions they are traditionally square; and over the years British brewers have come up with various ingenious systems such as the Burton Union set and the Brakspear double-drop system to skim off dead yeast and aerate the fermenting brew.

The Brewery Cat

The Result

So now we have our beer. What are we going to do with it? Well, it can be filtered, pasteurised, and carbonated before being put into barrel, bottle, or can; or it can simply be allowed to settle and condition briefly and then be packaged au naturel, complete with yeast and still fermenting slowly. The former is known as brewery-conditioned, the latter as cask or bottle-conditioned. I need hardly tell you which, from the gustatory point of view, is preferable!

What comes out of all this is that a pint of beer is no simple matter, and not to be taken for granted. In fact, beer is as big a subject as wine - there are as many styles of beer as there are of wine, and they deserve to be treated with every bit as much respect. So next time you're thinking of ordering a bottle of wine to go with your dinner, don't! Try a beer instead. A dry stout with your half-dozen Whitstables; a Belgian wheat beer with your moules; a robust bitter with your steak; a rich, sweet, brown ale with your pudding. And don't just swig it, either! Nose it - breathe in those aromatic hops! Get a good mouthful and hold it on your tongue - taste that fruity, biscuity malt! And after swallowing pause a while, and let your papillae get to grips with the long, dry, bitter finish.

Now - wasn't that good?

London

Central

Lay and Wheeler in Leadenhall Market

55 Leadenhall Market, London EC3V 1LT
Telephone: +44(0)870 4016238
+44(0)20 7929 3536

Respected wine merchant Lay & Wheeler's wine bar in the city (the other is at 33 Cornhill, see entry) occupies a former meat cellar in rejuvenated Leadenhall Market, now a smart shopping/restaurant arcade located a short walk from Fenchurch Station. Brick-vaulted, with a light wooden floor, wine posters, comfortable furnishings and light jazz music, it is, in essence, an upmarket sandwich bar, frequented by City suits who enjoy fine wine with their lunchtime sandwich. Accompany a generously-filled rare roast beef with horseradish, or a poached salmon with dill mayonnaise sandwich, or a platter of Continental cheeses, with a bottle of vintage champagne or a Puligny-Montrachet 1er Cru from the extensive, well chosen list of wines. Blackboards list the sandwich of the week, perhaps chorizo sausage with sun-dried tomato, fine wine specials and 15 wines by the glass. Competent service from friendly staff.

Prices: Sandwiches and light lunches from £4.
House wine £14.
Last orders: Bar: 21.00. Food: 20.30.
Closed: Weekends and Bank Holidays.
Food: Sandwiches, light bites and canapes.
Other points: Private and corporate receptions.
Wine tastings. Extensive wine list.
Directions: Just off Bull's Head Passage in Leadenhall Market, very close to the Lloyds Building.
(Map 1, see inset)

Central

Lay & Wheeler on Cornhill

33 Cornhill, London EC3V 3ND
Telephone: +44(0)870 4016239
+44(0)20 7626 0044
33cornhill@lwwinebars.com
www.lwwinebar.com

Hard working City folk with a penchant for fine wine and seafood head for this slick and stylish wine bar close to the Stock Exchange. Owned by the Essex-based wine merchant Lay & Wheeler, it is housed in a former bank and, unlike Lay and Wheeler in Leadenhall Market (see previous entry), this conversion offers three distinctive venues. In light pine and looking like the deck of a liner, with a sweeping staircase leading up to the Gallery Restaurant, the lunchtime atmosphere is busy and business-like with suited traders ordering premier Cru wines to accompany delicious seafood and thick-cut sandwiches (rare roast beef with horseradish) from the downstairs Seafood Bar. On display are Colchester native oysters, huge Mediterranean prawns, smoked salmon and dressed crabs and lobster. Those with more time can discuss the market over a civilised lunch upstairs, a typical meal being watercress and smoked haddock soup, cumin seared monkfish with charred peppers and coriander sauce, with lemon tart to finish. Downstairs, in the former bank vault, a boardroom is available for meetings, private lunch and dinners, and tutored wine tastings. Incidentally, the wine list draws on Lay & Wheeler's award-winning portfolio of 1,000 bins, with many offered by the glass.

Prices: Restaurant main course in Gallery £9.95.
Bar snacks from £4.95. House wine £11.95.
Last orders: Bar: 22.00. Food: lunch 14.30; dinner 20.30.
Closed: Weekends and Bank Holidays.
Food: Modern European.
Other points: Private and corporate receptions, lunches and dinners on the Gallery restaurant and in the exclusive board room. Wine tastings.
Directions: Bank tube station. Exit 5, Cornhill.
Opposite the Royal Exchange building. 10 minutes walk from Liverpool Street station. (Map 1, see inset)

Central

Nag's Head

53 Kinnerton Street, London SW1X 8ED
Telephone: +44(0)870 4016240
+44(0)20 7235 1135
bugsmoran7@hotmail.com

Owned by the Moran family for over 30 years, the tiny Nag's Head is a cosy, homely and warmly traditional pub tucked away in a peaceful little mews a short stroll from Harrod's. In fact, this snug little gem could well be London's smallest pub and its atmosphere and location is more that of an old-fashioned village local than a bustling London boozer. Step inside and you'll find a low-ceilinged, panelled front bar and a narrow stairway that leads to a tiny back bar adorned with family memorabilia and photographs. A 1930s' What-the-butler-saw machine and a fortune-telling machine taking old pennies are popular features. The choice of piped background music is individual, perhaps folk, jazz or early show tunes. In addition to exemplary Adnams ales, pulled on attractive 19th-century handpumps, you can order a satisfying homecooked meal, perhaps chicken and ham pie, sausage, mash and beans, Mediterranean vegetable quiche, a daily roast, a range of cold meats from the salad bar, and decent sandwiches and ploughman's lunches. Please note that no credit cards are taken.

Prices: Bar main course £6. House wine £10.50.
Last orders: Bar: 23.00. Food: 21.30.
Closed: Rarely.
Food: British.
Real Ale: Adnams.
Other points: Children welcome over 14 years old.
Credit cards not accepted.
Directions: Nearest tube: Knightsbridge. Kinnerton Street runs between Motcomb Street and Wilton Place (off Knightsbridge). (Map 2, F6)

Central

Swag and Tails

10-11 Fairholt St, London SW7 1EG
Telephone: +44(0)870 4016244
+44(0)20 7584 6926
theswag@swagandtails.com
www.swagandtails.com

Secreted away in a warren of pretty residential mews in Knightsbridge village, the Swag and Tails is well worth seeking out after a hard day's shopping. Beyond the magnificent, flower-adorned façade lies a civilised yet informal bar, with original panelling, stripped wooden floors and open fires and, to the rear, a cosy, quieter dining area. Business suits, shoppers and well-heeled locals quickly fill the bar at lunchtime, attracted by the welcoming atmosphere and the modern, Mediterranean-style dishes listed on a constantly changing blackboard menu. Pop in to peruse the papers over a pint and a classic burger with fries, or linger longer over something more substantial. Follow wok-fried chilli and ginger squid with Asian greens and crispy noodles with roast pork loin chop with caramelised onion mash and honey jus, or deep-fried skate wing with basil and sweet potato mash and red wine sauce. Finish with white chocolate tart with rhubarb jam and blood orange sorbet, or a plate of Irish cheeses. There is an interesting list of wines with useful tasting notes. Note the hard-working licensees, Annemaria and Stuart Boomer-Davies, close the pub at weekends!

Prices: Main course from £10.95. Bar/snack from £7.50.
House wine £11.50.
Last orders: Bar: 23.00. Food: lunch 15.00; dinner 22.00.
Closed: Saturday, Sunday, all Bank Holidays and 10 days over the Christmas period.
Food: Modern British.
Real Ale: Marston's Pedigree, Bombardier Premium Bitter, John Smith Smooth.
Other points: No-smoking area. Dogs welcome in the bar in the evening. Children welcome in the restaurant.
Directions: From Harrods, cross road and turn into Montpelier Street; first left into Cheval Place, then the second right and first left. (Map 2, F5)

New from YOUNG'S SMILES BRISTOL I.P.A.
£2.40
ABV 4.5%

The Ship Inn, Wandsworth, South West London

North

The Drapers Arms

44, Barnsbury Street, London N1 1ER
Telephone: +44(0)870 4016234
+44(0)20 7619 0348

Mark Emberton's Islington pub may look traditional from the outside but within it is modern, stylish and top-class in every way. The high-ceilinged interior, with its deep-rose walls and original wooden flooring, has been cleverly remodelled and is a wonderful place to enjoy superb food, either relaxing on the comfy sofas by the fire, at the solid wooden tables by the bar, or at the collection of bench seating away to the left. Mark has breathed life into this pub and its name: the walls are filled with large contemporary 'drapery' themed photographs, and he delivers fantastic fresh ingredients skillfully tailored into superb dishes for his ever-returning clientele. In the bar, order a pint of Courage Best or one of 13 wines by the glass and tuck into some upmarket 'bar bites', perhaps chilli squid or chargrilled breads with hummus dip. For a real treat, visit the dining room upstairs. In this wonderful high ceilinged room where pale blue walls contrast with deep red velvet chairs, you can sample, perhaps, rock oysters with shallot vinaigrette, followed by herb-crusted cod with Puy lentils and a refreshing lemon tart with crème fraîche. In summer there is also a lovely paved terrace area at the back.

Prices: Restaurant main course from £9.
House wine from £11.50.
Last orders: Bar: 23.00. Food: lunch 15.00
(Sunday 16.00); dinner 22.30.
Closed: Rarely.
Food: Modern British.
Real Ale: Courage Best Bitter, Greene King Old Speckled Hen.
Other points: Dogs welcome in bar. Garden.
Children welcome.
Directions: Nearest tube is Highbury and Islington or Angel. (Map 1, see inset)

North West

The Duke of York

2A St Anne's Terrace, St Johns Wood,
London NW8 6PJ
Telephone: +44(0)870 4016236
+44(0)20 7722 1933
dukeofyorkpub@btconnect.com
www.thedukeofyork.com

Residents in affluent St John's Wood have a neighbourhood pub-restaurant to be proud of in the form of the Duke of York near the top end of the High Street, a mere five minutes stroll from the tube. The current incumbents, Brendan and Ally, have been at this refurbished Victorian pub for four years and have succeeded in creating a stylish interior with a welcoming and informal atmosphere, and developing interesting, modern European menus. So, expect comfortable bar and dining areas with a subtle Moroccan influenced décor. Food is freshly prepared on the premises, including bread, and menus range from an all day menu with changing lunchtime options to a more elaborate evening carte. During the day tuck into soups, fresh pasta meals, imaginative warm salads, decent sandwiches, perhaps tuna and cheese foccacia or chargrilled steak baguette. Alternatively, you could try the wild mushroom risotto with fresh Parmesan and white truffle oil or the honey roasted duck. In the evening, start with steamed Shetland mussels with lemongrass and coconut milk, then follow with herb-crusted Barnsley lamb chop or corn-fed breast of chicken stuffed with mushroom duxelle, and finish with a classic, homemade sticky toffee pudding. Summer al fresco seating at pavement tables.

Prices: Restaurant main course £9.50. Bar main course from £3.50. House wine from £10.95.
Last orders: Bar 23.00. Food: 22.30.
Closed: Rarely.
Food: Modern British.
Real Ale: Greene King Old Speckled Hen,
John Smiths Smooth.
Other points: No-smoking area. Children welcome.
Dogs welcome. Pavement tables.
Directions: Nearest tube St John Woods. Top end of St Johns Wood High Street. (Map 2, A5)

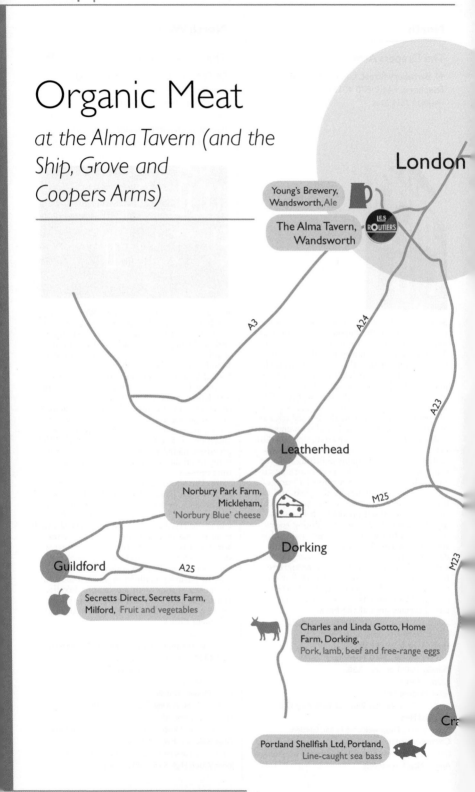

Organic Meat

at the Alma Tavern (and the Ship, Grove and Coopers Arms)

London

Young's Brewery, Wandsworth, Ale

The Alma Tavern, Wandsworth

LES ROUTIERS

A3

A24

A23

Leatherhead

Norbury Park Farm, Mickleham, 'Norbury Blue' cheese

M25

Dorking

Guildford

A25

M23

Secretts Direct, Secretts Farm, Milford, Fruit and vegetables

Charles and Linda Gotto, Home Farm, Dorking, Pork, lamb, beef and free-range eggs

Cra

Portland Shellfish Ltd, Portland, Line-caught sea bass

A205

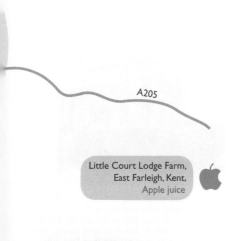

Little Court Lodge Farm,
East Farleigh, Kent,
Apple juice

The Gotto empire extends to four pubs in London and their farm in Surrey and has become well known for its fantastic food and drink. The food aspect of the business has always been a priority of theirs since they acquired the Ship twenty years ago and made it one of the first gastro pubs. Since then the Ship has been joined by the Alma, the Coopers and the Grove, all dotted around London and all excelling in the ambition of serving up first-rate food based on good quality ingredients, sourced carefully and expertly cooked. With the purchase of their Surrey farm they are able to rear their own sheep, pigs, cows, ducks and geese and although they cannot produce all the meat used in the pubs, they very carefully source from likeminded individuals that adhere to the same kind of farming practices. They saw that mass food production had changed the face of agriculture in the UK. - farms churning out bland produce quickly and in large quantities with little regard for the quality of the end product. The Gotto's have instead focused on sourcing animals from good stock, feeding them good food, making sure they lead a happy life and humanely slaughtering them. The farm is recently organic as well, making sure the land is free from fertilizers and pesticides. This self-contained business is unique with fashionable issues like food traceability and accountability easily taken care of, a factor that is becoming more and more important in this day and age.

South West

The Alma Tavern

499 Old York Road, Wandsworth,
London SW18 1TF
Telephone: +44(0)870 4016229
+44(0)20 8870 2537
drinks@thealma.co.uk
www.thealma.co.uk

Conveniently located across from Wandsworth station and close to Young's brewery, the Alma is part of Charles Gotto's well-run little empire of distinctive, atmospheric pubs, all of which have a strong emphasis on food (see the Ship, the Coopers Arms and the Grove). The Victorian tavern's classic green-tiled façade, adorned in summer with hanging flower baskets, immediately stands out. In the unexpectedly stylish atmosphere of the airy central room, an eclectic mix of painted pine and cast-iron tables, gilded mosaics of the Crimean Battle of Alma, and a fine art deco fireplace range around a huge island bar counter. At the back, the dining room has terracotta-painted walls, a famous pale blue frieze of nymphs and a comfortable, sophisticated dining atmosphere. Using organic and rare breed meats from Gotto's Surrey farm and other carefully sourced produce, the imaginative, popular menu may offer seafood chowder and duck, tarragon and Madeira pâté for starters, followed by game pie with roast winter vegetables, lamb's liver with onion mash, or Tunisian chicken with pumpkin and chickpeas, with hot chocolate pudding to finish. Sandwiches and lighter bites are also available. Besides the first-class Young's ales, you'll find a superb selection of wines.

Prices: Main course from £10. House wine £13.
Last orders: Bar: 22.50. Food: lunch 16.00
(Sunday 16.00); dinner 22.30 (Sunday 22.00).
Closed: Rarely.
Food: Modern British.
Real Ale: Youngs PA, Youngs SPA, Youngs Waggledance.
Seasonal ales available from Youngs.
Other points: Dogs welcome in the bar. Licence for
Civil Weddings.
Directions: Opposite Wandsworth Town Railway Station. (Map 1, see inset)

South West

The Bridge Pub and Dining Rooms

204 Castelnau, Barnes, London SW13 9DW
Telephone: +44(0)870 4016230
+44(0)208 563 9811
thebridgeinbarnes@btinternet.com
www.thebridgeinbarnes.co.uk

A ten minute walk across the Thames from Hammersmith tube and you will be in leafy Barnes. The Bridge Pub in Castelnau Road used to be a dingy, down-at-heel locals' bar until Murray Harris bought it in late 2002. Two years on, following a marvellous refurbishment and the addition of Australian chef Sarah Pope, the Bridge is now an upmarket gastropub that appeals to well-heeled foodies. Beyond the long, stylish bar is the 'Dining Room' bit, a lovely conservatory dining room, resplendent with lush plants and greenery and an ideal venue for sunny lunches or a candlelit dinner. Modern, Italian influenced food is freshly prepared on the premises using first-class ingredients. Monthly changing menus may include risotto primavera with shelled peas and asparagus, pasta with broccoli, pinenuts and Parmesan, an excellent fillet of brill with potato rösti, asparagus and tomato and thyme dressing, and oven-baked quail. Expect a quality list of wines, a raft of cocktails to challenge any West End bar, and Marston's Pedigree and Wells Bombardier on handpump. Spend lazy summer weekends and long lunches with the locals out on the wonderful garden terrace - well worth the trip out of the city.

Prices: Restaurant main course from £10.
House wine £11.50.
Last orders: Bar: 23.00. Food: lunch 15.00; dinner 20.30.
Closed: Rarely.
Food: Modern British with Italian and
Australian influences.
Real Ale: Marston's Pedigree, Bombardier
Premium Bitter, Ruddles Best.
Other points: No-smoking area. Garden and decked
seating area. Children welcome.
Directions: Travelling from Hammersmith; the Bridge
Pub is 200 yards over Hammersmith Bridge on the left
hand side. (Map 1, see inset)

South West

Bull's Head and Stables Bistro

373 Lonsdale Road, Barnes, London SW13 9PY
Telephone: +44(0)870 4016231
+44(0)20 8876 5241
jazz@thebullshead.com
www.thebullshead.com

The Thameside setting of this imposing 17th-century pub would be a draw in itself, but what really pulls crowds from miles around is the top-class modern jazz and blues groups that have made the Bull's Head internationally famous for over 40 years. Landlord Dan Fleming knows his jazz and attracts many American bands; nightly concerts are from 8.30-11pm (also 2-4.30pm on Sundays), held in a separate room with a genuine jazz club atmosphere; it's well worth paying the admission charge just to enter this famous room. Back in the bustling bar, alcoves open off the main area around the island servery, which dispenses Youngs cask-conditioned ales, over 80 malt whiskies and some 240 bottles of wine, 30 offered by the glass. All the food is cooked from fresh ingredients and served from noon until it's finished (they then can make sandwiches). Typical choices include soup and ciabatta, roast of the day with potatoes and three vegetables, steak and kidney pie, and treacle tart. The former Stables Bistro now houses Nuay's Thai Bistro with a Thai kitchen brigade, but you can also order at the bar in the main pub and be served there, or order authentic Thai food to takeaway.

Prices: Main course from £4.50. Thai main course from £4.75. Wine from £10.50.
Last orders: Bar: 23.00. Food: 22.00.
Closed: Rarely.
Food: Traditional British served at lunchtime. Thai food served in the evening.
Real Ale: Youngs Bitter.
Other points: No-smoking area. Children welcome in daytime.
Directions: Five minutes walk along the river from Barnes Bridge station. (Map 1, see inset)

South West

The Coopers Arms

87 Flood Street, London SW3 5TB
Telephone: +44(0)870 4016232
+44(0)20 7376 3120
drinks@thecoopers.co.uk
www.thecoopers.co.uk

Charles Gotto's civilised Victorian pub stands on a quiet corner site in Chelsea's affluent back streets. A popular neighbourhood local with a vibrant atmosphere within its light, airy and comfortable open-plan bar which attracts a well-heeled clientele in search of superior bar food and decent wines. Pine furnishings, pot plants, vintage ocean liner posters, framed Mac cartoons, and daily papers on a large table set the scene. Like Gotto's other pubs, the Ship, the Alma in Wandsworth and the Grove in Balham, modern menus list a good selection of freshly prepared dishes, with meat, game and eggs supplied by Gotto's organic Surrey farm. The daily chalkboard may list smoked salmon and scrambled eggs, leek and potato soup, and seared scallops and chorizo salad for a light snack or starter. For something more substantial choose, perhaps, chargrilled tuna with stir-fried vegetables in an oyster sauce, Angus rib-eye steak with pepper sauce and french fries, or chargrilled lamb steak with roast balsamic vegetables and herbed yoghurt. If you have room, try the rich chocolate torte for pudding. There are tip-top Young's ales, as well as an upstairs function room that is popular for wedding celebrations; Chelsea Registry Office is just around the corner.

Prices: Main course from £9. House wine £13.
Last orders: Bar: 23.00. Food: lunch 15.00; dinner 21.30.
No food Sunday evening.
Closed: Rarely.
Food: Modern British.
Real Ale: Youngs PA, Youngs SPA, Smiles Bristol IPA.
Seasonal ales from Young's Brewery.
Directions: Sloane Square tube station. (Map 2, G5)

South West

The Grove

39 Oldridge Road, Balham SW12 8PN
Telephone: +44(0)870 4016237
+44(0)20 8673 6531
drinks@thegroveatbalham.co.uk
www.thegroveatbalham.co.uk

The Grove is the latest addition to Charles Gotto's highly successful mini-empire of pubs across London (see The Ship, The Alma and Cooper Arms), complementing their organic Surrey farm. The Grove is a striking, Victorian corner building with a casual, gastropub feel (plain wooden tables and simple decor). With a light and airy bar, and a raised restaurant area where moulded walls, modern artwork and smart gilt mirrors add charm and character, this is a thriving neighbourhood pub. Already popular with well-heeled Balhamites and local artisans, it is the place to come for tip-top Young's ales, great wines by the glass and, in keeping with Charles's other pubs, excellent modern pub food. Typically, tuck into fresh asparagus with tomatoes and gorgonzola salad, or Caesar salad for starters or a light lunch, then, for something more substantial, order pork and leek sausages with mash, homemade burger with crispy onion rings and basil pesto, double chocolate stout and steak pie, Gotto's Home Farm lamb fillet with olives and rosemary, or saffron chicken with Italian potato and pancetta salad. For pudding, do try the quite delicious chocolate brownie pudding. Cracking Sunday lunches (order your joint in advance), a super al fresco patio for summer drinking and ever-popular pig-roasts.

Prices: Restaurant main course from £9. Bar main course from £4. House wine £13.
Last orders: Food: 22.00.
Closed: Never.
Food: Modern British.
Real Ale: Youngs Bitter, Youngs Special. 1 guest beer.
Other points: Children welcome. Dogs welcome. Garden and pagoda.
Directions: Between Balham and Clapham South tube station. From Clapham South go straight down Balham Hill and turn right on to Oldridge Road.
(Map 1, see inset)

South West

The Ship Inn

Jews Row, Wandsworth, London SW18 1TB
Telephone: +44(0)870 4016243
+44(0)20 8870 9667
drinks@theship.co.uk
www.theship.co.uk

Approach this Victorian pub by road and you pass a bus station and a concrete works, so not the most inspiring route. Take the river walk instead, and enter the pub via the delightful, two-level terrace, complete with rose-covered rustic trellis, barbecue and summer bar; the pub really makes the most of its riverside location. Within, you'll find a light, airy conservatory bar that makes a pleasant, airy, most un-London-like venue, with its bare boards, central wood-burning stove, motley collection of old tables and chairs, and an open-plan kitchen that produces good-quality food. Although owned by Young's, it is the flagship pub of Charles Gotto's select empire of gastropubs. Gotto is passionate about food and sources quality produce, including Shorthorn beef, rare breed pork and lamb, and game and eggs from his own organic farm in Surrey. On the short daily-changing menu you may find pork terrine with beetroot and cherry compote, roast pork cutlet wrapped in proscuitto with Calvados sauce, and poached haddock with parsley mash and chive beurre blanc. Specialist cheeses are sourced from small independent producers. Naturally, the beer is good, and there's a wine list of decent labels, with a choice of 10 by the glass.

Prices: Main course from £10.70. House wine £13.
Last orders: Bar: 22.50. Food: dinner 22.00 (Sunday lunch 16.00).
Closed: Rarely.
Food: Modern British.
Real Ale: Youngs PA, Youngs SPA, Youngs Triple A, Youngs Winter Warmer (when in season).
Other points: Garden.
Directions: Nearest train station is Wandsworth Town. From here, make your way under the railway bridge. Follow signs to Wandsworth Bridge, Jews Row is the last road on the left before the river. (Map 1, see inset)

West

The Red Lion

13 St Marys Road, Ealing, London W5 5RA
Telephone: +44(0)870 4016242
+44(0)20 8567 2541
red.lion@virgin.net

The Red Lion appears to be nothing more than a typical, traditional brass, dark wood, and smoked glass London pub, with its pumps dispensing Fullers ales. But the glamour of film beats at its heart. The walls of Studio Six, as the pub is lovingly called by the neighbouring Ealing Studios (where they have five studios), reflect this with an array of wonderful black and white photos and colourful posters. Unusually for London, this is a real family business, run by Jonathan and Victoria Lee, with son Kieran cooking in the kitchen. What's more, Victoria's cousin is the main supplier for fresh wild Scottish salmon, venison, wild duck, local pheasant, and black pudding. Here you can tuck into wild boar and apple sausages with mustard mash and onion gravy, swordfish steak sandwich with salad, a gourmet burger topped with Brie and bacon, or rack of lamb with crushed new potatoes, balsamic, tomato and basil sauce, with homemade syrup and ginger pudding to finish; good Sunday lunches. On warm evenings, the walled terrace is transformed for candlelit al fresco dining. And, you can't ignore this little pub when the most famous Guinness served at the bar was Sir Alec!

Prices: Restaurant main course from £8.95. Bar main course from £3.50. House wine £10.50.
Last orders: Bar: 23.00. Food: lunch 14.30 (Sunday 16.00); dinner 21.30. No food Sunday evening.
Closed: Rarely.
Food: Modern British.
Real Ale: Fuller's London Pride, Fuller's Chiswick, Fuller's ESB. 1 guest beer.
Other points: Dogs welcome in the bar. Garden.
Directions: Hanger Lane exit A40 take A406 south. Turn right onto Uxbridge Road and left at Marks and Spencers. Tube: Ealing Broadway. (Map 1, see inset)

England

Bath

The Hunters Rest Inn

King Lane, Clutton Hill, Bath BS39 5QL
Telephone: +44(0)870 4016001
+44(0)1761 452303
paul@huntersrest.co.uk
www.huntersrest.co.uk

Originally built as a hunting lodge for the Earl of Warwick in 1755, this striking rural inn is set at the end of a winding country road with views over the Cam Valley to the Mendips. Within, a stone bar is surrounded by a number of inter-connecting rooms, most filled with a selection of wooden and brass-topped tables and chairs; one leads into the bright conservatory. Old farm paraphernalia hangs from walls, dried hops adorn the beamed ceilings along with brass plates, hunting pictures and brass horns. Food is traditional, and the specials locally-sourced, and runs from filled ciabatta rolls and hearty ploughman's lunches to a giant beef and Stilton pie and lamb steak with red wine, garlic and herbs. Sea bass fillet with lemon butter sauce may appear on the specials menu. Wednesday night is family night, and kids can make use of the miniature railway in the back garden. All four bedrooms are individually decorated; each comes with bags of character, and a teddy bear. Victorian fittings complement the roll-top baths in two of the bathrooms. In addition, telephones come with data links and TV with video.

Rooms: 5. Double from £80, single room from £60, family room from £125.
Prices: Set lunch £12.50 and dinner £16.50. Restaurant main course restaurant from £10. Main course bar from £6. House wine £8.50.
Last orders: Bar: lunch 15.00; dinner 23.00. Food: lunch 14.00; dinner 21.30 (Friday and Saturday 22.15).
Closed: Never.
Food: Traditional English.
Real Ale: Bass, Butcombe Bitter, Wadworth 6X, Exmoor Ale, Smiles.
Other points: No-smoking area. Children welcome. Dogs welcome in the bar. Garden. Car park.
Directions: Between A39 and A37, near Chelwood and Farmborough. Phone for directions. (Map 5, F2)

Barkham

The Bull Inn

Barkham Road, Barkham, Wokingham,
Berkshire RG41 4TL
Telephone: +44(0)870 4016002
+44(0)1189 760324
barkhambull@barbox.net
www.thebullatbarkham.com

South of Reading and the M4 and close to California Country Park, the Bull Inn is a traditional village pub that oozes character and history. The main building was originally a brewhouse and the restaurant extension was, surprisingly, a working blacksmith's forge from 1728 until it closed in 1982. The original forge takes centre stage in the room and the scorch marks are still visible on the adjacent beams. Here, linen-clothed tables beneath huge exposed beams create a more formal setting for chef-proprietor Adrian Brunswick's traditional country cooking. Wife Susie oversees the large and attractively refurbished bar, dispensing Adnams ales and well chosen wines to locals and intending diners. Expect a modern twist to familiar dishes, perhaps calf's liver on a rocket potato cake, lamb rump served with dauphinois potatoes and a mint and redcurrant jus, king prawns with chilli sauce, and seared tuna with tomato and fresh herb salsa. Lighter lunchtime dishes.

Prices: Set lunch (2 course) £15.50 (includes a half bottle of house wine). Restaurant main course from £8. Bar main course from £5.50.
House wine £10.95.
Last orders: Bar: lunch 14.50; dinner 22.50 (Sunday 22.20). Food: lunch 14.15; dinner 21.15.
Closed: Rarely.
Food: Traditional British.
Real Ale: Adnams Broadside, Courage Best Bitter, Adnams Best, Old Speckled Hen. 1 guest beer.
Other points: No smoking in restaurant. Dogs welcome. Patio. Children welcome. Car park.
Directions: Exit10/M4. Head towards Wokingham and follow signposts to Barkham, the Bull Inn is in the centre of Barkham. (Map 5, F4)

Charvil

The Land's End

Charvil, Twyford, Berkshire RG10 0UE
Telephone: +44(0)870 4016246
+44(0)118 934 0700
www.greatmeals.co.uk

Landlord Stephen Bedford left his hugely
successful village pub (The Bell, Ramsbury,
Wiltshire) in late summer 2003 and reap-
peared some months later at the Land's End,
a pub so remote and difficult to find it's
hard to believe you're near Reading and the
M4. Perservere down the windy lane off the
A3032 and, just before an impressive ford,
you will find this 1930s whitewashed pub.
Inside, low ceilings with exposed beams,
an eclectic mix of wooden furnishings on
a red carpet, and red walls adorned with
tasteful prints, create a cosy and intimate
atmosphere, best enjoyed in winter when the
open log fires are crackling away. Quaff a
pint of Brakspear Bitter while perusing the
blackboard menus and settle in the bar or
in the more formal dining area for starters
of leek and potato soup, black pudding with
caramelised pear or confit of duck leg. For
main course, try one of the fish specialities,
perhaps, sea bass with seared scallops and
chives, or tuck into a hearty beef stroganoff,
chargrilled sirloin steak with hand-cut chips,
or rack of lamb with port wine sauce. Leave
room for sticky toffee pudding or a tangy
lemon tart. The rustic summer garden is very
peaceful indeed.

Prices: Restaurant main course from £9. Bar main
course from £6. House wine £11.
Last orders: Bar: 23.30. Food: lunch 14.00; dinner 21.00.
Closed: Rarely.
Food: Modern Pub Food.
Real Ale: Brakspear Ales.
Other points: No-smoking area. Dogs welcome.
Garden. Children welcome. Car park.
Directions: Exit10/M4. Get onto the A329 and then the
A4. At the roundabout take the A3032 and then the
first right down Park Lane. (Map 5, E4)

Newbury

The Bunk Inn

Curridge Village, Newbury,
Berkshire RG18 9DS
Telephone: +44(0)0870 4016003
+44 (0)1635 200400
www.thebunkinn.co.uk

Travel weary M4 drivers in need of a bed
can now pass the faceless Chieveley Travel
Inn, for Mickey and father Jack Liquorish
have extended their ever-popular Bunk Inn
to include six executive style bedrooms. All
are kitted out with quality fabrics and fittings, smart en suite facilities, and a host of
added extras (32-channel TV) that ensure a
comfortable stay. The accommodation should
also appeal to those looking for a bustling
and informal pub and the present food set up
should not disappoint either, as sound traditional favourites rub shoulders with modern
pub dishes on the daily chalkboard menu and
weekly changing carte. Take comfort in bangers and mash or a 'Bunk' long loaf snack. Or
head for the attractive conservatory dining
room for deep-fried Brie with apple and cider
chutney, grilled organic salmon with fennel
and saffron sauce, and the locally famous
slow-roasted lamb shoulder with port and
redcurrant gravy. Finish with steamed ginger
and apple sponge, strawberry bavarois, or a
plate of cheese with chutney. Altogether, the
welcoming beamed bar, stone-floored restaurant with local paintings and fresh flowers,
and a front terrace with upmarket tables and
chairs create a civilised atmosphere.

Rooms: 6. Double room from £80, single from £65.
Prices: Main course restaurant from £9.95. Main
course bar from £5.95. House wine £12.50.
Last orders: Bar: 24.00. Food: lunch 14.30 (weekend
15.00); dinner 22.00 (Sunday 21.30).
Closed: Rarely.
Food: Traditional and Modern British.
Real Ale: Fuller's London Pride, Wadworth 6X, Arkells
3B's. 1 guest beer.
Other points: No-smoking area. No dogs in restaurant
or rooms. Children welcome. Garden. Car park.
Directions: Curridge is signposted off B4009 3 miles
north of Newbury. Junction 13/M4. (Map 5, F3)

Newbury

The Yew Tree Inn

Hollington Cross, Andover Road, Highclere,
Newbury, Berkshire RG20 9SE
Telephone: +4490)870 4016004
+44(0)1635 253360
eric.norberg@theyewtree.net

This former 16th-century coaching inn is situated just south of Highclere on the edge of the Hampshire Downs beside the A343 and is a useful lunch spot for Highclere Castle visitors. Full of charm and character with ancient beams, and a huge inglenook fireplace, the light wood furnishings lend a contemporary air to this stylishly refurbished dining pub. Several interconnecting rooms, with linen draped tables, whitewashed walls and standing timbers comprise the smart dining areas. Head chef Gonzo Moore freshly prepares a sensibly short 'bill of fare' that's imaginative in style and utilises local produce. Dishes include a starter or main course portion of crayfish and herb risotto with Parmesan cheese, or Eric's traditional Swedish gravadlax served with a dill and mustard sauce. Alternatively, order game and pork terrine, move on to duck confit with bubble-and-squeak and honey and orange jus, calf's liver with bacon, horseradish mash and onion gravy, or steamed sea bass with stir-fried bok choi, spring onion and ginger and a chilli and red pepper salsa. Finish, perhaps, with frosted berries with hot white chocolate sauce. Then, head upstairs to one of the six en suite rooms, all tastefully furnished and equipped to a high standard.

Rooms: 6. Double from £60, prices include breakfast.
Prices: Restaurant main course from £8.95.
House wine £9.95.
Last orders: Bar: 23.00. Food: lunch 15.00 (Sunday 16.00); dinner 22.00 (Sunday 21.00).
Closed: Rarely.
Food: International.
Real Ale: Fuller's London Pride.
Other points: No-smoking in restaurant.
Dogs welcome. Garden. Car park.
Directions: Exit 13/M4. A34 to Highclere and A343 towards Andover; pub just past Highclere. (Map 5, C3)

Waltham-St-Lawrence

The Star Inn

Broadmoor Road, Waltham-St-Lawrence,
Reading, Berkshire RG10 0HY
Telephone: +44(0)870 4016005
+44(0)1189 343486
james@thestar-inn.co.uk
www.thestar-inn.co.uk

Sound investment by both Wadworth Brewery and enthusiastic tenants James Barrons-Ruth and Jayne Barrington-Groves has seen the fortunes of this unassuming local in pretty Waltham St Lawrence improve in recent years. Spick-and-span throughout the traditional pub interior and outside (smart gravelled patio and neat rear garden), the Star draws folk from miles around for interesting wines and homecooked pub food. Although the lunchtime menu offers pub favourites for speed and convenience, James refuses to serve chips or any deep-fried foods, preferring to prepare everything on the premises. Typically, chicken Caesar salad, ham ploughman's, freshly made chilli and hearty soups will accompany the giant filled baps (bacon and mushroom), and excellent home-baked pizzas (anchovy and stuffed green olive) on the lunchtime board. Expect a touch more imagination in the evening, with James's seasonally changing menu and daily specials choice offering smoked salmon with honey and mustard marinade, roast duck with apricot, prune and port compote, and rib-eye steak with peppercorn, cream and brandy sauce. Tip-top Wadworth ales (Henry's IPA and 6X) as well as good bin-end and monthly wine specials.

Prices: Restaurant main course from £11.95. Bar main course from £5.95. House wine £11.95.
Last orders: Bar: lunch 14.30 (week-end 15.00); dinner 23.00. Food: lunch 14.00; dinner 21.30.
No food Sunday evening.
Closed: Rarely.
Food: Modern pub food.
Real Ale: Wadworth 6X, Henry's IPA.
Other points: No-smoking area. Well behaved children welcome. Garden. Car park.
Directions: Exit 8 or 9/M4, and then the A404 to White Waltham heading west through Cox Green on Broadmoor Road for two miles to Waltham-St-Lawrence. (Map 5, E4)

Wargrave

St George & Dragon

High Street, Wargrave, Berkshire RG10 8HY
Telephone: +44(0)870 4016006
+44(0)118 940 5021
www.stgeorgeanddragon.co.uk

The quite brilliant 'Orange Tree' pub concept, developed by Paul Hales and Paul Salisbury at the Orange Tree in the West Midlands (see entry), where run-down pubs are transformed into stylish gastropubs, is picking up momentum with four new openings down the M40 to London, with the Freemasons Arms in Hampstead opening in September 2004. This winning formula - open kitchen and a contemporary, almost minimalistic dècor - has worked a treat at this lovely Thames-side pub in pretty Wargrave. The spacious, open-plan interior has been beautifully reworked, with simple muted colours, Asian art and wooden floors setting the style in the comfortable, yet very informal drinking and dining areas. Like all the pubs in this select group, the simple, restrained interior is matched by a modern Italian-inspired menu. Breads, cheeses and olive oils are on display and prepared at a deli-style counter, and all dishes are freshly prepared in the open-to-view kitchen. Tuck into bowls of fresh pasta, pizzas from the oven, perhaps a 'Siciliana' topped with ham, artichoke, olives, mozzarella and tomato, Caesar salads, or sea bass with noodles, pak choi and red onion salsa. On fine days eat beside the Thames.

Prices: Restaurant main course from £8.95. Main course bar from £5.50. House wine £11.95.
Last orders: Bar: 23.00. Food: lunch 14.30 (Sunday 16.30); dinner 21.30 (no food Sunday evening).
Deli bar last orders 18.00
Closed: Rarely.
Food: Modern British with Italian influences.
Real Ale: Bass, Fuller's London Pride.
Other points: No-smoking in restaurant. Large terrace overlooking the river. Children welcome. Car park.
Directions: Exit8/9/M4. M404 then A4 towards Reading, then right to Wargrave. Right at crossroads for pub. (Map 5, E4)

Chalfont St Giles

The Ivy House

London Road, Chalfont St Giles,
Buckinghamshire HP8 4RS
Telephone: +44(0)870 4016007
+44(0)1494 872184
www.theivyhouse-bucks.co.uk

There have been big changes at this 17th-century brick-and-flint freehouse set in the heart of the Chiltern Hills with views across the Misbourne Valley. The new-look Ivy House now features an enlarged dining room, new toilets, a smart patio for al fresco eating and five en suite rooms. Although enlarged, the wood and slate-floored bar, with its old beams, cosy armchairs, wood-burning fires and fine old pictures retains its traditional charm and offers five changing real ales and a select list of wines (20 by the glass). A menu of modern British dishes prepared by chef/proprietor Jane Mears and her team reveals a happpiness to experiment with ingredients to produce unusual dishes - look to the blackboard for the day's creations. Starter choices include homemade soups and ragout of artichoke hearts, basil, sun-dried tomatoes and garlic. Main courses extend to roast salmon with pesto and Parmesan, chargrilled sirloin steak with creamy pepper sauce, and loin of lamb with redcurrant and mint sauce, plus winter casseroles, summer salads, pasta meals and homemade puddings, perhaps hot chocolate pudding and chocolate fudge sauce. Retire to one of the individually furnished bedrooms and wake up to a hearty breakfast.

Rooms: 5. Double room £95, single occupancy £75.
Prices: Main course from £8.50. House wine £10.95.
Last orders: Bar:lunch 15.00; dinner 23.00 (open all day at the week-end). Food: lunch 14.30; dinner 21.30 (all day at the week-end).
Closed: Never.
Food: Modern British/global.
Real Ale: London Pride, Wadworth 6X. 3 guest beers.
Other points: No-smoking area. Children welcome. Dogs welcome in the bar. Garden and courtyard. Car park.
Directions: Exit2/M40. Between Amersham and Gerrards Cross on the A413. (Map 5, E4)

Chalfont St Peter

The Greyhound Inn

High Street, Chalfont St Peter,
Buckinghamshire SL9 9RA
Telephone: +44(0)870 4016008
+44(0)1753 883404
reception@thegreyhoundinn.net
www.thegreyhoundinn.net

Striking 600-year-old inn set in a pretty village on the edge of the Chiltern Hills and within easy reach of the M40. Today, following lavish refurbishment, it cleverly combines contemporary elegance with the traditional character of such an ancient building, and provides a comfortable country retreat for good modern food and stylish accommodation. Escape the capital for a night or two in one of twelve beautifully appointed bedrooms, where exposed beams and solid oak beds blend well with en suite marble bathrooms, rain-drench showers and Molton Brown toiletries. Feeling pampered, head downstairs and sink into one of the deep sofas by the roaring fire in the low-beamed bar for a pre-dinner drink. The wood-panelled dining room has a light and airy feel, with chunky furnishings and access to an upmarket terrace. Food successfully combines traditional English dishes with contemporary influences, with such starters as classic prawn cocktail and scallops with rocket, red onion, crispy bacon and sweet chilli dressing. The style continues in mains of rib-eye steak with pepper sauce, and baked salmon with leeks, mussels and watercress sauce.

Rooms: 12. Double from £100, single from £90, family from £120.
Prices: Set lunch and dinner £12.50. Restaurant and bar main course from £8.50. House wine £12.50.
Last orders: Bar: 23.00. Food: lunch 15.00; dinner 22.00 (Sunday 21.30).
Closed: Rarely.
Food: Modern British.
Real Ale: Courage Best Bitter, London Pride.
Other points: No-smoking area. Dogs welcome in the bar. Garden. Children welcome. Car park.
Directions: Exit1/M40 and Exit16/M25. A40 towards Gerrards Cross; right on A413 towards Amersham, second roundabout on the left. (Map 5, E4)

Denham

The Swan Inn

Village Road, Denham,
Buckinghamshire UB9 5BH
Telephone: +44(0)870 4016009
+44(0)1895 832085

Weary M25 and M40 travellers should shun the faceless services for this creeper-clad pub in upmarket Denham, just a few minutes drive from exits 17 and 1 respectively. With fine houses and brick and timber cottages for neighbours, and a magnificent rear terrace and garden, the Swan must be the best motorway pit-stop for miles. Like its stylish siblings (Alford Arms, Frithsden; Royal Oak, Marlow - see entries), the Swan's single bar and informal dining area has been tastefully refurbished and features a rug-strewn floor, a comfortable mix of sturdy tables and cushioned settles, large prints, and a splendid open log fire. Food follows the tried and tested formula of a chalkboard and regularly changing printed carte delivering modern pub food. 'Small plates' may range from rustic breads with roast garlic, balsamic and olive oil for an appetiser, to starters/light meals such as wild mushroom risotto or chicken, bacon and red onion terrine with tarragon and caper dressing. More substantial offerings may include pork and leek sausages with mash and shallot gravy, lamb rump with ratatouille and herb pistou, or rib-eye steak with horseradish and parsley butter.

Prices: Restaurant main course from £9.75.
House wine £10.75.
Last orders: Bar: 23.00. Food: lunch 14.30
(Sunday 15.00); dinner 22.00.
Closed: Rarely.
Food: Modern British.
Real Ale: Courage Best Bitter, Courage Directors, Morrell's Oxford Blue.
Other points: Garden. Children welcome. Dogs welcome in the bar. Car park.
Directions: Exit1/M40 and exit17/M25. From M40 take the A412 Uxbridge to Rickmansworth Road and turn left in 200 yards for Denham. (Map 5, E4)

Marlow

The Royal Oak

Frieth Road, Bovingdon Green, Marlow,
Buckinghamshire SL7 2JF
Telephone: +44(0)870 4016010
+44(0)1628 488611

Fronted by a gravel terrace edged with rosemary, with bay trees in pots either side of the door, this lovely cream-painted cottage on the edge of Marlow Common has been refurbished with style by David and Becky Salisbury. Beyond a cosy snug (open fire, rug-strewn boards, terracotta walls, an array of scrubbed oak tables, chairs and cushioned pews), piped jazz, and a buzzy atmosphere characterise the beamed and open-plan bar and dining areas. Informality is the key here, eat anywhere with the choice extending to both the rear terrace and the beautifully landscaped garden in summer. Both chalkboards and printed menus deliver food that reveals a lot of imagination at work in the kitchen. 'Small plates' range from clam, cockle and mussel broth, to substantial dishes such as calf's liver and bacon on carrot mash with rosemary jus, or chargrilled rib-eye steak with smoked paprika and chilli butter. Try the rustic breads with roast garlic and olive oil for dipping, there are freshly-cut lunchtime sandwiches, imaginative side orders and good puddings. The Salisbury's 'Country Pub and Eating' philosophy can also be enjoyed at the Alford Arms at Frithsden and the Swan at Denham (see entries).

Prices: Restaurant main course from £9.75.
House wine £10.75.
Last orders: Bar: 23.00. Food: lunch 14.30
(Sunday 15.00); dinner 22.00.
Closed: Rarely.
Food: Modern British.
Real Ale: Fuller's London Pride, Brakspear Ales, Marlow Rebellion.
Other points: Children welcome. Dogs welcome in the bar. Garden. Car park.
Directions: Take A4155 towards Henley; right in 300 yards for Bovingdon Green. (Map 5, E4)

Double Chocolate Chip Ice Cream *at the Ivy House*

Jane Mears of the Ivy House in Chalfont St Giles is pretty sure double chocolate chip is the winning flavour with her customers, though pistachio comes a close second. She is also quick to point out that this isn't just any old ice cream, this is Beechdeans - an ice cream company that takes care of every step from 'cow to customer'. This involves milking a pedigree herd of 120 Jersey and 270 Fresian cows twice a day on the 600-acre family farm and producing 1.5 million litres of ice cream every year.

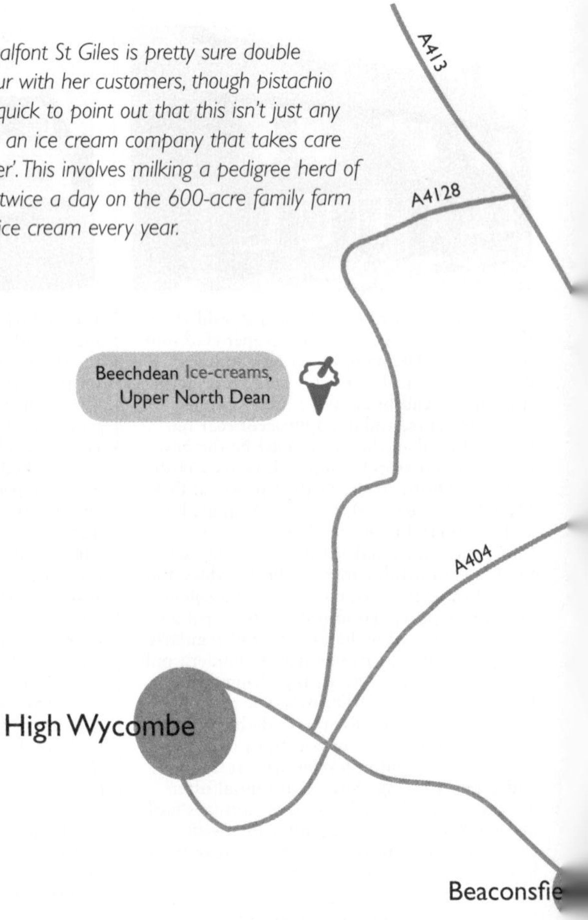

A413

A4128

Beechdean Ice-creams,
Upper North Dean

A404

High Wycombe

Beaconsfie

Based in the heart of Buckinghamshire's Chiltern Hills, Beechdean Ice Cream started in 1989 after Susie Howard took part in a one day ice cream making course, with a small machine and a van. Nowadays their ice cream can be found in all sorts of places ranging from the Albert Hall and Buckingham Palace to the Les Routiers listed Ivy House. This picturesque 17th-century brick and flint free house is well known for its fabulous food and sourcing of local produce. There are homemade soups on the blackboard and meats sourced from nearby butchers Goddens and Tom Robertsons as well as vegetables from D H Aldridge and eggs from Lower Bottom Farm, and for dessert, of course, three scoops of double chocolate chip.

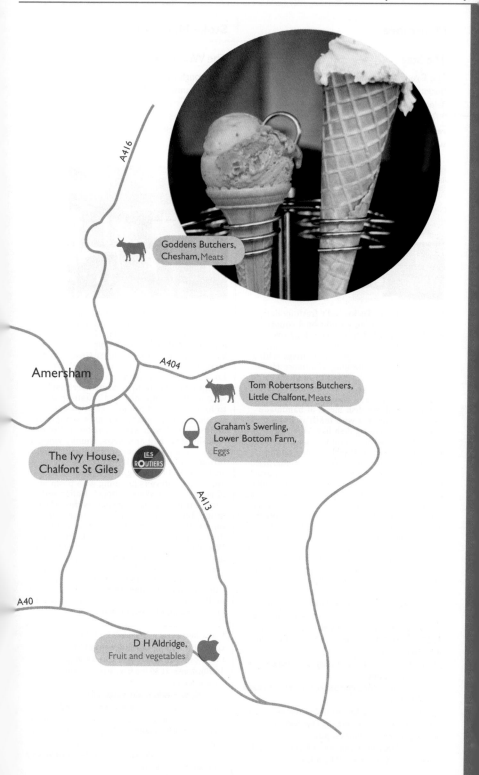

A416

Goddens Butchers,
Chesham, Meats

A404

Amersham

Tom Robertsons Butchers,
Little Chalfont, Meats

Graham's Swerling,
Lower Bottom Farm,
Eggs

The Ivy House,
Chalfont St Giles

LES ROUTIERS

A413

A40

D H Aldridge,
Fruit and vegetables

Mentmore

The Stag 🍷🍴

The Green, Mentmore,
Buckinghamshire LU7 0QF
Telephone: +44(0)870 4016011
+44(0)1296 668423
reservations@thestagmentmore.com
www.thestagmentmore.com

Mike and Jenny Tuckwood's fresh modern approach to running a traditional country pub has paid dividends since taking over this flagging rural inn some five years ago. It stands in a picture-postcard village with a lovely garden overlooking Mentmore House. The classic bar is the place to sample Charles Wells ales and some good bar food: sandwiches (hot beef and onion) and salads, for example, and one-dish meals of handmade local spicy sausages with mash and onion gravy, or an evening dish like Moroccan braised lamb with vegetable couscous. Imaginative, seasonally-changing evening menus are served in the stylishly modernised two-tiered restaurant, which has direct access to the garden. A plate of buffalo mozzarella (from a local buffalo herd) with balsamic and black pepper strawberries makes an unusual starter, with lobster ravioli in saffron broth and pork rillettes with crab apple jelly typical of other choices. Thoughtful attention to inherent flavours produces main courses such as roast cod with coconut and lemon sauce. An alternative to a dessert of baked American cheesecake is a plate of British cheeses.

Prices: Restaurant set lunch and dinner £28, main course £16. Bar lunch £4 or £6 and dinner £6 or £8.
Last orders: Bar: 23.00. Food: lunch 14.00 (bar food 15.30); dinner 21.00 (bar food 21.30); Sunday 20.30 (bar food 21.00).
Closed: Restaurant closed Monday lunch and evening.
Food: Modern British.
Real Ale: Charles Wells Bombadier, Charles Wells Eagle. Occasional guest beers.
Other points: No-smoking area. Children welcome at lunch and over 12 in the evening. Dogs welcome in the bar. Large garden. Limited car park.
Directions: Five miles north east of Aylesbury off A418 towards Leighton Buzzard. (Map 5, D4)

Stoke Mandeville

The Woolpack

Risborough Road, Stoke Mandeville, Aylesbury,
Buckinghamshire HP22 5UP
Telephone: +44(0)870 4016012
+44(0)1296 615970
www.woolpackstokemandeville.co.uk

One of four stylishly renovated pubs to open in 2004 by the dynamic team behind the hugely successful Orange Tree pub in the West Midlands. The Woolpack joins the Saxon Mill in Warwick, the St George and Dragon at Wargrave, and the group's first London venture, the Freemasons Arms in Hampstead (due to open September 2004), with more revamps of faded country pubs to follow across the South. The concept is simple and impressive, with pubs stripped out and reworked with wood or rushmat floors, squashy sofas and armchairs, chunky wooden furnishings, and a modern, minimalist look throughout. Trademark features include smart decked terracing, stone-fired ovens, and several dressers groaning with pasta jars, olive oils and baskets of bread. Italian-influenced menus are the same across this select group, but everything is freshly prepared on the premises with chefs interpreting the dishes as they wish. South of Aylesbury, the Woolpack offers 'little dishes' of squid, coriander, chilli and salsa, while 'leaves' feature chicken Caesar salad and crispy duck salad. There's also pizzas and pasta meals, more substantial dishes like rib-eye steak with Café de Paris butter, and daily chalkboard specials. Good ales and first-class wines.

Prices: Restaurant main course from £8.95. Main course bar from £5.50. House wine £11.95.
Last orders: Bar: 23.00. Food: lunch 14.30 (Sunday 16.30); dinner: 21.30 (no food Sunday evening).
Closed: Rarely.
Food: Modern British with Italian influences.
Real Ale: Bass, London Pride, Greene King IPA.
Other points: No-smoking in restaurant. Large garden and patio. Children welcome. Dogs welcome outside. Car park.
Directions: From Aylesbury take the B4443 signposted to Stoke Mandeville. (Map 5, E4)

Waddesdon

Five Arrows Hotel

High Street, Waddesdon, Aylesbury, Buckinghamshire HP18 0JE
Telephone: +44(0)870 4016013
+44(0)1296 651727
bookings@thefivearrowshotel.fsnet.co.uk
www.waddesdon.org.uk

Pitstone Windmill

Claydon House

A delightful Victorian confection (think turrets, gables and balconies) built by the Rothschilds' in 1887 to house the architects and craftsmen who were building Waddesdon Manor, Baron Ferdinand's Renaissance-style château is set on a hill in the vast estate behind the inn. Now a stylish small hotel-cum-inn run by Julian Alexander-Worster, you enter straight into the bar, from which open several civilised dining rooms with rug-strewn wood or stone floors, antique tables, and pictures from Lord Rothschild's collection. Locally sourced ingredients plus garden herbs influence the menu, crayfish tail salad with dill mayonnaise, for example, or salmon fishcakes with coriander jam. Thai marinated red mullet on soy noodles comes as a starter or main course, or there could be braised lamb shank with mint and sage gravy. To finish, choose between the cheese table or treacle tart and homemade honeycomb ice cream. There are also blackboard specials and lighter lunchtime meals like ploughman's lunches and steak and ale pie. The good wine list majors on the various Rothschild wine interests with eight by the glass. Eleven good-sized bedrooms are individually decorated with matching en suite bathrooms and boast all modern comforts. Both suites in the converted Courtyard Stables feature antique brass beds, and separate sitting areas.

Must See
- Waddesdon Manor
- Buckinghamshire Railway Centre, Quainton
- Claydon House, Middle Claydon
- Courthouse, Long Crendon
- Ascott, Wing
- Stowe House & Gardens
- Pitstone Windmill

Rooms: 11. Double room from £90, single from £70.
Prices: Main course from £13.50. House wine £12.50.
Last orders: Bar: lunch 15.00; dinner 23.00. Food: lunch 14.30 (Sunday 14.00); dinner 21.30 (Sunday 21.00).
Closed: Rarely.
Food: Modern British/Continental.
Real Ale: Fuller's London Pride.
Other points: No-smoking area. Garden. Car park.
Directions: Six miles north west of Aylesbury on A41.
(Map 5, D4)

Tourist Information Aylesbury +44(0)1296 330559
Where to Shop Aylesbury, Thame, Buckingham
Farmers Market Aylesbury (Tuesday)
Nearest Golf Course Aylesbury Park Golf Club
Cycling/Walking
Quiet lanes criss-cross the gently undulating Vale of Aylesbury linking attractive villages (Upper Winchendon, Brill, The Claydons) and places of interest (see above). See Pub Walk on page 266

Best Scenic Drives
South-east into the Chiltern Hills via Great Missenden, Amersham, Beaconsfield, High Wycombe and Henley-on Thames, returning via Stonor, Watlington and Thame. South-west to Oxford, Witney, Burford and the eastern Cotswolds.
Events and Festivals
Workshops, wine tastings and events at Waddesdon Manor (all year)
Thame Festival (June/July)

Brampton

The Grange Hotel

115 High Street, Brampton, Huntingdon,
Cambridgeshire PE28 4RA
Telephone: +44(0)870 4016014
+44(0)1480 459516
info@grangehotelbrampton.com
www.grangehotelbrampton.com

Nick and Susanna Steiger's redbrick hotel stands at one end of Brampton's meandering High Street. Built in 1773 and converted to a hotel in 1981, it has taken the Steiger's four years to restore and refurbish this attractive building back to its original Georgian elegance. Initial perceptions of this being a formal hotel ebb away as you venture beyond the lounge to the large modern bar, replete with Greene King ales, first-class wines, and ambitious modern food. Diners gather here to peruse Nick's imaginative bar menu, perhaps to order spaghetti with fresh crab, chilli, coriander and lime, or grilled sausages with onion mash and mustard sauce. Also available in the bar are the day's fixed-price menu and seasonally inspired carte which draws on supplies of fresh local produce, including rare breed meats from Denham Estate. Typically, begin with guinea fowl and artichoke terrine, follow with grilled sea bass with mussel and saffron broth, and round off with tarte tatin of mango with mango sorbet. Big upstairs bedrooms sport smart en suite bathrooms, CD players and large-screen TVs.

Rooms: 7. Double room from £80, single from £65, family from £100.
Prices: Set lunch and dinner £19.50. Restaurant main course from £8.50. Bar main course from £6.50. House wine £11.50.
Last orders: Bar: 23.00. Food: lunch 14.00; dinner 21.30 (no food served Sunday evening and residents only Sunday lunchtime).
Closed: First week of January.
Food: Modern British.
Real Ale: Greene King IPA. 2 guest beers.
Other points: No-smoking area. Dogs welcome. Garden. Children welcome. Car park. Licence for Civil Weddings.
Directions: A1/A14 interchange. B1514 past racecourse and turn into Grove Lane. (Map 6, C5)

Cambridge

The Green Man

Thriplow, Royston, Cambridgeshire SG8 7RJ
Telephone: +44(0)870 4016015
+44(0)1763 208855
www.greenmanthriplow.co.uk

In the heart of a small Cambridgeshire village stands this traditional looking village local, cream painted with attractive window boxes. Décor within is traditional with red patterned carpet, deep red walls, stripped tables, an open fire in a black metal grate, and a comfortable dining area with sofas in one corner. Beers change continually, with the emphasis on small breweries, so expect brews from Batemans, Milton and Wolf. The short global wine list reflects the menus and is changed regularly. The menus offer excellent value and evident passion in both compilation and cooking. Create your own dinner by selecting your main course, perhaps rib-eye steak or chicken supreme, your accompanying sauce, say creamy mushroom or pepper, then choose your desired side dishes from an impressive list. Precede with salmon fishcakes with tartare sauce, or chicken and bacon salad with balsamic dressing, and finish with crème brûlée with homemade shortbread. In addition, chalkboards list a good choice of daily specials. At lunch, tackle the sandwich 'kit', or opt for the locally made sausages with mustard mash and red wine gravy. Every two months there's a gourmet evening with matching wine list, and there's a popular Sunday lunch menu.

Prices: Set Sunday lunch £13.95. Restaurant main course from £7.50. Bar main course from £3.50. House wine £10.50.
Last orders: Bar: lunch 15.00; dinner 23.00. Food: lunch 14.00; dinner 21.00.
Closed: Sunday evening, all day Monday.
Food: Traditional/Modern British.
Real Ale: Klas Act. 4 guest beers.
Other points: No-smoking area. Children welcome. Garden. Car park.
Directions: Exit10/M11. Three miles south of junction off B1368. (Map 6, D5)

Heydon

The King William IV

Chishill Road, Heydon,
Cambridgeshire SG8 8PN
Telephone: +44(0)870 4016016
+44(0)1763 838773
www.kingwilliv.freeuk.com

Vegetarians will love this place, with over a dozen unusual dishes that have won awards for the licensee, Elizabeth Nichols, who has set the trend for more vegetarian cooking in pubs. Tuck into sweet chestnut potato cakes with wholegrain mustard sauce, goat's cheese and vegetable Wellington with saffron sauce, or Mediterranean vegetable moussaka with Greek salad. Meat lovers will not be disappointed with braised lamb shank with roasted garlic and red wine jus, or a classic steak and kidney pudding. A chalkboard lists lunchtime baguettes and local produce is used wherever possible on the menu. Although quite unremarkable from the outside, it is like an Aladdin's Cave within, overflowing with agricultural oddities, giant bellows, cast iron cauldrons, wrought-iron lamps, casks, decorative plates, heavy beams, tiled floors and rustic tables, some of them suspended by chains from the ceiling. Beyond this jumble of artefacts is the decorative stone bar counter that dispenses top-notch ale from Adnams, Fuller's, Greene King and local micro-breweries. It may be very atmospheric on a winter's evening, but escape the dark interior on fine summer evenings and enjoy a drink on the decking terrace, complete with teak furnishings and outdoor heaters.

Prices: Main course from £7.95. House wine £12.25.
Last orders: Bar: lunch 14.30; dinner 23.00. Food: lunch 14.00 (Sunday 14.30); dinner 22.00 (Sunday 21.30).
Closed: Rarely.
Food: Modern European.
Real Ale: Fuller's London Pride, Adnams, Brains Rev James. 2 guest beers.
Other points: No-smoking area. Children welcome. Garden. Car park.
Directions: Three miles east of Royston off B1039. Two miles from Exit 9 and 10 of the M11. (Map 6, D5)

Keyston

Pheasant Inn

Keyston, Huntingdon, Cambridgeshire PE18 0RE
Telephone: +44(0)870 4016017
+44(0)1832 710241
pheasant.keyston@btopenworld.com

At the heart of the village, beneath a huge sycamore tree, sits the Pheasant Inn. Formed from classic 16th-century English cottages, with dark thatch, a mass of floral planters and al fresco tables and chairs out front making you a temporary part of this picture-postcard scene. Within, it is quintessentially 'olde England': leather upholstery, the odd stuffed bird, hunting and shooting prints, a mass of blackened beams, brick inglenooks, flagstone floor and stripped boards. There's nothing 'olde worlde' about the cooking, however. Whether you eat in the informal lounge or in the more formal dining room, the menu's the same with no restrictions as to how much or how little you eat. Pressed terrine of confit chicken with herb mayonnaise, Thai duck salad with cucumber noodles, slow-roast pork hock with potato and apple cake and root vegetables, pot-roast guinea fowl with asparagus, girolle mushrooms and pancetta cream, and hot chocolate fondant with crème fraiche for pudding show modern food cooked with skill and assurance, and based on prime raw materials. The delights of the wine list are a joy to behold, with some 40 of the 100 well-chosen bins priced at around £20, with 20 available by the glass.

Prices: Set lunch £14.95. House wine £11.50.
Last orders: Food: lunch 14.00; dinner 21.00 (Sunday 21.00).
Closed: Rarely.
Food: Modern British.
Real Ale: Adnams. 3 guest beers.
Other points: No-smoking areas. Dogs welcome daytime only. Children welcome. Car park.
Directions: Village signed off A14 west of Huntingdon. (Map 5, C4)

Three Horseshoes, Madingley, Cambridgeshire

Madingley

Three Horseshoes

High Street, Madingley, Cambridge,
Cambridgeshire CB3 8AB
Telephone: +44(0)870 4016018
+44(0)1954 210221

The quintessential rural look of this white
painted and very picturesque thatched inn
gives way to stylish country chic and a lively
cosmopolitan atmosphere as you step inside
this early 1900s building. The Victorian
orangery look does justice to the original
architecture, mixing a light Mediterranean
feel with period elegance through pastel-
coloured waxed wood, stripped boards,
old-style foodie prints, brick fireplaces, lots
of light wood, leather-topped bar stools and
banquettes. Moving through to the conservatory restaurant, though similar in design
and with an identical menu to the bar area,
white linen, wicker chairs, lots of shrubs and
indoor plants growing up a trellis create a
relaxed mood. Richard Stokes's confident
cooking is a sound interpretation of the
Huntsbridge Group's policy of seasonal food
using prime raw materials. Thus, a typical
spring meal could bring risotto of peas, broad
beans, mint vermouth and pecorino, roast
turbot marinated with green olives, oregano
and lemon, or lamb rump with chorizo, green
bean salad and roast chilli salsa, followed by
strawberry and red wine sorbet. As with all
Huntsbridge places, there is a superb choice
of wines, offering the great and godly as well
as the unusual, with 34 halves listed.

Prices: Bar main course from £9.50.
House wine £11.50.
Last orders: Bar: lunch 14.00; dinner 21.00. Food: lunch
14.00 (Sunday 14.30); dinner 20.30.
Closed: Rarely.
Food: Italian.
Real Ale: Adnams Southwold. 1 guest beer.
Other points: No-smoking area. Restaurant no
smoking. Children welcome. Garden. Car park.
Directions: Two miles west of Cambridge. From Lon-
don leave the M11 at the A1303 exit. From the north
take the A14 then A1307. (Map 6, D5)

Chester

The Pheasant Inn

Higher Burwardsley, Tattenhall, Chester, Cheshire CH3 9PF
Telephone: +44(0)870 4016019
+44(0)1829 770434
reception@thepheasant-burwardsley.com
www.thepheasant-burwardsley.com

The Pheasant lies hidden down twisting narrow lanes high in the Peckforton Hills on the popular Sandstone Trail close to Peckforton Castle. A rambling place, once a farm and, surprisingly, an ale-house here since the 17th-century, the oldest part is the setting for the beautifully refurbished wood-floored bar, which has a bright, modern feel and claims to house the largest log fire in Cheshire. A tasteful contemporary style extends to the imposing, stone-flagged conservatory restaurant that looks over a tiered patio and, beyond, across the Cheshire plain towards Chester Cathedral and North Wales - a stunning spot from which to savour a pint of local Weetwood ale or one of eight wines by the glass. Game terrine or monkfish brochettes with saffron rice and red pepper coulis may preceed pan-fried sea bass with tomato and spinach tian or duck with wild berry and thyme jus. In addition, there are interesting daily specials and good puddings include toffee and date pudding with butterscotch sauce. The old barn has been skillfully converted into eight very comfortable bedrooms, including two suites, and spotless bathrooms. Two further bedrooms, housed in the pub proper, boast original beams and memorable views.

Shropshire Union Canal

Rooms: 10. Double room from £80, single from £65, Family room from £100, suite from £90.
Prices: Lunch £5-£20 and dinner £8-£20.
House wine £12.95.
Last orders: Bar: 23.00. Food: lunch 14.30 (Sunday 14.00); dinner 21.30 (Sunday 20.30).
Closed: Never.
Food: Modern British.
Real Ale: Weetwood Best, Eastgate, Old Dog, Ambush. 4 guest beers.
Other points: No-smoking area. Children welcome. Garden. Car park.
Directions: A41 south of Chester; 1 mile after Flatlow Heath turn left signposted to Burwardsley. Turn right in Tattenhall and take an immediate left. At the post office in Burwardsley, bear left up Higher Burwardsley Road to the inn. (Map 7, G4)

Must See
- Chester
- Beeston Castle: 13th-century ruin.
- Stapeley Water Gardens: many varieties of water lillies thrive in lakes, pools and waterfalls.
Local activities
Fishing on the River Weaver and the Shropshire Union Canal.

Events and Festivals
Nantwich and South Cheshire Agricultural Show (July)
Jazz Festival (Easter weekend)
Nantwich Folk Festival (Aug)
Chester

Tourist Information Nantwich +44(0)1270 610983
Where to Shop Chester, Nantwich, Northwich
Tarporley, Whitchurch
Farmers Market Nantwich (last Sat of month)
Kelsall (3rd Sat of month)
Nearest Racecourse Chester
Nearest Golf Course Carden Park

Where to Walk
Plenty of good waymarked walks in the area. For something more adventurous, try the Sandstone Trail which opened in 1974 and explores the central Cheshire sandstone ridge, rising to over 700 ft. The walk can be completed in 3 day-long sections of about 11 miles each.
See also Pub Walk on page 268

Mellor

The Oddfellows Arms

73 Moor End Road, Mellor, Stockport,
Cheshire SK6 5PT
Telephone: +44(0)870 4016020
+44(0)161 449 7826

Forming part of a ridge-top terrace of grit-stone cottages affording fine views across the Peak District, the three-storey Oddfellows Arms was built in 1700 to cater for the needs of mill workers from the many woollen mills that once thrived in the area. In 1860, the Oddfellows Society (a forerunner of the modern day trade union movement) required a meeting room and approached the landlord and over the years the name stuck. Within, it's rather like walking into someone's home. Beyond the flagged main bar there's a carpeted lounge and a cosy snug with log-burning stove, and throughout you will find an eclectic mix of furnishings and walls festooned with old prints and unusual display cases filled with church keys and fishing equipments. This is the place to settle with a jar of Adnams or Phoenix Arizona, but most people are here for the excellent food, whether bar snacks of Catalan cassoulet, Goan monkfish curry, a thick pea and ham soup, or a full-blown three course meal. Seafood is a speciality, say, whole snapper steamed Cantonese style, or fillet of cod in ale batter. Meat dishes can include shoulder of lamb with rosemary or rib of beef. The global wine list is fairly priced. See Pub Walk on page 270.

Prices: Sunday lunch £11.45. Set lunch £14 and dinner £20. Main course from £10. House wine £8.45.

Last orders: Bar: lunch 15.00; dinner 23.00. Food: lunch 14.30 (Sunday 14.00); dinner 21.30.

Closed: Monday, 3 weeks in the summer.

Food: International.

Real Ale: Marston's Bitter, Phoenix Arizona, Adnams Southwold. 1 guest beer.

Other points: No-smoking area. Children welcome. Dogs welcome in the bar. Small patio. Car park.

Directions: J1/M60. From Stockport follow the A626 to Marple and then follow signs to Mellor. (Map 8, F5)

Tarporley

The Fox and Barrel

Forest Road, Cotebrook, Tarporley,
Cheshire CW6 9DZ
Telephone: +44(0)870 4016021
+44(0)1829 760529
info@thefoxandbarrel.com
www.thefoxandbarrel.com

Martin and Peterene Cocking's thriving food pub stands beside the A49 north of Tarporley in unspoilt Cheshire countryside. Named the Fox and Barrel after a former landlord let a pursued fox escape to the cellar, it is worth seeking out for the genuine welcome, interesting seasonal menus and a tip-top pint of Bass. Beyond the snug bar, with its huge log fire, china ornaments and jugs, mix of tables and chairs, and daily newspapers, the half-panelled dining area sports a rug-strewn wood floor and rustic farmhouse tables topped with church candles. Interesting menus list 'lite bites' such as salmon and dill fishcakes with lemon mayonnaise, a bowl of mussels, and roast ham ploughman's, all served with a basket of own-baked bread. More inventive restaurant meals take in smooth liver pâté with red onion marmalade, homemade crab cake with spring onion and ginger, Barbary duck breast on spiced noodles with honey, ginger and soy syrup, or fillet steak with peppercorn sauce. Puddings include spiced raisin and ginger pudding with local Snugbury's ice cream. There's a good choice of wines with 15 by the glass, malt whiskies, a secluded summer patio for al fresco eating, and live New Orleans jazz every Monday.

Prices: Set lunch £14.50. Main course from £8.95. Bar/snack from £4.25. House wine £9.95.

Last orders: Bar: lunch 15.00; dinner 23.00 (all day during the week-end). Food: lunch 14.30; dinner 21.30 (Sunday 21.00).

Closed: Rarely.

Food: Modern pub food.

Real Ale: Bass, Marstons Pedigree, John Smiths Cask. 1 guest beer.

Other points: No-smoking area. Garden. Car park.

Directions: On the main A49, adjacent to Oulton Park race circuit, on the Warrington side of Tarporley. (Map 7, G4)

Wrenbury

The Dusty Miller

Wrenbury, Nantwich, Cheshire CW5 8HG
Telephone: +44(0)870 4016022
+44(0)1270 780537
admin@dustymill-wrenbury.co.uk
www.dustymiller-wrenbury.co.uk

The position of this handsomely converted 19th-century watermill is lovely, beside the Llangollen branch of the Shropshire Union Canal and next to a striking counter-weighted drawbridge. The River Weaver also flows through the pub garden and picnic tables among rose bushes on a raised gravel terrace are popular with locals and narrowboat owners enjoying pints of Robinsons Ales and summer hog roasts. The impressive modern interior has tall arched windows facing the water, hunting prints on terracotta walls and an eclectic mix of tables and seating. Good bar food is built around quality local and organic ingredients and ranges from starters of Shropshire Blue cheese paté with fruit chutney, to mains of jugged beef braised with red wine, onions and mushrooms, or braised salmon fillet on chive mash with prawn butter sauce. A chalkboard lists fresh fish from Fleetwood, perhaps naturally smoked haddock and baked prawns with melted cheddar cheese, and a light lunch menu lists decent sandwiches, for example black pudding and smoked bacon. To finish, there may be sloe gin ice cream with warm berry compote, or Eton Mess - meringue, whipped cream and strawberries. Alternatively, order a plate of cheese from a menu that lists individual makers.

Prices: Main course from £9.95. House wine £12.75.
Last orders: Bar: lunch 15.00; dinner 23.00. Food: lunch 14.00; dinner 21.30 (Monday 20.30, Sunday 21.00).
Closed: Monday lunchtime.
Food: Traditional and Modern British.
Real Ale: Robinson's Best, Robinson's Hatters Mild. 6 (seasonal) guest beers.
Other points: No-smoking area. Children welcome. Garden. Car park.
Directions: Signposted from the A530 Nantwich to Whitchurch Road. (Map 7, G4)

Darlington

The County

13 The Green, Aycliffe, Darlington,
Co Durham DL5 6LX
Telephone: +44(0)870 4016023
+44(0)1325 312273
www.the-county.co.uk

'Quality is paramount', so states chef-patron Andrew Brown on the County's website. He won Raymond Blanc's first scholarship in 1995 and then worked with the master in the kitchen's at Le Manoir aux Quat' Saisons, so Andrew knows about 'quality', namely careful cooking of first-class, fresh local produce. But to find it in a stylishly modernised pub overlooking Aycliffe's pretty village green near Darlington is a real surprise. The light, airy bar and bistro have adopted a rustic-chic look, the pared-back décor featuring chunky tables and padded pine chairs on wooden or tiled floors. In the main, the place offers first-class modern British cooking in an informal but civilized pub setting, but drinkers are made very welcome and real ale enthusiasts will find four brews on tap. Open sandwiches, freshly-battered haddock, and sausages and black pudding mash may appear on the bar menu. In the bistro, materials run to crab and prawn risotto with lobster sauce, halibut with Welsh rarebit crust, pesto new potatoes and tomato salad, and confit shoulder of lamb with Mediterranean vegetables and mint couscous. Leave room for an excellent pudding, perhaps rich lime and lemon cheesecake. Good value global list of wines.

Prices: Main course from £10.75. Bar meal from £7.50.
House wine £11.45.
Last orders: Bar: lunch 14.00 (Sunday 15.00); dinner 23.00. Food: lunch 14.00; dinner 21.15.
Closed: Sunday evening.
Food: Modern British.
Real Ale: Wells Bombardier Premium Bitter, Theakston Best. 2 guest beers.
Other points: No-smoking area. Children welcome. Car park.
Directions: Exit59/M1. Towards Aycliffe village on the A167, turn right into the village and then right immediately on to The Green. (Map 8, C5)

Romaldkirk

The Rose and Crown at Romaldkirk

Romaldkirk, Barnard Castle, Co Durham DL12 9EB
Telephone: +44(0)870 4016024
+44(0)1833 650213
hotel@rose-and-crown.co.uk
www.rose-and-crown.co.uk

High Force

Must See
- Barnard Castle
- Raby Castle: 14th-century castle built for Nevill family and surrounded by 200-acre parkland.
- Bowes Museum: 19th-century French-style chateau with fine collection of paintings, furniture and tapestries.
- High Force: England's highest waterfall (70ft).
- Killhope Lead Mining Centre

Barnard Castle

Built in 1733 as a coaching inn, the imposing, stone-built Rose and Crown stands beside the Saxon church and one of the beautifully maintained greens in the most picturesque of Teesdale villages. Since arriving here in 1989, Christopher and Alison Davy's tireless enthusiasm and dedication to providing high standards of hospitality, service and cooking has created one of the finest all-round inns in the country. Much of this success can be attributed to consistent cooking that is inspired by the seasons and backed by first-class local produce (served in the cosy lounge bar, and in the smart bistro-style Crown Room). Lunchtime filled baps are well presented and traditional favourites such as kidney and mushroom pie are always cooked with flair. Weekly changing menus may also list lamb's liver with black pudding mash and shallot gravy and confit of duck leg with orange sauce. Exemplary puddings are typified by hot walnut and syrup tart, but there's perfectly-selected local cheeses (Cotherstone, Blue Wensleydale). Four-course dinners are served at elegantly clothed tables in the civilised, part-panelled restaurant. The spotlessly maintained en suite bedrooms (two superb suites and five equally impressive courtyard bedrooms), have creaking floorboards, beams, stripped stone walls, well-chosen antique furniture, stylish contemporary fabrics, and a host of extras. See Pub Walk on page 272.

Rooms: 12. Double/twin room from £96.
Prices: Set lunch £14.95 and dinner £26. Bar main course from £7.95. House wine £12.95.
Last orders: Bar: lunch 15.00; dinner 23.00. Food: lunch 13.30; dinner 21.30 (Sunday 21.00).
Closed: Rarely.
Food: Modern British.
Real Ale: Black Sheep Best, Theakston Best.
Other points: No-smoking area. Children welcome. Car park.
Directions: Six miles north west of Barnard Castle on the B6277 towards Middleton-in-Teesdale. (Map 8, C5)

Tourist Information
Barnard Castle +44(0)1833 690909
Where to Shop Barnard Castle, Durham
Farmers Market Barnard Castle (1st Sat of month)
Best Scenic Drives
B6277 and unclassified road to St John's Chapel, A689, B6295 and B6305 to Hexham, return via B6306 and

B6278. A66 and minor roads to Grinton and Reeth, B6270 to Keld, return to A66 via Tan Hill and Sleightholme.
Events and Festivals
Teeside Thrash - music and dance (May)
Barnard Castle Meet Annual Carnival (May)

Launceston

The Springer Spaniel

Treburley, Launceston, Cornwall PL15 9NS
Telephone: +44(0)870 4016025
+44(0)1579 370424
thespringer@wagtailinns.com
www.wagtailinns.com

Richard Beaman takes food seriously at his solid, unassuming roadside pub south of Launceston. The main bar has a high-backed settle and two farmhouse-style chairs fronting a wood-burning stove, comfortable wall benches, rustic tables and a relaxing, chatty atmosphere - no intrusive music or games here. Richard is gradually smartening up the interior and restoring the pub to its former glory, including refurbishment of the separate beamed dining-room. Emphasis in the kitchen is on the use of fresh local ingredients, including game from nearby estates, fish landed at Looe, and daily produce from Plough to Plate, the Cornish farmers cooperative. For a light snack choose local ham and eggs, ciabatta sandwiches, steak and ale pie, or a potted local game pâté starter. More substantial fare, listed on the main menu and daily-changing chalkboards (also served in the bar), may include the likes of rack of Cornish lamb with a mustard and herb crust and redcurrant and mint dressing and fillets of sea bass with a roast pepper butter. Quality of food is matched with good service, a well-chosen list of wines (seven by the glass), and tip-top West Country ales - Sharps Doom Bar, Cornish Coaster and Springer Ale - on handpump.

Prices: Main course restaurant from £8.95.
Main course bar from £4.95. House wine £9.95.
Last orders: Bar: lunch 15.00; dinner 23.00.
Food: lunch 14.00; dinner 21.00.
Closed: Rarely.
Food: Traditional and Modern British.
Real Ale: Sharp's Cornish Coaster, Sharp's Doom Bar Bitter, Sharp's Springer Ale. 1 guest beer.
Other points: No-smoking area. Children welcome. Garden. Car park.
Directions: Beside A388 midway between Launceston and Callington. (Map 3, F4)

Lostwithiel

Royal Oak

Duke Street, Lostwithiel, Cornwall PL22 1AG
Telephone: +44(0)870 4016026
+44(0)1208 872552
mghine@aol.com

An unassuming, stone-built, 13th-century inn just off the main road in the original capital of Cornwall and reputedly linked to nearby Restormel Castle by a smuggling or escape tunnel. Catering for all tastes, the lively, slate-flagstoned public bar is genuinely local, attracting a good loyal following who seek out the choice of real ales, including Sharp's Own Bitter and tip-top brews from Lostwithiel's Keltek micro-brewery. By contrast, the comfortably furnished and carpeted lounge bar is very much geared to a dining clientele. Close inspection of a fairly standard, and lengthy, printed menu (and of the additional blackboard selection) will reveal some good homecooked dishes, for which Eileen Hine is justly renowned, served in very generous portions. Her excellent 'cow pie' (steak and kidney marinated and cooked in real ale) is legendary, but look out for her delicious homemade soups, crab au gratin and locally caught whole plaice with chips, alongside good sandwiches and hearty ploughman's lunches. Puddings include a homemade treacle tart or apple pie served with thick clotted cream. Upstairs bedrooms have recently been upgraded, all are spacious, well decorated, and furnished with a mix of period and pine furniture.

Rooms: 8. Double room from £75, single from £43.
Prices: Restaurant main course from £8.25. Bar main course from £5.95. House wine £9.95.
Last orders: Bar: 23.00. Food: lunch 14.00; dinner 21.15.
Closed: Rarely.
Food: Traditional English.
Real Ale: Fuller's London Pride, Marston's Pedigree, Bass, Keltek Exe Valley. 6 guest beers.
Other points: No-smoking area. Children welcome. Garden. Car park.
Directions: Just off the A390 in the town-centre. (Map 3, F3)

Mitchell

The Plume of Feathers

Mitchell, Truro, Cornwall TR8 5AX
Telephone: +44(0)870 4016027
+44(0)1872 510387
enquiries@theplume.info
www.theplume.info

In an area devoid of decent pubs, Martyn Warner's inspired transformation of a run-down 16th-century coaching inn off the A30 is a real oasis for discerning locals and weary travellers bound for Penzance. Now a stylish pub-restaurant with rooms, the refurbished bar and dining areas sport pine tables topped with candles and fresh flowers, painted half-boarded walls, stripped old beams and striking modern art. Careful conversion of barns has created five extremely comfortable bedrooms, all modelled on Olga Polizzi's Tresanton Hotel at St Mawes and kitted out with handmade pine furniture, iron or brass beds, large-screen TVs, modern art, and marble-tiled en suite bathrooms. An interesting range of modern European dishes mixed with British classics, run to tapas with chargrilled bread, handmade Cornish pasty with fries, Caesar salad and green Thai chicken with coconut cream. Dinner is a tad more serious, offering the likes of Cornish scallops with fresh herb salsa, glazed lamb shank with savoy cabbage and red wine jus, and plenty of imaginative fishy specials, perhaps seared tuna on roasted vegetables with red pepper juice and basil oil. Typical puddings include banana sticky toffee pudding, or finish with Cornish cheese and oatcakes. Expect Sharp's Doom Bar and three guest ales on tap.

Rooms: 5. Double room from £65, single from £48.75.
Prices: Main course from £7.25.
House wine £10.25-11.25.
Last orders: Bar: 23.00. Food: 22.00.
Closed: Rarely.
Food: Modern European/British.
Real Ale: Sharp's Doom Bar Bitter. 3 guest beers.
Other points: No-smoking area. Children welcome.
Dogs welcome in the bar. Garden. Car park.
Directions: At the junction of A3076 and A30, seven miles from Newquay. (Map 3, F3)

Port Gaverne

Port Gaverne Hotel

Port Gaverne, Port Isaac, Cornwall PL29 3SQ
Telephone: +44(0)870 4016029
+44(0)1208 880244. Freephone 0500 657867
www.portgavernehotel.co.uk

Graham and Annabelle Sylvester's charming 17th-century inn is peacefully situated in a sheltered cove just 50 yards from the beach. Since taking over in early 2002 the Sylvester's have gradually upgraded and refurbished this famous coastal inn and the 15 very good value bedrooms sport a fresh, comfortable look and gleaming modern bathrooms. The ship-shape, characterful pubby bar has a polished slate floor, a big log fire, Sharp's ales on tap, and first-rate traditional bar food in the form of ploughman's, ham and egg and seafood pie. A tiny snug bar with collections of old local photographs and a genuine ship's table, and an equally beamed and pleasant restaurant with fresh flowers lend a wonderful lack of formality. Noted for very fresh fish and a commitment to local produce, the Port Gaverne succeeds admirably in balancing good food and hospitality to all comers with a wholly acceptable degree of Cornish idiosyncracy. Dinner could produce homemade crab soup, monkfish wrapped in bacon with orange and ginger sauce, Port Isaac lobster, and a selection of regional cheeses as an alternative to pudding. Good value list of wines. Wonderful coastal path walks and magical summer sunsets.

Rooms: 15. Double/twin from £70, single from £35, family from £70.
Prices: Set dinner £25. Sunday lunch £10.95. Bar main course from £4.95. House wine £10.95.
Last orders: Bar: 23.00. Food: lunch 14.30; dinner 21.30.
Closed: 1 - 14 February.
Food: Traditional and Modern British.
Real Ale: Bass, Sharp's Doom Bar Bitter.
Other points: No-smoking area. Garden. Children welcome. Dogs welcome overnight. Car park.
Directions: Follow Port Isaac signs from A30 north of Camelford and A389 from Wadebridge via the B3314. (Map 3, F3)

St Breward

The Old Inn

Churchtown, St Breward, Bodmin Moor, Cornwall PL30 4PP
Telephone: +44(0)870 4016030
+44(0)1208 850711
darren@theoldinn.fsnet.co.uk
www.theoldinnandrestaurant.co.uk

A low white-painted stone cottage that claims to be the highest pub in Cornwall at 700 feet, set on the edge of Bodmin Moor in a true Cornish village. The weathered carved stone cross set in the front lawn is said to be of Saxon origin and parts of the bar date back over 1,000 years - when it was an alehouse for the builders constructing the parish church. Beyond the deep entrance porch, the strongly traditional interior exudes charm and atmosphere, with slate floors, part-exposed walls, thick beams, oak settles, a roaring winter log fire in the huge granite fireplace, and a newly extended dining area. Tools, traps, brasses and banknotes enhance the inn's rural character. Food at the Old Inn is wholesome, unpretentious and not for the faint-hearted - portions are very generous! Walkers, locals and moorland trippers tuck into hearty pub favourites like ploughman's, homemade pies and curries and Charlie Harris's garlic sausages and chips, all washed down with a tip-top pint of Sharps local ale - try the excellent Doom Bar. Locally reared beef provides the excellent steaks, and fresh fish, notably the huge battered cod, is landed at nearby harbours along the north Cornish coast.

Prices: Main course from £6.95. House wine £11.95.
Last orders: Bar: 23.00. Food: lunch 14..00. dinner 21.00.
Closed: Rarely.
Food: Modern British /Cornish.
Real Ale: Sharp's Doom Bar Bitter, Sharp's Special, Bass. Eden Ale as guest beer.
Other points: No-smoking area. Garden. Children welcome. Car park. 120 seat restaurant available for functions.
Directions: Follow signposts for St Breward from A30, or B3266 Bodmin to Camelford road. (Map 3, F3)

St Keverne

The White Hart Hotel

The Square, St Keverne, Helston, Cornwall
TR12 6ND
Telephone: +44(0)870 4016031
+44(0)1326 280325
www.whitehartcornwall.co.uk

Overlooking the square and church in the heart of this pretty village on the Lizard Peninsula, this 18th-century inn serves as a thriving community local and as a dining pub. Divers, walkers and tourists mingle with locals in the welcoming, wood floor bar as this popular pub is close to Flambards Theme Park and an easy stroll from the coast path and one of the best diving sites in the country. New owners Mark and Lesley Saffill took over the pub just before we went to press and there are plans to smarten up the exterior and refurbish the bar and dining areas. Head for the latter, where exposed beams, sea-grass matting and local art are the backdrop for hearty traditional bar food and daily fish specials like sea bass wrapped in bacon. Typically tuck into a generous mixed ploughman's lunch, local ham, egg and chips, or a large plate of scampi and chips. Alternative choices run to prime fillet steak, pasta and vegetarian dishes. Don't forgo the excellent crab sandwiches if you are here at lunchtime - or the indulgent, weekend-long Crab Festival in mid-July. There's comfortable cottagey accommodation in two en suite bedrooms.

Rooms: 2. Double room from £50, single from £35.
Prices: Restaurant main course from £5.00. Bar snack from £4.50. House wine £8.95.
Last orders: Bar: lunch 14.30; dinner 23.00. Food: lunch 14.00; dinner 21.00.
Closed: Rarely.
Food: Traditional Pub Food. Seafood.
Real Ale: Sharp's Doom Bar Bitter, Greene King Abbot Ale. One guest beer in Winter, two in Summer.
Other points: No-smoking area. Dogs welcome. Children welcome. Garden. Car park.
Directions: Village on B3293 11 miles south east of A3083 and Helston. (Map 3, G3)

The Lizard

Cadgwith Cove Inn

Cadgwith, Ruan Minor, Helston,
Cornwall TR12 7JX
Telephone: +44(0)870 4016032
+44(0)1326 290513
enquiries@cadgwithcoveinn.com
www.cadgwithcoveinn.com

A tiny fishing hamlet of thatched cottages on the rugged and beautiful Lizard coastline is the appealing setting for this 300-year-old pub, formerly the haunt of smugglers. In front of the plain, whitewashed building a sunny patio affords drinkers views across the old pilchard cellar to the peaceful cove. Down the lane is the shingle beach and the colourful fishing vessels that provide the inn with freshly-caught mullet, sea bass, gurnard, and the best crab and lobster on the peninsula. Furnished simply and decked with mementoes of bygone seafaring days, the two bars, both with open fires, serve five real ales, notably Sharp's Doom Bar Bitter. Expect traditional homemade pub food, but note and try the delicious white crab meat sandwiches or the famous crab soup served with thick crusty bread. Fish fanciers should look no further than the blackboard, which lists the daily catch, or plump for the ever-popular beer-battered haddock and chips. Alternatives include a real Cornish cheese lunch - perfect with a pint after an invigorating coastal walk. Seven simply equipped bedrooms.

Rooms: 7, 2 with private bathrooms.
From £25 per person.
Prices: Set lunch from £10 and dinner from £13. Restaurant main course from £5.95. House wine £8.95.
Last orders: Bar: lunch 15.00 (Thursday 17.00); dinner 23.00 (all day during the weekend). Food: lunch 15.00; dinner 21.30.
Closed: Check for seasonal variations.
Food: Seafood and Traditional European.
Real Ale: Wadworth 6X, Marston's Pedigree, Sharp's Doom Bar Bitter, Flowers IPA. Guest beers.
Other points: Children welcome. Dogs welcome. Garden and patio.
Directions: Off A3083 9 miles south of Helston. (Map 3, G3)

Ambleside

Drunken Duck Inn

Barngates, Ambleside, Cumbria LA22 ONG
Telephone: +44(0)870 4016033
+44(0)15394 36347
info@drunkenduckinn.co.uk
www.drunkenduckinn.co.uk

Wordsworth

Must See
- Rydal Mount:
Wordsworth's home.
- Bridge House
- Hawkshead
Courthouse: 15th-
century and all that
remains of the village
manorial buildings.
- Hill Top: Beatrix
Potter wrote many of
her famous children's
stories here.

Hawkshead

Take the Tarn Hows turning at Outgate off the B5286 to this 17th-century inn standing high in the hills at a lonely crossroads, with spectacular views across distant Lake Windermere to its backdrop of craggy fells. Walkers, tourists and avid foodies love the place, all drawn to this isolated spot for the views, home-brewed beers, first-class modern cooking and stylish accommodation, so weekends at the Duck can get hectic. Beyond the traditional bar, three adjoining rooms feature original beams, open fires, stripped settles, antiques and a wealth of landscape and sporting prints; the residents lounge is particularly elegant and comfortable. Justifiably popular food makes good use of fresh local produce, the simpler lunchtime menu offering potted Flookburgh shrimps, beer-battered cod with chunky chips, and lamb cutlets with redcurrant jus. More elaborate evening dishes may open with quail confit and garlic tartlet with sauté foie gras and cep oil dressing, with baked red snapper with fig, lemon and vanilla confit among the main course options. Warm rhubarb and custard tart with crumble ice cream may appear on the list of homemade puddings. As well as beer brewed behind the inn, you will find 20 wines by the glass. Overnight guests are housed in stylish, individually designed bedrooms, all with modern creature comforts and impeccable bathrooms.

Rooms: 16. Double room from £85, single from £63.75.
Prices: Main course from £8.95. House wine £9.50.
Last orders: Bar: 23.00. Food 21:.00.
Closed: Rarely.
Food: Modern British.
Real Ale: Barngates Cracker Ale, Barngates Tag Lag, Barngates Chester's Strong and Ugly, Barngates Catnap. 1-2 guest beers.
Other points: Car park. Garden. Children welcome. Fly Fishing. Dogs welcome in public areas.
Directions: Exit 36/M6. Take the A592 from Kendal to Ambleside. Follow signs to Hawkshead on the B5286 and turn right after two and a half miles. (Map 7, D3)

Tourist Information Ambleside +44(0)15394 32582
Where to Shop Grasmere, Hawkshead, Windermere
Farmers Market
Kendal Market Place, last Friday of the month (not Dec)
Where to Walk
Within the Lake District National Park's 866 square miles lies an enormous variety of terrain and choice of paths and tracks. Keep to the valley floors or take one of the very pleasant walks along the shores of the lake between Windermere and Hawkshead. If you've a real sense of adventure, try the summits of Great Gable, Scafell Pike and Helvellyn. Wainwright's long-distance Coast to Coast Walk or the 70-mile Cumbria Way.
Events and Festivals
Grasmere Lakeland Sports and Show (Aug)
Ambleside Daffodil and Spring Flower Show (March)

Appleby-in-Westmorland

Tufton Arms Hotel

Market Square, Appleby-in-Westmorland,
Cumbria CA16 6XA
Telephone: +44(0)870 4016034
+44(0)17683 51593
info@tuftonarmshotel.co.uk
www.tuftonarmshotel.co.uk

An unusual and rather evocative conversion of a 16th-century building which became a Victorian coaching inn, beautifully restored by the Milsom family in 1989 to reflect the ambience of that period: attractive wallpapers, lots of prints in heavy frames, drapes, old fireplaces and large porcelain table lamps. The heavily-balustraded main staircase is a magnificent feature. Light lunch and supper menus are served in the clubby bar, with a more formal choice available in the stylish restaurant with its conservatory extension. Cooking is of a high standard, be it rack of Cumbrian fell-bred lamb, or game from the local Dalemain Estate, where Nigel Milsom regularly arranges shooting parties (along with fishing, a major attraction for many guests). Fish is delivered from Fleetwood, to create, perhaps, paupiette of lemon sole stuffed with smoked salmon with a dill white wine sauce. There is a French accent to the carefully selected, well-annotated wine list of 160 bins, although other parts of Europe and the new world get a look in, too. Bedrooms vary from suites with period fireplaces, antique furnishings and large old-style bathrooms, to more conventional well-equipped en suite rooms with good proportions, but there are some compact and simply-furnished rooms to the rear.

Rooms: 21. Double/twin from £95.
Prices: Set dinner £24.50. Restaurant main course from £9.75. Bar main course from £6.95. House wine £9.50.
Last orders: Bar: 23.00. Food: lunch 14.00; dinner 21.00.
Closed: Rarely.
Food: Traditional English and French.
Real Ale: Boddingtons, Worthington's Best.
Other points: Children welcome. Dogs welcome overnight. Car park. Licence for Civil Weddings.
Directions: Exit38/M6. Take the B6260 to Appleby via Orton. (Map 7, C4)

Armathwaite

The Dukes Head

Armathwaite, Carlisle, Cumbria CA4 9PB
Telephone: +44(0)870 4016035
+44(0)1697 472226
hh@hlynch51.freeserve.com
www.dukesheadhotel.co.uk

A long-standing favourite in the beautiful Eden Valley among ramblers, bird-watchers and fishing folk (who come in search of the finest trout and salmon in the North of England), Henry Lynch's homely whitewashed inn remains firmly traditional. It retains an instant appeal for those with plenty of time to linger and reminisce, making it a peaceful base from which to explore this unspoilt area. The half-dozen cottagey bedrooms are simply and traditionally furnished, the most popular being the three with en suite bathrooms. Downstairs, beyond the civilised lounge bar, with its stone walls, open fires, sturdy oak settle and tables, and antique country prints, you will find a locals' bar, a neat dining room, and a glorious garden that borders the River Eden. One menu operates throughout, and offers a straightforward range of well prepared dishes that make excellent use of fresh local ingredients, including hot potted Solway shrimps, game in season, and cumberland sausage made by a local butcher. There's a good choice of salads, omelettes and sandwiches. A typical meal may begin with locally smoked salmon and prawns, followed by tuna loin with lime, coriander, chilli and garlic butter, or stuffed roast duck and apple sauce, with bread-and-butter pudding to finish.
See Pub Walk on page 274.

Rooms: 5, 2 not en suite. Double room from £52.50, single from £32.50.
Prices: Main course from £6.45.
Set Sunday lunch £12.95. House wine £12.00.
Last orders: Bar: lunch 15.00; dinner 23.00.
Food: lunch 13.45; dinner 21.00.
Closed: Rarely.
Food: Traditional British.
Real Ale: Jennings Cumberland Ale. I guest beer.
Other points: No smoking in the restaurant . Children welcome. Dogs welcome. Garden. Car park.
Directions: Off A6 7 miles south Carlisle. (Map 7, C4)

Broughton in Furness

The Blacksmiths Arms

Broughton Mills, Broughton in Furness,
Cumbria LA2 6AX
Telephone: +44(0)870 4016036
+44(0)1229 716824
blacksmitharms@aol.com
www.theblacksmitharms.com

New owners Sophie and Michael Lane, formerly at Routiers member The Merchant
House in Norwich, bring invaluable experience to the 16th-century Blacksmiths Arms, a
gem of a pub tucked away in the wonderfully
named Lickle Valley. Festooned with colourful hanging baskets, with roses and flower-
beds bordering the sheltered front patio, it
was once a farmhouse with a little shop in
the back and, in those days, opened as an inn
in the evening only. It is said that Coleridge
stopped here for a rum butter sandwich on
his way to visit Wordsworth. The interior
has a country cottage feel with uneven stone-
flagged floors and higgledy-piggledy rooms
awash with memorabilia and old prints. The
Lane's have maintained the pub's reputation
for good food and for sourcing produce from
the surrounding area, notably game from
shoots and locally reared and slaughtered
beef. At lunch, tuck into french onion soup,
potted shrimps, Cumberland sausage with
black pudding mash and red onion gravy,
decent baguettes and sandwiches. Evening
additions may run to peppered salmon fillet
and duck breast pan-roasted with lemon and
honey, served with wilted spinach and red
wine and thyme sauce. Accompany with an
excellent pint of Jennings Cumberland Ale or
farmhouse cider.

Prices: Main course from £9. House wine £9.50.
Last orders: Bar: 23.30. Food: lunch 14.00 (no food on
Monday lunch); dinner 21.00.
Closed: Monday lunch in the winter.
Food: Traditional and Modern British.
Real Ale: Jennings Cumberland Ale.
Other points: No-smoking area. Dogs welcome.
Children welcome. Patio. Car park.
Directions: Exit36/M6. A590, follow the signs to
Broughton in Furness and Broughton Mills is two miles
the other side. (Map 7, D3)

Cockermouth

The Pheasant

Bassenthwaite Lake, Cockermouth,
Cumbria CA13 9YE
Telephone: +44(0)870 4016037
+44(0)17687 76234
info@the-pheasant.co.uk
www.the-pheasant.co.uk

Originally a 500-year-old farmhouse, the
long and low Pheasant Inn, just off the A66
west of Keswick, looks like the archetypal
Victorian roadside inn as it was converted in
1778 to a popular ale house. Now more of
a country house with the cosiness of an old
coaching inn, it is the period appeal of the
Pheasant that is memorable. The characterful old building delivers a great red-painted
bar, a very civilized and gracious drawing
room (where hot and cold bar snacks are
served), a dining room, crackling log fires,
old prints, and highly polished period furniture. Lunch or dinner in the low-ceilinged
dining room offers plenty of choice. Modern
British in outlook, the kitchen produces rack
of Cumbrian lamb with minted mash and
red wine jus and grilled sea bass on crushed
potatoes with roast lobster cream and tomato
confit. Chicken liver and brandy pâté and
ginger panna cotta with banana and lime,
top and tail main course choices. Many of
the wines on an eclectic list are priced under
£20. Bedrooms have been refurbished and
offer comfortable accommodation with some
of the furniture made by a local joiner/cabi-
net maker. Rooms have good space and are
well-appointed with extras, but TVs are on
request.

Rooms: 15 en suite. Double/twin from £130.
Prices: Set lunch £19.95 and dinner £27.95.
House wine £13.25.
Last orders: Bar: 22.30. Food: lunch 14.00; dinner 21.00.
Closed: Rarely.
Food: Traditional British and French.
Real Ale: Cumberland Ale, Theakston Ales, Bass.
Other points: No-smoking area. Garden. Children
welcome over eight years old.
Directions: Located midway between Keswick and
Cockermouth and signposted from the A66.
Exit 40/M6. (Map 7, C3)

Coniston

The Black Bull

1 Yewdale Road, Coniston, Cumbria LA21 8DU
Telephone: +44(0)870 4016038
+44(0)1539 441668
i.s.bradley@btinternet.com
www.conistonbrewery.com

Donald Campbell stayed at this 400-year-old coaching inn when attempting his ill-fated water speed records on Coniston Water, an event commemorated in the name of the inn's Bluebird Bitter which is brewed in the micro-brewery adjacent to the pub. Other famous luminaries that have enjoyed the inn's hospitality include the poet Coleridge and Turner the artist, perhaps inspired by its location in the shadow of Coniston's 'Old Man' mountain. Today's Lakeland explorers will find the en suite accommodation homely and traditional, the seventeen clean and comfortable bedrooms (some have recently been refurbished) being split between the main inn and the converted coach house, the latter featuring modern pine-furnished rooms. Enjoy an award-winning pint in the traditionally furnished bar, with its exposed beams, open fires and Campbell memorabilia, or relax on the terrace to the rear of the pub. The wide-ranging bar menu caters for all tastes, from sandwiches, ploughman's and salads to local Esthwaite smoked trout, generous Cumbrian grills (10oz cumberland sausage), and a selection of homemade vegetarian dishes. Or, there is a separate evening restaurant menu featuring such classic dishes as steak chasseur, roast duck with fruit sauce, and the Black Bull's speciality plum pudding.

Rooms: 15. Room from £39.50 per person.
Prices: Main course from £7.25. House wine £10.
Last orders: Bar: 23.00. Food: 21.00.
Closed: Rarely.
Food: Modern British.
Real Ale: Coniston Bluebird Bitter & Old Man Ale.
Other points: No-smoking area. Garden. Children welcome. Car park.
Directions: On A593 eight miles south of Ambleside. J36/M6. (Map 7, D3)

Ennerdale

The Shepherd's Arms Hotel

Ennerdale Bridge, Lake District National Park, Cumbria CA23 3AR
Telephone: +44(0)870 4016039
+44(0)1946 861249
reception@shepherdsarmhotel.co.uk
www.shepherdsarmhotel.co.uk

Val and Steve Madden's relaxed and informal country inn is a welcome sight for walkers tackling Wainwright's arduous Coast to Coast Walk - this is Stop 2 on the trail. In the homely bar you'll find a pleasant sitting area with bookcase and open fire, as well as the bar area proper, where tip-top ales - Coniston Bluebird, Timothy Taylor's Landlord, Jennings Bitter and guest ales - are dispensed on handpump. There is also a rear conservatory with french doors leading out to gardens, which border a lovely, fast flowing stream. The decorative theme is high Victorian, particularly in the restaurant. Although the demand is not for fancy food, Steve insists that all ingredients are authentic and local: blackboards and a specials' list feature local game and meats. The bar menu may offer steak and real ale pie, as well as soups, sandwiches and salads. In the restaurant, expect leek and potato soup, half-shoulder of Herdwick lamb with garlic and mint gravy, and chocolate and orange sponge with fudge sauce. The wine list is very reasonably priced, with a good global spread and comes with helpful tasting notes. Pleasant en suite bedrooms have views, homely touches and period furnishings.

Rooms: 8, 2 with private facilities. Double/twin from £63. Single occupancy from £40.
Prices: Set dinner £18.95. Main course from £6.95. House wine £9.95.
Last orders: Bar: 23.00. Food: lunch 14.00; dinner 21.00.
Closed: Rarely.
Food: Modern British.
Real Ale: Coniston Bluebird, Jennings Bitter, Tetley's Cask, Timothy Taylor Landlord. 4 guest beers.
Other points: No-smoking area. Children welcome. Dogs welcome overnight. Car park.
Directions: Village signposted off A5086 Egremont to Cockermouth road. (Map 7, C3)

Eskdale

The Burnmoor Inn

Boot, Eskdale, Cumbria CA19 1TG
Telephone: +44(0)870 4016040
+44(0)1946 723224
enquiries@burnmoor.co.uk
www.burnmoor.co.uk

An attractive old pebbledash Lakeland inn, originally built as a farm in 1578, nestling in a tiny hamlet in the Eskdale Valley, a beautiful, lush and unspoilt part of western Cumbria. Across the Esk by an old stone bridge are bridleways to Eel Tarn and Wasdale Head. Converted to a pub in 1764, it has a homely bar with a crackling log fire, walls crammed with local adverts, and a row of handpumps dispensing tip-top local ales, including brews from Great Gable, Tirril, Barngates and Jennings. Hearty food is served in both the bar and cosy, cottagey restaurant, with dishes ranging from sandwiches and jacket potatoes, to a Cumberland tatie pot of lamb, beef and black pudding. A specials' board could list the likes of a casserole of Isle of Jura venison, homemade puddings like raspberry and apple pie, and own-grown herbs, summer vegetables and salads are a feature. Much of the menu is homemade, but if not, that fact is honestly stated. The nine bedrooms are simply furnished in a bright, rural style. Colourful walls, crisp white floral duvets, amusing animal prints and views over the surrounding fells provide a comfortable base. Poor reception dictates the peace of a TV-free environment; all rooms have radios. See Pub Walk on page 276.

Rooms: 9. Room from £30 per person. Double room four nights for the price of three all year, and three nights for the price of two November-March.
Prices: Set lunch £12 and dinner £16. Main course from £7.50. Bar main course from £7. House wine £10.
Last orders: Bar: 23.00. Food: lunch 17.00; dinner 21.00.
Closed: Rarely.
Food: Traditional English.
Real Ale: Jennings Bitter, Jennings Cumberland Ale, Black Sheep Best, Great Gable Ales, Barngates Ales, Tirril Ales. 3 guest beers.
Other points: No-smoking area. Garden. Children welcome. Car park.
Directions: From the south, exit 36/M6. Head to Newbridge, Greenodd and the Broughton-in-Furness; then head towards Ulpha, drop down into Eskdale and the turn right into Boot. (Map 7, D3)

Hawkshead

Queen's Head Hotel

Main Street, Hawkshead, Ambleside, Cumbria LA22 0NS
Telephone: +44(0)870 4016041
+44(0)15394 36271 / +44(0)800 137263
enquiries@queensheadhotel.co.uk
www.queensheadhotel.co.uk

A delightful 16th-century village inn-cum-hotel in the heart of the Lake District National Park, popular with tourists and walkers. The black-and-white painted frontage hides an interior full of period character: traditional beamed bars with open fires, and ales dispensed by bow-tied barmen, perhaps Robinsons Bitter and the aptly named Cumbria Way. Fifteen small, prettily decorated bedrooms are charming, in a smart rural-chic style, taking in coordinating floral fabrics and colours, and brass, canopied and four-poster beds. Rooms at the front have the best views over the village. The inn may be traditional in its look, but the food on offer ranges far and wide. The salad bar brings Cumbrian roast beef with watercress, chilli, radish and soy sauce, or the separate Herdwick lamb menu could include lamb Henry with rosemary scented sauce. Otherwise, a meal could include Westmorland pie (ham, potatoes, onions, cheese and red wine), or Woodhall's cumberland sausage with ale and white onion sauce. There's a good vegetarian menu. Look out for the Cirt Clog (20 inches in length), made in 1820 for a local man who contracted elephantiasis.

Rooms: 14, 2 not en suite, two with private bathroom. 2 four-poster beds and 2 family rooms. Double room from £34 per person, single from £47.50.
Prices: Main course lunch from £7.25.
House wine £10.95.
Last orders: Bar: 23.00. Food: lunch 14.30; dinner 21.30.
Closed: Rarely.
Food: Modern British.
Real Ale: Cwmbran Double Hop, Robinson's Best Bitter, Cumbria Way. 1 guest beer.
Other points: No-smoking area. Children welcome.
Directions: Exit 36/M6. A590 to Newby Bridge, then second right for Hawkshead. (Map 7, D3)

Milnthorpe

The Wheatsheaf Hotel

Beetham, Milnthorpe, Cumbria LA7 7AL
Telephone: +44(0)870 4016042
+44(0)15395 62123
wheatsheaf@beetham.plus.com
www.wheatsheafbeetham.com

Just off the A6, a mile or so north of the Lancashire border, Mark and Kathryn Chambers' atmospheric 16th-century inn stands by the River Bela and church in peaceful Beetham. Behind a facade of black-and-white gables and leaded windows are three interlinked bars, all distinguished by dark, heavy wood panelling, exposed beams, warming log fires and comfortable soft furnishings. It's a place that appeals to those looking for a restful atmosphere. Seasonal menus are built around local produce and run to the likes of soup, sandwiches and salads, as well as crab and salmon fishcakes or braised lamb shank with red wine and redcurrant gravy in the bar at lunchtime. In the evening, head for the first-floor restaurant and, perhaps, tuck into filo parcels of melting Cumbrian cheese with tomato chutney, or seared scallops with confit new potatoes and a ginger and honey soy reduction. The Wheatsheaf's own-recipe sausages are served with cumberland gravy, or there could be beef fillet with roasted garlic and shallots and horseradish mash among the interesting main dishes. Finish with lemon and lime pie with Chantilly cream. Bedrooms are attractively and individually decorated.

Rooms: 6. Doubles/twins from £65. Winter breaks available from £40 per night per room.
Prices: Restaurant main course from £6.95. Bar/snack from £2.95. House wine £10.95.
Last orders: Bar: lunch 15.00; dinner 23.00. Food: lunch 14.00 (Sunday 14.50); dinner 21.00 (Sunday 20.30).
Closed: Rarely.
Food: Modern and Traditional British.
Real Ale: Flowers IPA, Jennings Cumberland Ale. 2 guest beers.
Other points: Three non-smoking dining rooms. Small dogs welcome. Garden. Children welcome. Car park.
Directions: One mile south of Milnthorpe off A6. J35/M6. (Map 7, D4)

Penrith

The Highland Drove Inn

Great Salkeld, Penrith, Cumbria CA11 9NA
Telephone: +44(0)870 4016043
+44(0)1768 898349
highlanddroveinnn@btinternet.com
www.highland-drove.co.uk

Set close to the rear of the church in a picturesque Eden Valley village, this archetypal village inn resembles a white-washed old farmhouse with its old wooden porch and abundance of flowers. Within, there's an attractive brick and timber bar, old tables and settles in the main bar area, a separate games room, and a lounge area with a log fire, dark wood furniture and tartan fabrics. Landlord Donald Newton has created a good all-round country inn renowned for its conviviality and popular food, the latter nearly always served in Kyloes Restaurant upstairs. With its hunting lodge feel, it is the core of Donald's business, but the bar is still very much a locals' bar, and an important part of the community - the balance is well kept. Utilising local produce the kitchen produces satisfying country cooking that takes in lamb's kidneys with mustard, juniper and cream, then mains of sea bass fillets with pepperonata, risotto and rocket pesto, or rabbit and bacon pie, with sticky toffee pudding to finish. Cracking beers and good wines by the glass. Bedrooms are well equipped and nicely decorated.

Rooms: 3. Soon to be 5. Double/twin from £50.
Prices: Set lunch £12.95 and dinner £18.50. Restaurant main course from £8.95. Bar snack from £4.95. House wine £9.95.
Last orders: Bar: lunch 15.00; dinner 23.00 (open all day Saturday). Food: lunch 14.00; dinner 21.00 (Sunday 20.30).
Closed: Monday lunchtime.
Food: Eclectic Bistro.
Real Ale: John Smiths Cask, Theakston Black Bull.
Other points: No-smoking area. Dogs welcome. Garden. Children welcome. Car park.
Directions: Exit40/M6. Take A66 eastbound, then A686 towards Alston. Turn left B6412 for Great Salkeld. (Map 7, C4)

Penrith

Queen's Head Inn

Tirril, Penrith, Cumbria CA10 2JF
Telephone: +44(0)870 4016044
+44(0)1768 863219
bookings@queensheadinn.co.uk
www.queensheadinn.co.uk

Long, rambling and typically Cumbrian stone pub once owned by the Wordsworth family in the early 1800s, with a rental document in the bar signed by the great poet William himself. Within is what you'd expect for a village pub of this age: low heavy beams, thick walls, old oak panelling, and four blazing log fires, one in a grand inglenook with the original hooks for curing meat. Food, however, is bang up-to-date, with seasonal menus featuring a good range of traditional home-cooked meals. Lunch in the bar could take in a ploughman's with local farmhouse cheeses, or something more substantial like braised shoulder of local lamb with redcurrant gravy. Brewer's pudding, a steamed suet pudding with steak and rich Tirril ale gravy, and specials like grilled tuna with lime and ginger appear on the restaurant menu. Nursery puddings include sticky toffee pudding with hot toffee sauce. A century after the pub ceased brewing beer in 1899, landlord Chris Tomlinson revived the brewery and the now locally famous Tirril Brewery brews four ales, all of which are served in the flagstoned bar. Seven attractively furnished bedrooms.

Rooms: 7. Double from £65, single from £35.
Prices: Restaurant main course from £9. Bar main course from £7. House wine £10.50.
Last orders: Bar: lunch 15.00; dinner 23.00 (open all day Friday and weekend). Food: lunch 14.00; dinner 21.30 (Sunday 21.00).
Closed: Rarely.
Food: Modern and Traditional British.
Real Ale: Tirril Ales. 1 guest beer.
Other points: No-smoking area. Dogs welcome. Garden. Children welcome. Car park.
Directions: Exit40/M6. A66 east then A6 south through Eamont Bridge. Right at Crown Inn; follow Ullswater Road for 2 miles to Tirril. (Map 7, C4)

Sedbergh

Dalesman Country Inn

Main Street, Sedbergh, Cumbria LA10 5BN
Telephone: +44(0)870 4016045
+44(0)15396 21183
info@thedalesman.co.uk
www.thedalesman.co.uk

An unassuming, comfortably modernised 16th-century former coaching inn, festooned in summer with rampant floral displays, and popular with walkers exploring the nearby Howgill Fells. It stands in an old market town close to less strenuous strolls along the River Dee. Stripped stone and beams, farmhouse chairs and stools around copper-topped tables, and log-effect gas fires set the scene in the rambling, open-plan bar and dining room where you can enjoy good homemade food prepared from local produce. Arrive early for the excellent value lunchtime menu that features beer battered fish and chips, homemade Angus beef burgers, and Dalesman Club sandwiches. Influenced by the seasons and changing fortnightly, the evening carte may extend the choice to chargrilled lamb steak with aubergines and tomato and chilli salsa and chicken with bacon and mushroom risotto. Evening bar food ranges from chargrills and homemade pies to various platters and salads. For pudding choose steamed ginger pudding, or Wensleydale cheese with cranberry sauce. Seven spacious and comfortably furnished bedrooms are cottagey in style.

Rooms: 7. Rooms £30 per person.
Prices: Set lunch £10 and dinner £18. Main course from £8. House wine £8.
Last orders: Bar: 23.00. Food: lunch 14.00 (Friday, Saturday, Sunday 14.30); dinner 21.00 (Friday and Saturday 21.30).
Closed: Rarely.
Food: Modern British and traditional pub food.
Real Ale: Black Sheep Best (on Bank Holidays), Tetley's Bitter, Dalesman. 1 guest beer.
Other points: No-smoking area. Children welcome. Car park.
Directions: On A684 11 miles east of Kendal; 5 miles from Junction 36/M6. (Map 7, D4)

Ullswater

Brackenrigg Inn

Watermillock, Lake Ullswater, Penrith, Cumbria CA11 0LP
Telephone: +44(0)870 4016046
+44(0)17684 86206
enquiries@brackenrigginn.co.uk
www.brackenrigginn.co.uk

From the elevated front terrace and glorious gardens of this 18th-century inn you can enjoy sweeping views across Lake Ullswater, a position that is unrivalled in the area. An appealing homely feel is retained throughout the unpretentious interior, thanks in part to the attractive panelled bar with polished floor boards, open log fire, cracking local ales, and those views over the surrounding countryside, and the carpeted lounge-cum-family dining room with its polished mahogany furniture. The separate restaurant is also traditionally appointed and has splendid views. A sound local reputation for well executed, contemporary food has been built up over the years. The bar menu is built around local produce and available in the bar, lounge and terrace. Choices include smoked haddock aïoli, Watermillock-made cumberland sausage with apple mash, and cod battered in lemon and dill-scented batter with chunky chips. The restaurant table d'hote may list smoked cheese, ham and leek tartlet, followed by duck confit with champ and mixed bean broth, and caramelised rice pudding. En suite bedrooms are well decorated and furnished.

Rooms: 17. Double from £27 per person. Single from £32. Superior rooms and suites also available.
Prices: Set Sunday lunch £9.95. Set dinner £18.95. Restaurant main course from £10.50. Bar main course from £8.25. House wine £10.95.
Last orders: Bar: 23.00. Food: lunch 14.30; dinner 21.00.
Closed: Never.
Food: Modern British.
Real Ale: Black Sheep Ales, Jennings Cumberland Ale, Tirril Ales, Theakston Ales. 3 guest beers.
Other points: No-smoking area. Dogs welcome overnight. Garden. Children welcome. Car park.
Directions: On A592 6 miles from Exit40/M6. (Map 7, C4)

Air-Cured Ham and Bacon

at the Brackenrigg Inn

Richard Woodall is an extraordinary company. Situated in the small village of Waberthwaite it is one of the oldest family businesses in the world. Now into it's 7th and 8th generation of family members it is famous for its traditionally cured hams, bacon and sausages. Using the same recipes and techniques as the Woodall's of over 170 years ago and with the expertise of many generations knowledge in refining it has resulted in a fantastic product. Indeed, the Royal Family has awarded their sausage with the Royal Warrant. It helps that from start to finish the pig is in the hands of Richard Woodall, the company farming their own herd of around 180 sows in large straw-filled barns with natural light and fresh air and in a completely chemical and preservative free environment. There is a real feeling of tradition at Richard Woodall's, the business is even in the original premises! Further inland, the Brackenrigg Inn, in the small hamlet of Watermillock near Ullswater keeps a constant supply of Woodall's air-cured ham and bacon whilst sourcing their Cumberland sausage (that they might serve with delicious apple mash) from Adam Jackson and his farm a stones throw away.

Jennings Brewery, Cockermouth, Cumberland Ale

Cockermouth

A66

A595

Whitehaven

Lake District

A595

Woodall's, Nillom, Air-cured ham and bacon

The Brackenrigg Inn, Ullswater | Food Map

Thornby Moor,
Carolyn and Leonie Fairbairn,
Oak smoked cumberland cheese
A595
Tirril Microbrewery,
Ale
Penrith
Adam Jackson, Watermillock,
Cumberland sausage and other meats
Keswick
LES ROUTIERS
Brackenrigg Inn,
Watermillock, Ullswater
NationalPark
A592
A591
Ambleside
Windermere
A592
Smoked
Shortback

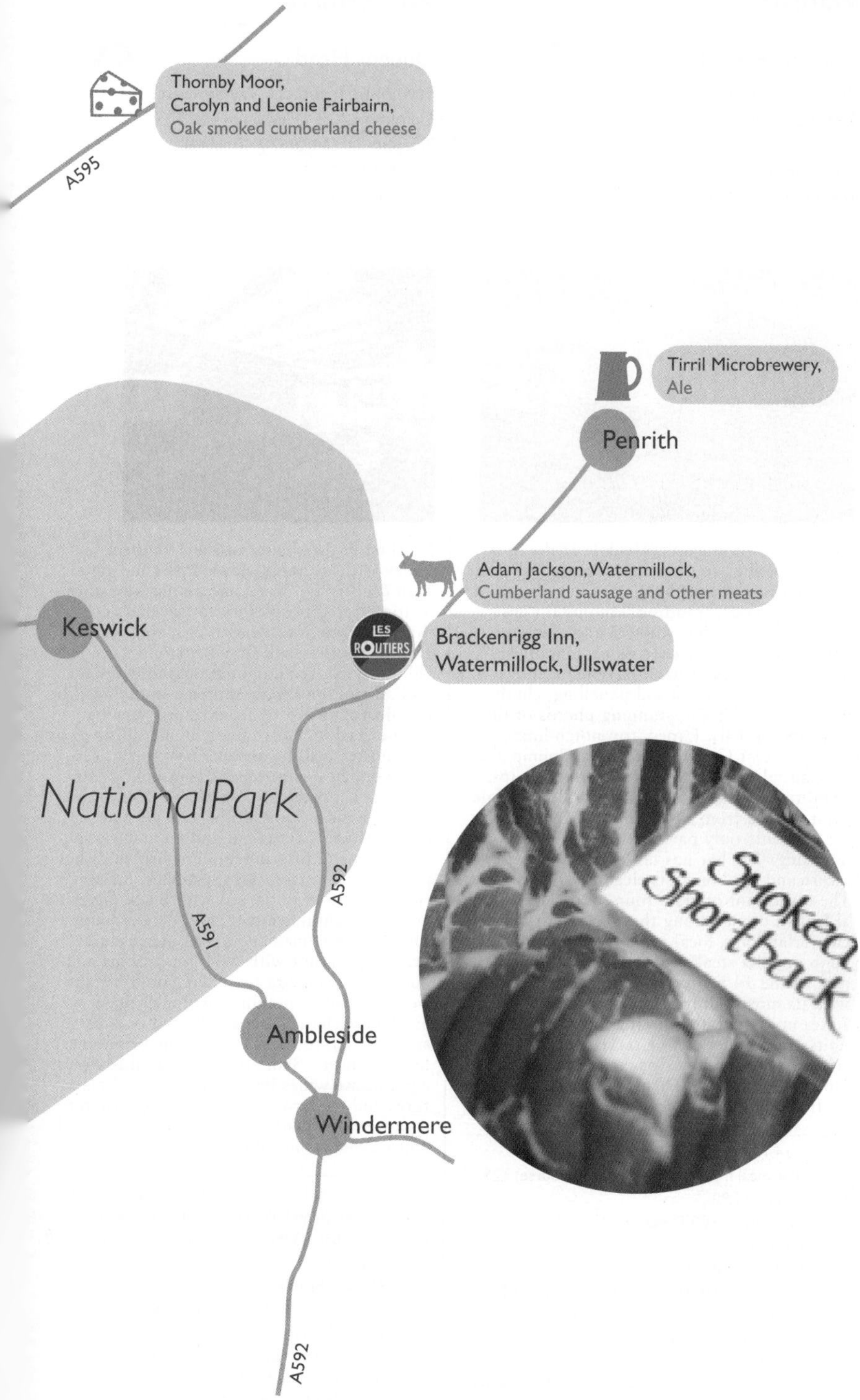

Wasdale

Wasdale Head Inn

Wasdale, Gosforth, Cumbria CA20 1EX
Telephone: +44(0)870 4016047
+44(0)19467 26229
wasdaleheadinn@msn.com
www.wasdale.com

At the head of unspoilt Wasdale at the foot of Great Gable, in a setting of romantic grandeur, with steep fells by way of backdrop, this is a famous, traditional mountain inn popular with serious walkers and climbers. Ritson's bar, named after its first landlord (the world's biggest liar), has high ceilings, a polished slate floor, wood panelling, climbing memorabilia and stunning photos of the surrounding fells. Expect top-notch home-brewed Great Gable beers on handpump and substantial food in the form of thick soups, Cumbrian sausages and ham and Borrowdale trout, served from a hot counter. By contrast, the residents-only part of the building is imposing. The bar has large Tudoresque furniture and the lounge is elegantly furnished. The restaurant offers a four-course, traditional British dinner along the lines of air-dried Cumbrian ham, local farm-reared Herdwick lamb or fillet steak, and classic puddings. The pick of the 14 bedrooms is the garden room, with its muslin-draped four-poster. Four suites in a separate building have kitchen units, and dinner can be served for you to reheat. The Christmas package is legendary. No turkey or telly? Then the Baa Humbug! Stuff the Bloody Turkey! break is for you.

Rooms: 14. Room from £49 per person.
Prices: Bar meal from £6. Set dinner (4 course) £25.
House wine £11.90.
Last orders: Bar: 23.00. Food: 21.00.
Closed: Rarely.
Food: Traditional British.
Real Ale: Great Gable Wasd'Ale, WryNose, Scafell, Yewbarrow.
Other points: Totally no smoking. Children welcome.
Dogs welcome overnight. Garden. Car park.
Directions: Wasdale Head is signed off A595 between Egremont and Ravenglass. (Map 7, D3)

Windermere

Queens Head

Townhead, Troutbeck, Windermere,
Cumbria LA23 1PW
Telephone: +44(0)870 4016048
+44(0)1539 432174
enquiries@queensheadhotel.com
www.queensheadhotel.com

Nestling in the shelter of the Troutbeck Valley with stunning views, this atmospheric 16th-century inn has come a long way since it first offered hospitality to travellers on the Windermere to Penrith coaching route. Today's tourists will find a first-class inn providing stylish accommodation and excellent food. Tradition reigns supreme in the bustling bar, distinguished by its extraordinary bar counter fashioned from a genuine Elizabethan four-poster bed, by antique beams, settles and wooden furniture, and a rambling interior that's a maze of cosy alcoves and little rooms. Food is bang up-to-date with an excellent-value set menu and an ambitious evening menu offering modern British dishes prepared from fresh local produce. Starters run to white bean parfait with black olives and sweet chilli dressing, and decent soups served with homemade bread. After mains of, say, pheasant with wild mushrooms and herbs with Madeira jus, there could be classic sticky toffee pudding. At lunch there are sandwiches, warm salads and one-dish specials. Tip-top ales favour Cumbrian microbrewery beers. Short list of affordable wines; eight house wines by the glass. Period features and modern comforts characterise the stylish, individually decorated bedrooms; all enjoy memorable valley views.

Rooms: 14. Double room from £75, single from £60.
Prices: Set lunch and dinner £15.50. House wine £10.
Last orders: Bar: 23.00. Food: lunch 14.00; dinner 21.00.
Closed: Rarely.
Food: Modern British.
Real Ale: Coniston Bluebird, Boddingtons, Jennings Cumberland Ale, Hawkshead. 2 guest beers.
Other points: No-smoking area. Children welcome.
Dogs welcome in the bar. Car park.
Directions: J36/M6. Take the A590/591 to Windermere and then take A592 towards Ullswater. (Map 7, D4)

Ashbourne

The Red Lion Inn

Main Street, Hognaston, Ashbourne,
Derbyshire DE6 1PR
Telephone: +44(0)870 4016049
+44(0)1335 370396
lionrouge@msn.com
www.lionrouge.com

Fantastic smells from the kitchen will encourage you to linger longer than a pint and tuck into some great pub food at Pip Price's unpretentious 17th-century inn close to Carsington Reservoir. With its oak beams, quarry tiles strewn with colourful rugs, three roaring log fires and papers and magazines to peruse, the cosy bar is really hard to leave. Add piped classical music and an eclectic mix of old farmhouse tables and study pews and you have a super country pub. Local drinkers fill the bar early and late in the evening; at other times food is the emphasis in the candlelit room and the intimate back room. Blackboards list the imaginative choice of modern pub food. Soundly cooked dishes, carefully prepared from fresh local produce and served on enormous white plates, range from a starter of chicken liver parfait with redcurrant sauce, to mains of rib-eye steak with red wine and shallot sauce. Lighter meals include smoked haddock and spring onion fishcakes, and there's comforting homemade nursery puddings. Expect a warm welcome, friendly service and, if staying overnight, excellent accommodation in three very comfortable and tastefully decorated en suite bedrooms. Book the Yellow Room, with its huge pine bed, quality armchairs, cast-iron fireplace and village views.
See Pub Walk on page 278.

Rooms: 3. Double room from £80, single from £50.
Prices: Main course from £7.95. House wine £10.95.
Last orders: Bar: lunch 15.00; dinner 23.00. Food: lunch 14.00 (Sunday 14.15); dinner 21.00.
Closed: Monday lunch.
Food: Modern and Traditional British
Real Ale: Marston's Pedigree, Bass, Old Speckled Hen.
Other points: No-smoking area. Children welcome over 10 years. Car park. Most credit cards. No Dogs.
Directions: J25/M1. From Ashbourne take B5035. After four miles turn right for Hognaston. (Map 8, G5)

Beeley

The Devonshire Arms

Beeley, Matlock, Derbyshire DE4 2NR
Telephone: +44(0)870 4016050
+44(0)1629 733259
jagrosvenor@devonshirearmsbeeley.co.uk
www.devonshirearmsbeeley.co.uk

Beeley stands in a sleepy valley between the River Derwent and the high moorland of the Peak District, a short stroll from the southern fringes of Chatsworth Park. The village inn, the handsome Devonshire Arms, was converted from three stone cottages in 1747 and soon became a thriving coaching inn serving the route between the Peak District and London. The comfortably civilised interior is comprised of three attractive beamed rooms, with stone-flagged floors, roaring log fires, cushioned antique settles, farmhouse tables, and tasteful prints, and a separate taproom where the hordes of walkers with muddy boots are made very welcome. Traditional homecooked bar food is available all day and ranges from freshly made soups with crusty bread, Devonshire ploughman's with four cheeses and homemade piccalilli, to beef and horseradish suet pudding, braised knuckle of lamb with rosemary sauce, and sirloin steak with pepper sauce. Friday is fresh fish night, so arrive early to sample beer-battered cod and chips, tuna Niçoise and a mammoth seafood platter. On Sunday note the special Victorian breakfast (booking essential), complete with Bucks Fizz and newspapers. Excellent Black Sheep and Theakston ales on draught, a good-value list of wines, and numerous malt whiskies.

Prices: Main course from £6.75. House wine £9.75.
Last orders: Bar: 23.00. Food: 21.30.
Closed: Rarely.
Food: Traditional and Modern British.
Real Ale: Black Sheep Best, Black Sheep Special, Bass, Marston's Pedigree, Theakston Old Peculiar, Ruddles Best. Two guest beers.
Other points: No-smoking area. Garden. Children welcome. Car park.
Directions: Junction 28/M1. Take the A6 and then on to the B6012 to Beeley and Chatsworth. (Map 8, G5)

Castle Donington

The Nags Head Inn 🍷

Hill Top, Castle Donington,
Derbyshire DE74 2PR
Telephone: +44(0)870 4016051
+44(0)1332 850652
idavisonc.@aol.com

Chef-landlord Ian Davison's rather plain-looking 19th-century pub is undoubtedly the best food pub for miles and, as it's just a short drive from East Midlands Airport, Castle Donington motor racing circuit, and the M1 (junction 24), it bustles with activity and booking a table is advisable, especially at lunchtimes. Ian offers a good selection of modern pub dishes in the traditionally furnished bar, with its open winter fires, and in the bright and informal dining areas, each furnished with chunky pine tables on seagrass and attractive french prints on colour-washed walls. Blackboards offer a range of interesting sandwiches such as tomato, mozzarella and pesto on warm ciabatta, and light dishes such as beef stir-fry with rice, and smoked cod kedgeree. For something more substantial try the beef, mushroom and red wine casserole, lamb shank with mustard mash, or aubergine, black olive and polenta layer with sun-dried tomato dressing. Finish with homemade bread-and-butter pudding or treacle oat tart. Beers range to Banks Mild, Marston's Pedigree and Mansfield Bitter, while the list of wines offers six house wines by the glass.

Prices: Restaurant main course from £12.95. Bar meal from £4.95. House wine £11.95.
Last orders: Bar: lunch 14.30; dinner 23.00. Food: lunch 14.00; dinner 21.15. No food on Sunday evening.
Closed: 26th December to 2nd January.
Food: Modern British.
Real Ale: Marston's Pedigree, Banks's Mild, Mansfield Bitter.
Other points: No-smoking area. Dogs welcome in the bar. Garden. Car park.
Directions: Three miles from the M1; J23A/J24. Pass entrance to East Midlands Airport; right at traffic lights at Donington Park, then round the airport. Pub on edge of Castle Donington. (Map 8, G6)

Hardwick

Hardwick Inn 🏳

Hardwick Park, Chesterfield,
Derbyshire S44 5QJ
Telephone: +44(0)870 4016052
+44(0)1246 850245
batty@hardwickinn.co.uk
www.hardwickinn.co.uk

Dating from around 1600 and built of locally quarried sandstone, this striking building was once the lodge for Hardwick Hall and stands at the south gate of Hardwick Park. The hall is owned by the National Trust, so the inn draws much of its trade from visitors exploring the magnificent park and lovely Elizabethan hall; it can be very busy at weekends. The inn, owned by the Batty family for three generations, has a rambling interior that features good period details such as stone-mullioned windows, oak ceiling beams and large stone fireplaces with open fires. Simple furnishings include upholstered wall settles and mahogany tables, while one room has a fine 18th-century carved settle. Traditional bar food (served all day) takes in ploughmans lunches, and a whole range of steaks, jacket potatoes and sandwiches, with blackboard daily specials offering hearty homemade pies, and a feature of the pub, fresh fish delivered daily from Scarborough. Look out for beer-battered cod or haddock, and crab or lobster salads, or opt for one of the daily carvery roasts, usually including topside of beef and local lamb, served with roast and boiled potatoes, Yorkshire pudding and three vegetables.

Prices: Set lunch £12.20 and dinner £13.20 in the carvery restaurant. Bar main course from £5.95.
House wine £7.75.
Last orders: Bar: 23.00. Food: lunch 21.30 (Sunday 21.00).
Closed: Rarely.
Food: Traditional British.
Real Ale: Theakston Old Peculier, Theakston XB, Ruddles County Ale, Marston's Pedigree, Greene King Old Speckled Hen.
Other points: No-smoking area. Children welcome. Garden. Car park.
Directions: Exit29/M1. A6175, then left and follow the tourist board signs to the pub. (Map 8, G6)

Wykeham Arms, Winchester, Hampshire

Ashprington

Waterman's Arms

Bow Bridge, Ashprington, Totnes,
Devon TQ9 7EG
Telephone: +44(0)870 4016053
+44(0)1803 732214

Situated on the banks of the River Harbourne at the top of Bow Creek, the Waterman's is a favourite summer venue for al fresco drinking with resident ducks and, if you are lucky, kingfishers to keep you company. Bow Bridge is mentioned in the Domesday Book and the inn has been in other lives a smithy, brewery, and a prison during the Napoleonic Wars. Tardis-like inside, a series of neatly furnished rooms radiate away from the central bar, all filled with a mix of rustic furniture, old photographs, brass artefacts and other memorabilia. Homecooked food caters for all tastes, from light snacks of filled baguettes, crab sandwiches, Caesar salad, daily pasta meals, and mussels cooked in white wine, cream and onion sauce, to more hearty dishes such as half shoulder of lamb, steak, mushroom and ale pie, and steaks from the grill. The inn has fifteen comfortable bedrooms, including five bedrooms in a side extension overlooking the flower-filled garden, each neat with floral, cottagey fabrics and co-ordinating friezes, attractive, dark-stained modern furniture and smart en suite facilities. Telephones and TVs are standard throughout. A peaceful base from which to explore the South Hams.

Rooms: 15. Double room from £69, single from £54, family room from £79.
Prices: Main course from £7.95. Bar meal from £4.95. House wine £8.95.
Last orders: Bar: 23.00. Food: dinner 21.30.
Closed: Rarely.
Food: Traditional English.
Real Ale: Wadworth 6X, Bass, Otter Ale.
Other points: No-smoking area. Children welcome. Garden. Car park.
Directions: Follow A381 out of Totnes towards Kingsbridge. Halfway up the hill, turn left at the sign for Ashprington and the Waterman's Arms. (Map 4, F5)

Dartmouth

The Floating Bridge Inn

Coombe Road, Dartmouth, Devon TQ6 9PQ
Telephone: +44(0)870 4016054
+44(0)1803 832354

Perfectly located, overlooking the River Dart where the town's Higher 'floating bridge' Ferry docks, and below the Britannia Naval College, this former ferry keeper's cottage has been refurbished by enthusiastic owners Jim and Gay Brent. Without spoiling the traditional atmosphere, the Brents have smartened up the pine-panelled bar, filled with Naval College memorabilia, and popular with visiting yachtsmen, tourists and college students. Equally popular on sunny days is the new roof terrace, one of the few places in Dartmouth where you can drink and dine with a glorious river view. In the dining room, evening candlelight and a warm welcome now draw folk in for Jim's food, in particular the summer chalkboard list of locally-caught fish, crab and lobster. Freshly-prepared dishes from the main menu range from firm pub favourites such as garlic prawns, seafood mornay and prime English steaks to smoked haddock and mustard chowder, scallops with orange butter sauce and an excellent rack of lamb with caramelised shallots and red wine. In the bar, tuck into a decent sandwich filled with fresh local crab, or choose the homemade steak and kidney pie or large battered fresh cod served with chips and peas.

Prices: Set lunch and dinner £15. Restaurant main course from £12. Bar snack from £2.50, bar main course from £4.95. House wine £8.
Last orders: Bar: 23.00. Food: lunch 14.00; dinner 22.00 (bar food served all day).
Closed: Rarely.
Food: Traditional pub bar food. Seafood.
Real Ale: Courage Best Bitter, Directors Bitter, Wadworth 6X. 1 guest beer.
Other points: No-smoking area. Dogs welcome. Roof terrace. Children welcome.
Directions: Next to Higher Ferry slipway. (Map 4, F5)

Exeter

The Twisted Oak

Little John's Cross Hill, Ide, Exeter,
Devon EX2 9RG
Telephone: +44(0)870 4016055
+44(0)1392 273666
info@thetwistedoak.co.uk
www.thetwistedoak.co.uk

Following major refurbisment, April 2004
saw the opening of Martin Bullock's second
pub-restaurant (see New Inn, Shalfleet, Isle
of Wight). Well placed just off the A30,
a mile or so west of Exeter, the red brick,
clematis and ivy-clad Twisted Oak stands
beside a picturesque Saxon bridge in rural
isolation close to the village of Ide. Rustic
traditional charm and contemporary minimal-
ism blend well throughout the wood-floored
bar, with its rich russet walls, leather sofas
and polished wooden tables, and through the
carpeted lounge into the new conservatory
dining room, the latter enjoying views across
the secluded garden. Menus are built around
local seasonal produce, with a modern twist
given to such traditional classics as local sausages with creamy mash and shallot gravy or
rump steak with chunky chips and red onion
confit. Alternatively, tuck into lunchtime salads and filled baguettes, roast cod with tomato and cardamom sauce and noodles, grilled
mussels with sauce Romesco and fries and,
for pudding, try the baked cheesecake with
caramelised strawberries. Chalkboards list the
day's delivery from Looe fish market. Three
real ales can be found on tap. Families are
made most welcome with a good children's
menu and and a large play area.

Prices: Restaurant main course from £9.95. Bar main
course from £6.95. House wine £9.95.
Last orders: Bar: lunch 15.00; dinner 23.00.
Food: lunch 14.30; dinner 21.30.
Closed: Never.
Food: Modern British.
Real Ale: Marston's Pedigree, Wadworth 6X,
O'Hanlons Fire Fly. 1 guest beer.
Other points: No-smoking area. Dogs welcome in
garden only. Car park.
Directions: Exit31/M5. Ide is just off A30 to Okehamp-
ton. Twisted Oak is just outside the village. (Map 4, F5)

Lynton

The Staghunters Hotel

Brendon, Lynton, Devon EX35 6PS
Telephone: +44(0)870 4016056
+44(0)1598 741222
enquiries@staghunters.fsnet.co.uk
www.staghunters.com

A great base for exploring Exmoor, Lorna
Doone country and the magnificent north
Devon coast, this friendly, family-run hotel
stands on the site of an old abbey (the chapel
has been incorporated into the lounge), deep
in the Doone Valley beside the babbling East
Lyn River. Pretty, cottagey bedrooms are
comfortably appointed, all are en suite, two
have four-poster beds; residents have their
own sitting room to relax in following an
invigorating day on the moor. Homely, simply
furnished bars offer a short menu of good
country cooking, say soup, grilled sardines,
or cottage pie with garlic bread and salad,
washed down with a pint of Exmoor Gold.
In the restaurant, which has lovely views
across the garden, there could be local trout
poached in white wine, or large pork chop
pan-fried with sage, apple and cider and
finished in cream. All are served with good,
fresh vegetables, and the menu is extended
by a daily specials board. Trout and salmon
fishing can be arranged on six miles of river
at Water Authority rates, pets are welcome,
there's stabling for visiting horses, and golf
can be arranged at nearby Saunton Golf
Club.

Rooms: 12. Double room from £60, single from £40,
family from £70.
Prices: Set dinner £16.95. House wine £8.50.
Last orders: Bar: lunch 14.30; dinner 23.00. Food: 21.30
(bar); 20.30 (restaurant).
Closed: Rarely.
Food: Traditional British.
Real Ale: Exmoor Stag, Exmoor Gold.
Other points: No-smoking area. Children welcome.
Garden. Car park.
Directions: Follow the A39 from Lynton towards Por-
lock, the Staghunters Hotel is signposted to the right
approximately five miles from Lynton. (Map 4, D5)

Modbury

The California Country Inn

California Cross, Modbury, Ivybridge,
Devon PL21 0SG
Telephone: +44(0)870 4016057
+44(0)1548 821449

California Cross reputedly takes its name from the large numbers of men who, obeying the urge to 'Go West', used to congregate at major crossroads waiting for the stagecoach to take them on their journey to the New World. A celebrated landmark throughout the 19th century, the California Inn was an important staging post between Dartmouth and Plymouth. Although much extended, reminders of its famous past can be seen in the old prints, photographs and artefacts that adorn the walls throughout the rambling, carpeted bar and Coachman's Restaurant. New owner Tony Bell is an experienced publican and he is gradually stamping his mark on the place, introducing new menus with the help of head chef Tim Whiston. In addition to draught and traditional beers there's a traditional pub menu in the bar, ranging from sandwiches and homecooked ham ploughman's to steak and kidney pie, battered cod and chips and chargrilled steaks. In the restaurant there's always changing and imaginative carte, or look to the chalkboards for the days specials, with local produce and meats used throughout.

Prices: Set lunch £10.50, set dinner £20. Restaurant main course from £8. Bar main course from £6.95. House wine £9.
Last orders: Bar: 23.00. Food: lunch 14.00; dinner 21.00.
Closed: Rarely.
Food: Traditional British.
Real Ale: Bass, Hobson's Best.
Other points: No-smoking area. Dogs welcome. Garden. Children welcome. Car park.
Directions: Wrangaton exit on the A38, off the B3196. (Map 4, F5)

Salcombe

Victoria Inn

Fore Street, Salcombe, Devon TQ8 8BU
Telephone: +44(0)870 4016058
+44(0)1548 842604
ajcannon@aol.com

From the outside the Victoria has the look of a typical seaside town pub. Step inside and you'll find a swish, modern interior, the result of a year-long refurbishment programme by new owner Andrew Cannon. Flagstones, heavy beams, chunky wooden tables and chairs, open log fire and pictures of old Salcombe feature in the cool bar area. Wind your way upstairs to a comfortable lounge bar and more formal dining area, both with stunning views across Salcombe harbour. Menus state that everything is freshly prepared from Devon produce, so look out for local butcher meats, fresh fish landed along the coast, locally made cheeses and ice cream, and hand-cut chips from Devon potatoes. Lunch brings a thick and creamy shellfish chowder, honey-roasted Devon ham with free range eggs and chips, and chicken and ham pie with suet-crust pastry. Cooking moves up a gear in the evening. With that view to gaze at, begin with Salcombe scallops with garlic and parsley butter, move on to John Dory on buttered tagliatelle and chervil and white wine cream sauce, and finish with a rich dark chocolate and whisky mousse. To drink, try a pint of West Country ale or one of eight wines by the glass.

Prices: Set lunch £12.95, set dinner £19.95. Restaurant main course from £9.95. Bar main course from £4.95. House wine £10.75.
Last orders: Bar: 23.00 (Sunday 22.30).
Food: lunch 14.30; dinner 21.00.
Closed: Rarely.
Food: Modern British.
Real Ale: Dartmoor Best, St Austell Tinners Ale, St Austell Tribute, Black Prince.
Other points: No-smoking area. Dogs welcome. Garden. Children welcome.
Directions: Town Centre. (Map 4, G5)

Slapton

The Tower Inn

Church Road, Slapton, Kingsbridge,
Devon TQ7 2PN
Telephone: +44(0)870 4016059
+44(0)1548 580216
towerinn@slapton.org
www.thetowerinn.com

The 14th-century Tower Inn takes its name from the ancient ruins of a tower it stands beside, all that remains of a monastic college; the inn was built in 1374 to accommodate the artisans building the college. The college has long gone, the pub endures and can be found tucked away in a sleepy village just inland from Slapton Sands. Six hundred years on and guests continue to be warmly welcomed, more recently by Annette and Andrew Hammett who bought the pub in December 2003. The welcome is followed by pints of local ale and plates of good modern pub food. Expect hearty sandwiches (try the local crab) and more traditional dishes like sausage and mash at lunch. From the evening menu begin with sautéed scallops and prawns with crème frâche and chilli jam, move on to slow cooked lamb shank on mash with a stew of peas, flageolets, garlic and parsley or roast sea bass with glazed crab mashed potatoes, finished with a lime and tarragon sauce. Local fish and game specials. Stone walls, open fires, scrubbed oak tables and flagstone floors characterise the interior, the atmosphere enhanced at night with candlelit tables. There are three cottage-style ensuite bedrooms and a super rear garden.

Rooms: 3. Room from £55.
Prices: Restaurant main course from £9.
House wine from £10.
Last orders: Bar: lunch 14.30 (Sunday 15.00); dinner 23.00. Food: lunch 14.15 (Sunday 14.30); dinner 21.30.
Closed: Rarely.
Food: Modern British.
Real Ale: Adnams Southwold, St Austell Tribute, Badger's Tanglefoot, Tower Ale. 1 guest beer.
Other points: No-smoking area. Garden and courtyard. Children welcome. Car park.
Directions: Off A379 between Dartmouth and Kingsbridge. (Map 4, G5)

Stokenham

The Tradesmans Arms

Stokenham, Kingsbridge, Devon TQ7 2SZ
Telephone: +44(0)870 4016060
+44(0)1548 580313
nick@thetradesmansarms.com
www.thetradesmansarms.com

Tucked away in the heart of the picturesque old village, this 14th-century part-thatched cottage is named after the men who traded in Dartmouth and stopped at the pub for their first night en route home to Kingsbridge. Comprising a simply furnished main bar with stone fireplace, wood-burning stove and heavy beams, and an equally informal dining room, it is now the domain of affable landlord Nick Abbot, who retreated to Devon following years running a hectic gastropub in the Chilterns. Life may be a tad easier now but Nick, and chef Tim Hoban, are still passionate about offering good food and, in particular, locally sourced produce. Meats and fish are smoked on the premises, fish is from day boats at Brixham and Plymouth, scallops are dived for in Start Bay, vegetables are grown four miles away, and Sutton Plymouth Pride is brewed along the road. This translates to pan-fried scallops with chorizo sausage, tagliatelle with clams, crab meat and white wine, crab cakes with sweet chilli jus, braised lamb shank with mint and rosemary gravy, and whole grilled lemon sole on changing menus. Light lunches of hot sandwiches, daily curries and various omelettes.

Prices: Set lunch and dinner £21.50. Restaurant main course from £7.95. Main course bar from £4.95. House wine £11.95.
Last orders: Bar: 23.00 (during summer months open all day at the weekend). Food: lunch 14.30; dinner 21.30.
Closed: Rarely.
Food: Modern British.
Real Ale: Brakspear Ales, Sutton Plymouth Pride.
Other points: No-smoking areas. Dogs welcome. Garden. Children welcome. Car park.
Directions: Just off the A379, between Dartmouth and Kingsbridge, a mile inland from Torcross. (Map 4, G5)

Totnes

The Sea Trout Inn

Staverton, Totnes, Devon TQ9 6PA
Telephone: +44(0)870 4016061
+44(0)1803 762274
enquiries@seatroutinn.com
www.seatroutinn.com

A warm welcome heralds a pleasant stay at this attractive 15th-century inn tucked away in the peaceful Dart Valley. The inn has become a firm favourite among both locals and visitors, especially fishermen, for its reliable food and comfortable accommodation in ten bedrooms, all decorated in cottage style with co-ordinating fabrics and darkwood furniture, with bathrooms featuring attractive fish tiles. A fishing theme runs through the pub, some specimens mounted in showcases, others depicted in paintings or on plates. Bar areas are traditional in character, the neat, rambling lounge bar sporting pine furnishings and open fires. The beamed public bar is a popular retreat for locals quaffing the full range of Palmers ales. From a wide-ranging bar menu, choose sandwiches and salads, or something hearty like homemade steak and ale pie, ham, egg and chips, whole Brixham plaice or, naturally, local trout with lemon butter sauce. More imaginative restaurant food is served in the conservatory dining room which overlooks the sheltered patio-style garden. Here, set-price menus list fresh Brixham fish and locally sourced meats.

Rooms: 10. Double room from £50, single from £39.50.
Prices: Set Sunday lunch £14.95. Set dinner £21.50.
Main course from £8.95. House wine £9.25.
Last orders: Bar: lunch 16.00; dinner 23.00. Food: lunch 14.00 (Sunday 14.30); dinner 21.00 (Friday and Saturday 21.30).
Closed: Never.
Food: Modern British.
Real Ale: Palmers IPA, Palmers Bicentenary 200, Palmers Copper and Gold Ale. 1 guest beer.
Other points: No-smoking area. Garden. Children welcome. Car park.
Directions: Off A384 between Totnes and Buckfastleigh. (Map 4, F5)

Trusham

Cridford Inn

Trusham, Teign Valley, Devon TQ13 0NR
Telephone: +44(0)870 4016062
+44(0)1626 853694
cridford@eclipse.co.uk
www.cridfordinn.co.uk

This carefully restored ancient longhouse is Devon's oldest domestic dwelling dating from 1081. Heavily thatched with a charming interior, the two interconnecting bars display original and huge beams, rustic stone fireplaces and floors, and the earliest example of a domestic window in Britain. In the separate dining room you can see a mosaic date stone in the preserved Saxon stone floor, fine oak pillars and small stained-glass windows. In general, the food on offer is traditional pub fare ranging from sandwich platters and the generous Cridford brunch at lunchtime, to Sawadee king prawns coated in tempura batter with chilli sauce, beer-battered cod and chips, smoked haddock florentine and rump steak in the evening. Additional evening specials may include salmon with cider, cream and tarragon sauce and Malaysian-born Jasmine's very authentic curries, perhaps beef rendang (cooked in coconut and spices) or green Thai chicken curry served with rice and coriander. Tip-top handpumped ales include Sharp's Doom Bar Bitter. Upstairs, four simple, yet comfortably furnished bedrooms are all individually decorated; all have well-equipped en suite bathrooms.

Rooms: 4. Double room £60, single from £50.
Check for seasonal variations.
Prices: Set lunch £12 (2 course). Set dinner £17.
Main course from £6.50. House wine £10.70.
Last orders: Bar: lunch 15.00; dinner 21.30.
Food: lunch 15.00; dinner 21.30.
Closed: 8-28 January.
Food: Traditional pub food and South-East Asian.
Real Ale: Badger Best, Sharp's Doom Bar Bitter, Old Speckled Hen, Spitfire, Trusham Ale, Sharp's own.
Other points: No-smoking area. Small garden. Children welcome. Dogs welcome. Car park.
Directions: From A38 take B3193, then right at first T junction to Trusham. (Map 4, F5)

Bridport

Shave Cross Inn

Shave Cross, Marshwood Vale, Bridport, Dorset
DT6 6HW
Telephone: +44(0)870 4016063
+44(0)1308 868358
roy.warburton@virgin.net
www.theshavecrossinn.co.uk

Fronted by a magnificent flower-filled sun-trap garden and set in a remote and peaceful spot in the heart of the beautiful Marshwood Vale, Roy and Mel Warburton's 14th-century, thatched cob-and-flint inn offers a cracking main bar, with huge beams, a stone floor, a roaring log fire in the inglenook, and rustic furnishings testifying to the pub's age. Marshwood-born Roy returned to his roots and bought the pub in April 2003 following three years in Tobago. With him came a Caribbean chef who has really spiced up the menu, noteworthy in an area renowned for traditional pub food. Look to the imaginative carte for such exotic offerings as jerk chicken salad with plantain, bacon and aïoli, roast Creole duck with cherry compote, and spicy-hot bouillabaisse crammed with white fish and seafood. Traditional tastes are well catered for on the bar/garden menu which lists freshly battered haddock and chips and rump steak, alongside decent ploughman's lunches (very local Denhay cheddar), and fresh crab sandwiches. Other than plantain, all produce is sourced from Dorset and Somerset, with tip-top ales from the local Branscombe Vale and Quay Breweries.

Prices: Set dinner £26. Bar main course from £6.95.
House wine £9.75.
Last orders: Bar: lunch 15.00; dinner 23.00. Food: lunch 15.00; dinner 21.30 (Sunday 20.00).
Open all day in the summer.
Closed: Monday, except Bank Holidays.
Food: Traditional British, Caribbean and International.
Real Ale: Branscombe Vale & Quay Brewery Ales.
Other points: No-smoking area. Dogs welcome. Garden. Children welcome (play area available). Car park. Thatched skittle alley. Function room.
Directions: Take Broad Oak road left off B3162 north of Bridport; pub in 3 miles. (Map 4, E6)

Cerne Abbas

The Royal Oak

23 Long Street, Cerne Abbas, Dorchester,
Dorset DT2 7JG
Telephone: +44(0)870 4016064
+44(0)1300 341797
royaloak@cerneabbas.fsnet.co.uk

David and Janice Birch's striking thatched and creeper-clad pub nestles in a picture-book village below Cerne's chalk giant etched into the Dorset Downs. Built with stone from the nearby ruined Benedictine abbey, it dates from the 16th-century and was once a blacksmith's shop and a popular coaching stop. Now a thriving village local with a traditional interior featuring flagstone floors, open log fires, beams and bric-a-brac, it not only attracts hungry walkers and tourists on the Hardy Trail but local diners in search of hearty and genuinely homecooked food that utilises first-class produce from local suppliers. Regular menus range from pub favourites such as ham, egg and chips, to specialities of local venison sausages with mash and onion gravy, and Dorset lamb shank with apricot, cranberry and rosemary sauce. Additive- and hormone-free steaks are sourced from accredited herds and served with a choice of sauces. Daily dishes on the handwritten menu extend the choice and may include pan-fried scallops with chillies, and red mullet on coriander mash with lemon butter sauce. Round off with apple and blackberry crumble. There are five real ales on handpump, 13 wines by the glass and an enclosed rear garden.

Prices: Starters from £3.95. Main course from £7.95.
House wine £10.65.
Last orders: Bar: lunch 15.00; dinner 23.00. Food: lunch 14.00; dinner 21.30 (Sunday 21.00).
Closed: Rarely.
Food: Traditional/Modern British.
Real Ale: Quay Best Bitter, Butcombe Bitter, St Austell Tinners Ale, & Tribute, Old Speckled Hen. Guest beers.
Other points: No-smoking area. Courtyard garden and decking. Children welcome.
Directions: Off A352 Dorchester to Sherborne road. (Map 5, G1)

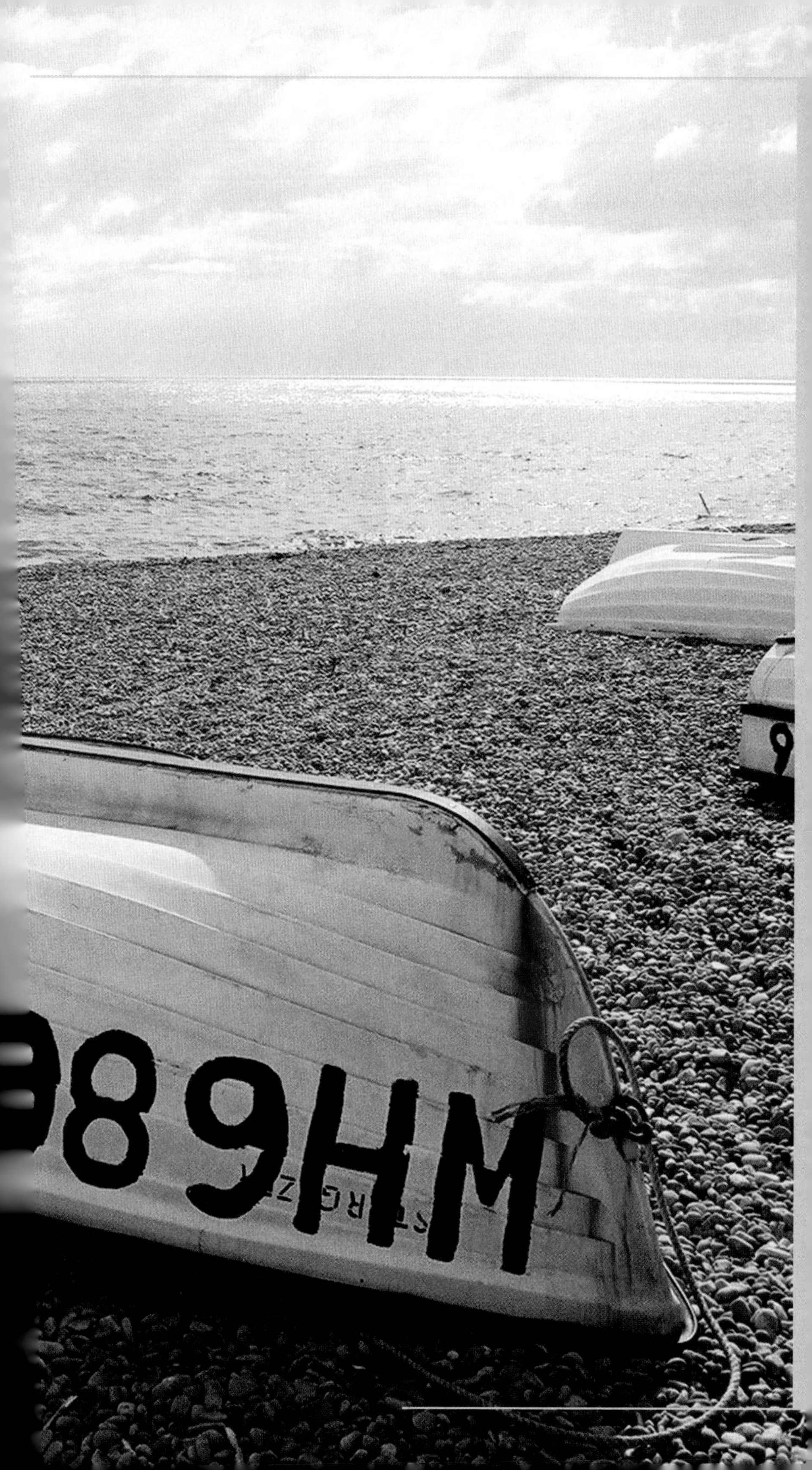
89HM

Corscombe

The Fox Inn

Corscombe, Dorchester, Dorset DT2 0NS
Telephone: +44(0)870 4016065
+44(0)1935 891330
dine@fox-inn.co.uk
www.fox-inn.co.uk

Former accountant Clive Webb bought the famous Fox just over a year ago and, you'll be pleased to hear, hasn't changed a thing. His pretty little thatched pub of stone and cob, built in 1620 as a cider house, is located down a web of narrow lanes deep in unspoilt Dorset countryside. It's everybody's idea of the perfect country pub, with two charming beamed bars, one with a huge inglenook fireplace, stone-flagged floors and gingham-clothed tables, the other filled with old pine furniture and chatty locals. No modern-day intrusions here or in the plant-festooned rear conservatory with its sturdy, long wooden table. Food at the Fox is country pub cooking at its best, with all dishes freshly prepared from quality Somerset and Dorset produce, including local estate venison with celeriac purée and rich game sauce, and rack of Dorset lamb with rosemary gravy, and the blackboard features fresh fish from West Bay - sea bass roasted with sea salt and rosemary. Other dishes that have impressed include mussel and bacon chowder, and local braised rabbit with olives, lemon and thyme. Puddings range from sticky toffee pudding to lemon crème brûlée. Accompany a first-class meal with a pint of Exmoor Ale or a fine wine (six by the glass). Tucked under the heavy thatch with rural views are four cottage en suite bedrooms. See Pub Walk on page 280 and outside close-up on page 332.

Rooms: 4. Double room from £75, single occupancy from £55.
Prices: Main course from £8.50. House wine £10.50.
Last orders: Bar: lunch 15.00; dinner 23.00. Food: lunch 14.00; dinner 21.00 (Friday and Saturday 21.30).
Closed: Rarely.
Food: Modern British.
Real Ale: Exmoor Ale, Fox Ale.
Other points: No-smoking area. Garden/conservatory. Well-behaved children welcome. Car park.
Directions: From Yeovil, take A37 towards Dorchester. After one mile turn right towards Corscombe; pub in 5 miles. Alternatively, take the A356 from Crewkerne to Maiden Newton for five miles. (Map 5, G1)

View of Dorchester from Maiden Castle

Must See
Beaminster, Forde Abbey, Sherborne Castle, Mapperton Gardens, Abbotsbury, Maiden Castle

Best Views Pilsdon Pen, Golden Cap, Hardy's Monument, Eggardon Hill
Villages to Visit Cerne Abbas, Abbotsbury, Evershot

Mapperton Gardens

Tourist Information Dorchester +44(0)1305 267992
Where to Shop Sherborne, Beaminster, Dorchester
Farmers Market Bridport
Nearest Racecourse Taunton
Nearest Golf Course Halstock
Local Activities
Fossil hunting, horse riding, beaches, cycling, fishing

Best Scenic Drives
A35 between Axminster and Dorchester. B-roads between Beaminster and Lyme Regis.
Events and Festivals
Yeovilton International Air Show (July)
Dorchester Music and Arts Festival (April)

Fontmell Magna

The Crown & Coach House

Fontmell Magna, Shaftesbury, Dorset SP7 0PA
Telephone: +44(0)870 4016066
+44(0)1747 811441
oldcoachho@msn.com

Shop/café owner Liz Neilson bought The Crown in March 2003, then, following much needed refurbishment, promptly moved her food/restaurant business across the road into the pub and installed chef Robin Davies, formerly at the Clarence Hotel, Dublin, in the kitchen. The combined talents of Liz and Robin have transformed the pub from a village local to a popular food pub, where local produce, small suppliers and fresh food are taken seriously. Bread is baked on the premises, fish is delivered daily from Poole, meat is sourced from local traceable herds, farms in the Blackmore Vale supply dairy produce, and the cheeseboard features the local Ashmore cheddar. Robin's menus may list classic pub dishes, perhaps roast leg of Dorset lamb, rib-eye steak and chips, and fresh plaice with prawns and garlic butter, but the quality of the ingredients and their presentation are first class. Alternatives may include cod fillet with pesto crust and roast organic chicken with home-made bread sauce. Good puddings (Dorset apple cake, treacle tart), Hall and Woodhouse beers, and good-value wines. Cosy and comfortable bedrooms are light and airy with an old fashioned and Victorian feel to them.

Rooms: 3, 2 with private bathrooms. Double from £55.
Prices: Restaurant main course from £8.95. Bar main course from £6.95. House wine £7.
Last orders: Bar: open all day. Food: lunch 14.30 (Saturday and Sunday until 15.00); dinner 21.00 (Saturday 21.30).
Closed: Rarely.
Food: Classic British with traditional French influences.
Real Ale: Badger Tanglefoot, Badger Best.
Other points: No-smoking area. Dogs welcome. Garden. Children welcome over 9 years old. Car park.
Directions: On A350 south of Shaftesbury. (Map 5, G2)

Braintree

Green Dragon

Upper London Road, Youngs End, Braintree, Essex CM77 8QN
Telephone: +44(0)870 4016067
+44(0)1245 361030
green.dragon@virgin.net
www.greendragonbrasserie.co.uk

Adorned with flower-filled hanging baskets all year round, this classic 18th-century inn was formerly a private house and stables, the latter housing the Barn and Hayloft restaurants, with their stripped brick walls and fine old ceiling beams. The neat garden to the rear has an aviary and children's play area and really comes into its own in summer. Within the pub, the lounge and Parlour bars done in yellows and browns with lots of original beams, red carpets, banquettes and traditional pub furnishings, provide a cosy atmosphere in which to relax with a pint of Greene King ale, or a decent glass of wine. The same blackboard and extensive printed menus are served throughout, but the range of light snacks to proper dishes offers great flexibility. Traditional pub staples are made from scratch with good ingredients, so tuck into sausages, mash and onion gravy, cottage pie, daily curry and pasta dishes, filled baguettes, or homecooked ham, egg and chips at lunch. There's more ambitious offerings from the Duke of Buccleuch's estate beef (rib-eye with garlic butter) and speciality seafood dishes like hot potted shrimps and seared tuna with salsa. You will find the pub hard beside the A131 close to the Essex County Showground.

Prices: Set lunch £12 and dinner £16.50. Main course from £7.50. House wine £9.
Last orders: Bar: lunch 15.00; dinner 23.00. Food: lunch 14.00; dinner 21.00 (Friday and Saturday 22.00, Sunday 20.00).
Closed: Rarely.
Food: Traditional British.
Real Ale: Greene King IPA, & Abbot Ale. 1 guest beer.
Other points: No-smoking area. Children welcome over eight years old. Garden. Car park.
Directions: M11 Stansted exit. Take A120 to Braintree then A131 towards Chelmsford. (Map 6, D6)

Clavering

The Cricketers

Clavering, Saffron Walden, Essex CB11 4QT
Telephone: +44(0)870 4016068
+44(0)1799 550442
info@thecricketers.co.uk
www.thecricketers.co.uk

Oak ceiling-beams and pillars bear witness to the 16th century origins of the large, neatly maintained pub overlooking Clavering's green and cricket pitch. It is owned and run by Trevor and Sally Oliver and it was here that young Jamie Oliver first discovered his passion for cooking. Within, are highly polished wood tables, gleaming brass knick-knacks and glasses, a log fire, and the place has a pleasant, well cared for atmosphere. Light floods in due to the modern open-plan layout. From quite an extensive bar menu there could be stuffed roulade of corn-fed chicken with tarragon and green peppercorn mayonnaise, or sautéed calf's liver and bacon with red onion gravy, with blackboard specials changing everyday. Fish features in a big way with perhaps monkfish and scallops with tomato and haricot bean ragout, or whole plaice, grilled on the bone, served with lemon, sea salt and thyme. The restaurant offers an imaginative set dinner menu with plenty of choice at each course and a blackboard lists a great selection of wines by the glass. Six bedrooms are located in the inn and the adjacent Pavilion has eight en suite bedrooms, all decorated to a very high standard with quality oak furniture and stylish fabrics.

Cambridge

Audley End

Where to Shop
Saffron Walden, Cambridge Farmers Market Ugley (3rd Sat of month)
Villages to Visit Head east of the M11 to the Essex villages of Thaxted (fine windmill), Finchingfield and Great Bardfield.

Rooms: 14. Double/twin room from £100, singles from £70.
Prices: Set lunch from £20 and dinner from £26.
Bar main course from £6.50. House wine £9.50.
Last orders: Bar: 23.00. Food: lunch 14.00; dinner 22.00.
Closed: Rarely.
Food: Modern European.
Real Ale: Adnams Southwold & Broadside.
Other points: No-smoking area in restaurant. Garden. Children welcome. Car park.
Directions: Exit8/M11. Take the A120 west; turn right onto the B1383 to Newport; turn left along B1038 for Clavering. (Map 6, D5)

Tourist Information
Saffron Walden +44(0)1799 510444
Must See
- Audley End, Saffron Walden: beautiful Jacobean mansion set in a magnificent landscaped park.
- Duxford Imperial War Museum
- Wimpole Hall & Home Farm, SE Cambridge
- Cambridge: Fitzwilliam Museum; University Botanic Garden; colleges.
- Linton Zoological Gardens

Where to Walk
The gently rolling landscape around Thaxted has good paths linking sleepy villages with windmills and charming cottages. There is also a good network of tracks around Saffron Walden which extend into the parkland of Audley End House. Enjoyable towpath and meadow walks across Wimpole Hall Estate.
Events & Festivals Duxford Airshow (September)
Regular events at Audley End House
Flying Legends Show, Duxford Airfield (July)

Colchester

The Peldon Rose Inn

Mersea Road, Peldon, Colchester,
Essex CO5 7QJ
Telephone: +44(0)870 4016069
+44(0)1206 735248
peldon@lwwinebars.com

Colchester-based wine merchant Lay & Wheeler bought this historic 600-year-old timbered pub back in 2001 and have worked their magic in restoring this locally famous old smugglers inn, which stands close to the causeway to Mersey Island. Conjure up images of smugglers discussing contraband in the ancient bar, where old-world charm abounds in standing timbers, 'skull-shattering' beams, antique mahogany tables, huge log fires and leaded-light windows, and in the adjacent dining area with its wonky timbered walls, tiled floor and upholstered chairs. The spacious, light and comfortably stylish rear conservatory is very contemporary by comparison. Bar food utilises locally sourced produce, notably Mersea Island fish and oysters. Follow pork and game terrine with red onion marmalade with, say, simply grilled Dover, whole local plaice or cod with decent chips and salad, or braised venison with smoked bacon and field mushrooms. There's a good sandwich choice, pasta meals and ploughman's lunches, while homemade puddings include chocolate pecan nut tart and steamed apple pudding. Not surprisingly, the short wine list is of superior quality, offering good tasting notes and close to 20 by the glass. Stylishly simple en suite bedrooms sport contemporary colours and furnishings.

Rooms: 3. Double/twin room from £60.
Prices: Restaurant main course from £6.75.
House wine £9.95.
Last orders: Bar: 23.00. Food: lunch 14.15; dinner 21.00 (Friday and Saturday 21.30). Summer until 21.30.
Closed: Rarely.
Food: Modern and Traditional British.
Real Ale: Adnams. Greene King IPA. 1 guest beer.
Other points: No-smoking area. Garden. Children welcome. Car park.
Directions: On the B1025 south of Colchester, close to the causeway to Mersea Island. (Map 6, D6)

Earls Colne

The Carved Angel

Upper Holt Street, Earls Colne, Colchester,
Essex CO6 2PG
Telephone: +44(0)870 4016070
+44(0)1787 222330
enquiries@carvedangel.com
www.carvedangel.com

A fine 15th-century building refurbished with style and panache by Melissa and Michael Deckers in 2000. Now a thriving contemporary gastropub with a relaxing, bright and airy conservatory area with deep fireside sofas, and a separate dining area furnished with smart pine tables and quirky paintings. Although the focus here is on first-class pub food, the Deckers have preserved the traditions of a country village pub, namely real ale from Adnams and Greene King, blazing log fires, comfortable seating and a convivial, informal atmosphere. Food is taken seriously, and the evolving blackboard menus list an imaginative range of modern British dishes, with odd forays abroad for inspiration. Speciality breads dipped in olive oil and balsamic vinegar pots left on the table preceed warm black pudding and bacon salad. Move on to pan-roasted sea bass with chilli sauce and mixed leaves, or chargrilled rib-eye steak with parsley butter sauce. Leave room for lemon and lime cheesecake with raspberry coulis or a plate of French and English cheeses. There is also a good-value set lunch menu and regular theme nights that celebrate regional cuisines. Excellent wines include Michael's special selection; 14 by the glass. Super decked terrace for al fresco dining.

Prices: Set lunch £9.95. Restaurant main course from £10.95. House wine £10.25.
Last orders: Bar: lunch 15.00; dinner 23.00. Food: lunch 14.00 (Saturday and Sunday 15.00); dinner 21.00 (Friday and Saturday 21.30)
Closed: Rarely.
Food: Modern European.
Real Ale: Adnams, Greene King IPA. 1 guest beer.
Other points: No-smoking area. Garden. Children welcome. Car park.
Directions: Exit7/M11. Follow the A1124 towards Halstead and follow the signs to Earls Colne. (Map 6, D6)

Horndon-on-the-Hill

Little Canfield

Bell Inn & Hill House

High Road, Horndon-on-the-Hill,
Essex SS17 8LD
Telephone: +44(0)870 4016071
+44(0)1375 642463

Lion and Lamb

Stortford Road, Little Canfield, Dunmow,
Essex CM6 1SR
Telephone: +44(0)870 4016072
+44(0)1279 870257
info@lionandlamb.co.uk
www.lionandlamb.co.uk

Located in the village centre a few doors from one another, John and Christine Vereker's 500-year-old Bell Inn offers a friendly rustic, pubby ambience including beams, scrubbed wooden tables, flagstone floors and five changing micro-brewery real ales; Hill House next door has a private dining room and ten beautifully furnished en suite bedrooms. The inn has been in Christine's family for over 60 years and is renowned by dint of its culinary ambition, but it is definitely still a pub. Either book in the restaurant or take first come, first served in the bar where, if no table is vacant, they take your name and you wait, propping up the bar in true pub fashion, until one is free. The menu, chalked up on several boards, is lengthy and lively, and reflects a contemporary understanding of modern ideas. Typically, begin with scallop and avocado ravioli with curried onions and crab jus, and follow with pot-roast lamb with mint jus, or poached halibut with sesame salt and cauliflower purée. The selection of British cheeses should gladden the hearts of wine lovers who want to continue exploring the Bell's outstanding wine list. Five striking, individually designed suites at the inn.

From the new A120 (Dumnow West junction), take the B1256 for a mile to find this popular family dining pub which dates from the 18th century. Both the character bar and modern dining room extensions feature open brickwork, log fires, exposed pine, huge oak beams, rustic furnishings, and a wealth of decorative memorabilia. Outside is a large garden, with a children's Wendy house making it a popular spot for families at weekends and now much quieter thanks to the new bypass. The varied menu (served all day) is a cut above the norm, with traditional favourites done well - Sunday lunch rare roast rib of beef with Yorkshire pudding, for example - and plenty of modern touches such as local handmade Dunmow sausages with mash and onion gravy, roasted salmon with coriander and chilli crust or Thai chicken, and the odd adventurous dish like chargrilled kangaroo. Fish comes directly from Billingsgate. For a light snack try a homemade quiche or a hearty cheese ploughman's lunch. The small family owned Ridleys Brewery in Essex provide beers that are worth sampling; 12 wines are offered by the glass. The pub is just a few miles from Stanstead Airport.

Rooms: 15. Rooms from £50. Suites from £85.
Prices: Restaurant main course from £12.
House wine £10.50.
Last orders: Bar: lunch 14.30 (Sunday 16.00); dinner 23.00. Food: lunch 13.45 (Sunday 14.15); dinner 21.45. No food served Bank Holiday Mondays.
Closed: Never.
Food: Modern British.
Real Ale: Bass, Greene King IPA. 5 guest beers.
Other points: No-smoking area. Dogs welcome overnight. Children welcome. Courtyard. Car park.
Directions: Exit30/31 M25. A13 for Tilbury then A128; follow the tourist signs from there. (Map 6, E6)

Rooms: 3. Double room from £65,
single occupancy £60.
Prices: Sunday set lunch £16. Restaurant main course from £8.50. Bar main course from £5.
House wine £10.75.
Last orders: Bar: 23.00. Food: 22.00.
Closed: Never.
Food: Traditional/Modern British/Australian influence.
Real Ale: Ridley's IPA, Old Bob & Prospect.
Other points: No-smoking area. Children welcome. Garden. Car park.
Directions: Exit 8/M11, B1256 east to Takeley and Dunmow. (Map 6, D6)

Cirencester

The Bell at Sapperton

Sapperton, Cirencester,
Gloucestershire GL7 6LE
Telephone: +44(0)870 4016073
+44 (0)1285 760298
thebell@sapperton66.freeserve.co.uk
www.foodatthebell.co.uk

Informality, a relaxing atmosphere, cracking ales and wines, and first-class food have been key ingredients to the roaring success of Paul Davidson's and Pat le-Jeune's stylishly refurbished 300-year-old Cotswolds pub. Civilised in every way, exposed stone walls, polished flagstones, bare boards, open log fires and individual tables and chairs set the style; added touches include tasteful wine prints, daily newspapers and fresh flowers. Use of fresh local produce has been vital to the popularity of the seasonally-changing menu and includes homemade bread, fish from Cornwall and local organic and rare breed meats, notably beef from the Cirencester Park herd and pork from Daglingworth across the valley. Follow Cerney goats' cheese panna cotta with roasted pimentoes and balsamic, or pressed venison terrine, with braised belly of 'Old Spot' pork with lime and ginger sauce, or English shorthorn sirloin steak with horseradish and Madeira glaze. Fishy options from the daily blackboard menus extend the choice to include, perhaps, seared king scallops with pancetta and stir-fried greens. A good walkers' snack menu lists a hearty three-cheese ploughman's. The wine list offers 14 by the glass and is strong on single-supplier wines. There's a secluded rear courtyard and landscaped front garden.

Prices: Main course from £9.75. Bar main course from £6. House wine £12.50.
Last orders: lunch 14.00; dinner 21.30.
Closed: Rarely.
Food: Modern British.
Real Ale: Uley Old Spot, Goffs Jouster, Hook Norton Best Bitter, Wickwar Cotswold Way.
Other points: No-smoking area. Garden. Children welcome over ten years old (before 18.30). Car park.
Directions: J15/M4, J11A/M5. Off A419 between Stroud and Cirencester. (Map 5, E2)

Cirencester

Wild Duck Inn

Ewen, Cirencester, Gloucestershire GL7 6BY
Telephone: +44(0)870 4016074
+44(0)1285 770310
wduckinn@aol.com
www.thewildduckinn.co.uk

Creeper-clad, with well-tended gardens and lawns, and a lavender-lined entrance path, this fine Elizabethan inn creates a favourable first impression. It stands in a sleepy rural backwater close to the Cotswold Water Park. The bar brims with character, atmosphere and cosy appeal, with big armchairs and rich burgundy walls festooned with old portraits and hunting trophies. The restaurant's labyrinth of small rooms offer dining space amid dark beams, more burgundy walls and wooden tables and chairs; the same printed menu is available throughout, along with daily-changing blackboard specials. The lively repertoire draws the crowds with its modern edge and realistic pricing, perhaps a one-course lunch of beer battered fish and chips, chicken Caesar salad, or a classic fish pie. Dinner could run to chicken liver and wild mushroom parfait with redcurrant jelly, and slow-roast belly pork with leek champ and cider gravy. The compact, globetrotting wine list offers some 30 by the glass, and the bar has five real ales. And, for those wishing to uncork a few bottles without driving home, 11 individually decorated en suite bedrooms offer traditional comforts, two in the oldest part of the building have four-posters.

Rooms: 11. Double room from £80, single from £60.
Prices: Main course from £6.95. House wine £9.95.
Last orders: Bar: 23.00. Food: lunch 14.00 (Sunday 14.30; dinner 22.00 (Sunday 21.30).
Closed: Rarely.
Food: Modern British.
Real Ale: Bombardier Bitter, Smiles Original, Theakston Old Peculiar, Theakston XB, Old Speckled Hen.
Other points: Children welcome. Dogs welcome overnight. Garden. Car park.
Directions: From Cirencester, take A429 towards Malmesbury. At Kemble turn left to Ewen. (Map 5, E2)

Zulu Warriors and Rare Breeds

at the Bell at Sapperton

Dave Tomlin's
Country Butcher,
Huntley, Beef

A40

The Bell at Sapperton uses only the finest meat from the finest butchers. A traditional country butcher in the heart of the Gloucestershire countryside, Dave Tomlin provides meat, home cured bacon and handmade sausages. With over 35 years experience it is no wonder his sausages win awards and the variety on offer is mind boggling. Dave Tomlin combines the traditional art of sausage making with an array of spices and flavours you would not have thought possible. You can gorge on the classic Gloucester Old Spot, the 'king among kings', or get stuck into the more exotic Zulu Warrior, an old South African recipe that combines pork with roasted coriander and cloves, or how about the Balearic which is a Mediterranean blend of tomatoes, mushrooms and leeks.

Chesterton Farm Shop, situated in the farmyard of a working farm and also used by the Bell was Britain's first accredited rare breeds butcher. Dave Tomlin has also been accredited by the Rare Breeds Survival Trust. This means they supply traditional British livestock breeds that have the old fashioned qualities that our grandparents might remember. They are breeds that thrive in non intensive, natural farming environments. They don't need growth promoters, hormones or the routinely fed antibiotics that are currently the cause of national concern. Because traditional breeds grow a little more slowly than modern ones, the meat develops a better, truer flavour. Unlike the bland sameness of modern meat, the meat from every traditional breed has its own special qualities, just as different varieties of apples do.

A38

Hobs House Bakery,
Chipping Sodbury, Bread

Bristol

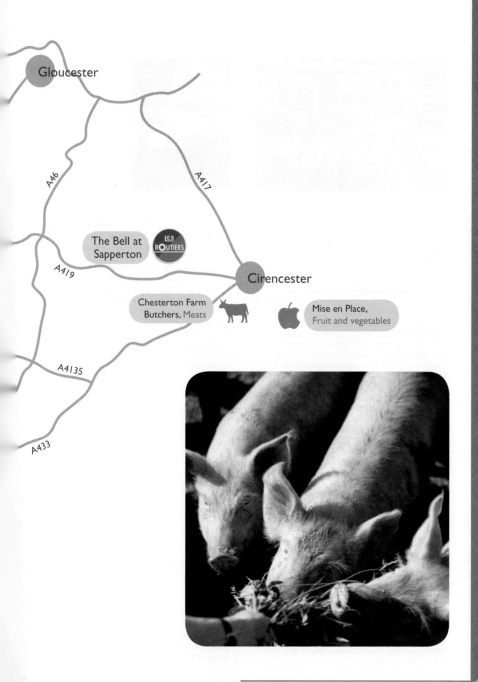

Gloucester

A46

A417

The Bell at Sapperton

LES ROUTIERS

A419

Cirencester

Chesterton Farm Butchers, Meats

Mise en Place, Fruit and vegetables

A4135

A433

Clearwell

The Wyndham Arms

Clearwell, The Royal Forest of Dean,
Gloucestershire GL16 8JT
Telephone: +44(0)870 4016075
+44(0)1594 833666
nigel@thewyndhamhotel.co.uk
www.thewyndhamhotel.co.uk

Set in several acres of glorious sloping gardens, woods and lawns, Nigel and Pauline Stanley's 600-year-old traditional inn stands at the heart of this medieval village. It is filled with oak beams, flagstones and exposed original red brick, the historic and very popular bar dispensing local Freeminer beers, Orchards Ciders, decent wines and a fabulous range of malt whiskies. Bedrooms at this civilised and well refurbished small inn, however, are much more recent (1990s) and in an adjacent building. They are spacious and well equipped with modern en suite bathrooms. Local foodstuffs feature prominently on both the bar and fixed price restaurant menus. These can include seasonal game from Lydney Park Estate, single herd meats, Gloucester Old Spot pork products and Brooks local ice cream. They are also active in the community cooperative for supplies of vegetables, salads and herbs, and local farmhouse cheeses. Translated on the menu, this brings ham hock and pork terrine with spiced pear chutney, monkfish tail with mash, ratatouille and tomato cream sauce, and lemon tart with a warm fruit coulis to finish.

Rooms: 18. Double room from £85, single from £45.
Prices: Restaurant main course from £8.95.
House wine £10.95.
Last orders: Bar: 23.00. Food: lunch 14.00 (Sunday 14.30); dinner: 21.30 (Sunday 21.00).
Closed: First week in January.
Food: Modern British.
Real Ale: Freeminer Bitter, Freeminer Speculation Ale.
Other points: No-smoking area. Children welcome. Dogs welcome overnight. Garden. Car park. Licence for Civil Weddings.
Directions: Exit2/M48. Via A48 and B4228 signed Forest of Dean. From A48 at Monmouth via A4176 and B4228, two miles from Coleford. (Map 5, E1)

Frampton Mansell

White Horse

Cirencester Road, Frampton Mansell,
Gloucestershire GL6 8HZ
Telephone: +44(0)870 4016076
+44(0)1285 760960
www.cotswoldwhitehorse.com

Shaun and Emma Davies have transformed the fortunes of this once derelict pub since taking on the challenge in 2001. Set hard beside the busy A419 and with an unprepossessing stone exterior, many would not give it a second glance as they speed by. But this is now a stylish pub-restaurant serving great food and wine. Venture in to find a stylishly-refurbished, individual interior with brightly-painted walls adorned with unusual modern art, sisal carpeted floors, chunky tables and colourful cushioned chairs. Modern menus are built around fresh produce from quality local suppliers: meat comes from Chesterton Farm butchers near Cirencester who specialise in rare and traceable breeds, game from local shoots, and fish is delivered twice-weekly from Looe in Cornwall. Top-quality local vegetables are used creatively; in addition, chips are handcut and bread is baked daily on the premises. From simpler lunchtime dishes like home-glazed ham, egg and chips, daily menus extend, perhaps, to beetroot risotto with grilled goat's cheese and basil pesto, roast partridge with caramelised apples and redcurrant jus, and skate wing with chinese cabbage and watercress butter sauce. Local ale comes from Hook Norton, Uley or Arkells breweries. Global wines focus on smaller growers; six by the glass or 50cl pot.

Prices: Restaurant main course from £8.95. Bar main course from £4.95. House wine £11.75.
Last orders: Bar: lunch 15.00; dinner 23.00. Food: lunch 14.30; dinner 21.45 (Sunday 15.00).
Closed: Sunday evening.
Food: Modern British.
Real Ale: Hook Norton, Uley Bitter.
Other points: Children welcome. Garden. Car park.
Directions: J15/M4. J13//M5. Between Cirencester and Stroud on the A419. On the main road, not in the village of Frampton Mansell itself. (Map 5, E2)

Kelmscott

The Plough at Kelmscott

Kelmscott, Lechlade, Gloucestershire GL7 3HG
Telephone: +44(0)870 4016077
+44(0)1367 253543
ploughatkelmscottgl7.fsnet.co.uk
www.theploughatkelmscott.co.uk

Tucked away down a narrow, dead-end lane in a peaceful Thames-side village and long a favoured watering-hole among Thames path walkers and the boating fraternity, the 17th-century Plough received a stylish makeover in 2002 and now operates as an upmarket gastropub-with-rooms. Despite its isolation, the village and the Plough bustle with visitors due to the proximity of Henry Morris's former country home. The interior has a stylish, contemporary rustic look, mixing original flagstones, crackling log fires and plenty of exposed brick and timbers with a semi-circle pine bar, modern wooden chairs and tables (with quality cutlery and glassware). Matching the surroundings is an imaginative modern British menu. On the bar menu you may find carrot and orange soup, fresh battered cod with hand-cut chips, local venison casserole, Thai crabcakes with plum sauce, and toasted open sandwiches. Evening dishes produce beef fillet on swede and carrot purée, colcannon, sweet roasted beetroot and a mustard and tarragon sauce. Of the eight en suite bedrooms, one is decorated in William Morris style. See Pub Walk on page 282.

Rooms: 8. Double from £75, single from £45, family room from £85.
Prices: Restaurant main course from £9.50. Lunch and bar snack from £4.95. Fish menu from £4.50. House wine £10.50.
Last orders: Bar: lunch 15.00; dinner 23.00. Food: lunch 14.30; dinner 21.00 (Saturday and Sunday all day).
Closed: Rarely.
Food: Classic and Modern British/French.
Real Ale: Hook Norton Ales. 2 guest beers.
Other points: Children welcome. Dogs welcome overnight. Garden. Live music and events.
Directions: Take A416 from Lechlade towards Faringdon; then follow signs to Kelmscott. (Map 5, E3)

Northleach

The Wheatsheaf Inn

West End, Northleach,
Gloucestershire GL54 3EZ
Telephone: +44(0)870 4016078
+44 (0)1451 860244
caspar@wheatsheafatnorthleach.com
www.wheatsheafatnorthleach.com

Quietly situated overlooking the broad main street in this celebrated Cotswold 'wool town', the stone-built 17th-century coaching inn has been stylishly revamped by brothers Caspar and Gavin Harvard-Walls over the past year. Expect classic period features like worn flagstone floors, big oak beams, blazing log fires and chunky wooden furnishings throughout the three, light and airy and connecting front rooms. The rustic bar deals in Hook Norton with changing guest ales and a blackboard menu. The classy, understated dining room is marginally more formal. Modern British favourites are inspired by what is available locally, warm pigeon salad with summer berries, and Gloucester Old Spot pork tenderloin with parsnip mash and cabbage, for example, or Bibury trout with watercress and bacon. Treacle tart, or apple crumble with custard are classic desserts, with local cheeses making a savoury alternative. Impeccable choices on a globally inspired wine list; 12 are offered by the glass. All eight en suite bedrooms have been refurbished and now match the effortless rustic chic of the downstairs.

Rooms: 8. Double/twin room from £60, single from £50, family room from £70.
Prices: Main course from £7. Bar/snack from £4. House wine £10.75.
Last orders: Bar 23.00. Food: lunch 15.00; dinner 22.00 (Sunday 21.00).
Closed: Never.
Food: Modern British.
Real Ale: Hook Norton, Wadworth 6X. 1 guest beer.
Other points: No-smoking area. Children welcome. Dogs welcome in bar. Garden. Car park. Licence for Civil Weddings.
Directions: Off A429 between Stow-on-the-Wold and Cirencester. Exit 15/M4. (Map 5, E2)

Farm House Cider
at the Wyndham Arms

A formerly overgrown and disused farm in the picturesque Wye Valley is now producing top quality Cider and Perry. The 200-year-old farm was bought by the fortuitously named Keith Orchard, who discovered in the overgrown orchard a host of Cider apple and Perry pear trees. He now produces many varieties, winners of recent, prestigious awards and sells it throughout the West Country to various shops and top restaurants and pubs, namely Les Routiers member, the Wyndham Arms. Situated in the Forest of Dean, this historic 600-year-old hotel in the heart of Cider and Perry country is heavily involved in promoting local foodstuffs - you will find Orchards produce behind the bar and, perhaps, cropping up in dishes such as Scrump Pork – braised pork fillet cooked in cider and apples. Meanwhile, if you fancy sampling this wonderful stuff one must cover the basics – the simple Farm House Cider, the adventurous 'Dabinett' Cider which at a mind-blowing 8.3% is the strongest and driest, and the unique 'Cannock' Perry, named after men that travelled from the Forest of Dean to work in the first Staffordshire foundries.

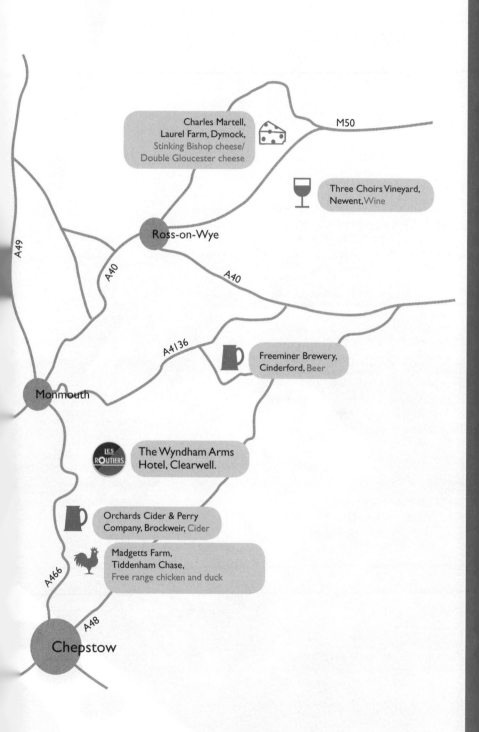

Charles Martell,
Laurel Farm, Dymock,
Stinking Bishop cheese/
Double Gloucester cheese

M50

Three Choirs Vineyard,
Newent, Wine

A49

Ross-on-Wye

A40

A40

A4136

Freeminer Brewery,
Cinderford, Beer

Monmouth

The Wyndham Arms
Hotel, Clearwell.

Orchards Cider & Perry
Company, Brockweir, Cider

Madgetts Farm,
Tiddenham Chase,
Free range chicken and duck

A466

A48

Chepstow

Painswick

Butchers Arms

Sheepscombe, Painswick,
Gloucestershire GL6 7RH
Telephone: +44(0)870 4016079
+44(0)1452 812113
bleninns@clara.net
www.cotswoldinns.co.uk ·

Part of Jonny Johnston's small Blenheim Inns
group of pubs, this mellow-stone pub dates
from 1620 and was originally a butchery for
deer hunted in Henry VIII's deer park. Note
the famous pub sign showing a butcher supping a pint of ale with a pig tied to his leg. It
is worth negotiating the narrow lanes for the
glorious views over the rolling Stroud Valley
from the sunny front terrace or steep garden
behind the pub. Added attractions include
the good range of beers - Hook Norton, Wye
Valley Dorothy Goodbody's Golden Ale and
Moles Best - and an interesting choice of traditional and modern pub food. The homely,
rustic bar and adjoining beamed dining room
are the setting for cooking that relies on
locally sourced raw materials such as handmade sausages from Jessie Smith in Dursley,
Texel lambs from Lypiatt Farm in nearby
Miserden, smoked fish from Severn and Wye
Smokery, and locally-grown vegetables. For
lunch, tuck into hearty homemade soups,
decent ploughman's or smoked haddock and
prawn pancakes, while at dinner choose, perhaps, from prime steaks, lamb shank braised
in honey and garlic with mash, roasted trout
fillet with a herb crust, and local pheasant
with bacon and peppercorn sauce.

Prices: Restaurant main course from £7.50. Bar snack
from £4. House wine £8.95.
Last orders: Bar: lunch 14.30 (Saturday 15.00); dinner
23.00. Food: lunch 14.30 (Sunday 15.00); dinner 21.30.
Closed: Never.
Food: Modern and Traditional British and European.
Real Ale: Hook Norton Best Bitter, Moles Best Bitter,
Wye Valley Dorothy Goodbody's Golden Ale.
Other points: No-smoking area. Children welcome.
Garden. Car park.
Directions: Junction 11a/M5. Just off the A46 between
Cheltenham and Stroud, near Painswick. (Map 5, E2)

Painswick

The Falcon Inn

New Street, Painswick,
Gloucestershire GL6 6UN
Telephone: +44(0)870 4016080
+44(0)1452 814222
bleninns@clara.net
www.falconinn.com

The Falcon, a handsome 16th-century coaching inn, is an unlikely setting to find the world's oldest bowling green. Standing opposite the parish church, this stone-built inn's colourful history also takes in the site of the first Masonic ceremony in Gloucestershire in 1794, and a period as the village courthouse. Interconnecting bar and dining areas are full of traditional character, the scene set by stone, tiled or carpeted floors, wood panelling, open log fires, and a mix of wooden benches and more formal furnishings. Jonny Johnston's careful sourcing of local produce, notably game from nearby shoots, locally-grown vegetables, and butchers meats, including belted Galloway beef, is evident on changing menus and the list of daily chalkboard dishes. Expect the likes of organic pork loin with cider, honey and apple sauce, braised venison with root vegetables, or best end of lamb with port and redcurrant sauce, and fish dishes such as organic Cockleford trout with red pesto. Twelve en suite bedrooms are split between the main building and the converted coach house. All are individually decorated with four-poster rooms located in the inn.

Rooms: 12. Double room from £68, single from £45.
Prices: Set lunch £12 and dinner £16. Restaurant main course £7.50. Bar snack from £4. House wine £8.95.
Last orders: Bar: 23.00. Food: lunch 14.30 (Sunday 15.00); dinner 21.30 (Saturday 22.00).
Closed: Never.
Food: Modern and Traditional British and European.
Real Ale: Hook Norton Best Bitter, Greene King IPA, Wadworth 6X. I guest beer.
Other points: No-smoking area. Children welcome. Dogs welcome overnight. Garden. Car park.
Directions: Junction 11a/M5. On A46 between Cheltenham and Stroud. (Map 5, E2)

Tetbury

The Trouble House

Cirencester Road, Tetbury,
Gloucestershire GL8 8SG
Telephone: +44(0)870 4016081
+44(0)1666 502206
enquiries@troublehouse.co.uk
www.troublehouse.co.uk

Ex-City Rhodes head chef Michael Bedford and his wife Sarah run this refurbished Wadworth pub in rural Gloucestershire, with great passion and enthusiasm. The setting may be rustic, with scrubbed tables, wooden floors, hop-adorned beams, open fires and pastel-painted walls, but Michael's inspired modern cooking continues to please, drawing restaurant tourists prepared to travel across the Cotswolds for a table - do book, as trade is brisk. Sound ideas and techniques, attention to detail and use of first-class ingredients results in honest, full-flavoured and robust cooking, notably confit of rabbit leg with Toulouse sausage, homemade pasta and mustard cream, or roasted cod with haricot beans, lentils and bacon. A deft touch is also evident with tomato and goats' cheese tart with mixed leaves, cured salmon with celeriac purée and a lemon and caper dressing, and crab risotto. Round off with glazed Basque tart or a plate of fine farmhouse cheeses. In addition to Wadworth 6X and Henry's IPA on handpump, expect a well-chosen and sensibly priced list of wines with 14 available by the glass. The Trouble House is uniquely named after a series of unfortunate events at the pub, namely agricultural riots, two suicides and a disastrous fire.

Prices: Main course from £13. House wine £13.50.
Last orders: Bar: lunch 15.00; dinner 23.00. Food: lunch 14.00; dinner 21.30.
Closed: Closed Sunday, Monday, 25 December - early January and one week in September .
Food: Modern British and French.
Real Ale: Wadworth Henry's IPA, Wadworth 6X.
Other points: No-smoking area. Dogs welcome in the bar. Garden. Car park.
Directions: One and a half miles from Tetbury along the A433 towards Cirencester. (Map 5, E2)

Winchcombe

The White Hart Inn

High Street, Winchcombe, Cheltenham, Gloucestershire GL54 5LJ
Telephone: +44(0)870 4016082
+44(0)1242 602359
enquiries@the-white-hart-inn.com
www.the-white-hart-inn.com

Church, Snowshill

Must See
- Sudeley Castle: Impressive old house blended into remains of a medieval castle. Rich furnishings, porcelain, fine tapestries and paintings, and splendid garden.
- Snowshill Manor: Cotswold Manor filled with extraordinary collections and a cottage garden.

Sudeley Castle

Behind the 16th-century stone exterior of this Cotswold's town-centre inn visitors will be treated to a taste of Swedish hospitality. Refurbished with impeccable taste in 2001 by Nicole Burr, who hails from Stockholm, a cool Scandinavian influence runs through the minimalist dining room, as well as the opulent Victorian restaurant, extending to the eight beautifully decorated bedrooms. It also influences the contemporary menus. What is traditional though is the pubby front bar where regulars quaff pints of local Stanney Bitter and tuck into ploughman's platters, big crusty baguettes, Scandinavian open sandwiches, or the house speciality smorgasbord platter - Swedish cold meats, seafoods and salads. In the restaurant, order venison with vodka marinated lingon berries, or something more traditional, perhaps local pheasant with redcurrant and pepper sauce. Beef and lamb come from the Sudeley Castle Estate, and other supplies are sourced as locally as possible. The Stable Bar offers Italian-style pizzas to eat in or take away. Individually designed and decorated bedrooms offer a high level of comfort, with modern facilities and luxury en suite bathrooms. The light and airy Carl Larsson Room, for example, has a stylish minimalist decor.

Rooms: **8.** Double from £70, single room from £55
Prices: Set lunch £12.95 and dinner £17.95. Main course restaurant from £11.95. Main course bar from £5.95. House wine £10.95.
Last orders: Food: 22.00.
Closed: Rarely.
Food: Modern British with Scandinavian specialities.
Real Ale: Old Speckled Hen, Wadworth 6X, Greene King IPA, Stanway Stanney Bitter.
Other points: No-smoking area. Children welcome. Patio. Car park. Meeting facilities.
Directions: Exit 9/M5. In the centre of Winchcombe on the B4362 Cheltenham to Stratford road. (Map 5, D2)

Tourist Information Winchcombe +44(0)1242 602925
Where to Shop Cheltenham, Stow-on-the-Wold
Farmers Market Winchcombe (3rd Saturday of month)
Nearest Racecourse Cheltenham
Nearest Golf Course Cleeve Hill
Where to Walk
The Cotswold Way, a 100-mile path from Chipping Campden to Bath passes through Winchcombe and some of the choicest scenery is to be found close to Winchcombe, notably between Broadway and Stanton and across Cleeve Common. From the town you can follow trail to Hailes Abbey and Belas Knap. Lovely circular walk to Sudeley Castle (see Pub Walk on page 284).
Events & Festivals
Winchcombe Horse Show (May)
National Hunt Festival, Cheltenham (March)
Prescott Speed Hillclimb Championship (May)

Crondall

The Hampshire Arms

Pankridge Street, Crondall, Farnham,
Hampshire GU10 5QU
Telephone: +44(0)870 4016083
+44(0)1252 850418
paulychef@hantsarms.freeserve.co.uk
www.thehampshirearms.co.uk

Serious investment by chef-proprietor Paul
Morgan in early 2004 has seen big changes
at his unpretentious pub secluded away in a
Hampshire village. Paul's energy and enthusiasm has been deflected away from the kitchen
into the fabric of the pub to complement the
style and quality of his food. So, the homely
bar has been smartened up, sofas now front
the log fire in the cosy lounge, the once tired-
looking restaurant has been remodelled and
refurbished in modern style, toilets are now
rather swish, and a new extension houses
Paul's grill restaurant. His passion for fresh
food and quality ingredients extends to making everything on the premises, including
breads, ice creams and chocolate petit fours.
Seasonally changing menus offer an intelli-
gent and well balanced range of modern dishes. This might translate as fennel and orange
soup or pan-fried scallops with celeriac purée
and a fish and chive butter sauce to start.
Herb-crusted lamb on black olive mash with
a ratatouille of vegetables and lamb's kidneys
could follow, or monkfish wrapped in Parma
ham with pea risotto and a lobster and shallot sauce. Alternatively, order a first-class
steak from the grill menu. Round off with
baked rice pudding with rhubarb compote.
Filled baguettes and lighter dishes are also
available at lunchtime.

Prices: Main course from £14.50. House wine £9.95.
Last orders: Bar: lunch 15.00; dinner 23.00. Food: lunch
14.00; dinner 21.30. No food Sunday evening.
Closed: One week over Christmas.
Food: Modern British.
Real Ale: Greene King Abbot Ale, Greene King Ruddles
Best, Greene King IPA. 1 guest beer.
Other points: No-smoking in the restaurant. Garden.
Children welcome. Dogs welcome in bar area.
Directions: Exit 5/M3. Take the A287 for Farnham, turn
off at Crondall. (Map 5, F4)

Eversley

The Golden Pot

Reading Road, Eversley, Hampshire RG27 0NB
Telephone: +44(0)870 4016084
+44(0)118 973 2104
jcalder@golden-pot.co.uk
www.golden-pot.co.uk

Having taken over this 18th-century, creeper-
clad brick pub from good friends, landlord
John Calder was committed to maintaining
the pub's reputation as a dining destination in
north Hampshire. Naturally the unique and
locally famous rösti menu remains a regular
fixture every Monday evening - toppings
include praprika chicken with tarragon cream
sauce, and bacon, onion and melted cheese.
With John came chef Lewy, who, with admi-
rable dexterity, prepares an extensive menu
from fresh ingredients in his small kitchen.
Bar meals and interesting daily blackboard
specials, say crab fishcakes with spicy tomato
sauce, smoked haddock risotto, and whole
grilled plaice with sorrel butter are served
throughout the two civilised and relaxing
bar areas. From the carte, served in the more
formal dining areas, typical starters include
grilled scallops and prosciutto with sautéed
leeks, or a bowl of moules marinière. Among
the main courses, poached pear and a juniper and thyme sauce accompany pan-fried
haunch of venison, and mushroom risotto is
served with honey and orange glazed breast
of guinea fowl. Sunday lunches are very
popular, so are the puddings such as lemon
torte and summer pudding. A sound list of
wines is complemented by Greene King ales
on handpump.

Prices: Restaurant main course from £10. Bar main
course from £6.75. House wine £12.95.
Last orders: Bar: lunch 15.00; dinner 23.00. Food: lunch
14.15 (Sunday 14.00); dinner 21.15.
Closed: Sunday evening during the winter.
Food: Modern British.
Real Ale: Ruddles Best, Greene King Abbot Ale and IPA.
Other points: No-smoking area. Dogs welcome on a
lead. Garden. Children welcome. Car park.
Directions: Exit4/M3 and Exit11/M4. On B3272 north
of Yateley, south of Finchampstead. (Map 5, F4)

Fordingbridge

Rose and Thistle

Rockbourne, Fordingbridge,
Hampshire SP6 3NL
Telephone: +44(0)870 4016085
+44(0)1725 518236
enquiries@roseandthistle.co.uk
www.roseandthistle.co.uk

A delightful long and low whitewashed pub enjoying a tranquil setting in a pretty downland village on the edge of the New Forest, close to Rockbourne's famous Roman Villa and Cranborne Chase. Originally two 17th-century thatched cottages it boasts tasteful furnishings with polished oak tables and chairs, carved benches and cushioned settles, and features two huge fireplaces with winter log fires. Country-style fabrics, dried flowers, and magazines add to the civilised atmosphere. Quality pub food, served in the music-free lounge-cum-dining area, is up to date, and sensibly light and simple at lunchtimes. Note daily homemade soup, 'elegant' Welsh rarebit, local sausages and mash and onion gravy, and ploughman's lunches. Evening dishes are more elaborate, featured on a monthly-changing menu and daily specials' board. Typically, tuck into duck with black cherries and tarragon, local venison with chestnuts and spring onion, and fresh fish (also available lunchtimes), such as roast cod with lemon and black pepper crust, and John Dory stuffed with lime and coriander butter. There is traditional bread-and-butter pudding and seasonal game from local shoots. Also, Sunday roasts, good ales and wines, plus a lovely rose-filled garden.

Prices: Main course restaurant from £11. Main course bar from £7.45. House wine £10.45.
Last orders: Bar: lunch 15.00; dinner 23.00 (Sunday 20.00 October - March). Food: lunch 14.30; dinner 21.30. No food Sunday evenings during the winter.
Closed: Rarely.
Food: Modern British.
Real Ale: Fuller's London Pride, Strong's Best Bitter.
Other points: No-smoking in the restaurant. Children welcome. Garden. Car park.
Directions: Signed off A354 south of Salisbury and off Sandleheath road west of Fordingbridge. (Map 5, G2)

Selborne

The Selborne Arms

High Street, Selborne, Alton,
Hampshire GU34 3JR
Telephone: +44(0)870 4016086
+44(0)1420 511247
info@selbornearms.co.uk
www.selbornearms.co.uk

Nick and Hayley Carter's traditional and simply furnished local stands in the heart of Selborne village, famous for its connections with the pioneer naturalist Gilbert White, and the wonderful surrounding walks through glorious beech 'hangers'. The pub provides welcome refreshment to the many walkers and visitors that throng to this village, but the food is definitely a cut above the pub grub often found in such touristy destinations. Everything is freshly prepared by chef Nick and served in the two homely bars which sport hop-strewn beams and a huge fireplace with a roaring winter log fire. Weary walkers can quench parched throats with local micro-brewery beers, and can tuck into the good-value lunchtime buffet (soup, cold meats, cheese, salads and fresh crusty bread), or order one of Nick's speciality sandwiches, perhaps the 'Rubins', filled with salt beef, sauerkraut and pastrami. In addition to more traditional choices: homemade curry; ploughman's lunches; steak and kidney pie, the daily changing chalkboard menu may list smoked haddock fishcakes, and a main course of chargrilled Irish beef fillet topped with Stilton and served with a port wine sauce.

Prices: Restaurant main course from £6.95. Bar main course from £4.95. House wine £9.50.
Last orders: Bar: lunch 15.00; dinner 23.00 (open all day Saturday during the summer and Sunday all day). Food: lunch 14.00; dinner 21.00.
Closed: Rarely.
Food: Modern International.
Real Ale: Courage Best Bitter, Cheriton Pots Ale, Ringwood Fortyniner. 2 guest beers.
Other points: Garden with children's play area. Barbecue. Car park.
Directions: On B3006 4 miles south of Alton. (Map 5, F4)

Southampton

The White Star Tavern & Dining Rooms ★

28 Oxford Street, Southampton,
Hampshire SO14 3DJ
Telephone: +44(0)870 4016087
+44(0)2380 821990
manager@whitestartavern.co.uk
www.whitestartavern.co.uk

Two years on and Mark Dodd and Matthew Boyle's dream of creating a stylish bar and restaurant (and eventually a chic hotel) in what was a former seafarer's hotel in the days of the Titanic, is well on track. Southampton's first gastropub, in up-and-coming Oxford Street close to Ocean Village and West Quay, has proved a great success, drawing both a lively drinking crowd and discerning diners. Smart front bar lounge areas sport modern brown leather banguettes and cream walls adorned with shipping photographs and retro mirrors, yet retain the original flagstone floors and the period open fireplaces. Beyond the large wooden bar, lies the spacious, wood-floored and panelled dining rooms. Good use of fresh produce from Hampshire suppliers can be seen in 'light bites' like local sausages and mash, salmon confit with gribiche or a classic BLT baguette, and in the lunchtime carte with roast duck with warm red cabbage and tarragon jus. In the evening, seared scallops with spinach and blue cheese cream, and beef sirloin with fondant potato and foie gras jus, show the style; homemade breads and puddings (strawberry cheesecake with balsamic). Impressive list of cocktails, champagnes and vodkas; eight wines by the glass.

Prices: Restaurant main course evening meal from £11.50, lunch from £4. House wine £11.50.
Last orders: Bar: lunch 15.00; dinner 23.00 (Friday to Sunday open all day, April to October open all day). Food: lunch 15.00; dinner 21.30 (Friday and Saturday 22.00, Sunday 21.00).
Closed: Rarely.
Food: Modern British.
Real Ale: Fuller's London Pride, Bass, Courage Best.
Other points: No-smoking area. Children welcome week-ends during the day. Outside seating.
Directions: Exit14/M3. A33 to Southampton and head towards Ocean Village and Marina. (Map 5, G3)

Wherwell

White Lion

Fullerton Road, Wherwell, Hampshire SP11 7JF
Telephone: +44(0)870 4016088
+44(0)1264 860317

At the heart of a picture-postcard thatched village, just a short stroll from Hampshire's finest chalk stream, the River Test, this 17th-century coaching inn is a thriving community local with a loyal trade. It is also a popular lunchtime destination among walkers and cyclists exploring the beautiful Test Valley. Legend has it that shots fired at Wherwell Priory from Oliver Cromwell's cannons fell short, and one cannon ball fell down the chimney of the inn instead - where it can be seen to this day. Traditional English pub food cooked on the premises from carefully sourced fresh ingredients is the key to the popularity of the food here. Eat in the beamed bar where a warming log fire burns in winter, or in the homely dining room. Sample smoked trout from the Chilbolton Estate, handmade sausages and cooked meats from the renowned John Robinson butchers in Stockbridge, or homecooked specials like steak and mushroom pie and smoked haddock and prawn bake. There are good salad platters, ploughman's lunches, and decent home-baked ham, egg and thick-cut chips. Three homely bedrooms.

Rooms: 3. Double room from £49.50, single from £37.50.
Prices: Restaurant main course from £7.50. Bar main course from £5.50. House wine £9.95.
Last orders: Bar: lunch 14.30 (Saturday and Sunday 15.00); dinner 23.00. Food: lunch 14.00; dinner 21.00 (Sunday 20.30).
Closed: Rarely.
Food: Traditional English.
Real Ale: Ringwood Best Bitter, Courage Best Bitter, Directors Bitter.
Other points: No-smoking area. Dogs welcome overnight. Garden. Car park. Folk club.
Directions: Village signed off A2057 between Andover and Stockbridge. (Map 5, F3)

Winchester

The Wykeham Arms

75 Kingsgate Street, Winchester, Hampshire SO23 9PE
Telephone: +44(0)870 4016089
+44(0)1962 853834

Tucked away in the narrow streets near the Cathedral Close and Winchester College, the mellow, redbrick, 250-year-old 'Wyk' is one of the finest hostelries in the land. The rambling series of bars and eating areas are furnished with old pine tables and time-worn college desks, have four roaring winter fires, are adorned with a fascinating collections of hats, tankards, pictures, and military memorabilia. Modern pub food, alongside more adventurous evening choices, attracts food lovers from far and wide. From a seasonal lunch menu you could tuck into a Dexter beef open steak sandwich, grilled salmon with spicy prawn couscous annd chilli jam, or minted shoulder of lamb on bubble-and-squeak with wok-fried vegetables. In the evening there's an imaginative repertoire of dishes built around fresh ingredients. Begin with squid tempura with chilli dipping sauce, move on to roast duck with chorizo, borlotti bean, Puy lentil and red wine cassoulet, or baked turbot with roasted pepper, baby artichoke and asparagus couscous and caper salsa. Satisfying puddings may include lavender and vanilla panna cotta. A well-chosen list of wines favours Burgundy; 19 by the glass. Stylishly decorated and thoughtfully equipped bedrooms are split between the inn and Saint George, an annexe across the street.

Rooms: 14. Doubles/twin room from £95, single from £55. Suite £135 and four-poster £120.
Prices: Sunday lunch £14.50 (2 course) and £18.50. Restaurant main course dinner from £13.95. Bar main course lunch from £6. House wine £11.95.
Last orders: Bar: 23.00. Food: lunch 14.30 (Sunday 13.45); dinner 20.45. No food Sunday evening.
Closed: Never.
Food: Modern British.
Real Ale: Gales HSB, Gale's Butser Bitter, Gale's Best Bitter, Bass. Guest beer.
Other points: No-smoking area in restaurant. Dogs welcome in bar. Garden. Car park.
Directions: Close to Winchester College and the Cathedral. (Map 5, F3)

Winchester Cathedral

Broadlands

See page 85 for an interior shot.

Must See
- Winchester: Cathedral & Close, Great Hall, City Museum.
- Wolvesey Castle
- Hinton Ampner House
- Jane Austen's House, Chawton
- Marwell Zoo
- Mid-Hants Railway (Watercress Line), Alresford
- Broadlands, Romsey

Where to Walk
Easy strolls through the Itchen Valley watermeadows to St Catherine's Hill (fine views across Winchester), and along the woodland and downland trails at Farley Mount Country Park. Longer walks along the South Downs Way. Rewarding city strolls.
See also Pub Walk on page 286.

Tourist Information Winchester +44(0)1962 840500
Where to Shop
Winchester, Alresford, Stockbridge, Romsey
Farmers Market Winchester (last Sunday of month)
Nearest Racecourse Salisbury, Goodwood
Nearest Golf Course South Winchester Golf Club

Local Activities
Fishing, cycling, theatre, city walking tours.
Events & Festivals
Winchester Folk Festival (May)
Grange Park Opera, Northington (June)
Winchester Festival & Hat Fair (July)
Alresford Agricultural Show (September)

Kington

The Stagg Inn

Titley, Kington, Herefordshire HR5 3RL
Telephone: +44(0)870 4016090
+44(0)1544 230221
reservations@thestagg.co.uk
www.thestagg.co.uk

Steve and Nicola Reynolds's rustic rural local in tiny Titley plays host to farmers drinking Hobson's Bitter at the bar and avid 'foodies', here for some of the best pub food in the land. Local boy and Roux-trained chef Steve has a real passion for food, delving deep into the fine raw materials that the Welsh Borders has to offer, notably fruit, vegetables, rare breed meats and game from local organic farms, producing seasonally influenced menus that are simply described. He makes just about everything on the premises. With his assured, yet restrained touch, exemplary dishes could include a starter of pigeon breast with herb risotto and thyme juice and mains like duck breast with sweet-sour rhubarb sauce and organic salmon fillet with tomato and ginger sauce. Puddings bring a passion fruit jelly and panna cotta and a first-class selection of twenty local unpasteurised cheeses. Or, in the homely pine furnished bar, wash down excellent organic local pork sausages with Ralph's Radnor cider or one of ten wines by the glass. Retire to one of the two en suite bedrooms, or stay at the Old Vicarage, where Steve's mum has two en suite rooms with lovely views. See Pub Walk on page 288.

Rooms: 5. Double room from £70, single from £50.
Prices: Restaurant main course from £12.50. Bar main course from £7.50. House wine £11.90.
Last orders: Food: lunch 14.00; dinner 22.00 (Sunday 21.00).
Closed: Monday, the first two weeks of November, the Tuesday after Bank Holiday and May Day.
Food: Modern British.
Real Ale: Hobson's Best. 1-2 guest beers.
Other points: No-smoking area. Children welcome. Dogs welcome. Garden. Car park.
Directions: On B4322 between Kington and Presteigne. (Map 4, B6)

Berkhamsted

Alford Arms

Frithsden, Berkhamsted,
Hertfordshire HP1 3DD
Telephone: +44(0)870 4016091
+44 (0)1442 864480

On warm days tables spill out onto the sun-trap front terrace of David and Becky Salisbury's pretty pub which lies secluded away on the edge of the Ashridge Estate (NT). Truly a peaceful spot and worth finding (follow signs for Frithsden Vineyard) for first-class food served in an informal and very welcoming atmosphere. Styled 'country pub and eating' on the menu, it successfully blends a stylishly modernised interior, with its tiled and wooden floors, old scrubbed pine tables and attractive prints, with some imaginative modern British cooking that relies on quality local, free-range and organic produce. Listed on the carte or daily-changing chalkboard are 'small plates' of, say, seared scallops with pea purée and mint vinaigrette, or game terrine with apricot chutney. Eclectic main courses range from cod in red wine on creamy mash with roast vegetable, or smoked salmon fishcake on celeriac remoulade and greens, to chargrilled rib-eye steak with rosemary and garlic butter. Warm chocolate brownie and vanilla and elderflower crème brûlée are typical desserts. Great care is taken in presentation of dishes and flavours shine through. Good ales from Brakspear, Marston's and Morrell's and a raft of wines offered by the glass. See Pub Walk on page 290.

Prices: Restaurant main course from £9.50. House wine £10.75.
Last orders: Bar: 23.00. Food: lunch 14.30 (Sunday 15.00); dinner 22.00.
Closed: Rarely.
Food: Modern British.
Real Ale: Brakspear, Marston's Pedigree, Morrell's Oxford Blue, Flowers Original.
Other points: Children welcome. Dogs welcome in the bar. Garden/terrace. Car park.
Directions: Telephone for directions. (Map 5, E4)

Flaunden

The Bricklayers Arms

Hog Pits Bottom, Flaunden,
Hertfordshire HP3 0PH
Telephone: +44(0)870 4016092
+44 (0)1442 833322
goodfood@bricklayersarms.com
www.bricklayersarms.com

Within minutes of leaving the M25 (J18)
you are in rolling Hertfordshire countryside
and encountering peaceful villages secluded
away down winding lanes. Coated in Virginia
creeper, Flaunden's low cottagey tiled pub is
a peaceful, inviting spot, especially in summer when its country-style garden becomes
the perfect place to enjoy an alfresco pint of
ale. On cooler days, the recently refurbished,
timbered and low-ceilinged bar, replete with
blazing log fires, old prints and comfortable
traditional furnishings, are popular with both
local diners and walkers for modern pub
food. New owners Alvin and Sally Michaels
have smartened up the place and introduced
a good range of menus to suit all comers. In
the bar, follow a country stroll with thick-cut
sandwiches, a steaming bowl of chilli, or tuck
into a special of confit of duck with red wine
jus. In the evening, come for starters of pan-
fried foie gras and sherry jus, or fresh local
asparagus with hollandaise, then follow with
roast halibut with pink peppercorn sauce
or best end of lamb served with red wine
and shallot sauce. Finish with hot chocolate
pudding. Don't miss the summer Sunday barbeques and live jazz in the garden.

Prices: Restaurant main course from £10.95. Bar snack
from £5.95. House wine £10.95.
Last orders: Bar: 23.00.
Food: lunch 15.00 (Sunday 16.00); dinner 21.30
(Sunday 21.00)
Closed: Rarely.
Food: Modern British/French.
Real Ale: London Pride, Greene King Old Speckled
Hen, Greene King IPA, Archers Best.
Other points: No-smoking area. Dogs welcome.
Children welcome. Garden. Car park.
Directions: 10 minutes from Exit18/M25. Three miles
south west of Hemel Hempstead. (Map 5, E4)

Reed

The Cabinet

High Street, Reed, Hertfordshire SG8 8AH
Telephone: +44(0)870 4016093
+44(0)1763 848366
thecabinet@btopenworld.com
www.thecabinetinn.co.uk

TV chef Paul Bloxham has done a magnificent job in transforming this pretty, white
clapboard, 16th-century pub from a tired
boozer into a contemporary rural gastropub.
Original low beams and cottagey windows
have been retained and his thriving village
pub comfortably incorporates locals at the
bar drinking pints of Adnams, a 'snug' smoking room with high-backed tobacco-coloured
leather dining chairs, and a smart dining
room with soft colours, crisp table linen,
gleaming glassware, and fresh flowers. An
enthusiastic modern menu is built around
local ingredients with 70% purchased from
local farmers, including vegetables from an
organic nursery, 28-day aged Galloway beef
and rare breeds such as Tamworth pigs. The
bar lunch menu is a simplified version of
what's available in the restaurant - perhaps
a classic Caesar salad or duck risotto with
cognac and wild mushrooms. Dinner in the
dining room brings Scottish langoustines
with saffron mayonnaise, organic chicken
with cep and balsamic sauce, local Aylesbury
duck with Roman sauce, and Cornish hake
with bouillabaisse sauce. Outside, a spacious
outdoor dining room has been created, with
heaters extending the season and an open
kitchen with wood-burning rotisserie.

Prices: Set lunch £15.95-£19.95. Restaurant main
course from £13. Bar main course from £5.
House wine £12.50.
Last orders: Bar: lunch 15.00; dinner 23.00. Food: lunch
14.30 (Sunday 16.00); dinner 22.30
Closed: Monday and Sunday night.
Food: Modern French/British with American influence.
Real Ale: Nethergate, Adnams, Greene King.
Other points: No-smoking area. Dogs welcome in the
bar. Garden and terrace. Children welcome. Car park.
Directions: Off the A10 betwen Buntingford and
Royston. (Map 6, D5)

Watton-at-Stone

George and the Dragon 🍷

High Street, Watton-at-Stone,
Hertfordshire SG14 3TA
Telephone: +44(0)870 4016094
+44(0)1920 830285
georgeanddragon@virgin.net
www.georgeanddragon-watton.co.uk

It's a difficult pub to miss on the A602
between Hertford and Stevenage, as the
400-year-old George and Dragon dominates
the centre of the village and the exterior is
of pink-painted pebbledash. There's character in spades within the homely bars, as
exposed beams, open log fires, yellow stained
walls hung with paintings and old scrubbed
tables create a quaint rustic look. Welcome
touches from caring landlords Peter and
Jessica Tatlow include fresh flowers and the
day's newspapers. Despite the rather gentri-
fied trappings, this is still a real pub, offering local gossip, good drinking with tip-top
Greene King ales, and a guest beer on handpump. On a changing menu and daily blackboards, starters range from mini fishcakes
with olive and red onion salsa, salmon car-
paccio, to good homemade soups and pâtés.
Moroccan-style lamb shank, pan-roasted
pork fillet on garlic lentils with sun-dried
tomatoes and pesto vinaigrette, and prime
Aberdeen Angus steaks from the chargrill are
typical main courses. Millionaire's bun, which
is fillet steak in a toasted roll with salad
garnish, is popular, as are lighter options like
tuna, ginger mayonnaise and spring onion
sandwiches, fishcakes with lime and coriander sauce, and creamy tagliatelle with fresh
Parmesan.

Prices: Main course from £7.85. House wine £13.85.
Last orders: Bar: lunch 15.00; dinner 23.00. Food: lunch
14.00; dinner 22.00. No food Sunday evening.
Closed: Rarely
Food: Modern pub food.
Real Ale: Greene King IPA, Greene King Abbot Ale.
2 guest beers.
Other points: No-smoking in dining area. Children
welcome until 21.00. Garden. Car park.
Directions: In the centre of the village on the A602
between Hertford and Stevenage. (Map 6, D5)

Peel

Waterfall Hotel

Shore Road, Glen Maye, Peel,
Isle of Man IM5 3BG
Telephone: +44(0)870 4016095
+44(0)1624 844310
jim@breadner.co.uk

The former smugglers' haunt stands at the
head of one of the loveliest glens on the
island, Glen Maye, and the name relates
to its spectacular waterfall. The beach is a
short stroll away. This is a family run pub,
with three generations currently involved,
and the emphasis is on a warm welcome and
unpretentious, good quality food at reasonable prices, served all day. All meat served
is Manx (steaks are a speciality), queenies
are caught locally, as are fresh crab and fish,
and spices for the daily curry are imported
directly from Goa. If the famous fish and
chips or the aforementioned curries do not
appeal then a choice for a typical supper
could be pan-fried local scallops with a lime
and chilli butter, or perhaps lamb cutlets
in garlic and rosemary or mint marinade.
Whether sitting in the cosy beamed bar and
dining area, preferably by the roaring fire in
the winter months, or enjoying the warmth
on the sun patio in the summer months, this
charming pub has a comforting and relaxing
atmosphere which is enhanced by its glorious
setting.

Prices: Main course from £6.95. House wine £8.25.
Last orders: Bar: 23.00 (Sunday lunch 14.30; dinner
22.30). Food: 21.30 (Sunday lunch 14.00).
Closed: Rarely.
Food: Traditional English/International.
Real Ale: Okells, Jennings Cumberland Ale,
Black Sheep Best.
Other points: Smoking in bar area only. Children
welcome. Garden. Car park.
Directions: Three miles south of Peel on the coast
road. (Map 7, D1)

Hertfordshire Market Produce

at The Cabinet at Reed

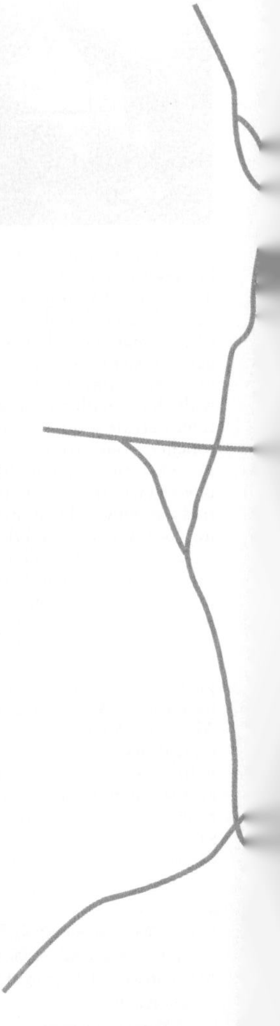

"I can put top quality, locally grown food on a plate for £15 to £20 like the Celtic Galloway beef which I get from a local farmer. I couldn't afford to do that in London, but I can here in Hertfordshire because of the fantastic ingredients I can buy locally. It takes time and care to find fresh ingredients locally, but I want to reflect the original character of the Cabinet, which would have offered everything in season."

Paul Bloxham, Head Chef and Owner, The Cabinet at Reed

Every third Saturday of the month a collection of representatives from Hertfordshire's farms and nurseries offering the best in beef, lamb, pork, chicken, preserves, game, eggs, vegetables, fruit and cakes gather at Sandon Village Hall for the Sandon Growers Market. Among the stalls are many of the food producers that help supply Paul Bloxham at The Cabinet at Reed. For example, Highbury Farm in Woodend (who have their own cold room cutting facility so they can offer lamb joints and cuts to meet individual requirements) supply Paul with lamb, whilst Beverly Burrows at Farrowby Farm in Hinxworth supplies free range, organic Berkshire pork loin that might be accompanied by smoked mushroom, pancetta ragoût and sprouting broccoli at The Cabinet dining table.

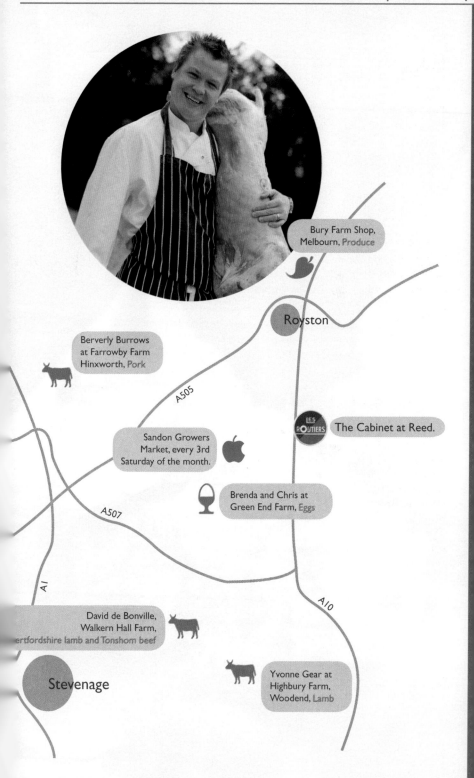

Bury Farm Shop, Melbourn, Produce

Royston

Berverly Burrows at Farrowby Farm Hinxworth, Pork

A505

LES ROUTIERS

The Cabinet at Reed.

Sandon Growers Market, every 3rd Saturday of the month.

Brenda and Chris at Green End Farm, Eggs

A507

A1

A10

David de Bonville, Walkern Hall Farm, ertfordshire lamb and Tonshom beef

Stevenage

Yvonne Gear at Highbury Farm, Woodend, Lamb

Paul Bloxham of The Cabinet at Reed, Hertfordshire

Bembridge

The Crab & Lobster Inn

32 Forelands Field Road, Bembridge,
Isle of Wight PO35 5TR
Telephone: +44(0)870 4016096
+44(0)1983 872244
allancrab@aol.com
www.crabandlobsterinn.co.uk

Follow signs to the Lifeboat Station in Bembridge to find this well established clifftop inn that affords magnificent views across the Solent and English Channel, particularly from the flower-adorned summer terrace. A popular watering hole for coastal path walkers, it also attracts locals and visitors for the fresh locally-caught seafood listed on daily-changing blackboards. Arrive early to bag a table as the nautically themed and traditionally furnished bar and dining areas fill quickly, especially during summer months. True to its name, house specialities are the crabs and lobsters that are caught on Bembridge Ledge all year round and served every which way - crab cakes, sandwiches and salads, and magnificent crab and lobster platters for two. Meaty alternatives on the straightforward bar menu include ham, egg, and chips, and chargrilled sirloin steak with mushrooms and fries. Wash them down with a pint of island-brewed Goddards Fuggle-Dee-Dum. From the restaurant carte, choose from a page of lobster specials or opt for whole Dover sole or, perhaps, pork fillet with fennel, rosemary and mustard sauce. Cosy en suite bedrooms are kitted out with modern comforts, and enjoy stunning sea views.

Rooms: 5. £35 per person per night including breakfast.
Prices: Restaurant main course from £8.25. Bar main course from £5.95. House wine £8.50.
Last orders: Bar: lunch 15.00; dinner 23.00 (open all day Saturday and Sunday). Food: lunch 14.30; dinner 21.30.
Closed: Never.
Food: Modern European.
Real Ale: Flowers IPA, Greene King IPA, Goddards Fuggle-Dee-Dum.
Other points: No-smoking area. Dogs welcome in the bar. Children welcome. Garden. Car park.
Directions: Follow signs to Lifeboat Station, the Crab & Lobster is signposted en route. (Map 5, G4)

Shalfleet

The New Inn

Mill Lane, Shalfleet, Isle of Wight PO30 4NS
Telephone: +44(0)870 4016097
+44(0)1983 531314
martin@thenew-inn.co.uk
www.thenew-inn.co.uk

Smack on the coast path and just a short stroll from Newtown Quay, this lovely cream-painted former fishermen's pub has long been a favoured watering-hole among the walking and sailing fraternity. Built in 1743 on the site of an old 'Church House' it oozes historic charm, and the original flagstone floors and inglenook fireplaces are thought to be from the original house. The beamed bars also quickly fill with diners, as the New Inn is famous for its fresh fish and seafood, with crab and lobster landed at Newtown Quay. Chalkboard menus list the market-fresh choice, perhaps up to 16 types and including local sea bass and plaice, hake with lemon and tarragon, haddock cooked in basil, red onion and tomato, and their mammoth seafood platter for two. Carnivores are not forgotten, the menu does extend to prime steaks (with all the trimmings), lamb shank with garlic mash, and game in winter. More traditional pub meals on printed menus include freshly-cut sandwiches (try the excellent crab), ploughman's lunches and ham, egg and chips. Wash a satisfying meal down with a first-class pint of Island-brewed Ventnor Golden or Goddards Fuggle-de-dum.

Prices: Set lunch and dinner from £18-£25. Main course restaurant from £12. Main course bar from £8. House wine £9.95.
Last orders: Bar: lunch 15.00; dinner 23.00. Food: lunch 14.30; dinner 21.30.
Closed: Rarely.
Food: Seafood.
Real Ale: Bass, Marston's Pedigree, Greene King IPA, Goddards Fuggle-Dee-Dum, Ventnor Golden.
Other points: No-smoking area. Dogs welcome. Garden. Children welcome. Car park.
Directions: On the main Newport to Yarmouth road (A3054), by the traffic lights in Shalfleet. (Map 5, G3)

Ashford

The Tiger Inn

Stowting, Ashford, Kent T25 6BA
Telephone: +44(0)870 4016098
+44(0)1303 862130
willettiger@aol.com
www.tigerinn.co.uk

The Tiger dates from 1676 when Amos Whittell was granted a licence to serve home-brewed ales and cider. A bit of its history is preserved on the exterior - embossed into the rendering are the words Mackeson Hythe Ales. The single front bar is rustic, unpretentious and full of rural charm, with stripped-oak floors, two warming wood-burning stoves, old-cushioned church pews, comfortable worn sofas, and sturdy scrubbed tables topped with candles, with a separate restaurant/function room to the rear. Generally filled with locals, the bar is relaxed and informal, and the homecooked food hearty. Chalked up on the blackboard, daily-changing dishes range from tiger prawns with red curry sauce and prawn crackers, and char-grilled chorizo salad with mint, coriander and sour cream salsa, to slow-roasted lamb shoulder with port and thyme sauce, steak and ale pie with puff-pastry crust, and Lincolnshire sausages with parsnip mash, sage and apple sauce. Alongside Everard's Tiger, naturally, tip-top ales include a micro-brewery guest ale. Don't miss the summer barbecues on the front patio, the annual beer festival, and the pub's famed traditional live jazz every Monday evening. Super walks across the North Downs.

Prices: Main course from £10. House wine £10.30.
Last orders: Bar: lunch 15.00; dinner 23.00. Food: lunch 14.00; dinner 21.00.
Closed: Monday lunch.
Food: Global.
Real Ale: Fuller's London Pride, Everards Tiger, Fuller's ESB, Shepherd Neame Master Brew Bitter, Shepherd Neame Spitfire. 1 guest beer.
Other points: No-smoking area. Dogs welcome. Children welcome. Garden. Car park.
Directions: Exit 11/M20. Take B2068 towards Canterbury, then turn left to Stowting. (Map 6, F7)

Bodsham

Froggies at the Timber Batts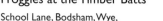

School Lane, Bodsham, Wye,
Kent TN25 5JQ
Telephone: +44(0)870 4016099
+44(0)1233 750237

Chef Joel Gross built up a great reputation at Froggies Restuarant in Wye, so when he headed deeper into the Kent countryside to the Timber Batts, a 15th-century pub in a remote hamlet, he knew they would follow. The place went from being just another rural pub popular with the walking fraternity, to one with an authentic French restaurant attached. The beamed and timbered bar has an inglenook fireplace the size of a small room and, on a lower level, a reception bar that also boasts an open fire, plus a sofa and comfortable seating. The restaurant has its own huge fireplace, more beams, plus old pine tables topped with candles. Favourites from Froggies of Wye days - superb stuffed mussels, a classic duck confit salad, perfect rack of lamb with herbs - are staples of the printed menu. Profiteroles and tarte tatin are classic puddings and there's a blackboard listing daily fish specials and bar snacks like croque monsieur. Sourcing is impeccable: game from local shoots, locally-grown vegetables, but cheeses are as totally French as the wine list, which includes the house wine grown and produced by Joel's cousin in the Loire Valley.

Prices: Set Sunday lunch £18. Set dinner £25. Restaurant main course from £12. Bar main course from £6. House wine £12.
Last orders: Bar: lunch 14.30; dinner 23.00. Food: lunch 14.30; dinner 21.30. No food Sunday evening.
Closed: Monday, the Tuesday after Bank Holiday Monday.
Food: Traditional French, Seafood and Game.
Real Ale: Adnams Best, Fuller's London Pride, Harvey's Sussex Best Bitter.
Other points: No-smoking area. Dogs welcome. Garden. Children welcome. Car park.
Directions: Village signed off narrow lanes south east of Wye and the A28. (Map 6, F7)

Bridge

The White Horse Inn

53 High Street, Bridge, Canterbury,
Kent CT4 5LA
Telephone: +44(0)870 4016100
+44(0)1227 830249
thewaltons_thewhitehorse@hotmail.com
www.whitehorsebridge.co.uk

In search of some rest and first-class refreshment off the busy A2 south of Canterbury then look no further than this 16th-century village pub, resplendent in summer with colourful hanging baskets. Two entrances can cause momentary confusion, one leads into the restaurant, the other straight into the traditional looking central bar, which has a magnificent log burning inglenook, wood panelling, and beamed ceiling. This comfortable room dispenses pints of Masterbrew, very good wines (8 by the glass), and some excellent bar food that utilises fresh produce from local suppliers. Ben Walton spent some time at the late, Michelin-starred Sandgate Hotel near Folkestone, and brings a touch of class to the kitchen. His good-value brasserie menu delivers upmarket salads, Whitstable oysters with shallot vinegar for starters and satisfying main dishes like confit duck leg with mash and apple sauce, and roast monkfish with herb, garlic and lemon butter. Move into the small, stylish restaurant and the cooking impresses with its technique and flair. Start with pressed oxtail terrine with beetroot relish and mustard dressing, perhaps, followed by beef fillet with red wine and thyme gravy, with prune and treacle tart to finish.

Prices: Set lunch £13.95 (Tuesday-Saturday), Sunday set lunch £23.50. Set dinner £19.50 (Tusday-Thursday) and £23.50 (Friday and Saturday). Restaurant main course from £12.50. Bar snack from £4. House wine £12.
Last orders: Bar: lunch 15.00; dinner 23.00 (Sunday 16.00). Food: lunch 14.30; dinner 21.30.
Closed: Sunday and Bank Holiday evenings.
Food: Modern English.
Real Ale: Shepherd Neame Master Brew. Guest beers.
Other points: No-smoking area. Garden. Children welcome. Car park.
Directions: South of Canterbury off A2. (Map 6, F7)

Kentish Cobnuts

at the White Horse Inn

Henry Bryant in Hernhill supplies the White Horse with apples from his orchard to make its delicious Apple and Cider Granite (the cider half is supplied by Neals Place Farm in nearby Blean). Mr Bryant also has a hand in their Poached Pears with Raspberry Sauce, Roasted Cobnuts and Vanilla Ice Cream (as does Amery Court Farm and Dargate Dairy) by providing chef Ben Walton with organically grown pears and the infamous Kentish Cobnut. More cobnuts are grown in Kent than anywhere else, hence their popularity and formation of such organisations as the Kentish Cobnuts Association. For those of you who don't know a Kentish cobnut when you see one, it is a type of hazelnut, just as a Bramley is a type of apple. Children played an early version of 'conkers' with hazelnuts; the game was called cobnut, and the winning nut the cob – the name stuck. Cobnuts are marketed fresh and consequently can usually only be bought when in season, typically from about the middle of August through to October. At the beginning of the season the husks are green and the kernels particularly juicy. Nuts harvested later on have brown shells and husks, and the full flavour of the kernel has developed. Fresh or roasted, crumbled as a Crème Brulee topping, or on a praline ice cream, cobnuts will always be a staple on the White Horse menu.

Syndale Valley Cheesemakers, Faversham, Cheese

Faversham

M2

A251

Ashford

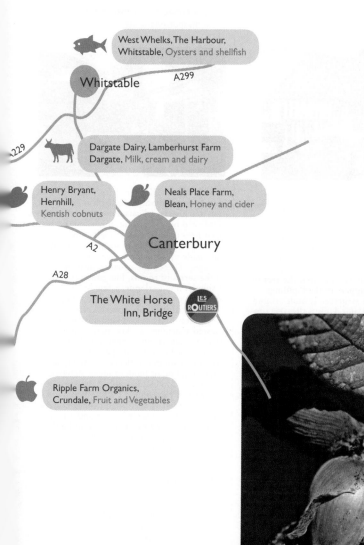

West Whelks, The Harbour,
Whitstable, Oysters and shellfish

Whitstable

A299

A229

Dargate Dairy, Lamberhurst Farm
Dargate, Milk, cream and dairy

Henry Bryant,
Hernhill,
Kentish cobnuts

Neals Place Farm,
Blean, Honey and cider

Canterbury

A2

A28

The White Horse
Inn, Bridge

LES ROUTIERS

Ripple Farm Organics,
Crundale, Fruit and Vegetables

www.cobnuts.co.uk

Chillenden

Griffins Head

Chillenden, Canterbury, Kent CT3 1PS
Telephone: +44(0)870 4016101
+44(0)1304 840325

An architectural gem of a building nestling in a tiny farming hamlet amid rolling open countryside. Dating from 1286, the Griffin's Head is a fine black-and-white, half-timbered Wealden hall house that was originally built as a farmhouse to serve the local estate. Although ale and cider were brewed on the premises for the workers, it was only granted a licence in 1753 so that the rector could hold tithe suppers in the buildings. The present Tudor structure is built around the original wattle and daub walls, remains of which can be viewed in one of the three unspoilt rooms, which also feature flagstone floors, exposed brick walls and beams, old scrubbed pine tables and church pews. Here, the full complement of cask-conditioned Shepherd Neame ales, interesting bin end wines and a splendid choice of champagnes, are served. Chalkboard menus list a good range of hearty dishes, including local estate game and asparagus in season, steak and ale pie, Barnsley chops (served with seasonal vegetables), mature Cheddar ploughman's lunches, homemade soups, and various fishy options. Finish with a good nursery pudding or a plate of cheese and a glass of port. Rambling roses and clematis fill the attractive garden, popular in summer for weekend barbeques.

Prices: Bar main course from £6. House wine £10.
Last orders: Bar: 23.00 (Sunday 18.00). Food: lunch 14.00; dinner 21.30.
Closed: Sunday evening.
Food: Traditional and Modern British.
Real Ale: Shepherd Neame Ales.
Other points: Garden. Car park.
Directions: Take the A2 from Canterbury, then left on the B2068 towards Wingham. Follow signs to Nonnington; the pub is 1 mile past Nonnington. (Map 6, F7)

Penshurst

Spotted Dog

Smarts Hill, Penshurst, Tonbridge,
Kent TN11 8EE
Telephone: +44(0)870 4016102
+44(0)1892 870253
thespotteddog@btopenworld.com
www.thespotteddog.net

Ben Naude and Kirsten Price, together with chef Nathan Ali, have brought talent, ambition and sheer enthusiasm to this atmospheric clapboard inn. Panelling, low-slung beams, open fires (one in a great inglenook), nooks and crannies are as you would expect of a pub made up of several early 16th century cottages. There's the usual traditional look to the series of rooms, but good taste keeps it simple: hop garlands, a few horse brasses, old photographs, various spotted dog motifs. Blackboards list daily specials, there are light lunch bites of Thai crab and coriander cakes, roasted vegetable, rocket, pesto and mozzarella foccacia, and linguini with sun-dried tomato, garlic pesto and pecorino, and an evening menu that reflects a contemporary understanding of modern ideas, definitely raising the food stakes above the norm for this part of the county. Crispy belly pork may be served with pickled cabbage, black pudding fritter, sautéed apple and a rosemary cream sauce, and braised shank of lamb could be accompanied with Puy lentils and basil jus. Yet the kitchen never loses sight of the fact that this is a pub - presentation is stylish not pretentious and portions generous without being overwhelming. Super summer terraces.

Prices: Bar main course from £8.95. Sandwiches from £5.25. House wine from £10.50.
Last orders: Bar: 23.00. Food: lunch 14.30; dinner 21.30 (Sunday 18.00).
Closed: Rarely.
Food: Modern European Food.
Real Ale: Harvey's Best Bitter, Larkins Traditional.
Other points: No-smoking area. Dogs welcome. No children under ten years old after 19.00. Dogs welcome in the bar. Terrace.
Directions: B2176 and B2110, through Penshurst village, third turning on the right. (Map 6, F5)

Stodmarsh

Red Lion

The Street, Stodmarsh, Canterbury,
Kent CT3 4AZ
Telephone: +44(0)870 4016103
+44(0)1227 721339
tiptop_redlion@hotmail.com

Robert Whigham's quirky 15th-century pub stands on a narrow country road in a sleepy village five miles from Canterbury. It adjoins the famous Stodmarsh Nature Reserve, so expect to find twitchers alongside folk in search of fine ale and food. Within, low ceilings, stone and wood floors, hop garlands, fresh flowers, candles on plain wood tables, and an open log fire, all add to the rustic charm of the tiny rooms. Beer is tapped direct from hop sack-covered barrels and the food is outstanding. A blackboard by the entrance displays a versatile, ingredient led menu, a mix of contemporary ideas and good country cooking that extends to proper buttery pastry for pies and delicious puddings. Local, free-range and organic ingredients make their way into the kitchen with game from local shoots, seasonal fruit and vegetables from nearby farms, and locally smoked ham all playing there part. Typically, tuck into pheasant and wild rabbit hotpot, chicken, leek and cider pie, local lamb stuffed with rosemary and garlic, or tackle Robert's damned good breakfast - local butcher sausages, bacon, own eggs, mushrooms, grilled tomatoes, even kidneys and T-bone steaks (from a local beef farm). Three simple double rooms (not en suite).

Rooms: 3, not en suite. Double room from £60.
Prices: Bar main course from £9.95.
House wine £10.95.
Last orders: Bar 23.00. Food: lunch 14.00; dinner 21.30.
Closed: Rarely.
Food: Traditional British using local produce.
Real Ale: Greene King Old Speckled Hen,
Abbot Ale & IPA.
Other points: Children welcome. Dogs welcome in the bar. Garden. Car park.
Directions: A257 east from Canterbury, follow signs left to Stodmarsh. (Map 6, F7)

West Peckham

Swan on the Green

West Peckham, Tonbridge, Kent ME18 5JW
Telephone: +44(0)870 4016104
+44(0)1622 812271
bookings@swan-on-the-green.co.uk
www.swan-on-the-green.co.uk

The glorious location at the heart of a sleepy Kent village, close to the church and overlooking a huge expanse of village green, combined with top-notch own-brewed beer and imaginative daily menus hint at why this pretty 16th-century pub is a roaring success. Within this former row of cottages, Gordon Milligan has renovated and decorated with restraint and good taste. The whole place is open plan with bare boards, beams, exposed brick contrasting with plain cream plastered walls, contemporary art, log fires, fresh flowers and chunky evening candles creating a surprisingly modern, light look that sits well with the age of the building. In addition, there are pale wood pews, wood tables, and kitchen chairs and a gleaming espresso machine. The simple lunch and adventurous evening menus change daily, with the former offering ploughman's of English cheeses, homemade Stilton burgers in warm ciabatta bread, and terrine of duck confit with salad. For dinner expect pan-fried scallops on guacamole with rocket, basil pesto and balsamic, then roast lamb fillet with rich raspberry and rosemary jus, or sea bass on sweet potato purée with wild mushroom and tarragon hollandaise. To drink, try a pint of Trumpeter Best or Whooper Pale, brewed in the Swan Brewery behind the pub.

Prices: Restaurant main course from £9.95.
House wine £11.
Last orders: Bar: lunch 15.00 (Saturday and Sunday 16.00); dinner 23.00. Food: lunch 14.00; dinner 21.30.
Closed: Rarely.
Food: Modern Pub Food.
Real Ale: Whooper Pale, Adnams Fisherman, Ginger Swan, Bewick, Swan on the Port Side, Black Swan, Swan Blonde and Swan Weisse.
Other points: Dogs welcome on a lead.
Children welcome. Car park.
Directions: West Peckham is off the B2016, half a mile north of the junction of A26/A228, north east of Tonbridge. (Map 6, F6)

Big Breakfasts
at the Red Lion

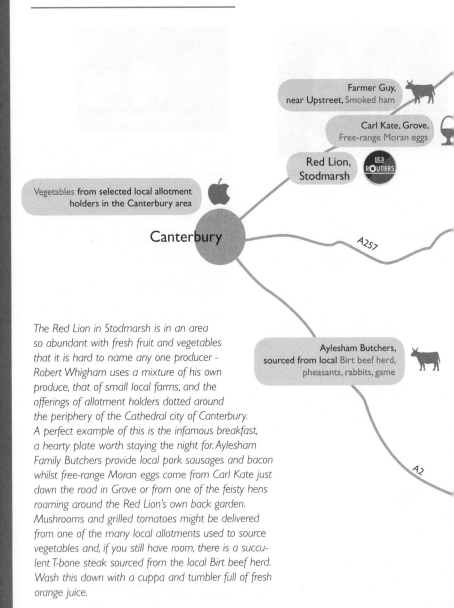

Farmer Guy, near Upstreet, Smoked ham

Carl Kate, Grove, Free-range Moran eggs

Red Lion, Stodmarsh

LES ROUTIERS

Vegetables from selected local allotment holders in the Canterbury area

Canterbury

A257

Aylesham Butchers, sourced from local Birt beef herd, pheasants, rabbits, game

A2

The Red Lion in Stodmarsh is in an area so abundant with fresh fruit and vegetables that it is hard to name any one producer - Robert Whigham uses a mixture of his own produce, that of small local farms, and the offerings of allotment holders dotted around the periphery of the Cathedral city of Canterbury. A perfect example of this is the infamous breakfast, a hearty plate worth staying the night for. Aylesham Family Butchers provide local pork sausages and bacon whilst free-range Moran eggs come from Carl Kate just down the road in Grove or from one of the feisty hens roaming around the Red Lion's own back garden. Mushrooms and grilled tomatoes might be delivered from one of the many local allotments used to source vegetables and, if you still have room, there is a succulent T-bone steak sourced from the local Birt beef herd. Wash this down with a cuppa and tumbler full of fresh orange juice.

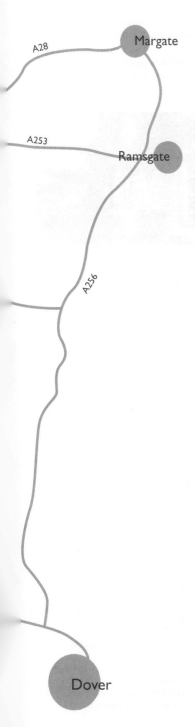

Downham

Assheton Arms

Downham, Clitheroe, Lancashire BB7 4BJ
Telephone: +44(0)870 4016106
+44(0)1200 441227
asshetonarms@aol.com
www.assheton-arms.co.uk

Downham remains splendidly preserved and virtually untouched since the day the Assheton family bought the village in 1558 and made it their home. With pretty stone cottages strung out along a stream, the village is devoid of TV aerials, dormer windows and street signs and is often used by film and television companies for period village scenes. In the best traditions of country life, the Assheton Arms is opposite the church, at the very heart of the place, with a cheerfully-warm traditional air and enthusiastic, long-serving landlords David and Wendy Busby. A single, beamed bar and the rambling adjoining rooms house an array of solid oak farmhouse tables and wing-back settees, a huge central stone fireplace, and a large blackboard that lists a good-value choice of honest, homecooked dishes. Using fresh local produce where possible, a typical menu may offer potted Morecambe Bay shrimps, ham and vegetable broth, or a ploughman's lunch with Chris Sandham's creamy Lancashire cheese. For something more substantial opt for the steak and kidney pie, casserole of venison, bacon and cranberry, Cumberland sausage and mash, or excellent fresh fish, perhaps sea bream with caper sauce. Arrive early as the pub bustles with local drinkers quaffing tip-top Marston's Pedigree.

Prices: Main course from £7.50. House wine £10.50.
Last orders: Bar: lunch 15.00; dinner 23.00. Food: lunch 14.00; dinner 22.00.
Closed: The first full week in January.
Food: Traditional British.
Real Ale: Marston's Pedigree, Moorhouses Pride of Pendle.
Other points: No-smoking area. Children welcome. Car park.
Directions: Off the A59, 3 miles north-east of Clitheroe. (Map 7, E4)

Hornby

The Castle Hotel

Main St, Hornby, Lancashire LA2 8JT
Telephone: +44(0)870 4016107
+44(0)1524 221204
information@diningroomhornby.co.uk
www.diningroomhornby.co.uk

Close to Hornby Castle in the town's picturesque main street, the small and intimate Castle Hotel was restored and refurbished back to its former coaching inn glory in 2002. Although it only has five tastefully decorated en suite bedrooms, the Castle is much more than a village inn, oozing luxury and style throughout the cosy lounge areas with deep sofas and crackling log fires, and elegant dining rooms. However, expect a friendly and informal atmosphere, and a great bar dispensing good ales. Although bar food is served in the lounges when quiet, for an informal meal head across the courtyard to the Castle Barns Bistro housed in well-converted outbuildings. Food is served throughout the day and from an impressive menu choice there may be starters of buttered brown shrimps, confit of duck with sweet orange dressing, or tomato and leek soup. Rustic and hearty main courses take in deep-fried bass with mushy peas and straw chips, linguine with hot smoked salmon and dill, and lamb steak with spring onion mash and red wine jus. Good sandwiches. Excellent fixed-price dinner menu in The Dining Room.

Rooms: 14, 2 with private bathrooms. Double room from £50, single from £40. Prices include breakfast.
Prices: Bistro restaurant main course from £6.95. Fine Dining restaurant main course from £17.95. House wine £10.95.
Last orders: Bar: 23.00. Food: Bistro 21.30. Fine Dining Restaurant 20.30.
Closed: Rarely.
Food: Modern European/Traditional English.
Real Ale: 3 guest beers available.
Other points: No-smoking area. Dogs welcome. Patio. Children welcome. Licenced for Civil Weddings.
Directions: Exit34/M6. Travel towards Hornby and the Castle Hotel is on the A683. (Map 7, D4)

Kirkham

The Villa Country House Hotel

Moss Side Lane, Wrea Green, Kirkham, Preston, Lancashire PR4 2PE
Telephone: +44(0)870 4016108
+44(0)1772 684347
thevilla@mercuryinns.com
www.villahotel-wreagreen.co.uk

Standing at the end of a long drive with views across open fields, it is hard to imagine that this striking mid-19th century building is just a few minutes drive from the M55 (junction 3) and the traditional resort attractions of Blackpool. Now a stylish hotel-cum-pub with 25 uniformly decorated bedrooms, all with en suite bathrooms and a host of extras, including air conditioning, it caters well for the local business trade as well as those seeking a comfortable and more peaceful base from which to visit Lytham's famous golf links or, perhaps, Blackpool. Smart public areas include an attractive pubby bar with comfy seating areas and a restaurant made up of three areas with panelling, heavy stonework, an open fireplace and french windows opening onto the gardens. The tables and furnishings add to the period and character. Menus are up-to-date, the bar snack menu listing speciality sandwiches and good salads. Freshly prepared dishes from the carte may include seared red mullet with asparagus and smoked salmon with dill and vermouth sauce, or braised shoulder of lamb with onion mash and red wine jus. Excellent value set-price lunch or early evening menu.

Rooms: 25. Single room from £80, double £90, family room from £90.
Prices: Set lunch and dinner (18.00-20.00 Monday-Friday) £15.95. Restaurant main course from £9.50. House wine £10.95.
Last orders: Bar: 23.00. Food: served all day, reduced hot menu 14.00-18.00.
Closed: Rarely.
Food: Modern British.
Real Ale: Jennings Bitter & Cumberland. 1 guest beer.
Other points: No-smoking area. Children welcome. Garden. Car park.
Directions: Just off the M55 (J3). (Map 7, E4)

Mawdesley

Red Lion

New Street, Mawdesley, Lancashire L40 2QP
Telephone: +44(0)870 4016109/4016110
+44(0)1704 822208/999
redlion@cybase.co.uk

Locals flock to Edward Newton's 19th-century whitewashed village inn for pints of Theakston and Black Sheep ales and the bustling 'community' atmosphere that pervades through the classic bar, replete with dartboard and piped music, to the colourful lounge and dining room. The furnishings and ambience are typical of a popular pub, with a feature made of the fireplace, and there are flowers, pictures and ornaments contributing to the overall charm of the place. Here, and in the Mediterranean-style conservatory, loyal regulars come for the food, which is good and reliant on local supplies and runs to own-grown herbs in the summer. Bar snacks, served at lunch on Wednesday to Saturday only, take in soup, triple-decker sandwiches, and hot spicy chicken salad with garlic mayonnaise. A set two- or three-course lunch and 'early doors' menu could include homemade pâté with tomato chutney, peppered rib-eye steak or minted lamb chops with red wine jus, and winter fruit crumble and custard. A carte extends the choice, running to crab and herb crumble with lemon and dill butter sauce, confit of duck with kumquat and lime jus, and grilled plaice with tartare sauce. A compact wine list with good choice under £15, offers four by the glass.

Prices: Set lunch £12 and dinner £13. Restaurant main course meal from £7.50. Snack from £2.50. House wine £11.
Last orders: Bar: 23.00. Food: lunch 14.00; dinner 21.00 (all day Sunday). No food Monday and Tuesday.
Closed: Rarely.
Food: Modern British.
Real Ale: Black Sheep Best, Theakstons, Websters.
Other points: No-smoking area. Garden. Children welcome. Car park.
Directions: Junction 27/M6. North on B5246 from Parbold, turn left into Malt Kiln Lane and continue to Mawdesley. (Map 7, F4)

Whitewell

Inn at Whitewell

Forest of Bowland, Whitewell, Clitheroe, Lancashire BB7 3AT
Telephone: +44(0)870 4016111
+44(0)1200 448222

A magnificent inn set amid the wild beauty of north Lancashire, well away from the hustle and bustle, standing next to the church and overlooking the River Hodder at the head of the Trough of Bowland. In fact, the 'inn' is Whitewell, yet despite its splendid isolation there is much to enjoy: eight miles of fishing rights, and the whole complex embraces a wine merchant, an art gallery, a shop selling homemade food products, and 17 individually decorated bedrooms. Inside, it's relaxed, laid back, even mildly eccentric, with a haphazard arrangement of furnishings, bric-a-brac, open log fires, heavy ceiling beams and colourful rugs throughout the stone-floored taproom, rambling dining areas and library. The atmosphere is truly unique, thanks to Richard Bowman and his staff who imbue this ancient hostelry with warmth, personality, and a pleasing quirkiness. The bar supper choice may include pork medallions with mustard sauce, with salads and substantial sandwiches appearing at lunchtime. Local produce features on the evening carte, perhaps breast of Goosnargh duck with tomato and bean cassoulet, and roast cannon of lamb with tarragon jus. It's worth saving space for pudding as well as specialist, prime-condition British and Irish cheeses. A superlative wine list completes the picture. Individual bedrooms are furnished with antique furniture, peat fires and Victorian baths.

Clitheroe Castle

Forest of Bowland

Must See
- Clitheroe Castle & Museum
- Ribchester Roman Museum
- Slaidburn Heritage Centre
- Forest of Bowland Fishing
Hotel residents have access to 7 miles of the River Hodder
Farmers Market Clitheroe (fortnightly Wednesday am)

Rooms: 17. Double/twin room from £89.
Prices: Restaurant main course from £12. Bar main course from £7.50. House wine £9.50.
Last orders: Bar: lunch 15.00; dinner 23.00. Food: lunch 14.00; dinner 21.30.
Closed: Rarely.
Food: Modern British.
Real Ale: Marston's Bitter, Taylor's Ales.
Other points: Children welcome. Dogs welcome overnight. Garden. Car park. Licence for Civil Weddings. Fishing.
Directions: Exit 32/M6 to Longridge. Centre of Longridge follow signs to Whitewell. (Map 7, E4)

Tourist Information Clitheroe +44(0)1200 442226
Where to Walk
An insight into the wild beauty of the Forest of Bowland can be enjoyed with walks along the River Hodder, across Dunsop Fell, up Wolf and Fairsnape Fell from Chipping, and through Beacon Fell Country Park. Cross the Ribble Valley for an invigorating ramble up Pendle Hill. Follow the Ribble Way for gentler strolls through the Ribble Valley. See also Pub Walk on page 292.
Events & Festivals
Royal Lancashire Show, Ribchester (July)
Hodder Valley Agricultural Show (September)
Ribchester Festival of Music & Art (June)
Clitheroe Folk Festival (June)

Wigan

The Mulberry Tree

9 Wrightington Bar, Wrightington, Wigan,
Lancashire WN6 9SE
Telephone: +44(0)870 4016112
+44(0)1257 451400

Having trained under the Roux brothers, chef
Mark Prescott headed north in 2000 to his
home village to take on this Victorian pub.
Stylish refurbishment followed and it now
stands out in Lancashire as a versatile, well
run pub-restaurant and Mark's talents bring
a high level of sophistication to this very
successful operation. As you enter, there is
a separate dining room to the left, an open-
plan dining area to the right, with the lounge
and smart, airy bar straight ahead. Subtle
lighting, pale eggshell walls, and a warm red
carpet, matched with light wood tables and
chairs, creates an uncluttered, modern look.
Young, hardworking staff bring a profes-
sional but not stuffy approach to service,
delivering superior lunchtime sandwiches,
salads, and dishes like roast salmon with
confit of savoy cabbage, red wine, shallots
and hollandaise. The dining room carte is
where more luxurious ingredients come into
play with ham hock and foie gras terrine
with black truffle and pistachios, but there
are more simpler dishes like roast Goosnargh
duck with green peppercorns and cranberries.
The well annotated wine list provides a great
deal of choice for under £20.

Prices: Restaurant main course from £9.95. Bar main
course from £8.50. House wine £13.50.
Last orders: Bar: lunch 15.00; dinner 23.00. Food:
lunch 14.00 (Sunday 15.00); dinner 21.30 (Friday and
Saturday 22.00).
Closed: Rarely.
Food: Classical French and Modern British.
Real Ale: Flowers IPA.
Other points: No-smoking area. No smoking in the
restaurant. Children welcome. Car park.
Directions: Exit27/M6. Head towards Parbold; immedi-
ate right after motorway exit by garage into Mossy Lea
Road for 2 miles. (Map 7, F4)

Hungarton

The Black Boy Inn

Main Street, Hungarton, Leicestershire LE7 9JR
Telephone: +44(0)870 4016113
+44(0)116 259 5410
markandrachel@theblackboyinn.fsbusiness.
co.uk

Back in 2001 when Mark and Rachel took
over the Black Boy, it was just another struggling village local offering basic pub food.
Fuelled with enthusiasm, they totally redecorated the place, laid a decking terrace for
summer dining, and then chef Mark set about
improving the menus. Diners from all over
south east Leicestershire now beat a path to
the door for good, imaginative pub food. It's
a relatively new building, so don't expect a
lot of character, just a simple open-plan look
with traditional pub-style tables and chairs
and an open fire making everything cosy in
winter, plus there is a very friendly atmosphere. Mark's menu offers a modern British
take with everything made from scratch on
the premises, all listed on a chalkboard that
delivers very good value for money. The
menu changes every six weeks, with smoked
chicken and beetroot salad or roasted pepper
and tomato soup as typical starter choices.
Main courses could take in lambs' liver, mustard mash and onion gravy, or salmon and
coriander fishcakes with tomato salsa, as well
as traditional favourites like beef, ale and
mushroom pie. Pecan pie with clotted cream,
or sticky toffee pudding make a great finish.
Everard's Tiger is the regular cask ale.

Prices: Restaurant main course from £6.95. Bar snack
from £3.50. House wine £9.50.
Last orders: Bar: lunch 15.00; dinner 23.00. Food: lunch
14.00; dinner 21.00 (Friday and Saturday 21.30).
Closed: Sunday evening, all day Monday.
Food: Traditional and Modern British.
Real Ale: Everard's Tiger. 1 guest beer.
Other points: No-smoking area. Garden. Children
welcome. Car park.
Directions: Seven miles east of Leicester off A47.
(Map 5, B4)

Nether Broughton

The Red House

23 Main Street, Nether Broughton, Melton Mowbray, Leicestershire LE14 3HB
Telephone: +44(0)870 4016114
+44(0)1664 822429
bookings@the-redhouse.com
www.the-redhouse.com

Sherwood forest

The latest additions to this stylishly revamped early Victorian house is the teak-decked courtyard and the Garden Bar and Grill housed in the old stables to the rear of the inn. They complete the impressive picture at this modern and very individual pub-restaurant with rooms, which successfully combines a relaxed atmosphere with contemporary luxury. The bar has a traditional feel (plenty of darkwood furniture), where chalkboards offer the day's bar menu, which includes a pasta, soup of the day, seared liver on thyme mash with rich jus, and a beef sandwich with horseradish cream. But modern styling distinguishes the restaurant with, for example, a bar that consists of a pine wood frame filled with old books. Or, for a change of scene, step through an arched walkway to the adjoining dining room that's filled with light from patio doors that look on to the new rear terrace. Here you can choose the likes of loin of venison with celeriac rösti and redcurrant jus, or roast cod with leek and potato chowder and tempura mussels, from a seasonally-inspired menu. Match this with an expansive, global wine list that is very keenly priced. Eight en suite bedrooms are imaginatively designed. As well as DVDs, there are goodies such as olives, pistachio nuts, mineral water, and freshly-baked cookies.

Must See Belvoir Castle, Burrough Hill Country Park, Great Central Railway, Leicester Museum & Art Gallery, DH Lawrence Birthplace Museum, Sherwood Forest Country Park & Visitor Centre

Belvoir Castle

Rooms: 8. Twin/double room from £50 per person.
Prices: Restaurant main course from £9.95. Bar snacks from £5. House wine £12.
Last orders: Bar: 23.00 (Sunday 22.30). Food: lunch 15.00 (Sunday 17.00); dinner 22.00 (Sunday 18.00).
Closed: Rarely.
Food: Modern British.
Real Ale: Marston's Pedigree, Belvoir Beaver Bitter. 2 guest beers.
Other points: No-smoking in the restaurant. Children welcome. Dogs welcome in the bar. Car park. Outside garden bar and open kitchen. Meeting room. Marquee facility.
Directions: Exit 25/M1, the A52, then the A606 to Melton. On the A606 between Nottingham and Melton Mowbray, five miles north of Melton. (Map 5, B4)

Tourist Information Melton Mowbray
+44(0)1664 480992; Nottingham 0115 915 5330
Farmers Market
Melton Mowbray (every Tuesday and Friday)
Where to Walk
Take a stroll along the Grantham Canal towpath around

Hose, Plunger and Redmile in the heart of the Vale of Belvoir. Excellent forest trails and marked walks through Sherwood Forest.
Events & Festivals Flower Festival, Belvoir Castle (May)
Robin Hood Festival, Edwinstowe (July/Aug)
Nottingham Carnival (Aug)

Mrs Kirkham's Lancashire Cheese

at the Red Cat

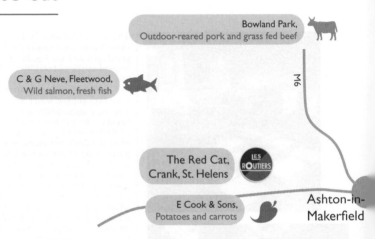

Bowland Park,
Outdoor-reared pork and grass fed beef

C & G Neve, Fleetwood,
Wild salmon, fresh fish

M6

The Red Cat,
Crank, St. Helens

LES ROUTIERS

Ashton-in-Makerfield

E Cook & Sons,
Potatoes and carrots

Lancashire is an area where traditional cheesemaking stretches back hundreds of years. When times were hard and meat a rarity, the poor folk of Lancashire made it into a filling meal. A casualty of the world wars, today there are only three farms making the real unpasteurised Lancashire cheese, and Mrs Kirkham's handmade, cloth wrapped, rather buttery and crumbly version is one. To make Lancashire in the traditional way is a laborious process. The curd made on one day is added to the previous day's curd – a tradition put down to the once poor roads in the area which made travelling slow and difficult. Hence, the curds were gathered each day and transported to the cheese house every few days.

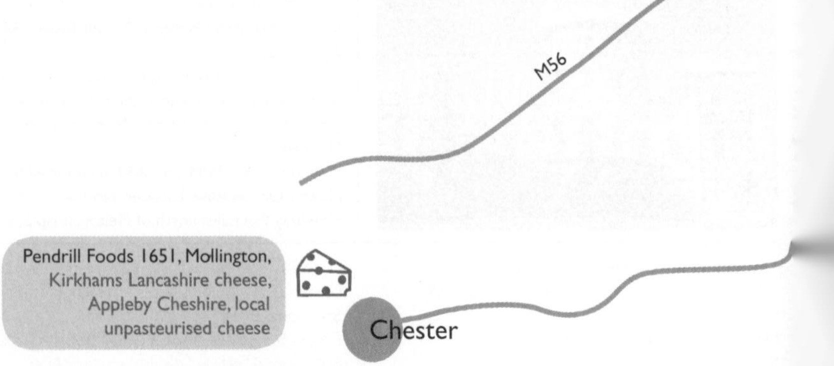

M56

Pendrill Foods 1651, Mollington,
Kirkhams Lancashire cheese,
Appleby Cheshire, local
unpasteurised cheese

Chester

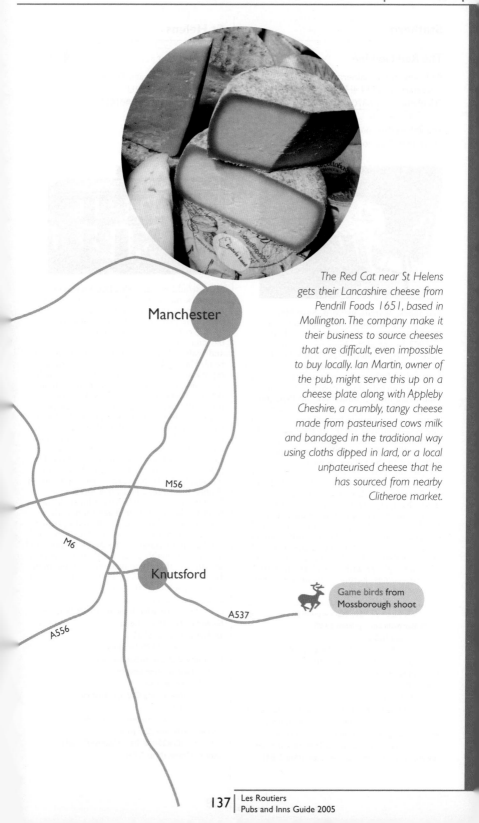

The Red Cat near St Helens gets their Lancashire cheese from Pendrill Foods 1651, based in Mollington. The company make it their business to source cheeses that are difficult, even impossible to buy locally. Ian Martin, owner of the pub, might serve this up on a cheese plate along with Appleby Cheshire, a crumbly, tangy cheese made from pasteurised cows milk and bandaged in the traditional way using cloths dipped in lard, or a local unpateurised cheese that he has sourced from nearby Clitheroe market.

Manchester

M56

M6

Knutsford

A537

A556

Game birds from Mossborough shoot

Stathern

The Red Lion Inn

Red Lion Street, Stathern,
Leicestershire LE14 4HS
Telephone: +44(0)870 4016115
+44(0)1949 860868
info@theredlioninn.co.uk
www.theredlioninn.co.uk

Ben Jones, Marcus Welford, Sean Hope and their mini-pub empire continue to thrive. Refurbishment of the 16th-century Red Lion in 2002 followed the huge success of their eponymous, Michelin star-rated Olive Branch at Clipsham and, unsurprisingly, business has been brisk. Informality, real ales, fine wines and good quality innovative and traditional food using local produce sum up their philosophy. The converted skittle alley dining room comes with low beams, terracotta walls and wood-burning stove. As the back of the menu indicates, there's a passion for quality suppliers: Brewster's Bitter on handpump is brewed in the village, game comes from the Belvoir estate, cheese, and sausages and fruits are sourced from local farms and dairies. There's something for everyone on the daily changing menu, including, perhaps, Caesar salad, roast pheasant with butternut pearl barley risotto, peas and tarragon, and smoked haddock with Welsh rarebit and bubble-and-squeak. Lunchtime additions include excellent sandwiches. Homely puddings like chocolate sponge with chocolate sauce finish off proceedings. Future plans include three en suite bedrooms.

Prices: Set lunch £13.50. Restaurant main course from £8.95. Bar main course from £4.95.
House wine £10.50.
Last orders: Bar: lunch 15.00; dinner 23.00. Food: lunch 14.00 (Sunday 15.00); dinner 21.30.
No food Sunday evening.
Closed: Rarely.
Food: Modern Pub Food.
Real Ale: Brewster Vale Pale Ale, Grainstore Olive Oil.
Other points: No-smoking area. Garden. Children welcome. Dogs welcome in the bar. Car park.
Directions: From A1; A52 towards Nottingham; left towards Belvoir Castle; Stathern left. (Map 5, B4)

St Helens

The Red Cat

8 Red Cat Lane, Crank, St Helens,
Merseyside WA11 8RU
Telephone: +44(0)870 4016116
+44(0)1744 882422
REDCAT@amserve.net

Most would not give this late Victorian red-brick pub a second glance but informed locals know that Ian Martin's unpretentious pub is the place to go for some inspired pub food. Venture into the traditional lounge bar and you will see the blackboard menu and realise that someone here knows proper food. Having battled against an inherited reputation for fairly basic pub staples, he has succeeded with a fresh, modern menu that delivers home-baked breads, seared loin of tuna with Niçoise salad or smoked chicken Caesar salad for starters, followed by loin of free-range Bowland pork with asparagus and girolle mushroom sauce, sea bass with oyster fritter and tomato and coriander sauce, or slow-roasted lamb with rosemary gravy. Ian's passion for local produce extends to sourcing vegetables from nearby farms, game from shoots at Rainford Hall, fish direct from Fleetwood, and unpasteurised local cheeses from Clitheroe market. Then there is the amazing wine list. You will be hard pressed to find another list anywhere that offers such a selection of classic wines and vintages - and at very reasonable prices. If there is one complaint, it is that there is no accommodation. Having to drive could spoil the enjoyment of sampling some great wines.

Prices: Set 2 course lunch and dinner £9.95. (Dinner between 18.00-19.15). Restaurant main course from £6.95. House wine £9.25.
Last orders: Bar: 23.00. Food: lunch 14.00; dinner 21.30. Food served all day on Sunday until 20.00.
Closed: First week of January.
Food: Modern British.
Real Ale: Greene King Old Speckled Hen, Theakston Best.
Other points: No-smoking area. Garden. Children welcome. Car park.
Directions: Exit23/M6. Take A580/A570 and follow signs to Crank. (Map 7, F4)

Bawburgh

Kings Head

Harts Lane, Bawburgh, Norwich,
Norfolk NR9 3LS
Telephone: +44(0)870 4016117
+44(0)1603 744977
anton@kingshead-bawburgh.co.uk
www.kingshead-bawburgh.co.uk

Sunny yellow walls, thick oak beams and standing timbers, roaring winter fires and a bustling atmosphere throughout four inter-linked rooms draw the crowds to this 17th-century building in the peaceful Yare Valley west of Norwich. Oozing old-world charm and named after Edward VII it looks across the River Yare and Bawburgh's old mill. Although landlord Anton Wimmer has created a thriving pub-restaurant offering good pub food, drinkers are welcome and local ale enthusiasts continue to beat a path to the door for first-class Woodforde's and Adnams ales. Uncomplicated dishes such as pan-fried scallops with crayfish cocktail and dressed rocket, and white onion, thyme and potato soup, or flash-fried calf's liver with bub-ble-and-squeak, dry cured bacon and onion gravy, represent a forgotten English cuisine, one that celebrates traditional country cooking with a fresh look and seasonal ingredients. Local produce plays a big part in the imaginative menu with the likes of Cromer crab and crayfish pâté, and a classy fish stew filled with bass, bream, scallops and organic salmon. Alternatively, try beer fillet with beetroot jus or beef battered local cod with chips, then round off with orange ricotta pudding. Short, global selection of wines.

Prices: Main course from £6.95. House wine £9.95.
Last orders: Bar: 23.00. Food: lunch 14.00
(Sunday 14.30); dinner 21.30.
Closed: Rarely.
Food: Traditional/fusion.
Real Ale: Woodforde's Wherry, Adnams, Courage
Directors Bitter, Greene King IPA.
Other points: No-smoking area. Children welcome.
Garden. Car park.
Directions: Take A47 west of Norwich, then B1108; pub
signposted down Harts Lane off B1108 in Bawburgh.
(Map 6, B7))

Brancaster Staithe

The White Horse

Brancaster Staithe, King's Lynn,
Norfolk PE31 8BY
Telephone: +44(0)870 4016118
+44(0)1485 210262
reception@whitehorsebrancaster.co.uk
www.whitehorsebrancaster.co.uk

The evocative bubbling call of the curlew and memorable views across breezy salt marsh to Scolt Head Island are among the magical treats that await you if visiting this stylishly refurbished village inn on the North Norfolk coast. Beyond the neat, white-painted front-age, drinkers will find a welcoming atmos-phere within the light and airy bar, kitted out in modern style with scrubbed pine. The rear conservatory dining room, with its adjoining summer sun deck and one of the finest views in Norfolk, is the place to linger over dinner. Reflecting the view, colours throughout are muted and natural, with found objects from the beach complementing contemporary art-work. Nick Parker's modern menus focus on fresh local fish and seafood, including oysters from Thornham and mussels harvested by Cyril just along the coast path. Start, per-haps, with smoked haddock chowder, move on to skate wing with Italian cannelini bean stew or corn-fed chicken with sweet pepper polenta. Sandwiches, salads and chargrilled rib-eye steak available for lunch. Original bedrooms are in the grassed-roofed exten-sion facing the marsh, designed in a wave to give every spacious room a piece of terrace. Bedrooms upstairs feature handsome modern furniture, simple clean lines, and soft colours.

Rooms: 15. Double room from £84, single supplement
£20 per night.
Prices: Main course from £9.50. House wine £10.80.
Last orders: Bar: 23.00. Food: lunch 14.00; dinner 21.15.
Closed: Rarely.
Food: Modern British.
Real Ale: Adnams Southwold, Fuller's London Pride,
Woodforde's Nelsons Revenge. 1 guest beer.
Other points: No-smoking area. Children welcome.
Dogs welcome overnight. Sun deck terrace. Car park.
Directions: On A149 between Hunstanton and
Wells-next-Sea. (Map 6, B6)

Cropwell Bishop and Colston Bassett Stilton

at the Red Lion Inn

Cropwell Bishop and Colston Bassett are two of just seven dairies in the world licensed to make Stilton cheese. By law Stilton can only be made in the three counties of Derbyshire, Leicestershire and Nottinghamshire. Gastropub and Les Routiers member, the Red Lion is a passionate supporter and whether it be White Stilton, Shropshire Blue or the 'King of Cheeses', the Blue Stilton, it will always take pride of place on a cheese plate of Somerset Brie, Lincolnshire Poacher, grapes and biscuits. Starting sometime in the late 18th-century Stilton was never actually made in Stilton, it in fact started from a farm in Melton Mowbray that sold the cheese to the famous Bell Inn, a staging post for coaches travelling to and from London and York. It is still made in much the same way as it was then, over 250 years ago, with traditional methods being used as much as possible. The milk is taken everyday from the same pastures and the same farms it has always been, despite production rates currently at over 1 million Stiltons per year. Cropwell Bishop is not quite as old, having started in 1950, but has a similar attention to tradition and detail with the original founders still sitting on the board to this day.

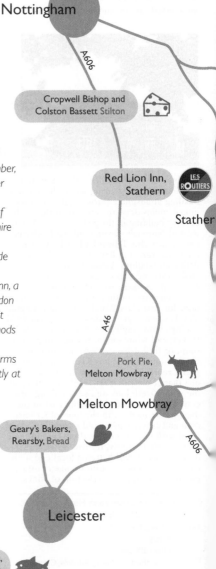

Nottingham

A606

Cropwell Bishop and Colston Bassett Stilton

Red Lion Inn, Stathern

LES ROUTIERS

Stather

A46

Pork Pie, Melton Mowbray

Melton Mowbray

Geary's Bakers, Rearsby, Bread

A606

Leicester

Holroyds Fish, Leicester, Fresh fish

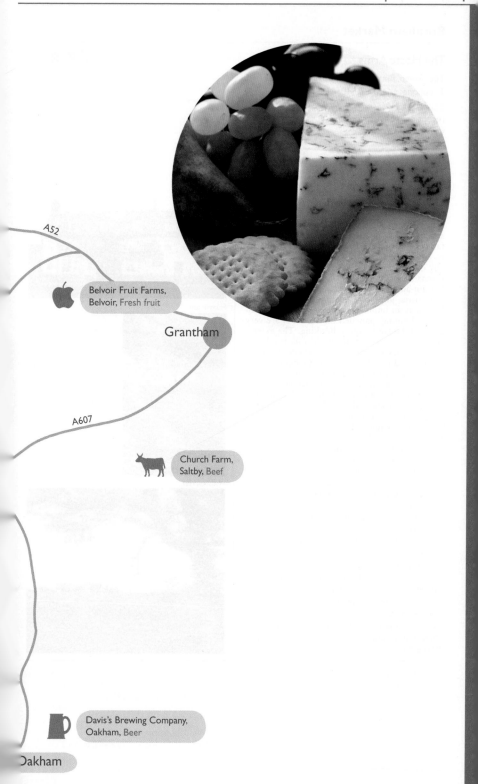

A52

Belvoir Fruit Farms,
Belvoir, Fresh fruit

Grantham

A607

Church Farm,
Saltby, Beef

Davis's Brewing Company,
Oakham, Beer

Oakham

Burnham Market

The Hoste Arms

The Green, Burnham Market, Norfolk PE31 8HD
Telephone: +44(0)870 4016119
+44(0)1328 738777
reception@hostearms.co.uk
www.hostearms.co.uk

Paul and Jeanne Whittome have worked wonders at this handsome 17th-century inn overlooking the village green in Burnham Market. Dedication and relentless enthusiasm for the property have transformed it into a rare combination of stylish pub, restaurant and upmarket hotel. Strong colours, tasteful fabrics, four-poster beds and handsome bathrooms characterise the comfortable, individually designed and very well equipped bedrooms (new Zulu wing) that are split between the inn and converted buildings to the rear. The rustic, unpretentious bar (no food served here) has an impressive range of East Anglian ales; adjoining, panelled dining areas are very comfortable and require booking. The extensive menu focuses on fresh Norfolk produce with a policy of sourcing ingredients from a 20-mile radius. Daily-changing menus may list grilled sardines with roasted peppers and Parmesan polenta or Burnham Creek oysters with red wine and shallot vinegar among the starters or snacks. Mains range from honey-glazed ham hock with minted green pea purée, to roasted cod with fennel, tomato and garlic casserole. For pudding there may be glazed lemon tart or mango and nougat parfait. There's a well chosen list of wines and a new Moroccan-inspired terraced garden.

Hunstanton

Holkham Hall

Must See
- Holkham Hall: classic 18th-century mansion located in a 3,000 acre deer park and including a pottery, museum and paintings by Rubens, Van Dyck and Gainsborough.
- Blakeney Point
- Castle Acre Priory
- Sandringham
- Heacham: one of England's largest lavender farms.

Rooms: 36. Double/twin from £108, single from £78. Children £20.
Prices: Restaurant main course from £9.25. House wine £11.95.
Last orders: Bar: 23.00. Food: lunch 14.00; dinner 21.00.
Closed: Rarely.
Food: Modern British with Pacific Rim influences.
Real Ale: Greene King IPA, Greene King Abbot Ale, Woodfordes Wherry. 1 guest beer.
Other points: No-smoking area. Dogs welcome. Children welcome. Garden. Car park.
Directions: Signposted off the B1155, five miles west of Wells-next-the-Sea. By the green in the village centre. (Map 6, B6)

Tourist Information Hunstanton +44(0)1485 532610
Where to Shop Old Hunstanton, Burnham Market.
Farmers Market Fakenham (4th Saturday of month)
Nearest Racecourse Fakenham
Nearest Golf Course Brancaster
Local Activities
The Norfolk Coast Cycleway runs from King's Lynn to Cromer and on to Great Yarmouth - a great way to explore the coastline.

Windsurfing takes place at Hunstanton and birdwatching is a perennial pastime on the North Norfolk coast.
The 93-mile Peddars Way and North Norfolk Coast Path - two routes joined together - is the region's best-known long-distance walking trail.
Events and Festivals
Hunstanton Music and Arts Festival (June/July)
King's Lynn Music and Arts Festival (July/Aug)
Windfeist Festival (windsurfing), Hunstanton (July)

Burnham Thorpe

The Lord Nelson

Walsingham Road, Burnham Thorpe,
Norfolk PE31 8HL
Telephone: +44(0)870 4016120
+44(0)1328 738241
enquiries@nelsonslocal.co.uk
www.nelsonslocal.co.uk

An unspoilt rural cottage in a sleepy village and named after England's most famous seafarer, who was born in the nearby rectory in 1758. The pub, originally called The Plough, pre-dates Nelson by over 100 years but was renamed in 1797 to honour Nelson's victory at the Battle of the Nile. A narrow, worn brick-floored corridor leads to a timeless, old-fashioned bar on the left boasting some magnificent high-backed settles and a few sturdy tables and plain chairs. Nelson memorabilia in the form of prints and paintings adorn the walls. New owners David and Penny Thorley may have installed a hatchway bar but top-notch ales are still drawn straight from the barrel in the adjoining tap room. A separate, cosy room with beams and open fire, the refurbished Victory Barn is available for functions, and there is a good-sized rear garden. Using fresh local produce, including game from Holkham Estate and seafood from coastal villages, daily menus range from sautéed crevettes with garlic butter and warm salmon salad, to monkfish with chilli and herb dressing, smoked haddock chowder, and rib-eye steak with pink peppercorn sauce. Don't leave without trying the rum concoction called 'Nelson's Blood'. See page 170 for an interior shot.

Prices: Restaurant main course from £8.95. Bar main course from £7.95. House wine £10.50.
Last orders: Bar: lunch 15.00 (14.30 during the winter); dinner 23.00. Food: lunch 14.00; dinner 21.00 (no food Sunday evening).
Closed: Monday during the winter.
Food: Traditional British/European.
Real Ale: Greene King IPA & Abbot Ale, Woodforde's Nelson's Revenge & Wherry. Guest ales.
Other points: No-smoking area. Children welcome. Dogs welcome in the bar. Car park. Garden. Childrens play area in garden. BBQ in the summer.
Directions: Off B1355 Burnham Market to Fakenham. (Map 6, B6)

Hevingham

Marsham Arms Inn

Holt Road, Hevingham, Norwich,
Norfolk NR10 5NP
Telephone: +44(0)870 4016121
+44(0)1603 754268
nigelbradley@marshamarms.co.uk
www.marshamarms.co.uk

Set back from the B1149, with an attractive creeper-clad façade, the wood beams and large open fireplace in the entrance are original features of this 18th-century country inn, built by local landowner Robert Marsham as a staging post for drovers travelling to Norwich market. In the comfortably modernised interior you will find local Adnams and Woodforde's ales on tap and a varied menu listing traditional homecooked bar food that relies on local lines of supply. Expect sound pub favourites like grilled bacon or hot sausage baguettes, garlic mushrooms, ploughman's lunches, seafood mornay, and steak and kidney pie with shortcrust topping. Steaks come from the local butcher, who also provides the meat for an excellent mixed grill; there's a popular help-yourself salad bar, and daily fish dishes on the chalkboard. Those looking for comfortable accommodation will find ten en suite bedrooms housed in a purpose-built block to the rear of the pub. Clean and tidy, and well-equipped, they make a good base from which to explore Norwich. Those on business, in particular, may find the location and informality of the inn more suitable than staying in a city-centre hotel.

Rooms: 10. Double room from £70, single from £48.
Prices: Lunch main course from £7.50.
House wine £9.50.
Last orders: Bar: 23.00 (Monday and Tuesday closed between 15.00-17.00). Food: lunch 15.00; dinner 21.30.
Closed: Rarely.
Food: Modern and Classic British/ethnic influences.
Real Ale: Adnams, Woodforde's, Bass, Greene King IPA. 2 guest beers.
Other points: No-smoking area. Children welcome. Garden. Car park.
Directions: North of Norwich Airport on the B1149 and two miles north of Horsford. (Map 6, B7)

Woodforde's Nelson's Revenge *at the Lord Nelson*

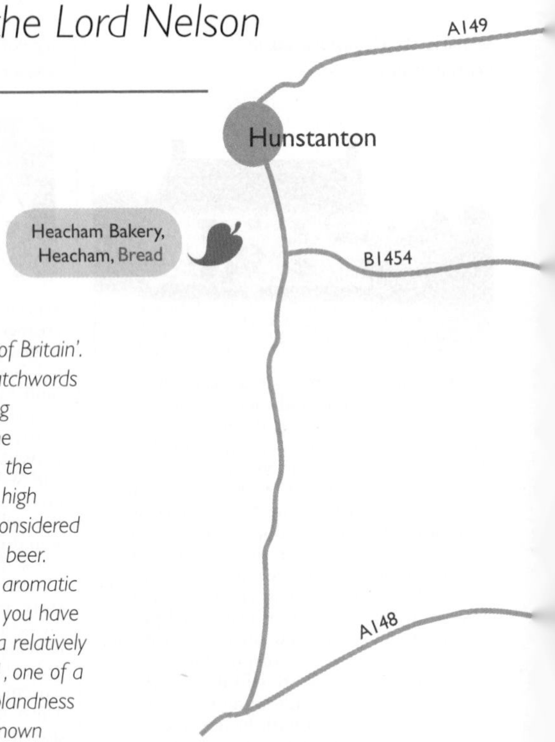

A149

Hunstanton

B1454

A148

On the Norfolk Broads lies the famous Woodforde's Brewery. The quality of the beers brewed here is not in doubt as amongst many awards they have twice won the supreme accolade of CAMRA's 'Champion Beer of Britain'. Care and attention to detail are the watchwords with the barley grown in the surrounding countryside and malted in Norfolk in the traditional style. A unique aspect is that the brewery has its very own borehole, this high quality water is low on nitrates and is considered very important in the production of the beer. Combine this with the finest bitter and aromatic hops and the brewery's own yeast and you have a winning combination. Woodforde's is a relatively young company having started in 1981, one of a wave of brewers rebelling against the blandness of the large brewing companies. Well known regionally they became nationally famous after their Norfolk Nog 'Old' Ale became Champion Beer of Britain. Since then awards have been coming thick and fast. As well as actually owning three pubs the beer can be found in numerous local pubs, one of these being the Lord Nelson. A pretty cottagey pub, named after Norfolk's favourite son, the pub has remained unchanged for years. With its stone flagged floors and original wooden settles it is like stepping back in time and makes a lovely setting for a pint of Woodforde's Nelson's Revenge.

Heacham Bakery, Heacham, Bread

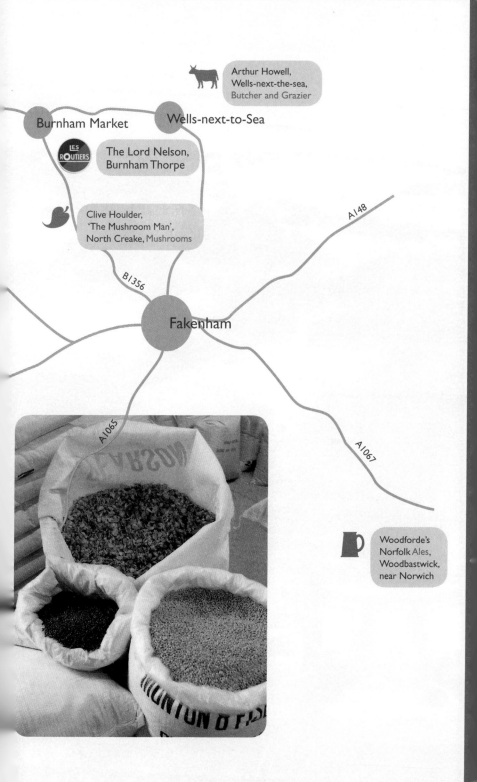

Arthur Howell,
Wells-next-the-sea,
Butcher and Grazier

Burnham Market

Wells-next-to-Sea

The Lord Nelson,
Burnham Thorpe

Clive Houlder,
'The Mushroom Man',
North Creake, Mushrooms

A148

B1356

Fakenham

A1065

A1067

Woodforde's
Norfolk Ales,
Woodbastwick,
near Norwich

The Victoria at Holkham, Norfolk

Holkham

The Victoria at Holkham

Park Road, Holkham, Wells-next-the-Sea,
Norfolk NR23 1RG
Telephone: +44(0)870 4016122
+44(0)1328 711008
victoria@holkham.co.uk
www.victoriaatholkham.co.uk

Viscount Coke's beautifully refurbished inn-cum-chic hotel stands at the entrance to Holkham Hall estate, just a short stroll from Holkham's magnificent sandy beach. An imposing brick building, built in the early 1800s to house the entourage of gentry visting the hall, it now offers accommodation to well-heeled visitors in eleven individually decorated, en suite bedrooms. Most have memorable marsh views across Holkham Nature Reserve, all are beautifully furnished with unique furnishings sourced from Rajasthan, alongside huge beds, and luxurious bathrooms. The colonial theme extends to the informal bar and brasserie: carved wood furniture, huge sofas, tables with fat candles, and a wealth of Indian artefacts. Menus focus on fresh, local produce, notably beef and seasonal estate game, as well as fish and seafood from the Norfolk coast, with lunch bringing warm crab linguine with spring onion, chilli and lime vinaigrette or Holkham venison burger with cranberry chutney. Equally accomplished dinners might include John Dory with olive-crushed potatoes, watercress and sauce vierge, and Holkham rib-eye steak with béarnaise. Woodforde's ales; 12 wines by the glass. See Pub Walk on page 294

Rooms: 10. Low season £55 and high season £70 and mid-season £70 - prices quoted are per person.
Prices: Main course restaurant from £7.
House wine £12.
Last orders: Bar: 23.00 Food: lunch 14.30; dinner 21.30 (Friday and Saturday 22.00).
Closed: Never.
Food: Modern British.
Real Ale: Woodforde's. 2 guest beers.
Other points: No-smoking area. Children welcome. Dogs welcome in the bar. Car park.
Licence for Civil Weddings.
Directions: On A149 3 west of Wells-next-the-Sea. (Map 6, B6)

Itteringham

Walpole Arms

The Common, Itteringham, Aylsham,
Norfolk NR11 7AR
Telephone: +44(0)870 4016123
+44(0)1263 587258
goodfood@thewalpolearms.co.uk
www.thewalpolearms.co.uk

Since 2001 this unspoilt brick and timber cottage in sleepy Itteringham has been run by BBC Masterchef producer Richard Bryan, with talented chef Andy Parle mastering the stoves in what has become a very busy kitchen. Discerning foodies travel to this exceptional pub-restaurant for first-class modern British and Mediterranean-inspired food. Daily menus reflect the passion for fresh local produce, notably Morston mussels, Cromer crab, lamb from the Walpole estate, organic beef from the National Trust's Felbrigg estate, venison from nearby Gunton Hall, and local farm fruit and vegetables. Typically, starters may include escabeche of mackerel, 'vol au vent' of foie gras with pear and grape chutney or pigeon terrine with shallot vinaigrette. Mains include a sizeable serving of Morston mussels steamed with onions, thyme and cream or calf's liver with black pudding, bubble-and-squeak and roast squash. Round off with rhubarb and stem ginger cobbler or almond parfait with citrus salad. There's the choice of dining in the rustic and informal opened-up bar, which retains plenty of original character, together with a dedicated lunchtime clientele, or book a table in the more formal dining room. Excellent East Anglian ales and a top-notch list of wines. See Pub Walk on page 296

Prices: Main course from £9. Bar main course from £5. House wine from £11.50.
Last orders: Bar: lunch 15.00; dinner 23.00. Food: lunch 14.00 (Sunday 15.00); dinner 21.30.
Closed: Rarely.
Food: Modern British.
Real Ale: Adnams Broadside, Adnams Best, Woodforde's Walpole. 1 guest beer.
Other points: No-smoking in the restaurant. Children welcome. Dogs welcome in the bar. Garden. Car park.
Directions: Off A140; go through Aylsham, past Blickling Hall, then take next right turn. (Map 6, B7)

Norwich

The Last Wine Bar and Restaurant

70-76 St George's Street, Norwich,
Norfolk NR3 1AB
Telephone: +44(0)870 4016124
+44(0)1603 626626
email@lastwinebar.fsnet.co.uk
www.lastwinebar.co.uk

Called 'The Last' because of its location in a Victorian shoe factory, this wine bar in an intriguing old building is set in the oldest quarter of Norwich. The space yields several dining areas and a lively upstairs bar. It has a distinctive atmosphere with an eclectic mix of customers - a cross section of young and old. The kitchen explores various Mediterranean styles, with the bar delivering good value dishes that run to charmoula chicken with roasted red onion salad, rib-eye steak and frites, or salmon fishcake with french beans and dill sauce, and bread and butter pudding for £13.60 for three courses. In the restaurant expect a weekly changing menu that could open with Mediterranean fish soup or fresh Cromer crab with avocado and lemon dressing, go on to pan-fried duck breast marinated in tamarind, and finish with vanilla cheesecake with caramel sauce. Some interesting specials include chargrilled squid with mussel and pepper salad and Serrano ham with Manchego cheese and pequillo peppers. The wine list is globally ranging with a good selection of wines by the glass.

Prices: Main course from £9.90. Bar meal/snack from £6.90. House wine £11.50.
Last orders: Food: lunch 14.30; dinner 22.30.
Closed: Sunday and Bank Holiday Mondays.
Food: Modern British/Mediterranean.
Real Ale: Adnams.
Other points: No-smoking areas. Terrace.
Directions: Locate St Andrews Hall at the top of St George's Street. Go over the bridge and past the Playhouse; on the left at the junction with Colegate. (Map 6, B7)

Norwich

The Wig and Pen

6 St Martins Palace Plain, Norwich,
Norfolk NR3 1RN
Telephone: +44(0)870 4016125
+44(0)1603 625891
info@thewigandpen.com
www.wigandpen.com

Arrive early, bag a window seat, or a table on the sunny front terrace, and savour the fabulous cathedral views over lunch at this partly modernised old beamed pub opposite the cathedral close. Log fires crackle in the original beamed bar, where legal related prints and pictures of the pub adorn the walls, and the welcoming atmosphere extends through to the modern dining extension. Expect to find lawyers and locals supping pints of ale at the bar, shoppers and tourists popping in for lunch and, in the evenings, a young, lively crowd here for the beer and live sport on the TV. Real ale enthusiasts are spoilt rotten. Brewery badges on the six handpumps may feature Oulton Ales Wet and Windy, Woodforde's Wherry and Adnams Old Ale - all kept in tip-top condition, great beer to wash down some hearty, traditional pub food. Dishes range from the tried-and-tested on the printed menu - sandwiches, baked potatoes, beefburger, ham, egg and chips and all-day breakfasts - to homecooked daily specials like broccoli and Stilton soup, Hungarian beef goulash, a good steak and kidney pie with short-crust pastry topping and rich gravy, and fresh fish supplied by Howards fishmongers along the road.

Prices: Restaurant main course from £7.50. Bar main course from £3.00. House wine from £8.95.
Last orders: Bar: 23.00. Food: lunch 14.30; dinner 21.00.
Closed: Sunday evening. Christmas Day, New Years Day.
Food: Traditional and Modern British.
Real Ale: 6 guest ales.
Other points: No-smoking area. Children welcome over 14 years old. Garden. Wheelchair access.
Directions: Adjacent to Norwich Cathedral. 100 yards from Maids Head Hotel Tombland. Walking distance from the River Wensum. (Map 6, B7)

Snettisham

The Rose and Crown

Old Church Road, Snettisham, King's Lynn, Norfolk PE31 7LX
Telephone: +44(0)870 4016126
+44(0)1485 541382
info@roseandcrownsnettisham.co.uk
www.roseandcrownsnettisham.co.uk

Find the cross monument in the village centre and you've found Anthony and Jeanette Goodrich's splendid Rose and Crown. Built in the 14th century to house the craftsmen working on the parish church, this attractive, flower-decked inn hides a warren of bars with heavy oak beams, uneven red-tiled floors, huge inglenook fireplaces and comfortable settles, a small informal dining room, and to the rear, a large garden room leading directly onto the sun-trap walled garden. The kitchen makes good use of the best seasonal and local produce, notably Cromer crab, Brancaster lobsters, oysters and mussels, and Sandringham Estate beef. At lunchtime expect decent sandwiches, perhaps crab, lemon and dill crème fraîche, grilled polenta, squid and chorizo salad, and classic dishes like steak and kidney pudding. Evening additions range from red mullet and king prawn tom yam with noodle broth to roast corn-fed chicken with corn mash and ginger stock. Good homemade puddings. Six real ales and 20 wines by the glass complement the food. Stylishly modern en suite bedrooms are individually decorated in bright colours with matching soft furnishings.

Rooms: 11. Double room from £45, single from £55.
Prices: Set lunch £10 (2-corse Monday-Friday). Restaurant main course from £8. House wine £11.
Last orders: Bar: 23.00. Food: lunch 14.00 (14.30 Saturday and Sunday); dinner 21.00 (21.30 Saturday and Sunday).
Closed: Rarely.
Food: Modern British.
Real Ale: Adnams, Greene King IPA. 4 guest beers.
Other points: No-smoking area. Children welcome. Dogs welcome overnight. Garden. Car park.
Directions: Off A149 between King's Lynn and Hunstanton. (Map 6, B6)

Warham

Three Horseshoes

Bridge Street, Warham, Wells-next-the-Sea, Norfolk NR23 1NL
Telephone: +44(0)870 4016127
+44(0)1328 710547

Warham is a sleepy rural backwater situated a mile from the North Norfolk coast. At its heart, close to the church, lies the Three Horseshoes, a timeless gem of a village local, comprising of a row of 18th-century brick and flint cottages. An old-fashioned atmosphere still infuses the charming three-roomed interior, delightfully unchanged since the 1930s. Gas lighting, stone floors, scrubbed tables, Victorian fireplaces and time honoured pub games, including a rare example of Norfolk 'twister', and an ancient one-arm bandit converted to take modern coins, will all fascinate. The hatchway bar dispenses tip-top East Anglian ales tapped from the cask, homemade lemonade, and local Whin Hill cider. Hearty country cooking is the order of the day here, with traditional Norfolk dishes based on local ingredients, including fish and game, highlighting both the unpretentious printed menu and interesting choice of daily specials. Typical choices range from Warham mussel soup and grilled local herrings, to pot-roast pigeon, chicken and leek pudding, and braised pheasant, with good accompanying vegetables, but no chips. Round off with a homemade nursery pudding. They don't take bookings so arrive early for a table if eating. There is homely bed and breakfast in the adjoining Old Post Office Cottage.

Rooms: 3, 1 with private bathroom. Rooms from £24.
Prices: Main course from £6.50. House wine £7.95.
Last orders: Bar: lunch 14.30; dinner 23.00.
Food: lunch 13.45; dinner 20.30.
Closed: Rarely.
Food: Traditional English.
Real Ale: Greene King IPA, Woodforde's Wherry. 1 guest beer.
Other points: No-smoking area. Children welcome. Dogs welcome overnight. Garden. Car park.
Credit cards not accepted.
Directions: Small turning off A149 between Wells-next-the-Sea and Stiffkey. (Map 6, B6)

The Crown Hotel, Wells-next-the-Sea, Norfolk

Wells-next-the-Sea

The Crown Hotel

The Buttlands, Wells-next-the-Sea,
Norfolk NR23 1EX
Telephone: +44(0)870 4016128
+44(0)1328 710209
reception@thecrownhotelwells.co.uk
www.thecrownhotelwells.co.uk

Standing at the foot of a peaceful tree-lined green is the 400-year-old Crown, a small hotel offering stylish accommodation and innovative modern cooking. New Zealand born chef-proprietor Chris Coubrough and his wife Jo took over just over a year ago and have redecorated throughout and upgraded all eleven en suite bedrooms. The inn retains its historic charm and character, especially in the Crown Bar with its huge log fire, ancient beams and flagged floor. Modern touches include brightly coloured walls and an uncluttered look; separate, more formal restaurant (set-price menus), and a light and airy rear conservatory dining area leading out to a modern decked terrace. Chris's bar food menu combines traditional favourites with modern British cooking. So, expect to find roast rack of lamb alongside garlic fried lambs' liver with black pudding fritter and dauphinois potatoes, or Bancaster mussels with tomato broth, and dishes like chicken Laksa with fragrant rice and coriander yoghurt. Try the Crown tapas slate, a black slate tile laden with European and Asian appetizers. Food is freshly prepared and presented with flair and imagination. Good East Anglian ales from Adnams and Woodforde's.

Rooms: 11. Double from £95.
Prices: Set dinner £29.95. Restaurant main course from £19.95. Main course bar from £7.95.
House wine £10.90.
Last orders: Bar: 23.00. Food: lunch 14.00 (Saturday, Sunday and and during peak season 14.30).
Dinner: 21.30.
Closed: Never.
Food: Modern British.
Real Ale: Adnams, Woodforde's Wherry.
Other points: No-smoking area. Dogs welcome in bar area only. Children welcome. Car park.
Directions: Centre of Wells-next-the-Sea. (Map 6, B6)

Winterton-on-Sea

Fisherman's Return

The Lane, Winterton-on-Sea,
Norfolk NR29 4BN
Telephone: +44(0)870 4016129
+44(0)1493 393305
fisherman_return@btopenworld.com
www.fishermans-return.com

After a long bracing walk across the dunes, or a day's exploration of the nearby Broads, the friendly and unpretentious bars of this 17th-century brick and flint pub, replete with warming wood-burners and local photographs and prints, are a welcome retreat in which to find good East Anglian ales (try a pint of Woodforde's Norfolk Nog) and some hearty home-cooked food. Formerly a row of fisherman's cottages, it is a traditional village pub where locals, fisherman and tourists exploring the coast are made truly welcome by John and Kate Findlay. A good summer family room (Tinho) in a timbered rear extension has pool table and games, and there's a lovely enclosed garden with a pets' corner and an adventure playground. The printed menu sticks to the traditional, but look to the blackboard for interesting daily specials such as hearty homemade soups and casseroles, Caister crab, mussels and mackerel, winter game dishes, boozy beef pie, and fresh fish like whole Dover sole, skate with capers and mushroom sauce, and hot Winterton smoked salmon. A tiny, flint-lined spiral staircase leads up under the eaves to three clean and modestly comfortable bedrooms of varying sizes, all with en suite bath or shower rooms.

Rooms: 3. Double from £70, single room from £45.
Prices: Main course from £8.25. House wine £10.75.
Last orders: Bar: lunch 14.30; dinner 23.00 (all day during the weekend). Food: lunch 14.00; dinner 21.00.
Closed: Rarely.
Food: Traditional English and Continental.
Real Ale: Woodforde's Wherry, Woodforde's Norfolk Nog, Adnams Best, Adnams Broadside. 1-2 guest beers.
Other points: No-smoking area. Children welcome. Dogs welcome overnight. Garden. Car park.
Directions: Eight miles north of Great Yarmouth off the B1149. (Map 6, B7)

Badby

The Windmill at Badby

Main Street, Badby, Daventry,
Northamptonshire NN11 3AN
Telephone: +44(0)870 4016130
+44(0)1327 702363
www.windmillinn.co.uk

Modernisation has done nothing to spoil the local village atmosphere in this 17th-century, honey-stoned and thatched inn, although it now functions as a small country hotel with good accommodation. In a pleasant, modern extension at the back are eight en suite bedrooms that are traditionally styled in keeping with the older building. Rooms are very well maintained and offer a high standard of comfort. The original pub is the very essence of an English country inn - picture-book pretty in a charming village, with two classic, beamed and flagstoned bars, one with a huge inglenook fireplace and both sporting cricketing and rugby pictures, plus real ale is drawn straight from the cask. Menus aims straight for the heart of traditional British cooking with some snappy updating. Loin of lamb, for example, comes wrapped in bacon with a redcurrant and port sauce, and burgers are made with venison and served with a creamy peppercorn sauce. Owners John Freestone and Carol Sutton are passionate about food and make the effort to source raw materials locally. Wines appeal to both fans of old and new world, styles are varied and prices ungreedy.

Rooms: 10. Double room from £69.50,
single from £57.50.
Prices: Main course from £8.25. House wine £9.50.
Last orders: Bar: lunch 15.30; dinner 23.00. Food: lunch 14.00; dinner 21.30 (Sunday 21.00).
Closed: Rarely.
Food: Global.
Real Ale: Flowers Original, Bass, Wadworth 6X, Fuller's London Pride. 1 guest beer.
Other points: No-smoking area. Garden. Children welcome. Car park.
Directions: Exit 16/M1. Three miles south of Daventry on A361; ten minutes from M1. (Map 5, D3)

Bulwick

Queen's Head

Main Street, Bulwick,
Northamptonshire NN17 3DY
Telephone: +44(0)870 4016166
+44(0)1780 450272

Situated in the heart of a pretty village opposite the church, this quaint 17th-century country pub, built of local Cotswold stone, has bags of character, and it's a great pit stop if you're travelling on the nearby A43. From the front door you enter a tiny drinking bar warmed by an open fire and dominated by plenty of timber joints and beams, with those wonky, uneven walls which indicate great age. New owners Geoff Smith and Angela Partridge, who took over in early 2004, continue to offer a good range of guest ales on handpump and have maintained the pub's reputation for good quality food by diligently searching for a good chef. Menus are modern British with influences from the Mediterranean, with imaginative offerings like chargrilled calf's liver on fried polenta with a fig vinaigrette, and tallegio cheese wrapped in Parma ham. Lunchtime meals include ploughman's and filled ciabatta sandwiches. Food is served in three small adjoining rooms, each strewn with rugs and furnished with classic wood furniture and knick-knacks. One room, with just a large dining table, can be used for private bookings.

Prices: Restaurant main course from £9.95. Bar main course from £6.50. House wine £9.95.
Last orders: Bar: lunch 14.30; dinner 23.00. Food: lunch 14.00; dinner 21.00 (Friday and Saturday 22.00).
No food Sunday evening.
Closed: Monday.
Food: Modern British with Mediterannean influences.
Real Ale: Batemans, Nethergate Suffolk County, Shepherd Neame Spitfire. 3 guest beers.
Other points: Totally no smoking in restaurant. Children welcome. Dogs welcome in bar only. Garden. Car park.
Directions: Just off A43 between Stamford and Corby. (Map 5, C4)

Oundle

Falcon Inn

Fotheringhay, Oundle,
Northamptonshire PE8 5HZ
Telephone: +44(0)870 4016131
+44(0)1832 226254

By night, the imposing, illuminated church serves as a golden beacon, visible for miles. Standing almost beside it in the main street of this historic village, the Falcon is a great village pub, run by Ray Smikle and John Hoskins of the Huntsbridge Group. Candles, fresh flowers, Windsor chairs, high-backed tapestry-covered chairs, some exposed stone, and discreet soft colours define the bar. The double conservatory dining room looks towards the church, providing a slightly more formal setting, with a mix of green director chairs and green Lloyd Loom chairs complementing the pale-green hand-painted walls. There's a snack menu chalked up on a board, but the printed, monthly-changing menu is offered in the bar as well as the dining room. This fits the bill nicely, aware of the rural location and tastes, but managing to be thoroughly modern. Thus, a May meal could open with a salad of asparagus, quails egg, olives, anchovy, Parmesan and chilli. Calf's liver with olive oil mash, bacon, spinach and red wine shallot sauce, could follow, with carmelised lemon tart with cherry compote, making a great finish. There are few wine lists of 100 bins that could be so indulgent, and with such an eclectic, esoteric and stimulating selection.

Prices: Set lunch £15.50. Restaurant main course from £9.75. Bar main course from £8.95. House wine £12.

Last orders: Bar: lunch 15.00; dinner 23.00.

Food: lunch 14.15; dinner 21.30.

Closed: Rarely.

Food: International.

Real Ale: Adnams Best, Greene King IPA. 2 guest beers.

Other points: No-smoking in the restaurant. Children welcome. Dogs welcome in the bar. Garden. Car park.

Directions: Village signposted off A605 between Oundle and Peterborough, one mile north of Oundle. (Map 5, C4)

Alnwick

Cottage Inn

Dunstan Village, Craster, Alnwick,
Northumberland NE66 3SZ
Telephone: +44(0)870 4016132
+44(0)1665 576658
enquiries@cottageinnhotel.co.uk
www.cottageinnhotel.co.uk

Purchased as a row of derelict cottages in 1975, the Cottage Inn was, briefly, a modest guesthouse before finally opening as a pub in 1988. The traditional beamed bar, with ancient exposed brick, dark wood panelling, and a substantial brick fireplace, is an atmospheric room, one where drinkers and diners mingle easily. There's a relaxed approach to eating: the same menu is available throughout, either in the bar, the plant-filled conservatory, or the medieval-styled Harry Hotspur restaurant. The smokery, Robsons of Craster, supply the Craster kippers served at breakfast, and as the lunch and dinner menus first course of kippers 'n' custard. There's also port and Stilton terrine, and a ramekin of pigeon pie to start, with mains running to shoulder of lamb hotpot, grilled tuna with lime butter, pan-fried lambs' liver with rich onion gravy and fresh crab and lobster direct from the Craster boats. Snacks, simpler dishes and Sunday lunches are also available. Local ales (Wylam Bitter, Cottage Inn Ale) are complemented by 12 reasonably priced wines by the glass. At the back, overlooking the pub's six-acre wooded garden, is a wing of peaceful ground-floor bedrooms. The 10 en suite rooms are fully equipped, comfortable and good value.

Rooms: 10. Double room from £69, single from £39. October-April special break offers.

Prices: Set dinner £14. Main course from £6.45. Bar/snack from £6.95. House wine £9.25.

Last orders: Bar: 24.00. Food: lunch 14.30; dinner 21.30.

Closed: Never.

Food: Traditional English and Scottish.

Real Ale: Cottage Inn Ace, Wylam Bitter. 2 guest beers.

Other points: No-smoking area. Children welcome. Garden. Car park. Adventure playground.

Directions: From A1 at Alnwick take B1340 towards Seahouses and follow Craster signs right. (Map 8, A5)

Alnwick

The Ship Inn

The Square, Low Newton on Sea, Alnwick,
Northumberland NE66 3EL
Telephone: +44(0)870 4016133
+44(0)1665 576262
forsythchristine@hotmail.com
www.theshipinnnewtonbythesea.co.uk

The preserved 'village green' is just a grassy area enclosed on three sides by fishermen's cottages, one of which is the unprepossessing and very traditional Ship Inn, and on the fourth side by the beach itself. The Ship is charming, largely as a result of Christine Forsyth, who runs the place with great enthusiasm, keeping the simply adorned bar spick-and-span and pulling pints of Wylam Gold Tankard for loyal regulars. Christine is a great champion of local and regional produce. Sit at plain scrubbed wood tables by the solid fuel stove and tuck into Boulmer crab sandwiches, ploughman's made with unpasteurised cheddar from Doddington Dairy, Craster kippers, or lobster caught by Gary in Newton Bay (50 yards from the pub). Meat comes from nearby farms and fish from Amble day boats. Lunch brings a good value mix of sandwiches, stotties (a kind of bread roll), soup and salads. The evening carte is equally good value, noted for sound country cooking that ranges from fish pie and venison and red wine casserole, to grilled red mullet with herb salsa. A 'serious' chocolate cake served with a rich dark chocolate and rum sauce makes an irresistible dessert.

Rooms: Self catering accommodation sleeps 4. £55 per night. From £250 per week.
Prices: Main course restaurant from £7.95. Main course bar from £3.50. House wine £8.95.
Last orders: Bar: 23.00. Food: lunch 14.30; dinner 20.00. No food Sunday and Monday evening.
Check for seasonal variations.
Closed: Rarely.
Food: Modern Pub Food.
Real Ale: Black Sheep Best, Gold Tankard, Landlords Choice. Guest beers occasionally.
Other points: Totally no smoking during food serving hours. Dogs welcome. Garden. Children welcome.
Directions: From A1 at Alnwick take B1340 towards houses, then B1339 and Ship signs. (Map 8, A5)

Kielder Water

The Pheasant Inn

Stannersburn, Kielder Water, Hexham,
Northumberland NE48 1DD
Telephone: +44(0)870 4016134
+44(0)1434 240382
enquiries@thepheasantinn.com
www.thepheasantinn.com

Just a mile from Kielder Water deep in unspoilt Northumberland countryside stands the Kershaw family's 400-year-old Pheasant Inn, formerly a farmhouse and a coaching stop. Refurbishment over the years has been painstaking and purposeful. All areas of this well-maintained building are meticulously clean, the decor cottagey and entirely appropriate to the style of the building and area; indeed, the Pheasant wears its comfortable look well. Polished wood tables and chairs add to the country look of the low-ceilinged dining room. The menu delivers sound, traditional country cooking, with the most popular dish being roasted Northumberland lamb with a rosemary and redcurrant jus. Lamb, beef and game come from a local butcher and fresh fish is from North Shields. Typically, start with roast tomato and red pepper soup, move on to sirloin steak with peppercorn sauce, or monkfish in herb butter, and round off with sticky toffee pudding or a plate of Northumberland farmhouse cheeses. There are homemade bar meals and super Sunday roasts. Eight bedrooms provide an excellent standard of accommodation. All the light, prettily decorated rooms have good en suite bathrooms. See Pub Walk on page 298.

Rooms: 8. Double/twin from £65, single from £35 and family from £75.
Prices: Evening main course from £9.25, lunch main course from £6.75. House wine £9.95.
Last orders: Bar: lunch 15.00; dinner 23.00. Food: lunch 15.00; dinner 21.00
Closed: Monday and Tuesdays, November to March.
Food: Traditional Pub Food.
Real Ale: Black Sheep Best, Timothy Taylor Landlord, Greene King Old Speckled Hen.
Other points: No-smoking area. Dogs welcome. Garden. Children welcome. Car park.
Directions: Follow signs to Kielder Water from B6320 at Bellingham, 17 miles north of Hexham. (Map 7, B4)

Longframlington

The Anglers Arms

Weldon Bridge, Longframlington, Morpeth,
Northumberland NE65 8AX
Telephone: +44(0)870 4016135
+44(0)1665 570271
johnyoung@anglersarms.fsnet.co.uk
www.anglersarms.com

A grand 18th-century coaching inn set beside an old stone bridge over the River Coquet. With a mile of private fishing, wonderful walking in the Cheviot Hills, and Northumberland's famous coast and castles just a short drive away, the Anglers provides the perfect base from which to explore this unspoilt area. Traditionally furnished bar and lounges are spacious and immaculately maintained, with warming log fires, plenty of wood panelling, fine old pictures and polished ornaments setting the appealing scene for supping pints of Bass and enjoying some popular bar food. Food is well sourced from quality suppliers, with local butcher meats and fish from the North Sea coast. From the traditional bar menu, start with pork and chicken liver paté with cumberland sauce, or tomato and feta salad, move on to grilled local trout, Border lamb cutlets on root mash with mint and rosemary sauce, or homemade steak and ale pie. More formal dining is in a refurbished Pullman railway carriage, where you can sample smoked breast of guinea fowl with pesto sauce. En suite rooms have brass or pine beds and peaceful rural views.

Rooms: 5. Double room from £60, single from £40, family from £90.
Prices: Restaurant main course from £14.95. Bar main course from £7.95. House wine £12.50.
Last orders: Bar: lunch 14.00 (Sunday 14.30); dinner 21.30 (Sunday 21.00). Food: lunch 14.30; dinner 21.30.
Closed: Rarely.
Food: Traditional British.
Real Ale: 3 guest beers available.
Other points: No-smoking area. Dogs welcome overnight. Children welcome. Garden. Car park. Licenced for Civil Weddings. Wheelchair access.
Directions: From A1 take A697 to Wooler & Coldstream, carry on to Weldon Bridge. (Map 8, A5)

Colston Bassett

Martins Arms Inn

School Lane, Colston Bassett, Nottingham,
Nottinghamshire NG12 3FD
Telephone: +44(0)870 4016136
+44(0)1949 81361

Built as a farmhouse in 1700 and formerly the Squire's residence on the Colston Bassett Estate, it was turned into an alehouse by the Martin family in 1844. Lynne Bryan and Salvatore Inguanta bought the pub in 1990 and transformed it into a very classy hostelry, furnishing the place with good taste. It exudes a quiet country-house atmosphere, with long curtains at the windows, cushions on upholstered chairs, a profusion of flowers, hunting prints on walls, and a splendid Tudor fireplace which came from the Hall. The bar itself almost seems an intrusion; however, you will find some top-notch real ale and impeccable wines from Lay & Wheeler. Good bar food includes speciality lunchtime sandwiches, ploughman's lunches featuring Colston Bassett Stilton, of course, and interesting light meals or starters like leek and cheese soufflé or smoked salmon and scrambled egg. Imaginative main dishes, served in both the bar and the smart, antique furnished dining room, range from spaghetti with garlic, clams, chilli and rocket to Tuscan-style lambs' liver with watercress mash, and seasonal game from nearby Park Farm Estate. Round off with an excellent homemade pudding or a plate of local cheeses. Lovely summer garden. See Pub Walk on page 300.

Prices: Set lunch £15-18 and dinner £25. Restaurant main course from £13.95. Bar main course from £9.50. House wine £12.75.
Last orders: Bar: lunch 15.00; dinner 23.00. Food: lunch 14.00 (Sunday 14.30); dinner 22.00 (Sunday 21.00).
Closed: Rarely.
Food: Modern British.
Real Ale: Bass, Black Sheep, Timothy Taylor Landlord, Greene King IPA & Old Speckled Hen, Batemans XB Bitter, Brakspear, Guest beers.
Other points: No-smoking area. Children welcome. Garden. Car park. Antique shop.
Directions: Off A46 east of Nottingham. (Map 8, G6)

Elkesley

The Robin Hood Inn

High Street, Elkesley, Retford,
Nottinghamshire DN22 8AJ
Telephone: +44(0)870 4016137
+44(0)1777 838259
robinhood1@clara.net
www.robin-hood-inn.co.uk

Keep going past the Little Chef (it's well worth those extra few miles) and take the Elkesley turning off the A1 to find this unassuming village local just yards from the busy dual carriageway. Pull into the car park and settle in the homely and comfortable lounge bar, or in the tiny dining room. Alan Draper has been offering weary travellers sustenance in the form of well-presented favourites like filled baguettes, ploughman's lunches, decent ham, egg and chips, and freshly-battered haddock and chips. Those intent on lingering longer should look to the main menu and the specials board for more ambitious alternatives, perhaps starters of salmon fishcake with steamed spinach and lemon butter sauce, or grilled scallops with artichokes, chorizo and aged balsamic. Follow with beef bourguignonne, pork sausages on creamy mash with caramelised onions, or pan-fried fillet steak with red wine sauce. Sweet-toothed diners can round off with caramelised lemon tart with pistachio ice cream or syrup sponge and custard. The varied and excellent-value midweek menu could entice you to go for four courses. Accompany with a pint of Pedigree or one of six wines available by the glass.

Prices: Set lunch and dinner from £13. Main course from £10. House wine £10.
Last orders: Bar: lunch 14.30 (15.00); dinner 23.00.
Food: lunch 14.00; dinner 21.00.
No food Sunday evening.
Closed: Rarely.
Food: Modern British.
Real Ale: Marston's Pedigree, Flowers IPA, Boddingtons.
Other points: No-smoking area. Children welcome.
Dogs welcome in the bar. Garden. Car park.
Directions: Two and a half miles south of Worksop, just off the A1. (Map 8, F6)

Tuxford

Mussel and Crab

Sibthorpe Hill, Tuxford, Newark,
Nottinghamshire NG22 0PJ
Telephone: +44(0)870 4016138
+44(0)1777 870491
musselandcrab1@hotmail.com
www.musselandcrab.com

Pubs and restaurants in land-locked Nottinghamshire are not renowned for offering great seafood, but this busy, energetic country pub, just a short drive from the A1, is clearly bucking the trend. Bruce Elliot-Bateman and chef Philip Wright firmly set out their stall when they aim to provide the freshest fish, whether native or exotic, with much of it delivered daily from Brixham. Choose from starters of crab bisque, oysters with chilli relish, or butterflied sardines dusted with Parmesan and deep fried. Main courses might be escolar cooked in foil with tomatoes, soy, coriander, white wine, lemon, leeks and ginger, or baked sea bass with roasted Mediterranean vegetables. Meat-eaters will not be disappointed with the huge mixed grill or game from local shoots. The stylishly refurbished interior offers various eating areas, a couple of bars with welcoming log fires, a mass of specials blackboards, and has all the wine list out on display. Then there are two distinct restaurant areas, one offering the period surroundings of a traditional oak beamed dining room; the other sheer vibrant Mediterranean, with terracotta and ochre hues. Gents - note the live goldfish in the plastic cistern above the urinals in the 'buoys' room.

Prices: Main course from £11. House wine £10.25.
Last orders: Bar: lunch 14.30 (Sunday 14.45); dinner 22.00 (Sunday 21.30). Food: lunch 14.30 (Sunday 14.45); dinner 22.00 (Sunday 21.00).
Closed: Rarely.
Food: Modern British.
Real Ale: Tetley's Cask.
Other points: No-smoking area. Dogs welcome in the bar. Garden. Car park.
Directions: From junction A57/A1 (Markham Moor), take the B1164 to Ollerton/Tuxford; the pub is 800 yards on the right. (Map 8, G7)

Bledington

The Kings Head Inn

The Green, Bledington, Kingham, Oxfordshire OX7 6XQ
Telephone: +44(0)870 4016139
+44(0)1608 658365
kingshead@orr-ewing.com
www.kingsheadinn.net

Oxford

A more delightful spot would surely be hard to find: facing the village green with its brook and border-patrolling ducks, this is surely the quintessential Cotswold pub. Dating back to the 15th-century, it stands smack on the Gloucestershire border in an immaculate stone village. Inside, the original bar is charming, full of low beams, ancient settles and flagstone floors, and a huge log fire burns in the inglenook, while the separate dining area is an informal setting for some imaginative pub food. Archie and Nicola Orr-Ewing are passionate about fresh local produce, notably free-range and organic ingredients, and, along with the fish delivered direct from Cornwall, all feature on the ever-changing menus. Modern influences on traditional English dishes can be seen in such starter choices as home-potted shrimps. Main courses include pork fillet with braised fennel, sweet potato mash and mustard cream sauce. Good homemade puddings run to lemon mousse with raspberry coulis, or regional cheeses. Lighter lunchtime choices are listed on the blackboard. There are tip-top Hook Norton and unusual guest ales on handpump and an interesting guest wine list that offers six by the glass. High standard, en suite bedrooms are split between the main building and the converted barn across the courtyard. All have been beautifully refurbished with modern facilities.

Must See
- Stow-on-the-Wold: Handsome market town.
- Chastleton House
- Rollright Stones, Little Rollright: Dramatic Bronze Age stone circle.
- Batsford Arboretum, Moreton-in-Marsh: Private collection of over 1000 rare species of trees spread over 50 acres. Also home to the Cotswold Falconry Centre: flying demonstrations.
- Bourton-on-the-Water: Touristy Cotswold village.

Rooms: 12. Double room from £70.
Prices: Set lunch from £15 and dinner from £20. Main course from £8.95. House wine £10.95.
Last orders: Bar: lunch 15.00; dinner 23.00. Food: lunch 14.00; dinner 21.30 (Sunday 21.00).
Closed: Rarely.
Food: Traditional/Modern British.
Real Ale: Hook Norton Best Bitter, Bass. 2 guest beers.
Other points: No-smoking area. Children welcome. Dogs welcome in the bar. Garden. Car park.
Directions: On the B4450 between Chipping Norton and Stow-on-the-Wold. (Map 5, D3)

Cotswolds

Tourist Information
Stow-on-the-Wold +44(0)1451 870083
Where to Shop
Stow-on-the-Wold, Burford, Cheltenham, Oxford
Farmers Market
Stow-on-the-Wold (2nd Thursday of month)
Classic Cotswold Villages
Take time to visit: Lower and Upper Slaughter;

Adlestrop; The Wychwoods; The Rissingtons; Cornwell. Head further afield to explore the charming small towns of Burford, Chipping Campden and Charlbury.
Events & Festivals
Gypsy Horse Fair, Stow-on-the-Wold (May)
Cornbury Music Festival, Charlbury (July)
Moreton Agricultural Show, Moreton-in-Marsh (Sep)

A M Bailey, Evesham,
Vegetables

Evesham

Cotswold Apple Juice

at the Kings Head Inn

One would expect to sup nothing but pure English nectar at the Kings Head in Bledington, a quintessential Cotswold pub complete with village green and ducks, and you will not be disappointed – on tap is the excellent Hook Norton Best Bitter, in the wine cellar are fine bottles from Haynes, Hanson & Clarke in Stow-on-the-Wold and, for a summer's day they serve Bensons pure English apple juice. Started in March 1999, Bensons is based in the heart of the Cotswolds. Rather like single grape variety wine they produce single variety apple juice; the traditional Cox with a sweet, full flavour, Bramley, one of their driest juices and an award winner ('Brammy Award' for the best Bramley Apple Juice in the year 2000) and supreme Jonagold with a flavour that lies between the two. They have also recently branched into some more adventurous concoctions, perhaps apple and raspberry or elderflower for the summer or rhubarb and cinnamon warmed up in the winter. You can find them at Farmer's Markets and, of course, at the Kings Head.

A40

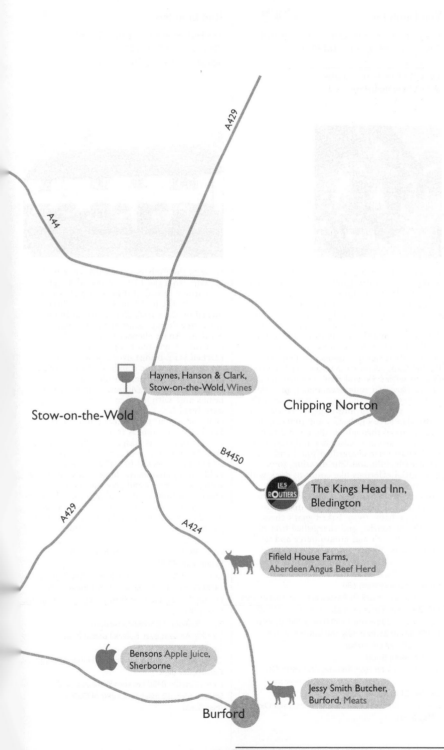

A429

A44

Haynes, Hanson & Clark,
Stow-on-the-Wold, Wines

Chipping Norton

Stow-on-the-Wold

B4450

A429

A424

LES
ROUTIERS

The Kings Head Inn,
Bledington

Fifield House Farms,
Aberdeen Angus Beef Herd

Bensons Apple Juice,
Sherborne

Jessy Smith Butcher,
Burford, Meats

Burford

Burford

The Lamb Inn

Sheep Street, Burford, Oxfordshire OX18 4LR
Telephone: +44(0)870 4016140
+44 (0)1993 823155
info@lambinn-burford.co.uk
www.lambinn-burford.co.uk

It's difficult to exaggerate the mellow charm of the 14th-century Lamb Inn, tucked down a quiet side street in this most attractive Cotswolds town. The golden stone façade is entwined with honeysuckle and roses, while within centuries of history are etched in the oak beams, mullioned windows, and antique settles that characterise the rustic bar and beautifully furnished lounges. Bruno and Rachel Cappuccini have refurbished the restaurant with style and flair, and upgrading of the fifteen en suite bedrooms is on-going. They vary in size and ooze cottagey appeal; all have antique furniture, pretty fabrics and many also have old beams and timbers. Bar meals, served throughout the ground floor, run from various sandwiches and starter or main course size chargrilled squid and rocket salad with chilli and lime dressing, to more substantial offerings like confit of duck with butternut squash and Swiss cheese mash. Cooking moves up a gear for dinner in the restaurant, the daily modern British menu listing, perhaps, twice-baked goat's cheese and thyme soufflé, and chargrilled beef fillet with spinach and potato purée and wild mushrooms. Wonderful walled garden.

Rooms: 15, Double/twin from £130.
Single occupancy from £80.
Prices: Set dinner £29.50. Restaurant main course from £10. Bar main course from £8. House wine £13.50.
Last orders: Food: lunch 14.30 (Friday and Saturday 15.00); dinner 21.30 (Friday and Saturday 22.00).
Closed: 28 - 29 December.
Food: Modern British.
Real Ale: Hook Norton, Adnams, Wadworth 6X.
Other points: No-smoking area. Dogs welcome. Garden. Children welcome.
Directions: Off A40 between Cheltenham and Oxford. (Map 5, E3)

Chalgrove

Red Lion Inn

115 High Street, Chalgrove, Oxford,
Oxfordshire OX44 7SS
Telephone: +44(0)870 4016141
+44 (0)1865 890625

Some of the timbers in this attractive building date from the 11th century, although the earliest record of it being a pub is 1637. Unusually, the Red Lion has always been owned by the parish church and once provided free dining facilities for the church wardens. Annie Shepherd has recently taken over this cream and red painted village inn, reached via a bridge over a small stream, and it is hoped that the standard of food remains good. The atmosphere inside is decidedly relaxed and unpretentious, from the bar and beams area with its open log fire and simple dark furnishings where locals gather for a chat and a pint, to the neat dining areas. Food currently ranges from traditional pub favourites such as lasagne and homemade pies, but the arrival of a new chef has also added daily specials like Thai crabcakes with mild chilli mayonnaise, honey roast duckling with a strawberry and green peppercorn sauce, and homemade puddings like blackcurrant crumble and ice cream. On sunny summer days you can sit in the front streamside garden or in the sheltered rear garden.

Prices: Restaurant main course from £6.95.
House wine £9.95.
Last orders: Bar: lunch 15.00; dinner 23.00. Food: lunch 14.00 (Sunday 14.30); dinner 21.00. Limited menu Monday, Tuesday. No food Sunday evening and May Day.
Closed: Rarely.
Food: Traditional British/International.
Real Ale: Adnams Best, Fuller's London Pride.
1 guest beer.
Other points: No-smoking area. Children welcome. Garden. Car park.
Directions: On B480 between Watlington and Stadhampton, 10 miles south east of Oxford. (Map 5, E3)

Charlbury

The Bull Inn

Sheep Street, Charlbury, Oxfordshire OX7 3RR
Telephone: +44(0)870 4016142
+44(0)1608 810689

Overlooking the main street of this handsome, small Cotswold town, the smartly refurbished and civilised Bull Inn dates from the 16th century and offers good old-fashioned hospitality and imaginative, freshly prepared food. Although under recent new ownership, the Bull remains a comfortable haven for Cotswolds weekenders, walkers enjoying the many footpaths that criss-cross the area (see Pub Walk page 302), and local diners. Behind the mellow stone exterior lies a most relaxing and tastefully furnished lounge and dining room. The equally welcoming bar area features wooden floors, heavy beams, and loyal locals quaffing pints of Hook Norton and Greene King ales. Visitors popping in for just a snack in the bar will find freshly made sandwiches, well cooked familiar pub dishes and a good range of daily specials on the chalkboard menu. At a recent inspection meal we enjoyed a rich chicken liver terrine, served with locally baked bread, and an excellent main course of beef fillet salad, followed by a plate of good farmhouse cheeses. Service was warm, attentive, friendly and efficient. To the side there is an attractive vine-covered terrace and, upstairs, three simple and immaculately clean en suite bedrooms.

Rooms: 4. Double room from £75-£85.
Prices: Set Sunday lunch £18.75. Restaurant main course from £10. House wine from £10.95.
Last orders: Bar: lunch 15.00 Sunday 16.00); dinner 23.00. Food: lunch 14.00 (15.00 Sunday); dinner 21.00 (Friday and Saturday 21.30)
Closed: Sunday evening, and during the day Monday.
Food: Modern British.
Real Ale: Hook Norton Best Bitter, Greene King Abbot Ale, Greene King IPA.
Other points: No-smoking area. Garden. Car park.
Directions: Village signposted off A40 along B4437 two miles north of Woodstock. (Map 5, D3)

Chipping Norton

The Chequers

Goddards Lane, Chipping Norton,
Oxfordshire OX7 5NP
Telephone: +44(0)870 4016143
+44(0)1608 644717
enquiries@chequers-pub.co.uk
www.chequers-pub.co.uk

The 16th-century Chequers has a strongly traditional look, with low ceilings, open fires and rugs on flagstone floors giving a very cosy feel, and the location, in the middle of a bustling market town, certainly draws some appreciative customers. Fuller's ales perfectly kept by landlord John Reid and food freshly prepared by wife and former home economics teacher Kay add to the appeal of this bustling pub-restaurant. The restaurant was originally an open courtyard, but it has been glassed over and is now conservatory-style with a high sloping glass roof. Here you will find a popular menu that utilses fresh produce from select local suppliers. Start with leek parcels filled with smoked cheddar, mushrooms and onion and served with a sweet balsamic dressing, or Thai fishcakes with sweet and sour dipping sauce. Continue with roast half shoulder of lamb with mint gravy, pork and leek sausages with mash and onion gravy, or roasted vegetable lasagne with mixed salad. Blackboard specials and lunchtime sandwiches, ploughman's and salads extend the choice. Accompany a good meal with a pint of Pride or one of 16 wines available by the glass.

Prices: Restaurant main course from £8.50. Bar main course from £5. House wine £9.50.
Last orders: Bar: 23.00. Food: 14.30 (Sunday 17.00); dinner 21.30.
Closed: Rarely.
Food: Modern British.
Real Ale: Fuller's London Pride, Fuller's Chiswick, Fuller's ESB. 1 guest beer.
Other points: No-smoking in the restaurant.
Directions: On the A44 between Oxford and Evesham and Oxford and Stratford. (Map 5, D3)

Christmas Common

The Fox and Hounds

Christmas Common, Watlington,
Oxfordshire OX49 5HL
Telephone: +44(0)870 4016144
+44(0)1491 612599

New owners took over this 15th-century
brick-and-flint cottage as we went to press
and it is hoped the high standards of food
will be maintained by Candice and Tess. It
was carefully transformed from a classic rural
ale house to a modern-day food pub back in
2001, without losing the original charm and
character. Much loved by Chilterns walkers
and cyclists, the timeless main bar retains its
red and black tiled floor, simple wooden wall
benches, and a blazing winter log fire in the
massive inglenook fireplace. Also, in time-
honoured fashion, Brakspear ales are drawn
direct from the cask. Beyond is the new, barn-
like dining room, replete with wooden floors,
high rafters, an eclectic mix of furnishings,
and french doors leading to the garden. Food
and drink has favoured the organic approach
with game from Stonor Park, farm-reared
meats, unusual cheeses, and organic ciders,
ales and wines. Lunch in the bar may include
doorstep sandwiches, Welsh rarebit, and roast
ham ploughman's with homemade pickles.
Served from an open-to-view kitchen, food in
the dining room is more imaginative. Expect,
perhaps, rib-eye steak with red wine sauce
and sticky toffee pudding.

Prices: Main course from £13. Bar meal from £7.
House wine from £12.
Last orders: Bar: lunch 15.00; dinner 23.00
(all day Saturday and Sunday).
Food: lunch 14.30 (Sunday 15.00); dinner 21.30.
Closed: Rarely.
Food: Modern British.
Real Ale: Brakspear Ales.
Other points: No-smoking in the restaurant. Garden.
Car park.
Directions: Exit 5/M40. Take the A40 in the direction
of Lewknor. Then follow signs to Christmas Common,
approximately three miles. (Map 5, E4)

Crays Pond

White Lion

Goring Road, Goring Heath, Crays Pond,
Oxfordshire RG8 7SH
Telephone: +44(0)870 4016145
+44(0)1491 680471
reservation@innastew.com
www.innastew.com

There's a real buzz locally about Stuart and
Caroline Pierrepont's gastropub in sleepy
Crays Pond. Business has been brisk ever
since they re-opened the doors following
refurbishment of this 300-year-old building
back in autumn 2002. Although there may
be an emphasis on dining at this now stylish
pub-restaurant, there's still a laid-back feel to
the homely, simply furnished bar where locals
congregate to quaff top-notch Greene King
ales. It is open all day (from 8.30am) for
breakfast, morning coffee, lunch and afternoon teas and is a great place to relax with
the daily papers. However, the serious action
takes place in the dining room and plant-
filled conservatory. Rug-strewn wood floors,
deep terracotta walls lined with unusual
prints, and simple furnishings set the scene
for the daily-changing menu with its emphasis on fish. The kitchen successfully combines
traditional favourites with modern ideas, say,
seared scallops with black pudding, celeriac
mash and pancetta, or chicken liver pâté
with onion marmalade. Follow, perhaps, with
suckling pig with roast pumpkin and apple
mash. Round off with chocolate and hazelnut
brownie.

Prices: Set lunch £18 and dinner £25. Restaurant
main course from £7.50. Bar main course from £4.95.
House wine £11.95.
Last orders: Bar: 23.00. Food: lunch 14.30 (Sunday
15.00); dinner 21.30. No food Sunday evening.
Closed: Monday.
Food: Modern British.
Real Ale: Greene King IPA, Greene King Abbot Ale.
Other points: No-smoking area. Dogs welcome in the
bar. Garden. Children welcome. Car park.
Directions: From Pangbourne cross toll bridge to
Whitchurch; pub in 2 miles. (Map 5, E3)

Crowell

The Shepherd's Crook

The Green, Crowell, Chinnor,
Oxfordshire OX39 4RR
Telephone: +44(0)870 4016146
+44(0)1844 351431
scrook@supanet.com

Daily deliveries of fresh fish are the highlight of the ever-changing blackboard menus at this honest, rural local by the village green, beneath the wooded escarpment of the Chiltern Hills. In fact, landlord Steven Scowen is passionate about the quality of the food he offers, sourcing meat and game from local farms and butchers, and using homegrown herbs and vegetables to accompany his wife's freshly-cooked dishes. Dine in the refurbished bar, with its tasteful mix of stripped brick, flagstones, oak beams and open fire, or at oak tables in the raftered dining room. Expect black pudding topped with pancetta, cheese ploughman's with homemade pickles and thick-cut sandwiches (salt beef, bacon and avocado) at lunchtime. The menu extends to king prawns with garlic and chilli, Oxford sausages with mustard mash and onion gravy, and steak and kidney pie in the evening. Suitable fishy options may be Cromer crab salad, and wild sea bass fillet with spring onion, ginger and garlic. Also of note are the well-kept handpumped ales (Steven's other passion), namely Bathams Best, Hook Norton Best, Timothy Taylor Landlord and guest brews, and an unusual list of wines that includes French wine from a private vineyard.

Prices: Main course restaurant from £10.
Main course bar from £5. House wine £11.95.
Last orders: Bar: lunch 15.00; dinner 23.00 (all day during the weekend). Food: lunch 14.30; dinner 21.30 (Sunday 21.00).
Closed: Rarely.
Food: Modern British/seafood.
Real Ale: Hook Norton, Taylor's Landlord, Enville Ale.
Other points: No-smoking area. Children welcome. Garden. Car park.
Directions: On the B4009 between Chinnor and Junction 6/M40 (Map 5, E4)

Faringdon

The Snooty Fox Inn

Littleworth, Faringdon, Oxfordshire SN7 8PW
Telephone: +44(0)870 4016147
+44(0)1367 240549

Initially, you walk into a large, mainly open-plan room with plenty of space, a few private dining areas with lots of oak beams, and wooden tiled flooring to the rear. Walking further into the pub, you come across the modern looking bar, a huge wine rack beside it, and lots of comfy sofas opposite. Here, Greene King IPA, Adnams and two guest ales are dispensed. The main part of the restaurant is more open, has real wood flooring and a big brick fireplace with an open fire (blazing in cooler months), while overhead the ceiling gets higher, exposing lots more timber beams. Chalkboards offer a wide-ranging list of reasonably priced wines, and seasonal menus may deliver starters of scallops and king prawns cooked in garlic butter with creamy cabbage and smoked bacon or smoked duck salad for starters. For a main dish, try Matt's half shoulder of lamb with honey and rosemary gravy, sirloin steak with mushroom and garlic sauce, pasta carbonara, and one of four Thai curries. Sandwiches, filled baguettes and a popular 'light eating' section of, say, home-cooked ham, egg and chips, or chicken and spring onion kedgeree are also available.

Prices: Restaurant main course from £9.95.
Bar snack from £7.95. House wine £11.
Last orders: Bar: lunch 15.00; dinner 23.00 (Open all day during the summer). Food: lunch 14.30; dinner 21.30 (Friday and Saturday 22.00).
Closed: Rarely.
Food: Modern Brasserie Food.
Real Ale: Greene King IPA, Adnams. 2 guest beers.
Other points: No-smoking area. Dogs welcome. Garden. Children welcome. Car park.
Directions: Exit 16/M4. On A420 Swindon to Oxford road, two miles east of Faringdon. (Map 5, E3)

REFRESHMENTS

NEXT DEPARTU
FROM THIS PLATF

GOATHLAND
NEWTON DALE
LEVISHAM
PICKERING

Henley-on-Thames

The Greyhound

Gallowstree Road, Rotherfield Peppard,
Henley-on-Thames, Oxfordshire RG9 5HT
Telephone: +44(0)870 4016148
+44(0)1189 722227

Looking every part the quintessential country pub, the picture-postcard black and white timbered Greyhound stands back from the road in the charmingly named village of Rotherfield Peppard. Its ancient brick and timber façade and wonky tiled roof is fronted by a glorious summer garden with colourful borders and tubs, and smart teak tables and cotton parasols. Step inside and you won't be disappointed with the woodblock floor, the crackling log fire in the brick fireplace and the inviting deep sofas in the classic beamed bar. Up a few steps and located in a converted pitch-roofed old barn is the main dining area, replete with rug-strewn wooden floors, hop-strewn rafters, and a real eclectic mix of furnishings. New owner Steve Wicks took over in early 2004 and has maintained the pub's reputation for quality pub food. Lunch in the bar could take in decent soup and sandwiches, bowls of fresh pasta and soundly cooked traditional pub dishes. 'Dinner at the Greyhound' is a tad more elaborate, a typical meal commencing with seared peppered tuna with wilted spinach and a honey and mustard dressing, followed by fillet steak on celeriac and spinach with a red wine and wild mushroom sauce.

Prices: Restaurant main course from £10.95. Bar main course from £9.50. House wine £13.50.
Last orders: Bar: 23.30. Food: lunch 14.30 Sunday 16.00); dinner 21.30.
Closed: Rarely.
Food: Modern British.
Real Ale: Greene King Old Speckled Hen, Fuller's London Pride. 1 guest beer.
Other points: No-smoking area. Dogs welcome. Garden. Children welcome. Car park.
Directions: On B481 between Reading and Nettlebed, just north of Sonning Common. Exit11/M4. (Map 5, E4)

South Stoke

The Perch & Pike Inn

South Stoke, Goring, Oxfordshire RG8 0JS
Telephone: +44(0)870 4016149
+44(0)1491 872415
edwinjtpope@aol.com
www.perchandpike.com

Tucked away in the peaceful Thames Valley village of South Stoke, just a short stroll from the river, is the charming Perch & Pike, a brick-and-flint pub that has been carefully refurbished and extended in recent years. However, the pub has improved markedly since the arrival of Edwin Pope and chef-partner Tim Sykes two years ago, their style and enthusiasm creating the perfect country retreat deep in rural Oxfordshire. Inside, the spick-and-span bar, complete with low-beamed ceilings, red tiled and brick floors and open fires, offers a cosy, traditional atmosphere in which to quaff a pint of Brakspear ale. In contrast, the ambience and decor in the restaurant in the manificent barn conversion is up-to-the-minute, with modern artwork on the walls and stylish furnishings on a light wood floor. Imaginative, monthly-changing dinner menus utilise fresh local produce. Typically, begin with chicken liver parfait with homemade chutney, then follow with game casserole or calves' liver and bacon with red wine and Dijon mustard mash, and finish with locally made ice creams, or pear and red wine tart. Expect equally enticing lighter lunches. Four chic, individually designed en suite bedrooms. See Pub Walk on page 304.

Rooms: 4. Double/twin room from £55.
Prices: Set lunch £15 and dinner £25. Restaurant main course from £12.95. Bar main course from £7.50. House wine £10.
Last orders: Bar: lunch 15.00 (Sunday 17.00); dinner 12.00. Food: lunch 14.30 (Sunday 15.00); dinner 21.30. No food Monday evening.
Closed: Sunday evening.
Food: Modern British.
Real Ale: Brakspear Ales.
Other points: No-smoking area. Dogs welcome. Garden. Children welcome. Car park.
Directions: North of Goring off B4009. (Map 5, E4)

Stoke Row

The Crooked Billet

Newlands Lane, Stoke Row, Henley-on-Thames,
Oxfordshire RG9 5PU
Telephone: +44(0)870 4016150
+44(0)1491 681048
www.thecrookedbillet.co.uk

Tucked away down a leafy country lane, Paul
Clerehugh's well-hidden little gem is a typically quaint village local that has upgraded
itself to pub-restaurant status, and is well
worth uncovering, so do ask for directions
when making that very essential booking. It
has the feel of a great winter pub, with small
intimate rooms with low, heavy-beamed ceilings, part quarry-tiled and woodblock floors,
rustic furnishings, and the roar of burning
logs in the inglenook fireplace. There has
never been a bar in the place (it was built in
1642), and pints of Brakspear are brought
up from the cellar. The lengthy, cosmopolitan
and adventurous weekly-changing menu has
plenty of interest and the food is unpretentious with a rustic, homely quality that
doesn't lose sight of its surroundings. From
the carte or the set lunch of two or three
courses choose, perhaps, potted foie gras and
chicken liver mousse with onion marmalade
or fresh tomato soup with rocket pesto, followed by roast hake with scallops, clams and
mussels, or excellent game dishes in winter.
There could be an exemplary summer pudding, with summer berry coulis, fresh strawberries and clotted cream. An enthusiastic
wine list roams the wine growing regions
of the world. Quailty live jazz adds to the
atmosphere.

Prices: Set lunch £14.95. House wine £12.
Last orders: Food: lunch 14.30; dinner 22.00.
Closed: Rarely.
Food: Modern British.
Real Ale: Brakspear Ales.
Other points: Garden. Car park.
Directions: Exit 8/9/M4 and follow signs for Henley,
then A4130 to Nettlebed. Turn left and follow signs to
Stoke Row. (Map 5, E4)

Witney

The Fleece

11 Church Green, Witney,
Oxfordshire OX28 4AZ
Telephone: +44(0)870 4016151
+44(0)1993 892270
fleece@peachpubs.com
www.peachpubs.com

Summer 2003 was a frantic time for Lee Cash
and Victoria Moon and their fledgling Peach
Pub Company. Within a crazy few months
their thriving little empire grew from one
pub (Rose and Crown, Warwick) to three,
taking in the One Elm in Stratford and this
stylish 10-bedroomed inn overlooking the
church green in upmarket Witney. Late summer refurbishment to the bar and dining
areas has seen the successful Peach Pub formula replicated here. The trademark leather
sofas around low tables, individual mirrors
and modern artwork on warm, earthy coloured walls, a laid-back atmosphere, and a
Continental-style opening time of 8.30am for
coffee and breakfast sandwiches has found
favour among Witney residents. Equally
popular is the all-day sandwich, salad and
deli-board menu, the latter offering starters
or nibbles with drinks of charcuterie, cheese,
fish and unusual antipasti. Modern main
menu dishes range from spicy smoked chicken
tagliatelle, to whole sea bass with sun-dried
tomato, artichoke and crushed potatoes, and
confit pork belly with creamed horseradish
and cabbage. Upgrading of the already stylish
en suite bedrooms during 2004 will see the
current decor and furnishings replaced with
warm, vibrant colours, funky/chic mirrors,
fabrics and furnishings.

Rooms: 10 Double/twin from £75, single from £65 and
family from £85.
Prices: Restaurant main course from £7.50. Bar main
course from £1.35. House wine £10.50.
Last orders: Bar: 23.00.
Closed: Rarely
Food: Modern European.
Real Ale: Greene King IPA, Old Speckled Hen,
Morland Original Ale.
Other points: Dogs welcome. Garden. Children
welcome. Car park.
Directions: In town centre by the Green. (Map 5, E3)

English 'Champagne'

at the Crooked Billet

Brookleas Fish Farm,
Wantage, Freshwater crayfish

Boze Down is now one of a few hundred vineyards in England and is one of even less producing world class wine. Situated on the sheltered southern slopes of the Chiltern Hills the soils in this chalk and flint area provide excellent drainage and encourage the vines to root deep into the chalk and bring up the nutrients needed to make memorable wine. The vineyard covers five acres and grows six varieties of white grape and four reds, this allows Boze Down to produce a wide range of complex wines. Against all the English elements and various hungry animals Boze Down takes great care to produce the best possible fruit and only to harvest it when the full flavour has developed. The care towards the final product extends to there being no herbicides and the vineyard being fertilised organically by sheep who graze there during the winter. They are particularly proud of their bottle fermented sparkling wine. Equally, they supply to just as enthusiastic publicans and restaurateurs such as the Crooked Billet in nearby Stoke Row where you can sample a glass of their English 'Champagne' with some home cured gravadlax salmon, a 1/2 dozen oysters or a grilled individual goat's cheese with artichoke hearts from Rowan Tree Goat Farm in nearby Leyhill.

A34

Doves Farm, Hungerfor
Spelt flo

Newbury

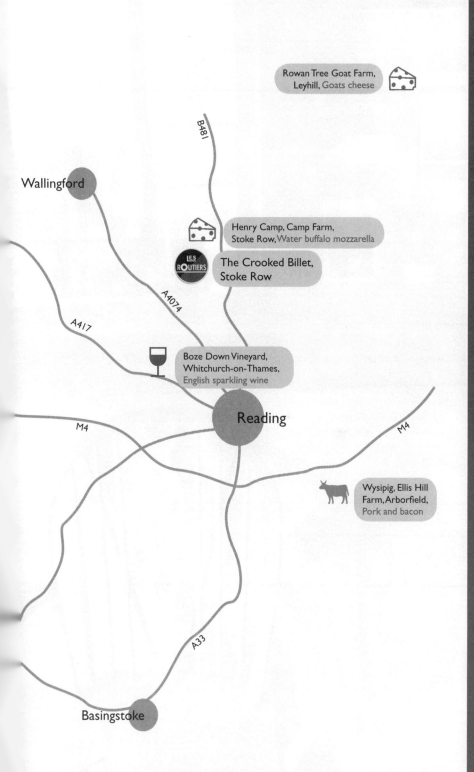

Rowan Tree Goat Farm, Leyhill, Goats cheese

B481

Wallingford

Henry Camp, Camp Farm, Stoke Row, Water buffalo mozzarella

LES ROUTIERS

The Crooked Billet, Stoke Row

A4074

A417

Boze Down Vineyard, Whitchurch-on-Thames, English sparkling wine

M4

Reading

M4

Wysipig, Ellis Hill Farm, Arborfield, Pork and bacon

A33

Basingstoke

ADMIRAL LORD NELSON
&
HIS HOMELAND

Cecil J. Isaacson

Hero's Country

The Lord Nelson, Burnham Thorpe, Norfolk

Clipsham

Olive Branch

Main Street, Clipsham, Oakham,
Rutland LE15 7SH
Telephone: +44(0)870 4016152
+44(0)1780 410355
info@theolivebranchpub.com
www.theolivebranchpub.com

Whilst retaining all of its pub qualities - space for just having a drink, a casual relaxed style which takes in both decor and service - Sean Hope, Ben Jones and Marcus Welford are to be congratulated for putting flesh on a brilliant gastropub vision, and for pulling in industry gongs for superlative pub food. With vaguely open-plan rooms within, styled in a pleasing eclectic manner, a pleasant sheltered paved area with tables and chairs without, this unpretentious old stone pub is a boon for travellers on the A1. Wine is obviously a passion, with blackboards detailing house specials, classics and up and coming producers from around the globe. Chalkboards list lunchtime sandwiches and the very good value set lunch. Otherwise, grab a menu and a table anywhere in the pub. Success at the Olive Branch is down to a philosophy of offering good quality innovative and traditional food using first-class local produce. There could be sweet pepper and chorizo soup, or potted shrimps with toasted Rearsby bread to start. Then chargrilled halibut with champ mash and crispy pancetta, or roast partridge with game chips and honey-roast vegetables, with chocolate roulade and Chantilly ice cream to finish. New for 2004 are a pub shop and wholesale wines.

Prices: Set lunch £15. Restaurant main course from £8.95. Bar main course from £6.75.
House wine £11.50.
Last orders: Bar: lunch 15.00 (Saturday and Sunday open all day); dinner 24.00. Food: lunch 14.00 (Sunday 15.00); dinner 21.30 (Sunday 21.00).
Closed: Rarely.
Food: Modern pub food.
Real Ale: Grainstore Olive Oil. 2 guest beers.
Other points: No-smoking area. Children welcome. Garden. Car park.
Directions: Off the A1 north of Stamford. (Map 5, B4)

Uppingham

The Old White Hart Inn

51 Main Street, Lyddington, Rutland LE15 9LR
Telephone: +44(0)870 4016153
+44(0)1572 821703

Truly a traditional local, this honey-coloured 17th-century stone pub stands by the village green with its pretty cottages and backdrop of the picturesque Welland Valley. Popular in summer for its charming walled garden and twelve floodlit pétanque pitches. Good bar food and more elaborate restaurant dishes are available within the traditionally furnished bar and dining areas. At lunchtime, relax in the cosy beamed bar with its splendid log fire and order, perhaps, mussels in white wine and garlic or, deep-fried Grimsby haddock from the specials board. There is a good range of lighter dishes, including toasted panninis. The seasonally changing evening menu may list duck liver parfait with tomato chutney, and pheasant with thyme jus, with daily fresh fish specials listed on the blackboard. Stuart East sources quality produce locally, in addition to shooting his own game, and making his own sausages. Five welcoming and well-appointed bedrooms are individually decorated to a high standard, one has an open fireplace and a huge bathroom with jacuzzi and separate large shower. Plans include three more en suite rooms. See Pub Walk on page 306.

Rooms: 5. Double room from £80, single from £55. Jacuzzi double room £85.
Prices: Set lunch and dinner £12.95 and £9.95 (2 course) - order before 19.30 available Monday-Friday. Main course from £9.95. House wine £11.
Last orders: Bar: lunch 14.00; dinner 23.00. Food: lunch 14.00 (Sunday 14.30); dinner 21.00.
Closed: Rarely.
Food: Traditional British.
Real Ale: Greene King IPA, Greene King Abbot Ale, Timothy Taylor Landlord. 1 guest beer.
Other points: No-smoking area. Children welcome. Garden. Car park.
Directions: South of Uppingham off A6003. (Map 5, C4)

Telford

The Hundred House Hotel

Bridgnorth Road, Norton, Shifnal, Telford, Shropshire TF11 9EE
Telephone: +44(0)870 4016155
+44(0)1952 730353/0845 6446 100
hundredhouse@lineone.net
www.hundredhouse.co.uk

From the outside the Hundred House is an unassuming, red-brick Georgian inn. It is a very different story once you step over the threshold: quarry-tiled floors, exposed brickwork, huge fireplaces, beamed ceilings, and some fine oak panelling show signs of sympathetic restoration. The personality of the inn gains from the inimitable input from the Phillips family since 1986. Sylvia's influence shows in the décor, with herbs and dried flowers from the inn's wonderfully luxuriant gardens adorning beams and tables. This enthusiasm extends to the excellent food on offer. Stuart Phillips sources local produce and cooks both a brasserie-style and full restaurant menu, enhanced by daily specials. He gives a distinctly modern touch to such dishes as breast of Hereford duck with orange sauce, and monkfish, salmon and scallop casserole with lobster and tarragon bisque. Delicious homemade puddings may include raspberry brûlée. Lighter dishes of steak and kidney pie and local pork sausages with mash and onion gravy are also on offer. Still very much the village local, however, expect to find five real ales and a well-chosen list of wines. Both names and colour schemes in the ten enchanting en suite bedrooms reflect the garden, incorporating brass bedsteads with patchwork covers, and even padded swing seats suspended from the rafters. The newly refurbished barn is now a function room.

Rooms: 10. Double room from £99, single from £75, family from £125.
Prices: Main course restaurant from £10. Main course bar from £7.95. House wine £12.50.
Last orders: Bar: lunch 15.00; dinner 23.00. Food: lunch 14.30; dinner 22.00 (Sunday 21.00).
Closed: Rarely.
Food: Modern British.
Real Ale: Phillips Heritage Bitter, Phillips Heritage Mild, Batemans XB Bitter, Everards Tiger Best Bitter, Highgate & Walsall Saddlers Strong Ale. 1 guest beer.
Other points: No-smoking area. Children welcome. Garden. Car park.
Directions: Beside the A442 midway between Bridgnorth and Telford. Exit4/M54. (Map 5, C1)

Ironbridge

Must See
- Wightwick Manor: reflects the style and influence of William Morris and the Arts and Crafts Movement.
- Boscobel House: where Charles II hid from Parliamentary troops in 1651.
- Ironbridge: insight into the origins of the Industrial Revolution.
- Aerospace Museum, Cosford.
- Dudmaston: 17th-century house containing fine furniture and Dutch flower paintings.
- Severn Valley Railway: take a classic ride on a restored railway.

Bridgnorth

Tourist Information Bridgnorth +44(0)1746 763257
Where to Shop Bridgnorth, Ludlow, Much Wenlock Shrewsbury, Church Stretton.
Farmers Market
Bridgnorth (3rd Friday of month)
Nearest Racecourse Wolverhampton, Ludlow

Local activities
Fishing on the River Severn, canoeing, horse riding and pony trekking
Events and Festivals
Folk Music Festival, Bridgnorth (Aug)
Haydn Music Festival (June)

Exford

The Crown Hotel

Park Street, Exford, Somerset TA24 7PP
Telephone: +44(0)870 4016156
+44(0)1643 831554
info@crownhotelexmoor.co.uk
www.crownhotelexmoor.co.uk

Selworthy

Must See
- Dunster Castle
- Culbone Church, West Porlock
- Valley of the Rocks, Lynmouth
- Lorna Doone Country
- Lyn & Exmoor Museum, Lynton
- Arlington Court

Villages to Visit
Selworthy,
Malmsmead,
Winsford,
Luccombe, Dunster

Dunster Castle

Long a favourite among the huntin', shooting' and fishin' set, the 17th-century Crown stands by the green in a lovely village and offers country pursuit followers a touch of luxury in the heart of Exmoor. The old coaching inn has been imaginatively styled; on one side you enter a pretty country hotel, on the other, a simple rural bar with hunting and shooting memorabilia, tables fashioned from old barrels, good bar food and well kept ales such as Exmoor Fox and Gold. There are seventeen, very comfortable en suite bedrooms, all are furnished with quality pieces, and are very well equipped. And comfort and elegance extend throughout the cosy reception rooms. Although refurbishment and upgrading has been on-going since Hugo Jeane took over in early 2003, the character of the hotel is being retained studiously. Chef Robert Skuse, who used to cook at the Clarence Hotel in Exeter, is very produce minded and prepares such dishes as goat's cheese brûlée with beetroot tarte tatin, line-caught sea bass with lobster vierge, and duck breast with confit leg, braised white beans and five spice sauce on the fixed-price menu in the restaurant. Daily bar food is equally up-to-date, perhaps featuring salmon fishcakes with tomato fondue, pan-roasted cod with tomato and herb crust, and glazed lemon tart.

Rooms: 17, 1 not en suite. Rooms from £47.50.
Prices: Set dinner £29 (5 course). Restaurant main course from £15. Bar main course from £7. House wine £11.50.
Last orders: Bar: lunch 14.30; dinner 23.00.
Food: lunch 14.30 (Sunday 14.00); dinner 21.30.
Closed: Rarely.
Food: Modern and Traditional French.
Real Ale: Exmoor Ale, Exmoor Gold. 1 guest beer.
Other points: No-smoking area. Garden.
Children welcome. Car park.
Directions: On B3224 midway between and A396 at Wheddon Cross (Map 4, D5)

Tourist Information Minehead +44(0)1643 702624
Farmers Market Minehead (1st & 3rd Fri of month)
Local Activities
Horse riding, wildlife safaris (4x4), deer watching, fishing, shooting.
Top Five Views
Valley of the Rocks, Lynmouth, Porlock Hill, Dunkery Beacon, Hanging Cleeve (Simonsbath), Winsford Hill.

Where to Walk
Exhilarating coast path walks between Minehead and Lynmouth. Inland, follow the trails up Dunkery Beacon, enjoy beautiful valley walks along the River Barle near Simonsbath, and Tarr Steps. See Pub Walk on page 308.
Events & Festivals
Dunster Show (August), Lyn & Exmoor Festival (June), Exford Show (August)

Exford

Exmoor White Horse Inn

Exford, Exmoor National Park,
Somerset TA24 7PY
Telephone: +44(0)870 4016157
+44(0)1643 831229
linda@exmoorwhitehorse.demon.co.uk
www.devon-hotels.co.uk

Situated opposite the River Exe in the heart
of this small village in the Exmoor National
Park, the White Horse is a lovely creeper-
clad 16th-century coaching inn. Popular
among the walking fraternity and as a base
for exploring Exmoor, the inn offers good
value en suite accommodation in bedrooms
that reflect the character of the inn. All have
a soft cottagey look that takes in soft pastel
colours and floral fabrics. Downstairs in
the comfortable, beamed and carpeted bar
there are country-themed prints adorning
the walls, open log fires, Exmoor ale on tap,
and an extensive menu listing traditional
pub meals. Look out for the inn's specialities, namely venison, pheasant and partridge
from the surrounding moors, locally caught
lobster and daily deliveries of fresh fish, and
the platter of Somerset cheeses - all from
select local suppliers. There is also a Sunday
lunch carvery. Tarr Steps, Dunkery Beacon,
the picture-postcard villages of Dunster,
Selworthy and Porlock, and the dramatic
north Somerset/Devon coast are all within
easy reach.

Rooms: 28. Double/twin room from £80,
single from £40.

Prices: Set dinner £30 (3 courses). Main course from
£12. Bar snack menu from £6. House wine £9.50.

Last orders: Bar: 23.00. Food: lunch 14.30; dinner 21.30.

Closed: Never.

Food: Traditional British using local produce.

Real Ale: Exmoor Ale, Old Speckled Hen, Marston's
Pedigree, Exmoor Gold. 1 guest beer.

Other points: No smoking in the restaurant and food
bar. Children welcome. Dogs welcome overnight.
Garden. Car park.

Directions: On B3224 midway between Simonsbath
and Wheddon Cross (A396) south of Minehead.
(Map 4, D5)

Mells

The Talbot 15th Century Coaching Inn

High Street, Mells, Frome, Somerset BA11 3PN
Telephone: +44(0)870 4016158
+44(0)1373 812254
roger@talbotinn.com
www.talbotinn.com

At the heart of this timeless feudal village
with its splendid church, magnificent manor
house and unspoilt stone cottages is the
Talbot Inn, a rambling, 15th-century coaching inn with an attractive walled garden and
a warren of friendly bars. Visitors take a step
back in time as they enter the cobbled courtyard and pass through a massive oak double
doorway. Within, in the company of old
prints, hop vines and attendant memorabilia,
Roger Elliott and his experienced team provide an object lesson in what good inn-keep-
ing is all about. Seasonal menus are safely
traditional in content, everything from crab
soup and pasta bolognese, perhaps, to pheasant breast with bacon and mustard and tarragon sauce, and evening Brixham fish specials
that might include roast cod with parsley and
garlic crust and lemon chive sauce. Butcombe
bitter is served direct from the cask, and
quality house French and world-wide alternatives are served by the glass. Stone steps lead
to bedrooms whose facilities offer a taste of
old-style country living with a host of modern appointments and brightly lit, practical
bathrooms. Follow a peaceful night's rest
with a massive country breakfast over the
morning papers.

Rooms: 8. Double room from £85,
single occupancy from £55.

Prices: Restaurant main course from £10.95. Bar snack
from £7.50. House wine £10.95. Sunday lunch £10.95.

Last orders: Bar: lunch 15.00; dinner 23.00. Food: lunch
14.00; dinner 21.30.

Closed: Never.

Food: Traditional British.

Real Ale: Butcombe Bitter. Up to two guest beers.

Other points: No-smoking areas. Garden. Children
welcome. Dogs welcome overnight. Car park adjacent.

Directions: Off A362 2 miles west of Frome.
(Map 5, F2)

Montacute

The Kings Arms Inn

Montacute, Somerset TA15 6UU
Telephone: +44(0)870 4016159
+44(0)1935 822513
kingsarmsinn@realemail.co.uk
www.greenekinginns.co.uk

A 17th-century hamstone inn standing opposite the church and Montacute House (NT)
in a very picturesque and unspoilt village,
that was once an ale house owned by the
abbey. Later it became a coaching inn on
the Plymouth-London route, where horses
were changed before the gruelling climb up
Ham Hill. Today's comfortable inn offers
characterful accommodation in fifteen en
suite bedrooms, all of which are spacious and
well equipped; some sporting comfortable
four-poster beds. Downstairs, the Windsor
Room is a relaxing lounge, but the Pickwick
Bar remains the centre of village life. Here,
Greene King ales are served, alongside popular bar meals that range from homecooked
ham sandwiches to steak and kidney pie with
shortcrust pastry. The daily-changing set-
price menu and evening carte is served in the
Cottage Restaurant. Start, perhaps, with pan-
fried chicken livers with raspberry dressing or
mussels in white wine, then follow with beef
fillet Rossini with pepper sauce, oven-baked
duck breast with cranberry and orange jus, or
lemon sole with parsley butter sauce. Follow
a relaxing night with a decent breakfast and
a walk on the National Trust's wooded St
Michael's Hill behind the inn.

Rooms: 15. Double room from £80, single room £65.
Prices: Set lunch from £12.95 and dinner from £21.95.
Main course from £11.95. Main course bar meal from
£7.95. House wine from £9.95.
Last orders: Bar: 23.00. Food: lunch 14.30; dinner 21.00.
Closed: Rarely.
Food: Modern British.
Real Ale: Greene King IPA, Greene King Abbot Ale.
Other points: No-smoking area. Children welcome.
Dogs welcome overnight. Garden. Car park.
Directions: Take A3088 from A303, signed Montacute
House. Exit 25/M5. (Map 5, G1)

Wells

The Crown at Wells and Anton's Bistrot

Market Place, Wells, Somerset BA5 2RP
Telephone: +44(0)870 4016161
+44(0)1749 673457
eat@crownatwells.co.uk
www.crownatwells.co.uk

In 1695 Quaker William Penn (founder of
Philadelphia) preached to a crowded market
place from an upper window of the historic
Crown, built in 1450 within sight of the
Gothic cathedral and Bishop's Palace. The
traditional, pubby Penn Bar is complemented
by Anton's, a more contemporary wine-bar-
cum-bistro. In the latter, dark-wood beams
are offset by half pitch-pine walls hung with
cartoons (originals by a well-known local
cartoonist after whom the bistro is named),
while stripped-pine tables, candles, newspapers, and subdued (evening) lighting offer an
informal, relaxed, more up-to-date atmosphere. Anton's dishes of generous proportions
continue the contemporary theme with the
likes of crab, prawn and salmon fishcake
with chilli and basil relish, followed, perhaps,
by braised Moroccan-style lamb shank with
couscous. Baked almond tart with praline ice
cream or West Country cheeses make a good
finish. Good value 'Les Routiers' menu available at lunchtime and early evening Sunday
to Thursday; traditional bar meals in the
Penn Bar. A 30-plus wine list offers 12 by the
glass. Bedrooms are all en suite and are decorated in keeping with the old traditional inn.
Some of the larger rooms at the front have
four-poster beds.

Rooms: 15. Double room from £85, single from £50.
Family room from £100.
Prices: Set lunch from £10.95. House wine £11.50.
Last orders: Bar: lunch 15.00; dinner 23.00. Food: lunch
14.30; dinner 21.30 (Sunday 21.00).
Closed: Never.
Food: Mediterranean.
Real Ale: Butcombe Bitter, Oakhill Best Bitter, Smiles
Best. 1 guest beer.
Other points: No-smoking area. Children welcome.
Dogs welcome overnight. Car park.
Directions: Centre of Wells. (Map 5, F1)

Wells

Fountain Inn and Boxer's Restaurant

1 St Thomas Street, Wells, Somerset BA5 2UU
Telephone: +44(0)870 4016162
+44(0)1749 672317
eat@fountaininn.co.uk
www.fountaininn.co.uk

Adrian and Sarah Lawrence's popular 16th-century pub was built to accommodate the builders working on Wells Cathedral. Today's guests come to sample pints of the local Butcombe Bitter and freshly prepared food in Boxer's Restaurant. The bar offers the main focal point on entry, along with a welcoming fire, but what hits you is the unpretentious nature of the place. Dark-wood furniture, simple tablecloths and a floral carpet happily clashing with the terracotta walls offer an almost 'Chelsea Kitchen' cult-style, no-nonsense bistro atmosphere, within a pub setting. This place is all about food, and there's a profusion of blackboards displaying the daily specials such as a starter of warm crab tartlet lightly spiced with chilli, ginger and lime. The printed menu cranks out a lengthy repertoire of familiar and more contemporary dishes: beef, ale and mushroom pie, beer battered cod and chips and ploughman's for lunch. Evening main courses take in monkfish wrapped in Parma ham with mustard beurre blanc and beef casserole. Portions are honest, robust, and prices reasonable. An 80-odd-bin wine list travels the globe. Beyond the bar there's Boxer's Restaurant (red and white chequered clothed tables and an air of country calm) serving the same menus.

Prices: Set lunch £9.75. Restaurant main course from £7.25. Bar main course from £3.50. House wine £9.95.
Last orders: Food: lunch 14.00 (Sunday 14.30); dinner 22.00 (Sunday 21.30).
Closed: Rarely.
Food: Modern British.
Real Ale: Butcombe Bitter, Courage Best Bitter.
Other points: No-smoking area. Children welcome. Car park.
Directions: Junction 22/M5. In the city centre, 50 yards from the cathedral. Follow signs for the Horringtons.
(Map 5, F1)

Wincanton

Old Inn

Holton, Wincanton, Somerset BA9 8AR
Telephone: +44(0)870 4016163
+44(0)1963 32002

Weary A303 travellers should look out for the Holton exit and head for this 17th-century former coaching inn for rest and refreshment. It enjoys a peaceful village setting and is popular locally for good straightforward pub food with produce sourced from local suppliers. The character beamed bar, dominated by a large stone fireplace with log-burning stove, boasts ancient flagstones, upholstered wooden settles, large refectory tables and a clutter of bric-a-brac, including polished copper pots and pewter mugs, and an interesting collection of key rings hanging from the beams by the bar counter. Sup a pint of local Butcombe ale or Wadworth 6X and tuck into a traditional bar meal, perhaps a ploughman's lunch with locally produced farmhouse cheddar cheese, roast beef and horseradish sandwich, lasagne, pork curry, or rump steak with all the trimmings. From the separate restaurant menu perhaps choose lamb cutlets with rosemary, or peppered steak flamed in brandy and cream. Meat from locally reared animals is supplied by quality local butchers. Book for hearty Sunday roasts. There's al fresco seating on the flower-filled front terrace.

Prices: Set menu £16.50. Main course from £8.25. Bar meal from £6.25. House wine £8.25.
Last orders: Bar: lunch 14.00; dinner 22.00. Food: lunch 14.00; dinner 22.00. Restaurant closed Sunday evening, bar meals available from 19.00.
Closed: Rarely.
Food: Traditional British.
Real Ale: Butcombe Bitter, Wadworth 6X, Otter Ale.
Other points: No-smoking in the restaurant. Children welcome in the restaurant. Dogs on leads welcome in the bar. Garden. Car park.
Directions: Off A303 2 miles south west of Wincanton.
(Map 5, G1)

Wookey Hole

The Wookey Hole Inn

Wookey Road, Wookey Hole, Wells,
Somerset BA5 1BP
Telephone: +44(0)870 4016164
+44(0)1749 676677
mail@wookeyholeinn.com
www.wookeyholeinn.com

The beautiful Mendip Hills rise up behind
this striking early Victorian pub and, to the
uninitiated, it looks like a traditional rural pub.
Step inside are you will find a vibrant, open-
plan bar and a distinct Mediterranean feel,
with soft muted colours against white, lots
of windows and skylights, and blond wood
tables and chairs well-spaced over wood or
stone floors. Quirky add-ons such as the
orange retro couch and unusual wall lighting (designed by owner Mark Hey) indicate
that this is more of a restaurant than a pub.
Modern menus open with the likes of vegetable, fish or meat antipasto. Mains range from
pan-seared scallops with thyme, ginger and
lemon butter to peppered rib-eye steak with
chunky chips and salad, and puddings include
a satisfying ginger pudding with ginger sauce.
Four guest real ales and eight Belgian beers
on tap. A seagrass stairway leads to five
funky bedrooms decorated in muted colours,
with interesting soft furnishings and lighting, contemporary art and big bathrooms.
Reclamation yards have been scoured to give
an interesting mix of old and new, juxtapos-
ing, for example, a Victorian bathtub and
square basin with a modern stainless-steel
loo, and all rooms have video and CD
players.

Rooms: 5. Room from £70.
Prices: Main course from £13. House wine £12.50.
Last orders: Food: lunch 14.30; dinner 21.30.
Closed: Rarely.
Food: Modern British.
Real Ale: 4 guest ales available.
Other points: Children welcome. Garden.
Directions: Follow the signs to Wookey Hole Caves
off the A371 between Cheddar and Wells. Exit22/M5
(Map 5, F1)

Stafford

The Holly Bush

Salt, Stafford, Staffordshire ST18 0BX
Telephone: +44(0)870 4016165
+44(0)1889 508234
geoff@hollybushinn.co.uk
www.hollybushinn.co.uk

The origins of this pretty thatched 14th-
century pub are thought to reach back to
1190. It is also reputed to be Staffordshire's
oldest licensed premises and England's second oldest. What is known for sure is that
the Holly Bush was once a baiting house
for asses, mules and ponies carrying salt to
nearby Stafford and beyond. It maintains its
historic charm throughout the cosy interior,
with carved heavy beams, a planked ceiling,
exposed brick walls, old oak furnishings,
open fires and intimate alcoves characterising
the main bar. Landlord Geoff Holland is passionate about using fresh local produce and
sources meat from W M Perry, an Eccleshall
butcher with his own abbatoir, and game
from local shoots. Among the good value
dishes on offer you will find homemade soups
or warm watercress, potato and bacon salad
for starters, followed by braised local estate
venison with chestnuts and celery, slow-
cooked lamb and barley stew and steak and
ale pie. Alternatives include poached plaice
with white wine and prawn sauce, and prime
steaks, including a 20oz T-bone. Expect good
lunchtime sandwiches and a chalkboard listing daily seafood specials. Round off with a
traditional pudding or a plate of Staffordshire
cheeses.

Prices: Main course from £6.95. House wine £7.25.
Last orders: Bar: lunch 14.30; dinner 23.00. Food: lunch
14.00 (all day Saturday and Sunday); dinner 21.30.
Closed: Rarely.
Food: Modern and Traditonal British.
Real Ale: Boddingtons, Marston's Pedigree. 1 guest beer.
Other points: No-smoking area. Garden. Car park.
Directions: Junction 14/M6. Four miles along A51 Stone
to Lichfield road, or half a mile from the A518 Stafford
to Uttoxeter road. (Map 8, G5)

Handmade Sausages

at the Holly Bush

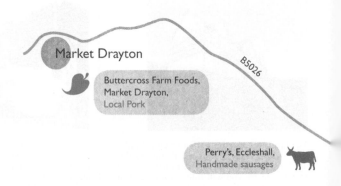

Market Drayton

Buttercross Farm Foods,
Market Drayton,
Local Pork

B5026

Perry's, Eccleshall,
Handmade sausages

*Whilst local venison is easily available from Cannock
Chase just south of Stafford, the Holly Bush sources
other meats such as beef, pork and lamb from the
traditional village family butcher, William Perry in
Eccleshall. In operation since 1927, it is one of the few
butchers' shops in Staffordshire that has its own
abattoir where sheep, pigs and cattle from within a
fifteen miles radius are slaughtered. Hence, customers
can be sure that meat is correctly hung to ensure its
prime eating quality. For instance, hindquarters of beef
are hung for 3-4 weeks before being offered for sale.
The current proprietor, Peter Bevan, has been here for
twenty-three years and his manager for twenty years.
Such expertise in the field helps make the classic
dishes such as the Holly Bush's slow-cooked lamb and
barley stew, and steak and ale pie sure winners. Landlord Geoff Holland also makes particularly good use of
Perry's selection of handmade sausages (they offer 14
varieties, but not all at once). Favourites are Stilton and
leek and sun-dried tomato. Washed down with a glass
of red wine or two sourced from the independent, family-owned wine merchant Whitebridge Wines in Stone
just a few miles up the A51, and you'll find it difficult
to leave at the end of an evening.*

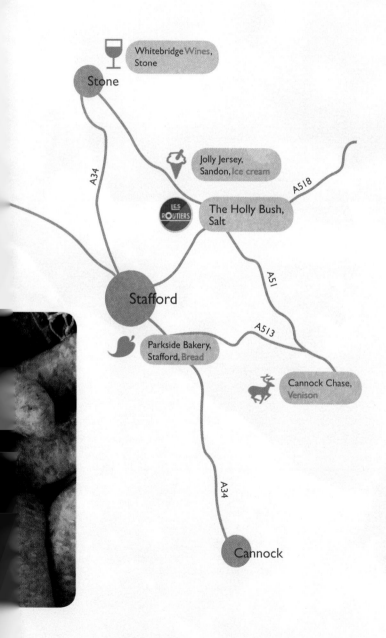

Whitebridge Wines, Stone

Stone

Jolly Jersey, Sandon, Ice cream

A34

A518

The Holly Bush, Salt

LES ROUTIERS

A51

Stafford

A513

Parkside Bakery, Stafford, Bread

Cannock Chase, Venison

A34

Cannock

Barnby

The Swan Inn

Swan Lane, Barnby, Beccles, Suffolk NR34 7QF
Telephone: +44(0)870 4016167
+44(0)1502 476646

Take Swan Lane off the A146 at Barnby to find this flower-adorned, pink-washed village local and, perhaps, the most extensive menu of fish and seafood to be found in a Suffolk pub. Unlike many, the quality and freshness here is first class thanks to pub owner and Lowestoft fish wholesaler, Don Cole, who supplies the pub with the best of the day's catch landed at the dock five miles away. Up to 80 different fish dishes are listed on the printed menu and an array of ever-changing blackboards in the bar. From local sprats traditionally smoked in Don's smokehouse, flour-fried slip sole, and fresh grilled sardines with garlic butter, the choice extends to longshore codling fillets, deep-fried in crispy batter, and turbot fillet in prawn and brandy sauce. The house speciality, however, is a 20oz Dover sole, simply grilled. In addition, expect to find oysters, dressed Cromer crabs, locally caught lobster, deep-fried fresh scampi and monkfish tails in hot garlic butter. All are accompanied with salad, new potatoes or chips and peas, and served throughout the traditionally furnished bar and restaurant. Both are crowded at lunch and dinner, so do book. A self-contained flat is available on a nightly basis.

Rooms: 3. Rooms from £40 per person.
Prices: Set lunch £13 and dinner £18. Restaurant main course from £7.95. Bar main course £3.95.
Last orders: Bar: lunch 15.30; dinner 23.30. Food: lunch 14.00; dinner 21.30.
Closed: Rarely.
Food: Seafood.
Real Ale: Adnams, Greene King Abbot Ale, Greene King IPA, Bass. 1 guest beer.
Other points: No-smoking area. Children welcome. Garden. Car park.
Directions: Off A146 east of Beccles. (Map 6, C7)

Bungay

St Peter's Hall

St Peter South Elmham, Bungay,
Suffolk NR35 1NQ
Telephone: +44(0)870 4016168
+44(0)1986 782322
stuart@stpetersbrewery.co.uk
www.stpetersbrewery.co.uk

Built in 1280 and extended in 1539 using 14th-century architectural salvage from nearby Flixton Priory, the impressive manor and surrounding farm buildings were refurbished in 1996 by John Murphy to provide the rather grand setting for his unique micro-brewery, and a highly individual bar and restaurant. Open at weekends only, the latter not only showcases the brewery's impeccable portfolio of bottled and draught beers, but offers a stylish menu created by chef Julian Williams. What's more, the ambience is unmatched anywhere else in the country. Cross the moat, enter a stone porch and drink and eat in high-ceilinged rooms filled with 17th- and 18th-century furnishings, notably some French choirstalls and a Bishop's chair, splendid Brussels tapestries, and fine stone fireplaces. Food, however, is right up to date, an enjoyable inspection dinner menu commenced with a good warm goat's cheese tart with leeks, thyme and baby spinach, then followed baked turbot with shellfish, spinach and crushed new potatoes, with excellent British farmhouse cheeses to finish. Alternatives may include potted shrimps, roast guinea fowl with baked squash, and cep mushroom sauce, and walnut tart. Open sandwiches at lunch are made with local Metfield organic bread.

Prices: Restaurant main course from £10.50. Lunch main course from £5.65. House wine £11.
Last orders: Bar: 23.00 (Sunday 22.30). Food: lunch 14.00; dinner 21.00.
Closed: Rarely.
Food: Modern British/International.
Real Ale: St Peter's Beers.
Other points: No-smoking area. Garden. Children welcome. Car park.
Directions: Brewery and Hall signed off A144 three miles south of Bungay. (Map 6, C7)

Cavendish

The George

The Green, Cavendish, Sudbury, Suffolk CO10 8BA
Telephone: +44(0)870 4016169
+44(0)1787 280248
reservations@georgecavendish.co.uk
www.georgecavendish.co.uk

Must See
- Lavenham: historic wool town.
- Kentwell Hall & Melford Hall, Long Melford
- Gainsborough's House, Sudbury
- Colne Valley Railway, Castle Hedingham

Farmers Market
Long Melford (3rd Saturday of month)
Sudbury (last Friday of month)

Villages to Visit
Cavendish, Clare, Kersey, Lavenham, Chelsworth, Stoke by Nayland; Thaxted and Finchingfield (both Essex)

Lavenham

Cavendish

The potential of this 600-year-old timber-framed building, beautifully situated beside the village green, was realised in March 2002 when Jonathan and Charlotte Nicholson took it on. With vision and sheer hard work they have transformed a faded village boozer into a smart and rather stylish pub-restaurant, replete with eye-catching mustard and green façade. Inside, everything has been stripped back, so that wood, exposed brick and standing timbers create a modern space offset by simple neutral colours. That this is a dining pub is obvious, tables laid up for eating fill every space, though don't be put off popping in for a drink as there's a small bar area for those just wanting a pint of Woodforde's Wherry or a glass of wine from a short, well annotated global wine list. Former Conran head chef Jonathan utilises fresh local seasonal produce and his inventive daily menus include a keenly priced two or three course lunch menu and a carte that may deliver starters of seared king scallops with chorizo, celeriac and sherry dressing, and foie gras and goose roulade with grape chutney. For main course there may be roast sea bass with asparagus and lemon and thyme veloute or Moroccan spiced lamb rump with roast sweet potato and stuffed pimento. Charlotte has created five stylishly simple en suite bedrooms upstairs, all boast charming village views.

Rooms: 5. From £37.50 per person.
Prices: Restaurant main course from £12.75. Bar snack/light lunch from £4.95. House wine £10.25.
Last orders: Bar: 23.00. Food: lunch 15.00; dinner 22.00.
Closed: Sunday evening and all day Monday.
Food: Modern British.
Real Ale: Nethergate Augustinian Ale, Woodforde's Wherry Best Bitter.
Other points: No-smoking area. Garden and terrace with heated canopies.
Directions: On A1092 between Haverhill and Long Melford. (Map 6, D6)

Tourist Information Sudbury +44(0)1787 881320
Where to Shop Sudbury, Cambridge, Ipswich
Nearest Golf Course Stoke by Nayland
Where to Walk
The 60-mile Stour Valley trail passes through Cavendish and the beautiful, gently rolling landscape around Sudbury, Long Melford, Lavenham and Clare is crosscrossed with well waymarked footpaths.

Cycling
South Suffolk is superb cycling country - gently rolling terrain and stunning views. Explore the quiet narrow lanes and villages between Long Melford and Bury St Edmunds, the web of lanes east of Lavenham, and across the Essex border around Thaxted.
Events & Festivals Lavenham Carnival (August)
Annual Re-creation of Tudor Life, Kentwell Hall (June)

Ipswich

The Ship Inn

Church Lane, Levington, Ipswich,
Suffolk IP10 0LQ
Telephone: +44(0)870 4016170
+44(0)1473 659573

Tranquil views over the Orwell estuary with
its bobbing boats and serene waterscape, a
nautical ambience and first-class fresh fish
dishes are among the attractions at this
immaculately whitewashed and impressively
thatched 14th-century pub. Just six miles
from Ipswich, the Ship is a popular lunchtime
venue, especially in summer when the flower-
festooned front and rear terraces fill up early.
The spick-and-span, low-ceilinged bar is
warmed by a big log fire and is adorned with
nautical bric-a-brac of all kinds. With hardly
a free table to be found at lunch or dinner (please book ahead), chef-patron Mark
Johnson's twice daily-changing chalkboard
menus have really proved a hit locally since
he, and wife Stella, took over in 2002. Mark
offers imaginative meals prepared from fresh
local produce, notably locally reared meats,
seasonal salads and vegetables, venison from
the Suffolk Estate, and excellent fish direct
from Lowestoft. Typically, start with platter
of homemade breads with olives, olive oil and
balsamic, or mussels steamed in white wine,
shallots, cream and garlic, then tuck into
steak, vegetable and Suffolk ale pie or grilled
mixed fish with garlic and herb mayonnaise.
Wash down with a pint of Adnams ale or one
of twelve wines available by the glass.

Prices: Main course lunch from £7.50. Main course
dinner from £9.50. House wine from £9.25.
Last orders: Bar: lunch 14.30; dinner 23.00. Food: lunch
14.00 (Sunday 15.00); dinner 21.30.
Closed: Sunday evening.
Food: Modern British.
Real Ale: Adnams Broadside, Adnams Best, Greene
King IPA.
Other points: No-smoking area. Garden. Children
welcome over 14 years old. Car park.
Directions: A14/A12 at Ipswich. Follow signs to
Levington via Bridge Road. (Map 6, D7)

Orford

The Crown and Castle

Orford, Woodbridge, Suffolk IP12 2LJ
Telephone: +44(0)870 4016171
+44(0)1394 450205
info@crownandcastle.co.uk
www.crownandcastle.co.uk

Must See
- Orford Castle
- Sutton Hoo Archaeological Site
- Woodbridge Tide Mill
- Minsmere Bird Reserve
- Leiston Abbey

Where to Walk
Follow the Suffolk Coast & Heaths Path or enjoy gentle forest and heathland walks
- Rendlesham Forest, Dunwich Heath - and riverside walks close to the River Deben, Shottisham, and the River Blyth, Southwold. See also Pub Walk on page 310.

Woodbridge Tide Mill

Southwold

The location of Ruth and David Watson's beautifully refurbished Victorian former pub, adjacent to a Norman castle with stunning views across the Ore estuary, is perfect. Having recreated their vision of a modern, stylish inn and bistro, the Watson's continue to improve and upgrade the facilities and fabric of the inn; bedrooms have been refurbished, the Trinity toilets remodelled and refitted, a new reception area created, and the bar stylishly restructured. In keeping with the setting, all 18 bedrooms are light and refreshingly simple. En suite bathrooms have quirky pebble-print tiles, luxury towels and toiletries. Downstairs, stripped wooden boards, polished tables and original artworks set the scene for some modern food that delves deep into Suffolk's rich larder. Casual lunches, also served on the terrace, may include home-cured salmon gravlax with fennel salad, and local cod with shellfish broth and rouille. Dinner from the fixed-price menu may begin with rabbit and prune terrine with apple chutney or spiced tiger prawns with Asian-style slaw and coriander dressing, followed by rump of Suffolk lamb with caramelised garlic and spinach pilaf and salsa verde, or Orford-caught skate with nut brown butter. Round off with warm squishy lemon and polenta cake with candied lemons and mascarpone. Well-chosen list of wines with tasting notes and bin end specials.

Rooms: 18. Double from £90, family from £130.
Prices: Main course restaurant from £13.50.
House wine £12.
Last orders: Food: lunch 14.00; dinner 21.00
(later on Saturdays).
Closed: 24-25 December (open to residents and only lunch to non-residents), 3-6 January.
Food: Global.
Real Ale: Greene King IPA, Old Speckled Hen.
Other points: No-smoking area and in the bedrooms. Children welcome (over nine years old in the restaurant). Dogs welcome overnight. Patio. Car park.
Directions: Take the A12 to Woodbridge and then follow the B1084 to Orford. (Map 6, D7)

Tourist Information Woodbridge +44(0)1394 382240
Where to Shop
Woodbridge, Ipswich, Southwold, Snape Maltings
Farmers Market
Woodbridge (2nd Saturday of month)
Local Activities
Birdwatching, sailing, boat trips, fishing, cycling

Nearest Racecourse Newmarket
Nearest Golf Course Aldeburgh, Woodbridge
Events & Festivals
Woodbridge Street Fair (June), Aldeburgh Music Festival (June), Snape Proms (August), Suffolk County Show, Ipswich (May/June)

Denham Estate Venison
at the Ship Inn

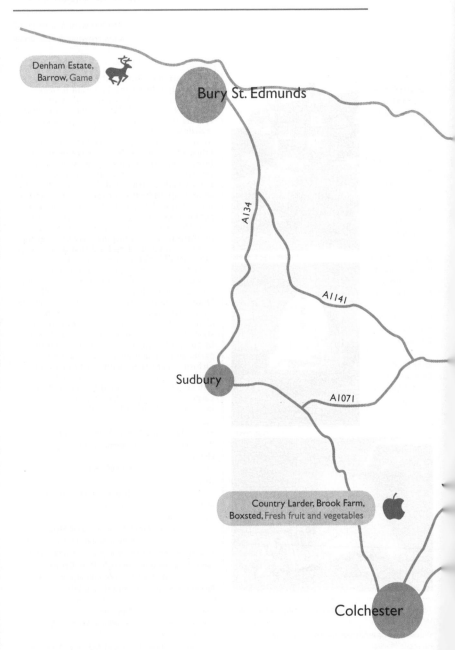

Denham Estate, Barrow, Game

Bury St. Edmunds

A134

A1141

Sudbury

A1071

Country Larder, Brook Farm, Boxsted, Fresh fruit and vegetables

Colchester

In a stunning part of Suffolk lies Denham estate, Europe's largest Fallow deer farm, 1200 acres of rolling countryside with a herd numbering up to 3000. This is good news for Les Routiers members The Ship Inn and the Pheasant at Keyston as this is where they source fantastic farmed venison. Denham produces both wild and farmed venison and with tight controls over health, diet, traceability and age (all animals are slaughtered under the age of 24 months and hung for a minimum of ten days) there is no doubt as to its quality. The science of rearing these deer is off set by the humane conditions these animals are kept in, an extensive natural, free-range and stress free environment, and grazed in meadows rich in clover, rye and timothy grasses. All other food, such as barley, hay and apples are home-grown on the estate and free of all additives, hormones or genetically modified substances.

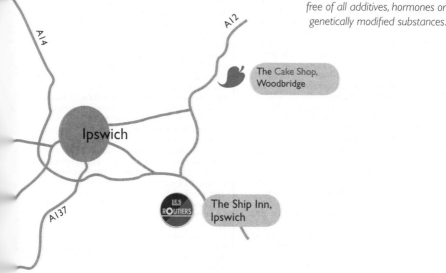

The Cake Shop, Woodbridge

Ipswich

The Ship Inn, Ipswich

Southwold

The Crown

High Street, Southwold, Suffolk IP18 6DP
Telephone: +44(0)870 4016172
+44(0)1502 722275
crownhotel@adnams.co.uk

Celebrated brewer and wine merchant, Adnams, take the credit for the stylish restoration of Southwold's central Georgian inn. From the outside the Crown looks stately, all white paintwork, with a flag flying and a wrought-iron sign hanging over the pavement. Inside, the town's martime past is echoed in a magnificent ship's binnacle, marine paintings and glazed screen in the Back Bar, whilst at the front, the Parlour is a buzzing mix of contemporary wine bar, brasserie and English village pub, and the centre of local life. Here you will find prime-condition Adnams beers, excellent wines (20 by the glass), and daily menus offering, perhaps, crab spring roll with Mersea oyster and seared scallop, as a precursor to crisp bass with pickled cucumber and sauce vierge that mark out the emphasis on fresh fish. However, seared livers with celeriac remoulade and braised lamb shank with pease pudding should assuage alternative appetites, and puddings may include chocolate brownie with warm chocolate sauce. Restaurant menus, set at two or three courses, add a further dimension to the kitchen's skills, while imaginatively selected wines and beautifully refurbished and maintained en suite bedrooms simply underline the thread of quality that runs throughout.

Rooms: 14, 1 with private bathroom. Double/twin from £110.
Prices: Set lunch £20.50 and dinner £29. Restaurant main course from £10. House wine £9.50.
Last orders: Bar: 23.00. Food: 22.00
Closed: Rarely.
Food: Modern British.
Real Ale: Adnams.
Other points: No-smoking area. Garden. Children welcome. Car park.
Directions: A1095 off A12 for Southwold. (Map 6, C7)

Walberswick

The Bell Inn

Ferry Road, Walberswick, Southwold, Suffolk IP18 6TN
Telephone: +44(0)870 4016173
+44(0)1502 723109
bellinn@btinternet.com
www.blythweb.co.uk/bellinn

Walberswick is a tiny village by the sea, overlooking the River Blyth and its auspicious neighbour Southwold. Standing by the green, the Bell is a fine old inn with an unbroken history dating back over 600 years. Inside, it looks every inch the classic Suffolk pub, with low beams, blazing winter log fires, flagged floors and high wooden settles in the rambling main bar. Very quaffable beers and the fine wines fittingly come from Adnams in Southwold and those staying the night have the choice of six comfortably furnished en suite bedrooms, including the Sea View Suite. Good food is based on simply prepared local produce among which local fish and seafood take pride of place. The repertoire encompasses all manner of options from a classic BLT sandwich, steak and kidney pie, and smoked haddock fishcakes in the bar, to romantic dinners in the candlelit restaurant on weekends. Weekly choices might include terrine of venison with juniper berries, pan-fried scallops with guacomole and bacon or local game casserole with Stilton dumplings. Apple and ginger crumble or excellent cheeses with quince jelly bring up the rear.

Rooms: 6. Double/twin from £70.
Prices: Restaurant main course from £7.25. Bar main course from £6.25. House wine from £11.95.
Last orders: Bar: lunch 15.00; dinner 23.00. Food: lunch 14.00 (Sunday and Bank Holidays 14.30); dinner 21.00. Open all day 21st July to end of August and school holidays.
Closed: Rarely.
Food: Modern British.
Real Ale: Adnams Bitter, Broadside, Fisherman & Oyster Stout.
Other points: No-smoking area. Dogs welcome. Garden. Children welcome. Car park. Boule court.
Directions: Take B1387 off A12 at Blythburgh for Walberswick. (Map 6, C7)

Alfold Crossways

The Alfold Barn

Horsham Road, Alfold Crossways, Cranleigh,
Surrey GU6 8JE
Telephone: +44(0)870 4016174
+44(0)1403 752288

Don't follow signs for Alford but keep to
the A281 Horsham Road to find this handsomely converted 16th-century barn. With
its vast beamed ceilings the pub is split into
two areas separated by an adjoining bar, the
latter sports a TV and is the domain of local
drinkers. A further spacious bar has deep
leather sofas and armchairs, old church pews,
flagstone floors, and cream-painted walls
adorned with quotes from Shakespeare. Next
door is the spacious dining area with old gar-
dening tools decorating the walls and beams.
Daily-changing lunch and dinner menus are
extensive and do come with an appetite as
portions are generous and not for the faint-
hearted. At a recent inspection meal, a basket
of warm bread rolls preceded a starter of
garlic and chilli mushrooms, followed by
an enormous whole sea bass grilled in herb
butter and accompanied by a dish of fresh
vegetables. Alternatives may include carrot,
potato and coriander soup, liver and bacon
casserole, and fillet steak with béarnaise
sauce. If you've room, try a pudding, perhaps
Eton Mess. Expect few frills, just good homecooked food using quality ingredients. Big
rear garden with play area and animal corner.

Prices: Main course restaurant from £8. Snacks from
£4.95. House wine £10.95.

Last orders: Food: lunch 14.00; dinner: 21.00 (Friday
and Saturday 21.30) No food all day Monday or
Sunday evening.

Closed: Sunday evening and Monday morning.

Food: Modern British.

Real Ale: Adnams Broadside, Youngs Best Bitter.
2 guest ales.

Other points: No-smoking area. Dogs welcome. Garden. Children welcome. Car park. Childrens play area.

Directions: Exit 11/M23. Midway between Guildford
and Horsham on the A281. (Map 5, F4)

Ockley

Bryce's

The Old School House, Ockley, Dorking,
Surrey RH5 5TH
Telephone: +44(0)870 4016175
+44(0)1306 627430
bryces.fish@virgin.net
www.bryces.co.uk

It is now 12 years since Bill Bryce bought
this roadside pub, formerly a boy's board-
ing academy with the old school bell still
hanging above the door, and established his
eponymous pub-restaurant in the heart of
the Surrey countryside. Fresh fish delivered
daily from London is the mainstay on the
printed menus and ever-changing blackboards
in both the informal beamed and carpeted
bar or in the more formal restaurant. Add
oysters, mussels and scallops from Loch Fyne
and the Pure Oyster Company at nearby
Faygate, and crab from Portland, and the Old
School House is a seafood lovers delight. Bill
prides himself on the quality and freshness
of his fish and understands that simplicity
in preparation and presentation ensures that
delicate flavours are allowed to shine. There
could be mackerel with crab and coriander
risotto alongside non-fishy dishes such as
lasagne and rib-eye steak and chips in the
bar. The main fish event, however, is reserved
for the set-price lunch and dinner menus,
where imaginative specials may include seafood mixed grill with hollandaise and crispy
grey mullet on wild mushroom and garlic
risotto. The wine list includes fourteen by the
glass, although feel free to delve into 'Bryce's
Special Cellar' for some classic vintages.

Prices: Set lunch £22 (two course) and dinner £27.50.
Bar main course from £7.50. House wine £12.50.

Last orders: Bar: lunch 15.00, dinner 23.00. Food: lunch
14.30; dinner 21.30.

Closed: Closed Sunday evenings in November, January
and February

Food: Seafood.

Real Ale: Gale's Butser Bitter, GB, Fuller's London Pride.

Other points: No-smoking in the restaurant. Children
welcome. Dogs welcome in the bar. Patio. Car park.

Directions: J9/M25. Eight miles south of Dorking on
the A29 (Map 6, F5)

West End

The Inn @ West End

42 Guildford Road, West End,
Surrey GU24 9PW
Telephone: +44(0)870 4016176
+44(0)1276 858652
greatfood@the-inn.co.uk
www.the-inn.co.uk

Take the A322 from the M3 (J3) for two miles to find Gerry and Ann Price's smartly refurbished pub-restaurant. On taking over in 2000, they changed the pub's name and locals now refer to it as the 'dot com'. However, Gerry's subtle inn sign, depicting a scene from Othello extolling the virtues of drinking with an Englishman, is an indication that there's good food and great wine to be found behind the ordinary exterior. Not only that, you'll find a light, modern and airy interior, with wooden floors, creamy yellow walls, tasteful check fabrics, crisp linen clothed tables, a warming wood-burner in the bar, and a relaxed, bustling atmosphere. Imaginative seasonal menus, enhanced by daily specials, list an eclectic range of modern British dishes. There are good-value set lunches, light bites (smoked haddock kedgeree), and a sandwich menu to go with a pint of London Pride, or a glass of wine from an enthusiasts' list. Follow homemade breads and chicken liver pâté with cumberland sauce, with roast pheasant with brandy jus, or pork belly with apple and celeriac mash and a honey and thyme jus. Round off with warm chocolate sponge, or a plate of cheese. New for 2004 - larger car park, boules pitches and an al fresco dining terrace.

Prices: Set lunch £18. Main course from £12.50.
Bar main course from £6. House wine £11.95.
Last orders: Bar: lunch 15.00 (Saturday 16.00); dinner 23.00. Food: lunch 14.30; dinner 21.30.
Closed: Rarely.
Food: Modern British.
Real Ale: Fuller's London Pride, Courage Best Bitter.
Other points: No-smoking area. Garden. Boules pitch. Dining patio. Car park.
Directions: On the A322 Guildford to M3 road, two miles south of J3/M3. (Map 5, F4)

Barcombe

Anchor Inn

Anchor Lane, Barcombe, Lewes,
East Sussex BN8 5BS
Telephone: +44(0)870 4016177
+44 (0)1273 400 414
www.anchorinnandboating.co.uk

Built in 1790, this white-painted inn stands
on the banks of the River Ouse, four miles
upstream from Lewes and surrounded by
peaceful Sussex countryside. Serious flooding
in October 2000 caused extensive damage
and a major revamp followed resulting in a
modern and more stylish interior. Visitors
can expect lots of oak beams, wood and flagstone floors, bright, light decoration, warm
lighting, crackling winter fires and a lovely
atmosphere. The restaurant is similar in style,
light and airy, but there is seating for diners in all areas of the bar. The menu offers
classic pub staples such as chilli and lasagne.
Daily specials are chalked up on a board and
offer the likes of roast salmon with coriander
and dill for starters, followed by noisettes of
lamb with rosemary jus and sirloin steak with
Burgundy sauce. A predominantly French list
of wines; ten wines by the glass. The draw,
especially in summer, is the large riverside
decking area with views directly to the river.
In addition, ancient boating rights stretch-
ing over two miles, mean that the inn has 27
rowing boats available for hire by the hour.
And there are three cottage-style en suite bedrooms with a comfortable feel.

Rooms: 3, 2 with private bathrooms. From £45 for
single occupancy.
Prices: Set lunch and dinner £15. Bar main course from
£6.50. House wine £10.95.
Last orders: Bar: 23.00. Food: 15.00; dinner 21.00.
Closed: Rarely.
Food: Modern British.
Real Ale: Harvey's, Badger Tanglefoot.
Other points: No-smoking area. Garden. Licence for
Civil Weddings. Children welcome. Car park. Fleet of
27 boats. Marquee events in the summer.
Directions: From Lewes take the A26 to Barcombe.
(Map 6, G5)

Lewes

The Rainbow Inn

Resting Oak Hil, Cooksbridge, Lewes,
East Sussex BN8 4SS
Telephone: +44(0)870 4016178
+44(0)1273 400334

Built of brick and flint in the 17th century,
the Rainbow makes the most of its attractive
corner site, with rustic benches on a flower-
filled front patio and a sun-trap enclosed
rear terrace replete with teak furnishings,
barbecue area, and distant South Downs
views. Inside, beyond the small rustic bar,
where you will find a cracking pint of local
Harveys ale, the civilised and warmly decorated dining areas sport an eclectic mix of
tables and chairs and a relaxed and informal
atmosphere. Chef-manager Luke Wilson
sources fresh local produce for his modern,
daily changing menus and chalkboard specials, the latter listing fresh Newhaven fish,
lamb from Park Gardens Farm in nearby
Ditchling and game in season. The printed
menu offering, say, prawn and chicken ravioli
with crispy leeks and saffron cream, followed
by roast breast of chicken stuffed with sun-
dried tomatoes, spinach and feta with basil
couscous and red pepper sauce, or roast cod
with Parmesan crust with chevil butter sauce.
Good puddings range from bread-and-butter
pudding to rhubarb crème brûlée. The short,
carefully selected global list of wines complements the menu. Two upstairs private dining
rooms are perfect for intimate dinner parties.

Prices: Set lunch £10.45 (2 courses). Restaurant main
course from £8.95. Bar main course from £3.95.
House wine £11.
Last orders: Bar: lunch 15.00; dinner 23.00. Food: lunch
14.30; dinner 22.00.
Closed: Rarely.
Food: Modern European.
Real Ale: Harvey's Sussex Bitter.
Other points: No-smoking area. Garden. Children
welcome. Car park. Private dining. Barbecue area.
Directions: On A275 3 miles north of Lewes.
(Map 6, G5)

Old Heathfield

Star Inn

Church Street, Old Heathfield,
East Sussex TN21 9AH
Telephone: +44(0)870 4016179
+44(0)1435 863570

Look for the village church and you will find this 14th-century pub with its roughly hewn golden stone, marvellous summer garden and impressive views across the High Weald. Built in the 14th century for the stonemasons constructing the church, it looks every inch the quintessential English country pub. The interior is equally atmospheric, with low, black beams, wood panelling and floors, rustic tables and chairs, a big inglenook fireplace, and an atmospheric vaulted upstairs dining room - all very cosy and welcoming. This is very much a food pub, with blackboards on the walls announcing what's on the menu. The focus is on fresh fish from Billingsgate or direct from boats in Hastings, with specialities like large cock crabs, lobster, fresh mussels, and first-class fish and chips proving very popular. Practically everything on offer is made on the premises, with non-fishy favourites, served in generous portions, taking in slow-cooked half shoulder of lamb, beef in ale pie, and cumberland sausage with mash and onion gravy. Expect a mammoth ploughman's, hearty soups and sandwiches at lunch, and homemade puddings may include bread-and-butter pudding. There's a decent selection of wines by the glass and local Harvey's and Shepherd Neame ales on tap.

Prices: Restaurant main course from £9.
House wine £12.50.
Last orders: Bar: lunch 15.00; dinner 23.00.
Food: lunch 14.15; dinner 21.15.
Closed: Rarely.
Food: Modern British.
Real Ale: Harvey's, Shepherd Neame Master Brew.
Other points: No-smoking area. Children welcome.
Dogs welcome. Garden. Car Park.
Directions: From the A265, turn onto the B2096 to
Old Heathfield. (Map 6, G6)

Rushlake Green

Horse and Groom

Rushlake Green, Heathfield,
East Sussex TN21 9QE
Telephone: +44(0)870 4016180
+44(0)1435 830320
chappellhatpeg@aol.com

A brilliant little pub dating back to 1673 in a quintessentially English setting on an unspoilt village green deep in rural Sussex countryside. Blackened beams, stripped wooden floors, crackling log fires, horse brasses, old prints and photographs, and soothing evening candlelight characterise the cosy, cottagey interior which oozes warmth and charm. Expect a warm welcome from landlord Mike Chappell and a chatty, relaxed atmosphere as the pub is popular with local drinkers and diners seeking out the very good bar food. An array of blackboards display the ambitious modern repertoire that is far removed from the usual pub staples. Produce is sourced locally, with venison, wild duck and pheasant from nearby Heathfield Park, fish from the south coast, tip-top ale from Harvey's Brewery in Lewes, and white wine from the village vineyard. Start with sautéed scallops with spring onions and bacon, then follow with roast leg of lamb or one of their good fresh fish and seafood dishes; say steamed turbot with samphire and mushroom sauce. Finish with plum and almond tart. Track this pub down in the summer and dine al fresco in the splendid cottage garden with its colourful flower borders and peaceful views.

Prices: Main course from £12.50. House wine £12.50.
Last orders: Bar: lunch 15.00; dinner 23.00.
Food: lunch 14.15; dinner 21.15.
Closed: Rarely.
Food: Modern British.
Real Ale: Harvey's. 1 guest beer
Other points: Children welcome. Dogs welcome. Fully
air conditioned. Garden. Car park.
Directions: Take the A265 towards Burwash. Turn right
on the B2096 to Battle and then right again at Chapel
Cross signed to Rushlake Green. The pub is on the
green. (Map 6, G6)

Chichester

The George & Dragon

51 North Street, Chichester,
West Sussex PO19 1NQ
Telephone: +44(0)870 4016181
+44(0)1243 785660
enquiries@gdchi.co.uk
www.georgeanddragoninn.co.uk

In March 2004 new owners Don Hoare and Jen Day took over this lovely little pub in Chichester's bustling town centre, long a favoured lunch time stop-off, where wooden floors, scrubbed pine tables, roaring log fires in pretty tiled fireplaces, and simple glass lanterns all make an inviting place for people to enjoy a break. Around the central bar, you will find a refreshing cross-section of visitors - shoppers, local businessmen, friends meeting for lunch, and tourists. Beyond the bar is the slate-floored conservatory restaurant and this opens out onto a small patio, which forms a wonderful barbecue area and summer sun trap for al fresco dining. Seasonal menus utilise fresh local produce, with the daily fixed-price menu listing, perhaps, grilled mussels with chilli, garlic and herbs, followed by braised shoulder of lamb with redcurrant jus, and homemade puddings. Good traditional bar meals range from fresh Selsey crab sandwiches to ham and eggs with bubble-and-squeak and chips. The pub's old flint and brick stable block has been beautifully renovated and contains ten stylish en suite bedrooms.

Rooms: 10. Double room from £75, single from £50.
Prices: Restaurant main course from £6.95. Bar snack from £3.50. House wine £10.50.
Last orders: Bar: 23.00. Food: lunch 14.30; dinner 21.15 (Sunday 21.30).
Closed: Rarely.
Food: Traditional and Modern British.
Real Ale: Adnams, Greene King Abbot Ale, Fuller's London Pride. Guest beers available.
Other points: No-smoking area. Dogs welcome. Patio/courtyard. Children welcome.
Directions: North of city; top end of North Street. (Map 5, G4)

Chichester

The Royal Oak

Pook Lane, East Lavant, Chichester, West Sussex PO18 0AX
Telephone: +44(0)870 4016183
+44(0)1243 527434
nickroyaloak@aol.com
www.sussexlive.co.uk/royaloakinn

Nick Sutherland's thriving gastropub-with-rooms stands in an upmarket village close to Chichester and rolling South Downs countryside on the edge of the Goodwood Estate. Flint-built 200 years ago and accessed via a pretty raised terrace, the charming little cottage comprises of an open-plan bar and dining area with crackling log fires, leather sofas, fat cream candles on scrubbed tables, and Sussex ales tapped from the cask. Classy modern British food draws the discerning and well-heeled from far and wide, the main menu and daily blackboard additions featuring quality fish and meats from London markets and vegetables from local organic farms. Typically, a meal may begin with crispy duck salad with honey, seasame, ginger and alfalfa, followed by Sussex pork and herb sausages, mash and balsamic onion jus, lamb steak with rosemary mash, or whole skate with prosciutto and potato salad. Lunchtime brings sandwiches, home-cooked ham, eggs and bubble-and-squeak, and there are good homemade puddings - crisp lemon tart with raspberry sauce. Decent wines include some interesting French classics; 12 by the glass. Few comforts have been overlooked in kitting out the six stylish bedrooms split between the main building and converted cottages to the rear. All feature pastel décor, smart, contemporary furnishings, high-spec CD players and flat-screen televisons, and quality tiled bathrooms with power showers. There is summer al fresco dining on the sheltered front terrace.

Chichester

Rooms: 6. Double/twin from £70.
Prices: Restaurant main course from £11.
House wine £9.95.
Last orders: Bar: 23.00. Food: lunch 14.30; dinner 21.30.
Closed: Rarely.
Food: Traditional English and Mediterranean.
Real Ale: Badger Best, Ballards, Badger Sussex Bitter.
Other points: No smoking in the bedrooms. Garden and terrace. Car park.
Directions: Village signposted off A286 Midhurst road a mile north of Chichester. (Map 5, G4)

Must See
- Weald and Downland Museum: fascinating collection of over 40 regional historic buildings.
- Bignor Roman Villa
- Parham House
- Petworth House
- Uppark House

Where to Walk
The South Downs Way runs east to west across the hills. Good walking along the coast near Selsey and Littlehampton and around Pagham and Chichester Harbours.

Weald and Downland Museum

Tourist Information Chichester +44(0)1243 775888
Where to Shop
Chichester, Midhurst, Petersfield, Arundel
Farmers Market
Every other Friday. Contact Chichester
Tourist Information
Nearest racecourse Goodwood
Nearest golf course Hunston

Best Scenic Drives
A286 north to Midhurst and Haslemere, diverting onto unclassified roads to visit Blackdown Hill. Return via B213, B2070, B2146 and B2141. A27 to Arundel, A284 and A29 to Pulborough, unclassified roads to Bignor and Sutton, East Dean and Charlton.
Events and Festivals Chichester Festival (July)
Goodwood Revival Weekend (September)

Midhurst

The Duke of Cumberland

Henley, Fernhurst, Midhurst,
West Sussex GU27 3HQ
Telephone: +44(0)870 4016185
+44(0)1428 652280
gaston.duval@btopenworld.com

Perservere up the steep narrow lane off the A286 to find this unspoilt 15th-century country pub, its rustic brick and stone walls covered with roses and wisteria, hidden away in wooded hills with views across the Weald. The tiny rustic bars exude atmosphere in spades, helped by painted, panelled walls, low beamed ceilings, quarry-tiled floors, scrubbed pine tables and benches, and open log fires. Gas lamps, old indentures, and blue and white plates decorate the walls. Relying on fresh produce, including organic beef from local farms, bar food combines both the modern and the traditional, the latter including ploughman's lunches, ham, egg and hand-cut chips, cod in 'hatter' batter, and a rump steak sandwich with horseradish. Alternatively, you may wish to order terrine of rabbit, pigeon and venison, pan-fried mackerel with cracked peppercorns and tomato compote, and rib-eye steak with anchovy butter. Specialities include grilled trout from the pub's own spring-fed pools and, given 24-hours notice, traditional roasts are served as a joint to the table. In summer, order a pint of Timothy Taylor Landlord, drawn straight from the cask, or a glass of Nyetimber 'champagne', and sup it on the brick terrace beside babbling streams.

Prices: Restaurant main course from £10.95. Bar main course from £6.95. House wine £11.50.
Last orders: Bar: lunch 15.00; dinner 23.00 (open all day during the Summer). Food: lunch 14.30; dinner 21.30. No food Sunday evening.
Closed: Rarely.
Food: Traditional and Modern pub food.
Real Ale: Adnams Broadside, Hook Norton Best Bitter, Shepherd Neame Spitfire. 3 guest beers.
Other points: Children welcome. Dogs welcome in the bar. Gardens with ponds. Car park.
Directions: Off A286 north of Midhurst. (Map 5, F4)

Partridge Green

The Green Man

Church Road, Partridge Green, Horsham,
West Sussex RH13 8JT
Telephone: +44(0)870 4016186
+44(0)1403 710250
info@thegreenman.org
www.thegreenman.org

There is something very special about this red-brick roadside pub. For proprietor William Thornton, the pub is the fulfillment of a personal ambition - he used to drive past the run down pub when visiting his mother. When the building came up for sale, he bought it and the results are remarkable. Refurbished with enthusiasm and taste, the place oozes stylish informality and reflects William's interests, through and through. His love of Spain can be found in everything, from the olive-patterned water jugs to the lashings of olive oil and bread on the table, and tapas on the menu (chorizo, anchovies, mussels in chilli oil). The interior is highly individual, which makes it feel more like a home than a pub: prints, a wood-burning stove. Food remains the central focus, with a typical meal opening with grilled goat's cheese with caramelised pear and wild rocket followed, perhaps, by lamb shank with orange mash and root vegetable jus, or smoked haddock on bubble-and-squeak with hollandaise, and a rich dark chocolate and rum tart to round things off. Salads and open club sandwiches are available at lunch only.

Prices: Set lunch £16 and dinner £22. Restaurant main course from £8.95. Bar main course from £4.95. House wine £11.50.
Last orders: Bar: lunch 15.00 (Sunday 16.00); dinner 23.00. Food: lunch 14.00 (Sunday 14.30); dinner 21.30. No food Sunday evening.
Closed: Rarely.
Food: Modern British.
Real Ale: Harvey's Sussex, King Horsham Best Bitter.
Other points: No-smoking area. Dogs welcome. Garden. Children welcome over five years old. Car park.
Directions: On B2135 south of A272. (Map 6, G5)

Cherington

Cherington Arms 🍷

Cherington, Shipston-on-Stour,
Warwickshire CV36 5HS
Telephone: +44(0)870 4016187
+44(0)1608 686233
www.hooknorton.tablesir.com/cheringtonarms

A small, quiet, 17th-century Cotswold village pub with a strong local feel, run by passionate and confident owners. The bar is deeply traditional in look with exposed brick walls, a red stone tiled floor, open fire, hop decorations and classic wooden pub furniture - a place to relax with a first-class pint of Hook Norton. Chalkboards list special dishes of the day, backed up by a printed bar menu ranging from roast beef and horseradish sandwiches to baguettes filled with char-grilled steak and caramelised onions, and ploughman's of mature cheddar with salad, pickles and a basket of bread. The restaurant is separate, a relaxing room with lots of character. In two tiers, one part has large oak pillars, carpeted floors, ceiling beams, and log burner, the other is wood-floored with square wooden tables. A piano sits in the corner and hops and china decorate the walls. A well balanced menu, a mixture of traditional and modern British, delivers good country cooking along the lines of chicken liver parfait with red onion marmalade, followed by rib-eye steak with Cafe de Paris butter and chunky chips, or wild mushroom and herb risotto. Sticky toffee pudding for dessert.

Prices: Restaurant main course from £7.50. Bar main course from £3.75. House wine £10.40.
Last orders: Bar: lunch 15.00; dinner 23.00 (open all day Saturday and Sunday in the Summer). Food: lunch 14.00; dinner 21.00. No food Sunday evening.
Closed: Monday lunchtime.
Food: Modern and Traditional British.
Real Ale: Hook Norton Best & Generation. Guest beer.
Other points: No-smoking area. Totally no smoking in restaurant. Dogs welcome. Garden. Patio. Children welcome. Car park.
Directions: Off A3400 between Chipping Norton and Shipston-on-Stour. Exit 11/M40. (Map 5, D3)

Lapworth

The Boot Inn

Old Warwick Road, Lapworth,
Warwickshire B94 6JU
Telephone: +44(0)870 4016188
+44(0)1564 782464
www.thebootatlapworth.co.uk

Modern brasserie style dishes highlight the specials board and stylish menu at this smartly refurbished, red-brick pub beside the Grand Union Canal, just minutes from the M42 (J4). Bustling bars sport an interesting mix of rustic tables and bench seating, rug-strewn quarry-tiled floors, impressive flower arrangements and a lively atmosphere, while the contemporary upstairs restaurant has a civilised dining ambience. Expect adventurous pub food with a distinct Mediterranean flavour, the choice ranging from rustic breads, roast garlic and olive oil and seared squid with sweet chilli and leaves on the list of 'first plates' to linguine with arrabiata tomato sauce and pecorino on the choice of 'pasta and leaves', and mains like fillet steak with smoked roast garlic, spinach and mascarpone mash. Classic British dishes are given a modern twist, perhaps haddock in tempura batter with pea purée and sauce gribiche. On the 'Puds and Stickies' menu you may find baked chocolate fondant with mint ice cream, accompanied by glass of Campbells Rutherglen Muscat from the excellent global list of wines. Impressive sandwich and filled baguette menu.

Prices: Restaurant main course from £9.
House wine £11.50.
Last orders: Bar: 23.00. Food: lunch 14.30 (Sunday 15.00); dinner 22.00 (Sunday 21.00).
Closed: Rarely.
Food: Modern European.
Real Ale: Wadworth 6X, Greene King Old Speckled Hen, Tetley's Bitter.
Other points: Dogs welcome. Garden. Children welcome. Car park.
Directions: Exit4/M42. A3400 from Hockley Heath south-west for two miles; Lapworth signposted left. (Map 5, C3)

Preston Bagot

The Crabmill

Preston Bagot, Claverdon,
Warwickshire B95 5EE
Telephone: +44(0)870 4016189
+44(0)1926 843342
www.thecrabmill.co.uk

A stylish Italian influence permeates the modern menus and the interior at this 15th century, brick-and-timber, former cider mill, peacefully located beside a leafy lane deep in Shakespeare country. Comfortably upmarket and appealing to a well-heeled clientele, expect to find a contemporary and often bustling bar area, replete with steely bar, wood floors and mirrored mustard walls, and a cosy, spilt-level lounge with leather sofas and deep armchairs. The main attraction, however, is the rustic Italian food served in the three individually themed and candlelit dining rooms, each divided by heavy beams and standing timbers. The Red Room (also known as the 'rude room') sports slightly risqué caricature pictures. Starters or light meals come in the guise of chicken liver parfait with brioche and onion jam, and mussels with apples, leeks, cider and crème fraîche. For a main course, consider duck confit with mashed sweet potato and wild mushrooms, Sicilian mutton pie with honey roast root vegetables, sirloin steak with onion tatin and wine jus, or a daily fish special of swordfish with herb and lemon polenta and oven-dried tomatoes. Add in imaginative bar meals, upmarket sandwiches, decent wines, and a super continental style patio garden and you have it all.

Prices: Restaurant main course from £10. Bar main course from £4.95. House wine £11.95.
Last orders: Bar: 23.00 (Sunday 18.00). Food: lunch 14.30 Sunday 15.30); dinner 21.30.
Closed: Rarely.
Food: Modern European.
Real Ale: Wadworth 6X, Greene King Old Speckled Hen, Tetley's Bitter.
Other points: No-smoking area. Dogs welcome. Garden. Children welcome. Car park.
Directions: Exit16/M40 and Exit4/M42. (Map 5, C2)

Stratford-upon-Avon

The One Elm

1 Guild Street, Stratford-upon-Avon,
Warwickshire CB37 6QZ
Telephone: +44(0)870 4016190
+44(0)1789 404919
theoneelm@peachpubs.com
www.peachpubs.com

In a prime location in the town centre, a stroll from the river and theatre, the One Elm mirrors the chic, contemporary look and style of menus to be found at Peach Pubs flagship pub, the Rose and Crown in Warwick. Since opening in 2003 business has been brisk, the successful formula working well in neighbouring Stratford. Opening at 9am for coffee and breakfast sandwiches, there is an informal, almost continental feel about the place, especially in the stylish front lounge area with its wood floor, bright painted walls, leather sofas and low tables displaying the day's newspapers. Beyond the central, open-to-view kitchen is the more formal dining area. From a deli chalkboard above the bar offering tapas-style starters or nibbles of charcuterie, cheese, fish, antipasti, and rustic breads, both lunch and dinner menus list interesting modern pub food. Enjoy starter or main course size moules marinière or begin with pan-fried red mullet with spicy couscous or cheddar and spinach double-baked soufflé. Follow with rack of lamb with saffron, chick pea and potato dahl or 35-day dry-aged rump steak from the chargrill, then round off with dark and white chocolate terrine. Well chosen wines with eight by the glass, including decent house champagne.

Prices: Restaurant main course from £7.50. Bar main course from £1.35. House wine £10.50.
Last orders: Bar: 23.00.
Closed: Rarely
Food: Modern European.
Real Ale: Greene King Old Speckled Hen, Greene King IPA, Fuller's London Pride.
Other points: Dogs welcome. Garden. Children welcome. Car park.
Directions: Exit15/M40. In the town-centre. (Map 5, D3)

The Rose and Crown, Warwick, Warwickshire

Warwick

The Durham Ox

Shrewley Common, Shrewley, Warwick,
Warwickshire CV35 7AY
Telephone: +44(0)870 4016191
+44(0)1926 842283
info@durham-ox.com

Ross Sanders and champion showjumper
Nick Skelton are the duo responsible for
restoring the fortunes of this big country pub.
Refurbished, rebuilt and remodelled inter-
nally it re-opened as a contemporary dining
pub in 2002 and business has been brisk.
The cream coloured brick facia overlooks the
car park, where you are likely to see Ferraris
parked alongside tractors, plus a massive beer
garden next to a 'horse park' that provides
waitress drinks service to the well-shod and
mounted. The food, both in its sourcing and
preparation, is taken seriously, with as much
fresh produce as possible procured locally.
'Grazing' boards list tapas-style light bite or
starter portions of chorizo or chilli's stuffed
with feta cheese, while from the carte you
can kick off with seafood chowder or salmon
and crab fishcakes with wilted spinach and
aïoli. Mains range from beer-battered cod
with fat chips to pan-fried sea bass with herb
risotto and sauce vierge, and aged Angus rib-
eye steak priced by the ounce. Imaginative
side orders and an excellent value set-price
menu. Team with Abbot Ale or Old Speckled
Hen, or one of 15 chosen wines by the glass.
One of the best pubs to have come out of the
highly competitive area of Warwickshire.

Prices: Set lunch £10 (2 course Monday-Friday January-
February only). Restaurant main course from £5.95.
Snack from £3.95. House wine £12.
Last orders: Bar: 23.00. Food: lunch 15.00; dinner 22.00.
Closed: Rarely.
Food: Modern British.
Real Ale: Greene King IPA, Old Speckled Hen & Abbot.
Other points: No-smoking area. Children welcome.
Dogs welcome in the bar. Large garden. Childrens play
area. Car park.
Directions: Junction 15/M40. Off A4177 between War-
wick and Solihull, 4 miles from Warwick. (Map 5, C3)

Warwick

The Rose and Crown

30 Market Place, Warwick,
Warwickshire CV34 4SH
Telephone: +44(0)870 4016192
+44(0)1926 411117
roseandcrown@peachpubs.com
www.peachpubs.com

Warwick had little to offer discerning pub-
going locals until chef Lee Cash and partner Victoria Moon formed the Peach Pub
Company and transformed this 18th-century
inn smack in the town's central Market
Place. Now, other than being a favoured
destination for food and accommodation,
the attractions include inspired touches such
as leather sofas bordering a long, low-slung
coffee table displaying a selection of the day's
newspapers, and a policy of opening early to
attract people throughout the day. There's a
dedicated dining area, but all tables are kept
free of cutlery to encourage a mix of drinkers and diners. A deli plate chalkboard offers
small tapas-style portions of cheeses, hams,
salami, marinated anchovies and peppers and
rustic breads. There is also a soup of the day
and risotto of the week. Two printed menus
offer a wide selection of options to suit the
occasion and time of day, opening at 8am
with breakfast sarnies, then offering shellfish
linguine, confit belly pork with pearl barley
and cider broth, and medallions of beef fillet with rosemary potatoes and horseradish
cream. Good global wine list offering six
by the glass. Five minimalist-style bedrooms
are tastefully decorated in different colour
schemes and are comfortably equipped and
appointed.

Rooms: 5. Doubles/twins from £65.
Prices: Restaurant main course from £7.50. Bar main
course from £6.50. House wine from £10.50.
Last orders: Bar: 23.00. Food: 22.00.
Closed: Rarely.
Food: Modern British.
Real Ale: Fuller's London Pride, Timothy Taylor
Landlord, Old Speckled Hen.
Other points: Children welcome. Dogs welcome.
Garden and terrace. Parking opposite. Private dining.
Directions: In the centre of Warwick. (Map 5, C3)

Warwick

The Saxon Mill

Coventry Road, Guys Cliffe, Warwick,
Warwickshire CV34 5YN
Telephone: +44(0)0870 4016193
+44(0)1926 492255
www.saxonmill.co.uk

Leave the M40 (J15) or take the A429 north
out of Warwick to locate the Saxon Mill pub,
the latest addition to the select 'Orange Tree'
group across the West Midlands. Paul Hales
and Paul Salisbury have an eye for finding the
right struggling pubs and transforming them
into stylish food venues appealing to young,
well-heeled professionals. With unrivalled
views across the River Avon and Guy's Cliffe
from its decked terrace, this beautifully renovated old mill is no exception. Naturally, the
modern, almost minimalistic interior décor
much loved at the Orange Tree - wood or
rushmat floors, simple muted colours, deep
sofas and chunky wooden tables and chairs -
has been replicated here and works well with
the original beams, open fires and bare brick
walls. You will also find dressers laden with
pasta jars and olive oils, and the trademark
features of open-to-view kitchen, stone-fired
ovens and the trendy, Italian-inspired menu.
Typically, tuck into a 'little dish' of goat's
cheese and balsamic onion tart with roasted
cherry tomatoes, or order one of the fired
pizzas, or opt for something more substantial
like calves' liver with pancetta, sage, onion
mash and red wine jus.

Prices: Restaurant main course from £8.95. Main
course bar from £5.50. House wine £11.95.
Last orders: Bar: 23.00. Food: lunch 14.30 (Sunday
16.30); dinner 21.30 (no food Sunday evening).
Deli bar last orders 18.00.
Closed: Rarely.
Food: Modern British with Italian influences.
Real Ale: Bass, Brew XI.
Other points: No-smoking area in restaurant. Water-
front seating. Children welcome. Dogs welcome in bar.
Car park.
Directions: A46 to Leek Wooton roundabout, then
A429 towards Warwick; pub in 400yds. (Map 5, C3)

Chadwick End

The Orange Tree

Warwick Road, Chadwick End,
West Midlands B93 0BN
Telephone: +44(0)870 4016194
+44(0)1564 785364
www.theorangetree.co.uk

The Orange Tree is the jewel in the crown
of this select group of country dining pubs
operated by Paul Hales and Paul Salisbury.
Set back from the A4141, this stylishly refurbished old inn exudes contemporary charm.
From the smart cream-painted and timbered
exterior to the modern, perhaps minimalistic
décor of the beautifully reworked interior, the
Orange Tree really impresses, indeed, it has
set the trend that numerous pubs are trying
to follow across the West Midlands. The rustic country setting and the simple, restrained
décor is matched by an interesting and unusual, Mediterranean-inspired menu. Authentic
wood-fired pizzas and robust meat dishes,
either cooked on an in-view rotisserie spit,
perhaps spit gammon with peaches and Dijon
mustard sauce, or duck confit with black
pudding, celeriac and apple from the stove,
draw the crowds. Further favourites include
homemade pasta dishes such as macaroni
with smoked haddock and spinach, delicious
warm salads, and fishy specials like whole
plaice with white beans, garlic and Parmesan.
An Italian deli-style counter displays a superb
range of breads, cheeses and olive oils. The
interesting wine list offers good value and a
global choice; Greene King ales on tap.

Prices: Restaurant main course from £7.95.
House wine £11.95.
Last orders: Bar: 23.00. Food: lunch 14.30 (Sunday
16.30); dinner 22.00. No food Sunday evening.
Closed: Rarely.
Food: Modern European.
Real Ale: Greene King IPA.
Other points: Dogs welcome. Garden. Children
welcome. Car park.
Directions: Exit5/M42. On the A4141, four miles
south-east towards Warwick. (Map 5, C3)

Wishaw

The Cock Inn

Bulls Lane, Wishaw, Sutton Coldfield,
West Midlands B76 9QL
Telephone: +44(0)870 4016195
+44(0)121 313 3960

Backing on to open fields in the sleepy village of Wishaw just minutes from the M42 (J9) and the Belfry Golf Course, this cracking country pub is a clone of the locally famous Orange Tree at Chadwick End (see opposite). The amazing success of the OT concept, which appeals to Birmingham's young and well heeled pub-goers, has seen the stylish interior dècor and dynamic food operation marketed as a brand, with new openings appearing in the Home Counties. Beyond the tasteful cream and beige, there is a spacious and very contemporary interior. Expect plush leather sofas, matching deep armchairs, modern wood tables and a fresh, minimalist feel. Sutton Coldfield residents need only drive to Wishaw to experience the Italian-inspired food that put the Orange Tree on the local culinary map. From 'little dishes' like fresh sardines with garlic and parsley and squid with coriander, chilli and salsa, the menu lists delicious warm salads (salmon Caesar with anchovy and Parmesan), fresh pasta meals and home-fired pizzas - 'Siciliana' with ham, artichoke, mozzarella and tomato. Robust main courses extend the choice to duck confit with mash and chilli jam and spit-roast chicken with garlic, lemon, aïoli and chips.

Prices: Restaurant main course from £7.95.
House wine £11.95.
Last orders: Bar: 23.00. Food: lunch 14.30; dinner 21.30.
Closed: Rarely.
Food: Modern British with Italian influences.
Real Ale: Brew XI. 1 guest beer.
Other points: Garden. Car park.
Directions: Exit9/M42. Take signs for Curdworth and Minworth. Take a sharp right at the White Horse pub and drive for one mile. (Map 5, C2)

Bradford-on-Avon

The Kings Arms

Monkton Farleigh, near Bradford-on-Avon,
Wiltshire BA15 2QH
Telephone: +44(0)870 4016196
+44(0)1225 858705
enquiries@kingsarms-bath.co.uk
www.kingsarms-bath.co.uk

This striking stone-built inn, dating back
to the 11th century when it was built as a
retreat for a nearby monastery, can be found
in a sleepy conservation village just a short
drive from Bradford-on-Avon and bustling
Bath. With its impressive stone-arched doorway and stone mullion windows it is clear
that the Kings Arms packs a lot of history
and, of course, ghosts; the place is said to
be haunted by a monk, a miner and a wail-
ing woman. Heavy beams, dark red-painted
walls and a stone-flagged floor give period
character to the Chancel Bar, but the restaurant, with wall-hung tapestries, church
pews, candelabras, and sturdy wooden tables
adorned with pewter plates, has a rather
ecclesiastical look. Note that the massive
inglenook fireplace in the restaurant is, reputedly, the largest in Wiltshire. Homecooked
food takes in the traditional in the bar: Bath
sausages, spring onion and bacon mash and
onion gravy, and rump steak with fat chips
and salad. In the evening, the kitchen puts the
emphasis on modern British dishes, notably
salmon fillet with roasted tomato sauce, and
Barnsley lamb chop with cumberland sauce.
To drink, try the excellent, locally-brewed
Butcombe Bitter or one of ten decent wines
by the glass.

Prices: Set Sunday lunch £13.50. Restaurant main
course from £10.20. Bar main course from £6.50.
House wine £10.95.
Last orders: Bar: lunch 15.00; dinner 23.00. Food: lunch
14.45; dinner 21.30.
Closed: Rarely.
Food: Modern British.
Real Ale: Butcombe Bitter, Wadworth 6X,
Wychwood Hobgoblin.
Other points: No-smoking in the dining area. Children
welcome. Dogs welcome in the bar. Garden. Car park.
Directions: A4 east from Bath, then A363 for Bradford-
on-Avon. Go under railway bridge and turn left in two
and a half miles for Monkton Farleigh. (Map 5, F2)

Brinkworth

Three Crowns

The Street, Brinkworth, Swindon,
Wiltshire SN15 5AF
Telephone: +44(0)870 4016197
+44(0)1666 510366
www.threecrowns.co.uk

Set back from the road, close to the village
church and green, Anthony and Allyson
Windle's 200-year-old stone pub is a bustling
dining destination. The traditional pubby bar,
furnished with a variety of old and new pine,
features two remarkable tables created from
huge 18th-century bellows and is the spot for
lunchtime snacks, namely enormous ploughman's lunches and filled double-decker rolls.
A comprehensive list of main courses is dis-
played on a huge blackboard that dominates
one wall of the pine-furnished conservatory
dining extension. Few people leave dissatis-
fied: portions are not for the faint-hearted,
and food quality is well above average. The
ambitious dishes make good use of local
produce, including locally farmed veal. Roast
guinea fowl is stuffed with apple, rosemary
and sausage meat, wrapped in bacon and
served with a red wine sauce flavoured with
chocolate. Good fish options include sea bass
baked with garlic butter, and traditional pie
lovers will be torn between classics such as
chicken, ham and mushroom, or lamb and
mint. Round off with a delicious homemade
pudding or a plate of cheese from an impressive cheeseboard selection.

Prices: Set lunch/dinner £15.20 (2 courses). Main
course from £12.95. Bar/snack £4.95.
House wine from £11.95.
Last orders: Bar: lunch 15.00 (Saturday 16.00, Sunday
17.00); dinner 23.00 (Sunday 22.30).
Food: lunch 14.00; dinner 21.30.
Closed: Rarely.
Food: Modern British and Traditional French.
Real Ale: Archers Best, Boddingtons, Castle Eden, Full-
er's London Pride, Wadworth 6X. 1 guest beer.
Other points: No-smoking area. Children welcome.
Dogs welcome in the bar. Garden. Car park.
Directions: J16/M4. A3102 towards Wootton Bassett,
then B4042 for five miles. (Map 5, E2)

Marlborough

The Barleycorn Inn

Collingbourne Kingston, Marlborough,
Wiltshire SN8 3SD
Telephone: +44(0)870 4016198
+44(0)1264 850368
www.barleycorninn.co.uk

David and Heather Wheeler have neatly refurbished this 17th-century coaching inn since taking over in 2000. It is a welcome pit-stop for travellers using the A338 south of Marlborough, offering six guest ales on handpump and good traditional pub food. Inside, you will find a simple yet convivial bar with pastel yellow walls, wooden floors and comfortable furnishings, and a separate dining room with stripped wooden floors, linen tablecloths, contemporary art and painted murals, and a striking blue and white theme to the decor. Food is homecooked and good value, the lunchtime choice including filled rolls and jacket potatoes alongside cheese omelette, steak and mushroom pie and locally-made sausages with mash and onion gravy. From the evening menu, order 'posh bangers' with horseradish mash, red wine and onion gravy, pork medallions with grain mustard sauce, or look to the daily chalkboard for Spanish-style mussels cooked in tomato, basil, garlic and cherry tomato and red onion tart to orange and thyme marinated salmon, and rib-eye steak with pepper sauce. A good summer garden hosts popular barbecue evenings.

Prices: Main course from £7.25. Bar/snack from £4. House wine £6.95.
Last orders: Bar: lunch 15.00; dinner 23.00. Food: lunch 14.15; dinner 21.30 (Sunday 21.00).
Closed: Rarely.
Food: Modern and Traditional English.
Real Ale: Wadworth IPA. 5 guest beers.
Other points: No-smoking area. Garden. Children welcome over 14 years old. Car park.
Directions: Exit 14/M4. On the A338, midway between Swindon and Salisbury, 10 miles south of Marlborough. (Map 5, F3)

Norton

The Vine Tree

Foxley Road, Norton, Malmesbury,
Wiltshire SN16 0JP
Telephone: +44(0)870 4016199
+44(0)1666 837654
info@thevinetree.co.uk
www.thevinetree.co.uk

The secluded 18th-century mill is set in unspoilt Wiltshire countryside, has a tranquil sun-trap summer terrace, a two-acre garden and, more importantly, a growing reputation for innovative modern pub food. Equally, it is popular with local drinkers in search of a decent pint or one of 20 wines by the glass. Partners Tiggi Wood and Charles Walker have smartened up the part stone-flagged interior, furnishing it in attractive pine and maintaining the open fires and evening candlelight. Eclectic menus draw on global influences, although fish from Cornwall is a speciality, as is local game in season, and where possible, they use organic produce. Starters and light meals may include chicken liver parfait with onion confit. For something more substantial try, perhaps, venison and juniper pie, or fishy specials like chargrilled tuna with olive and red papper tapenade. For pudding try the pink champagne and wild strawberry jelly. Impressive Sunday lunch menus include roast Cotswold pork and local farm chicken, and don't miss the popular summer barbecues. Just four miles north of M4 (junction 17).

Prices: Main course from £9.95. Snack from £5.75. Sunday lunch from £9.50. House wine £10.75.
Last orders: Bar: lunch 15.00; dinner 23.00. Food: Lunch 14.30 (Saturday and Sunday 15.00); dinner 21.30 (Saturday and Sunday 22.00).
Closed: Never.
Food: Modern British/Mediterranean influence.
Real Ale: Tiger Beer, Fuller's London Pride, Youngs Bitter, Fiddlers Elbow, Butcombe. Guest beers.
Other points: No-smoking area. Dogs welcome. Children welcome. Play area. 2 acre garden and terrace. Large car park.
Directions: Exit 12/M4. Take A429 towards Cirencester, left for Grittleton, then right in Norton to Foxley, bearing right over ford to pub. (Map 5, E2)

Sherston

Carpenters Arms

Easton Town, Sherston, Malmesbury,
Wiltshire SN16 0LS
Telephone: +44(0)870 4016182
+44(0)1666 840665

You will find this 300-year-old former farm-house on the edge of Sherston village, hard beside the B4040 towards Malmesbury. Whitewashed, with a tiled roof and more recent side extentions, and very much a lively community local, with cribbage and boules teams and a big telly in the bar, it has recently been taken over by Paul and Julie Smith who hail from Merseyside. An early inspection found a warm welcome, traditional pub food, tip-top Wadworth 6X on handpump, and a blackboard listing 10 wines by the glass, thus a useful pitstop following a visit to nearby Westonbirt's magnificent arboretum. Sit in one of the rambling inter-connecting rooms, all pleasantly modernised with wooden or tiled floors, a good mix of sturdy benches, simple pub chairs and tables, some of the latter sporting checked tablecloths, and tasteful bric-a-brac on high shelves. A conservatory extension leads into the delightful garden which overflows with plants and flowers, notably rambling roses and honeysuckle - perfect for summer alfresco eating and drinking. Simple pub food ranges from ploughman's lunches, Wiltshire ham, egg and chips, steak and kidney pie and filled baguettes at lunch, to such evening steak meals with all the trimmings.

Prices: Main course from £6.95. Bar meal from £4.50.
House wine £9.95.
Last orders: Bar: lunch 14.30 (Sunday 15.00); dinner 23.00. Food: lunch 14.00 (Sunday 14.30); dinner 21.00. No food Sunday evening.
Closed: Rarely.
Food: Modern British.
Real Ale: Flowers IPA. 2 guest beers.
Other points: No-smoking area. Children welcome. Garden. Car park.
Directions: Junction 16/17/ M4. Take the B4040 from Malmesbury heading towards Chipping Sodbury. (Map 5, E2)

Swindon

The Sun Inn

The Street, Lydiard Millicent, Swindon,
Wiltshire SN5 3LU
Telephone: +44(0)870 4016201
+44(0)1793 770425
thesuninnlm@yahoo.co.uk
www.cotswoldinns.co.uk

Close to Lydiard House and Park and the hustle and bustle of Swindon, the late 18th-century Sun Inn lies tucked away in a pretty conservation village. Part of Jonny Jonhston's small Blenheim group of pubs (see Falcon Inn, Painswick and Butchers Arms, Sheepscombe, Gloucestershire), its refurbished interior sports tiled and wooden floors, open log fires and exposed timbers, and retains much of the building's original charm and character. Food is freshly prepared from local produce, with meat supplied by Harts specialist butchers in Cricklade, smoked fish from Severn and Wye Smokery, and first-class vegetables from Mise en Place in Cirencester. Well presented lunch dishes may include warm ciabattas, pasta with tomato and chorizo, Wiltshire ham, egg and chips, and liver and bacon with mash and onion gravy. Evening additions and daily dishes may feature lime and chilli seasoned squid, hake with wild mushroom risotto, roast pork tenderloin stuffed with apricots, wrapped in bacon and served with a cider jus, deep-fried cod stuffed with pesto butter, and chargrilled fillet steak with peppercorn sauce. There is a short global list of wines (8 offered by the glass).

Prices: Restaurant main course from £7.50. Lunch menu from £4.50. Bar snacks from £2.50.
House wine from £9.95.
Last orders: Bar: lunch 15.00; dinner 23.00 (all day Sunday during the summer). Food: lunch 14.30 (Sunday 15.00); dinner 21.30 (Sunday 21.00).
Closed: Rarely.
Food: Modern and Traditional British and European.
Real Ale: Wadworth 6X, Flowers Original. Guest beers.
Other points: No-smoking area. Children welcome. Garden. Car park.
Directions: Junction 16/M4. Three miles west of Swindon. (Map 5, E2)

Tenbury Wells

The Fountain Inn

Oldwood, St Michaels, Tenbury Wells,
Worcestershire WR15 8TB
Telephone: +44(0)870 4016202
+44 (0)1584 810701
enquiries@fountain-hotel.co.uk
www.fountain-hotel.co.uk

In just four years Russell Allen has worked wonders at the Fountain, a traditional black and white 17th-century inn beside Oldwood Common. Having totally refurbished the interior and sympathetically extending the pub, he has recently added eleven smart en suite bedrooms to the business. He has also certainly made his name after installing an impressive (and very live) 1,000 gallon shark tank in the low-beamed bar. Press coverage following a shark attack on the head chef's arm boosted trade considerably, and now diners come from miles around, tucking into the likes of baked tuna marinated in garlic, olive oil and spice, while watching Hawaiian tangs patrolling the tank. Seafood is, of course, big business here, with fish bought direct from Birmingham market, but other produce is sourced more locally, notably Herefordshire beef and game from Bowket's of Tenbury, home-grown organic herbs and vegetables, and handmade local cheeses. With food served all day, the menu caters for all tastes, and that ranges from Worcestershire ploughman's, and beef and Fountain ale pie, to jumbo cod and chips and blackened red snapper. Try the award-winning Fountain Ale.

Rooms: 11. Double/twin room from £39.50.
Disabled suite available.
Prices: Main course from £6.95. Sunday lunch £12.95.
House wine £9.95.
Last orders: Bar: 23.00. Food: 21.00.
Closed: Never.
Food: Traditional British with Continental influences.
Real Ale: Adnams Best, Adnams Broadside, Fountain Ale, Wye Valley Ale, Hook Norton Ale. 5 guest beers.
Other points: No-smoking in the restaurant. Children welcome. Large garden. Car park. Shark aquarium.
Directions: One mile from Tenbury Wells on A4112 Leominster road. (Map 4, B7)

Tenbury Wells

Peacock Inn

Worcester Road, Tenbury Wells,
Worcestershire WR15 8LL
Telephone: +44(0)870 4016203
+44(0)1584 810506
james.vidler@btconnect.com
www.thepeacockinn.com

The Peacock, a rambling, ivy-clad 14th-century inn on the Shropshire border, enjoys views across the River Teme and boasts a charming interior that comprises several low-beamed and comfortably furnished rooms, notably the oak-panelled lounge with its blazing log fire, hop-strewn black beams and relaxing dining atmosphere. Quaff local Hobsons Best or one of ten wines by the glass in the lively locals bar, and tuck into fresh pasta dishes and good homemade pizzas from a bistro-style menu in the rear high-vaulted dining room. In the lounge bar the modern menu highlights local produce, notably excellent fish fresh from Birmingham market and local game. Choose, perhaps, monkfish with garlic and sun-dried tomato sauce, or freshly battered cod and chips. Alternatively, start with duck and green peppercorn terrine starter, or mussels cooked in garlic, white wine and cream, then follow with venison with caramelised shallots and a port and redcurrant sauce, or roast pheasant with wild mushrooms and red wine sauce. To finish try, perhaps, the lemon tart with raspberry coulis. The Peacock also offers overnight accommodation in three en suite bedrooms, including two with hand-crafted oak four-poster beds.

Rooms: 6. Double/twin room from £70.
Prices: Set lunch £15 and dinner £18. Main course from £10. Bar main course from £8. House wine £12.
Last orders: Bar: lunch 15.00; dinner 23.00.
Food: lunch 14.15; dinner 21.15.
Closed: Rarely.
Food: Traditional British/French.
Real Ale: Adnams Best, Hobson's Best, Hook Norton Old Hooky.
Other points: No-smoking area. Children welcome. Garden. Car park.
Directions: Exit6/M5. Two miles east of Tenbury Wells on the A456 Worcester Road. (Map 4, B7)

Wye Valley Fountain Ale

at the Fountain Inn

The Fountain Inn in Tenbury Wells serve their very own personalised real ale. Brewed down the road at Wye Valley Brewery, you'll get a pint of unfiltered, unpasteurised pure cask-conditioned ale, fermented malted barley, hops, yeast and water, just the way it should be. Founded in 1985 the Wye Valley Brewery is committed to using old traditional methods while using only the best quality raw materials. This philosophy has brought huge success and rapid expansion, indeed, it is now recognised as the leading cask ale brewery in the county. The awards are impressive and include 'Supreme Champion' at the 2002 CAMRA National Winter Beer Festival for the wonderfully named 'Dorothy Goodbody's Wholesome Stout' and four major awards, three of them again from CAMRA at the Great Welsh Beer Festival for Butty Bach (meaning 'my little friend' - a very appropriate name for some beer fanatics!). Our editor urges you not to stop there but also to sample their classic chestnut coloured Wye Valley Bitter or their smooth Hereford Pale Ale. Besides Fountain Ale the Fountain Inn features a selection of Wye Valley ales as does the Butchers Arms in Painswick, Gloucestershire.

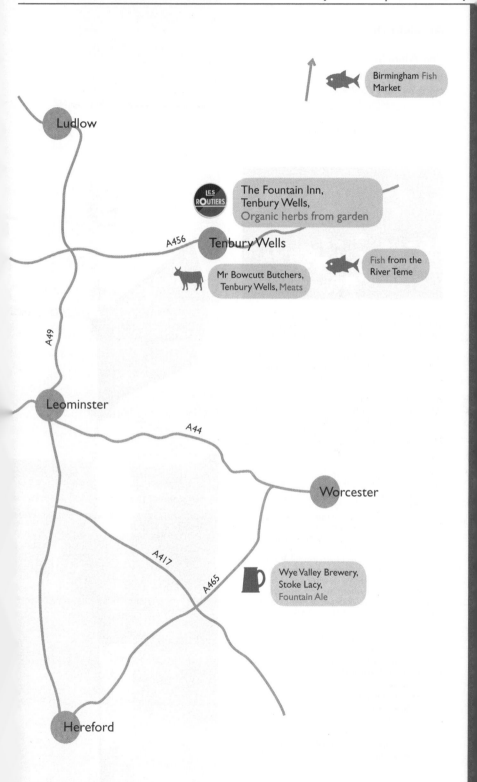

Birmingham Fish Market

Ludlow

LES ROUTIERS

The Fountain Inn,
Tenbury Wells,
Organic herbs from garden

A456

Tenbury Wells

Fish from the
River Teme

Mr Bowcutt Butchers,
Tenbury Wells, Meats

A49

Leominster

A44

Worcester

A417

A465

Wye Valley Brewery,
Stoke Lacy,
Fountain Ale

Hereford

Ampleforth

The White Swan

East End, Ampleforth, York,
North Yorkshire YO62 4DA
Telephone: +44(0)870 4016204
+44(0)1439 788239
www.whiteswanampleforth.co.uk

This comfortably modernised stone inn lies at the heart of Ampleforth on the edge of the Hambleton Hills and a short walk from the famous Catholic college that dominates the area. Following five years as head chef at the now closed Ryedale Country Lodge in Nunnington, Robert Thompson (and wife Gillian) took over the White Swan in April 2003. The past year has seen the food improve dramatically, the day's chalkboard menu now drawing locals and well-heeled 'parents' in for interesting, freshly prepared dishes. The 'country' bar at the front has a quarry-tiled floor and an open log fire and is where the locals congregate. Diners head for the more modern rear dining area, where comfortable wall bench seating and a mix of tables and chairs create a relaxed and informal atmosphere. From lunchtime sandwiches, the menu may list warm crab, cheese and chive tartlet with cucumber and chilli salsa, or local black pudding on cherry tomato and herb mash with shallot gravy for starters. Mains take in classics like battered Whitby haddock and an excellent steak and ale pie with short-crust pastry, and the more inventive, perhaps beef fillet with mushroom, brandy and mustard sauce. Shetered rear patio with views across the Vale of York.

Prices: Restaurant main course from £6.95.
House wine £10.50.
Last orders: Bar: lunch 14.30; dinner 23.00.
Food: lunch 14.00; dinner 21.00.
Closed: Rarely.
Food: Traditional British.
Real Ale: Tetley's Bitter.
Other points: No smoking in dining room. Patio.
Children welcome. Car park.
Directions: In the centre of Ampleforth on the main street opposite the Post Office. (Map 8, D6)

Bedale

The Buck Inn

Thornton Watlass, Bedale, Ripon,
North Yorkshire HG4 4AH
Telephone: +44(0)870 4016205
+44(0)1677 422461

Next to the village green cricket pitch - it's a four if the ball hits the pub wall, a six if it clears the roof - this is a traditional, well-run, friendly institution that has been in the experienced hands of Michael and Margaret Fox for over 17 years. The lounge, with upholstered wall benches, a shelf lined with old bottles, several mounted fox masks, and a fine mahogany bar counter is comfortably old-fashioned; adjacent to it is the newly refurbished dining room which overlooks the sheltered rear garden. At lunchtime good value dishes range from Masham rarebit (Wensleydale cheese with local ale topped with bacon) and deep-fried Whitby cod and chips to smoked haddock fishcakes and steak and kidney pie. Using locally sourced produce, equally traditional evening additions may include homemade chicken liver pâté and goat's cheese and tomato tartlet to start, followed by baked cod with avocado pear and tiger prawns, or the generous Buck mixed grill. At the bar you will find local Black Sheep and Theakston beers, and an impressive selection of malt whiskies. Stay the night in one of the comfortable cottagey bedrooms (5 en suite) and explore beautiful Bedale.

Rooms: 7, 2 with shared bathrooms. Double from £70, single from £50, family from £85.
Prices: Sunday set lunch £12.50. Restaurant main course from £9.50. House wine £9.95.
Last orders: Bar: 23.00. Food: lunch 14.00; dinner 21.15.
Closed: Rarely.
Food: Traditional British.
Real Ale: Black Sheep, Theakston Best, John Smiths. 2 guest beers.
Other points: No smoking in restaurant. Dogs allowed in bedrooms, not in bar. Garden. Children welcome. Car park.
Directions: From Bedale follow the B6268 towards Masham. After two miles turn right at signed crossroads. (Map 8, D5)

Coxwold

Abbey Inn

Byland Abbey, Coxwold, York,
North Yorkshire YO61 4BD
Telephone: +44(0)870 4016207
+44(0)1347 868204
jane@bylandabbeyinn.com
www.bylandabbeyinn.co.uk

The 18th-century creeper-clad inn takes its name from the romantic ruins of 12th-century Byland Abbey, which it overlooks, and both stand in an off-the-beaten track location below the Hambleton Hills. Daytime visitors can admire the views from the charming garden or wait until the Abbey floodlights come on at night. Flagstone floors, polished boards, exposed stone walls, oak beams and a big, open roaring fire are all complemented by heavy Jacobean dining chairs, stripped-oak tables, candlesticks, stuffed birds and objets d'art. In addition, the book-lined library can be used for private dining; it is all very civilised. The menu is classic modern British, with local ingredients shaping the repertoire. Crab, smoked haddock and prawn mousse with creamy tartare sauce may open proceedings on the dinner menu. Among main courses, look for rich game casserole with herb and nut dumpling and shank of local lamb with apricot and honey glaze. Accompany with Black Sheep beers or one of 16 wines by the glass. The three en suite bedrooms are stunning: two have great Abbey views, each is spacious with fabulous beds, and a mix of beams, soft colours and well-chosen period furniture giving a chic, country look.

Rooms: 3. Double room from £80-£120.
Prices: Main course from £7.95. House wine £11.50.
Last orders: Bar: lunch 15.00; dinner 23.00.
Food: lunch 14.00; dinner 21.00.
Closed: Monday lunch and Sunday evening.
Food: Modern British.
Real Ale: Black Sheep Ales, Tetley's Bitter.
Other points: No-smoking area. Garden. Children welcome. Car park.
Directions: From A1; A168 towards Thirsk, then A170 and A19 towards York. Left to Coxwold, then left for Byland Abbey. (Map 8, D6)

Escrick

The Black Bull Inn

Main Street, Escrick, North Yorkshire YO19 6JP
Telephone: +44(0)870 4016208
+44(0)1904 728245
www.theblackbullinn.net

Bedrooms at this traditional village inn are good value and make a peaceful country alternative to the city-centre hotels, yet you are only a ten minute drive from York. You will find Escrick along the A19 south of York and, once at the Black Bull, expect a friendly welcome from the Hall family and comfortable accommodation in ten bedrooms. One has a four-poster, all are freshly decorated with pastel colours and matching furniture, and are well-equipped with TV, alarm clocks, tea-making facilities and toiletries. The en suites with power showers are very well fitted, and as with the rest of the accommodation are meticulously clean. Downstairs, log fires warm a traditional bar that's filled with polished tables and pew bench seating, and there's an adjoining restaurant. Printed menus list classic homecooked pub dishes, ranging from sizzling skillets with peppered steak, or Cajun chicken, to hearty grills (fillet steak with Madeira sauce), lamb shank with red wine and rosemary sauce, and steak and ale pie with shortcrust pastry topping. Daily specials include pork medallions in a cream and whisky sauce or chicken cooked with coconut and cream. Salads, hot sandwiches and vegetarian dishes are also available.

Rooms: 10. Double room from £65, single from £42, four-poster £70.
Prices: Main course from £8. Sunday set menu £7.95. House wine £8.50.
Last orders: Bar: lunch 14.30; dinner 23.00. Food: lunch 14.30; dinner 21.30 (Saturday 22.00, Sunday 20.30).
Closed: Rarely.
Food: Traditional pub food.
Real Ale: 1 guest beer.
Other points: No-smoking area. Children welcome. Car park.
Directions: A19 five miles south of York. (Map 8, E6)

Fadmoor

The Plough Inn

Main Street, Fadmoor, Kirkbymoorside,
North Yorkshire YO62 7HY
Telephone: +44(0)870 4016209
+44(0)1751 431515

Overlooking the triangular green of this tranquil village high up on the edge of the North Yorkshire Moors, this stylishly refurbished old stone pub enjoys distant views across the Vale of Pickering to the Wolds. First and foremost the Plough is a great local and walkers' pub, serving a splendid pint of Black Sheep Bitter in its snug little bar replete with black-tiled floor, simple wall benches and wood-burning old range. However, imaginative pub food is drawing discerning local diners to this moorland oasis. Neil Nicholson sources meat from local farms and butchers, fresh vegetables from Kirkbymoorside, and fish is delivered direct from Hartlepool. Dinner may begin with steamed Shetland mussels in cream, white wine and dill, or duck and mango spring roll with sweet chilli and ginger dip. For main course, try the slow-roasted shank of lamb with red wine and rosemary sauce, roast pheasant with bacon braised barley and whisky cream sauce, or excellent fishy options like pan-fried monkfish with curried mussels. Firm favourites include freshly battered haddock with homemade tartare sauce, steak and kidney pudding and fillet steak au poivre. Good-value two-course lunch and Early Bird menus are also available.

Prices: Set lunch £11.25 (two course). Set early-bird dinner £14.50. Main course from £9.50. House wine from £10.95.
Last orders: Bar: lunch 14.30; dinner 23.00. Food: lunch 13.45; dinner 20.45.
Closed: Rarely.
Food: Traditional and Modern pub food.
Real Ale: Black Sheep Best. 1 guest beer.
Other points: No-smoking area. No dogs. Children welcome. Garden. Car park.
Directions: Kirkbymoorside; north for one and a half miles turn left and fork left to Fadmoor. (Map 8, D6)

Ferrensby

General Tarleton Inn

Ferrensby, Knaresborough,
North Yorkshire HG5 0QB
Telephone: +44(0)870 4016210
+44(0)1423 340284
gti@generaltarleton.co.uk
www.generaltarleton.co.uk

Turn off the A1 at Boroughbridge and heads towards Knaresborough to locate the 'GT', an 18th-century former coaching inn, where you are guaranteed a good meal and a comfortable bed. Little has changed since chef-patron John Topham bought Denis Watkins's share of the business back in 2003. Impressive brasserie-style food is served throughout a rambling, low-beamed bar which boasts open fires, a comfortable mix of country furnishings and some cosy nooks and crannies. Expect a varied choice of modern British dishes on the bar/brasserie menu, queenie scallops grilled with garlic butter and gruyère, for example, or rustic fish soup, perhaps an open sandwich of cream cheese, smoked salmon, bacon and mango chutney. Mains bring Ilkley pork sausages with mash and red onion gravy, rump of lamb with grillled Italian vegetables, and puddings may include sticky toffee pudding with caramel sauce, or, as an alternative, Yorkshire farmhouse cheeses. The adjacent dining-room, formerly a granary, offers a separate set menu. The well-chosen list of wines includes a dozen by the glass. Housed in a more recent extension are 15 uniformly decorated bedrooms.

Rooms: 14. Double/twin rooms £84.90, single £74.95.
Prices: Set lunch £9.95 and dinner £29.50.
House wine £11.75.
Last orders: Bar: lunch 15.00; dinner 23.00. Food: lunch 14.00; dinner 21.30 (Saturday 22.00).
Restaurant closed on Sunday.
Closed: Never.
Food: Modern British.
Real Ale: Black Sheep Best, Timothy Taylor Landlord, Tetley's Bitter. 1 guest beer.
Other points: No-smoking area. Dogs welcome (not in the bar). Garden. Children welcome. Car park.
Directions: A1 Boroughbridge take A6055 towards Knaresborough. (Map 8, E6)

Great Ouseburn

The Crown

Great Ouseburn, York,
North Yorkshire YO26 9RF
Telephone: +44(0)870 4016211
+44(0)1423 330430

The hands-on approach from the hard-working Gill family has ensured that standards of service and quality of food remain high at their classic Yorkshire pub, which stands in a picturesque village and conveniently close to the A1. Traditional it may be in appearance, being chock-full of character and interesting memorabilia, including that of the Tiller Girls dancing troupe who began their careers here, but the food is decidedly up-to-date with imaginative modern British dishes featuring on a variety of menus. From the extensive dining room carte you may begin with baked queen scallops with leeks, smoked bacon and mozzarella, before moving on to a memorable 'Moby Dick' fresh haddock in crisp beer batter, or roast duck with plum and ginger sauce. In the bar, opt for chargrilled British steaks, served with hand-cut chips, the Crown's legendary steak, ale and mushroom pie or Finnan haddock with poached egg. Leave room for banana bread-and-butter pudding or caramelised fig tarte tatin with caramel sauce. Good vegetarian options; set-price monthly menus and decent Sunday lunches. The well-annotated, wide-ranging wine list has been thoughtfully put together, offering good tasting notes and ten wines by the glass.

Prices: Brasserie 2-course set menu £12. Main course from £11. Bar main course from £6.50.
House wine from £9.80.
Last orders: Food: 21.30 (Sunday 21.00).
No food Monday-Friday lunch.
Closed: Rarely.
Food: Modern British.
Real Ale: Black Sheep, Hambleton Best, John Smiths.
Other points: No-smoking area. Children welcome. Garden. Car park.
Directions: Junction 48/A1. Off the B6265 between Boroughbridge and Green Hammerton. (Map 8, D6)

Harome

The Star Inn

High Steet, Harome, Helmsley, North Yorkshire YO62 5JE
Telephone: +44(0)870 4016212
+44(0)1439 770397
www.thestaratharome.co.uk

For seven years Harome's thatched village local was empty and neglected, then Andrew and Jacqui Pern, a young, talented and very enthusiastic couple, came down from the moors and saw its potential. Today, it shines like a beacon well beyond Yorkshire for the Pern's have transformed it into one of the finest inns in Britain. Indeed, Andrew's culinary talents haven't stopped at delivering outstanding pub food - the Star's kitchen also provides top-class goodies to their thriving organic food shop-cum-deli across the lane. The original 14th-century thatched building has low-beamed ceilings, wonky walls, hand-carved oak furniture, and a blazing winter log fire making up the civilised bar. There is a separate, beautifully decorated dining-room; booking is essential. The cooking makes full use of homegrown herbs and seasonal produce comes from a select network of local suppliers. Weekly-changing menus, enhanced by daily specials, blend imagination with bold and vibrant flavours, evident in a meal that could open with risotto of Rievaulx partridge with braised chestnuts, black trumpet mushrooms and roast hazelnut pesto. Next, try the wild turbot fillet with Yorkshire Blue rarebit, seared celery salad and Waldorf vinaigrette, and dark chocolate and orange tart with satsuma sorbet; then the coffee loft beckons for coffee and homemade chocolates. Accommodation is first-class, three are in a thatched 15th-century cottage nearby. Wake up to a delicious breakfast hamper; cooked breakfasts are extra, served in the 'Piggery'.

Rooms: 11. Double/twin room from £90.
Prices: Set lunch £20 and dinner £30.
Main course from £14. House wine £11.95.
Last orders: Bar: 23.00. Food: lunch 14.00; dinner 21.30;
Sunday lunch 18.00.
Closed: Monday.
Food: Modern British/Regional.
Real Ale: Black Sheep Best, John Smiths Cask,
Theakstons, Cropton Brewery. 2 guest beers.
Other points: No-smoking area. Children welcome.
No dogs. Garden. Car park.
Directions: The Star is two and a half miles south-east off the A170 between Helmsley and Kirkbymoorside. (Map 8, D6)

Must See
- Castle Howard, Malton: Magnificent 18th-century domed palace enjoying a dramatic setting of lakes, fountains and extensive gardens.

York

- Nunnington Hall
- Rievaulx Abbey: Beautiful and well preserved ruins of a Cistercian abbey founded in 1131 set in the peaceful Rye Valley.
- Helmsley: Lively small market town with ruined 12th-century castle and Duncombe Park.
- Ryedale Folk Museum, Hutton-le-Hole
- North Yorkshire Moors Railway, Pickering

Where to Shop
Helmsley, Easingwold, Malton and York Farmers Market
Cleveland Way, York

Castle Howard

Tourist Information Pickering +44(0)1751 473791
Where to Walk
For well waymarked and fairly easy circular walks head for Rievaulx Abbey, Sutton Bank, Farndale, Levisham,

Rosedale Abbey and Lastingham. OS Map: Explorer OL26 & 27. For more adventurous walking undertake sections of the Cleveland Way and Lyke Wake Walk.
Events & Festivals Jorvik Viking Festival, York (Feb)
Festival of Food & Drink, York (September)

Kirkham Abbey

The Stone Trough Inn

Kirkham Abbey, Whitwell-on-the-Hill, York,
North Yorkshire YO60 7JS
Telephone: +44(0)870 4016213
+44(0)1653 618713
info@stonetroughinn.co.uk
www.stonetroughinn.co.uk

Lovely views of Kirkham Abbey and the
Derwent valley are to be had from this well-
kept pub, and Castle Howard (of Brideshead
Revisited fame) is ten minutes away. The
bar area is split into three cosy lounge areas,
with plenty of open fires, flagstone floors and
fresh flowers. Exposed stone walls, nooks and
crannies and lots of little knick-knacks add
to the relaxed, homely atmosphere. Here, the
bar menu offers creamy fish pie topped with
cheddar mash, braised Flaxton lamb on roast
garlic mash with rosemary and redcurrant
jus, or lunchtime sandwiches with homemade
chips, and classic puddings - treacle tart with
vanilla ice cream. The restaurant goes in for a
more smart-casual look with large farmhouse-
style tables, crisp linen napkins and softer
lighting. Chef/proprietor Adam Richardson
uses as much local produce as possible, giving a strong regional identity to the food.
Starters, for example, might feature pan-fried
king scallops on pea purée with crisp Parma
ham and thermidor sauce, with mains offering beef fillet with horseradish crust and rich
red wine jus, or roast duck breast with pak
choi, fondant potatoes and oriental sauce.
There's a good rounded, global wine list with
some 60 wines, and four real ales on tap.
Excellent local walks.

Prices: Restaurant main course from £10.95. Bar main
course from £7.25. House wine £11.95.
Last orders: Bar: lunch 14.00; dinner 20.30.
Food: dinner 21.30; Sunday lunch 14.15.
Closed: Monday, except Bank Holidays.
Food: Modern British.
Real Ale: Timothy Taylor Landlord, Black Sheep Best,
Tetley's Cask, Theakston Old Peculiar, Malton Brewery
Golden Chance. 1-2 guest beers.
Other points: No-smoking area. Garden. Children
welcome. Car park.
Directions: One and a half miles off the A64 between
York and Malton, near Castle Howard, overlooking
Kirkham Abbey. (Map 8, D6)

Leyburn

The Friar's Head at Akebar

Akebar Park, Wensleydale, Leyburn,
North Yorkshire DL8 5LY
Telephone: +44(0)870 4016214/4016215
+44(0)1677 450201/450591
info@akebarpark.com
www.akebarpark.com

Peacefully located in rolling countryside
close to Leyburn, Akebar Park is the vision
of Joyce and Colin Ellwood who have transformed their historic farm into a popular
leisure facility, namely an 18-hole golf course
and caravan park. At its heart, however,
is the Friar's Head, a fascinating country
pub created fifteen years ago from old farm
workers cottages. Blazing log fires warm the
character bar, where old stone, brick and
heavy timbers have been used to great effect
in creating a traditional and very cosy pub
atmosphere. The best room is the Cloister
Restaurant, a superb conservatory-style garden room festooned with magnificent vines
and plants and enjoying great country views.
Here you can sit at massive, candlelit, stone
tables and tuck into some good modern pub
food prepared from fresh local produce. Meat
is sourced from local family butchers and
shoots at nearby Constable Burton Hall provide the seasonal game. Typically, begin with
beetroot mousse with mustard and horseradish mayonnaise, and move on to whole lemon
sole with lemon butter and herb sauce or
venison topped with pancetta with sloe gin
and redcurrant sauce. Round off with Seville
orange tart with marmalade ice cream. First-
class Yorkshire beer, decent wines and invigorating local walks.

Prices: Restaurant main course from £8. Bar main
course from £7. House wine £9.95.
Last orders: Bar: lunch 14.30; dinner 23.00. Food:
lunch 14.30; dinner 21.30 (Saturday 22.00).
Closed: Three days in February, phone to confirm.
Food: Modern British.
Real Ale: John Smiths, Theakston, Black Sheep.
Other points: No-smoking in the restaurant. Garden.
Children welcome. Car park. Driving range adjacent.
Directions: A1 Leeming Bar. A684 from west to Bedale,
then seven miles on A684 to Akebar Park. (Map 8, D5)

Wensleydale
at the Friars Head at Akebar

Despite a turbulent history which saw the dairy nearly close in the 1930's before the intervention of a local farmer and then being almost moved to Lancashire, it was rescued by passionate workers who still run the business and who managed a buy out to keep it in Yorkshire, Wensleydale Dairy is still heralded as the official maker of Real Wensleydale Cheese. Indeed, these Yorkshiremen really know their product - from the maturing of the English traditionals including Red Leicester, Double Gloucestershire and Sage Derby to the natural smoking or flavouring of cheese with ingredients such as pecan nuts or caramelised onions. However, it is the Wensleydale which is the highlight, whether it be the mild, slightly sweet 'fresh' white cheese or the ripe, blue version which takes six months to mature and has a smooth, creamy texture similar to Stilton but with a mellower flavour. Find it at the Friars Head at Akebar where you can wash a wedge down with a pint of first-class Yorkshire ale.

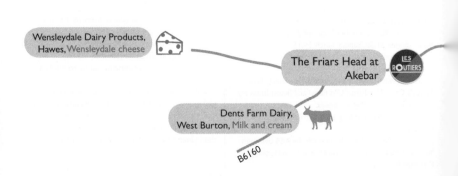

Wensleydale Dairy Products, Hawes, Wensleydale cheese

The Friars Head at Akebar

LES ROUTIERS

Dents Farm Dairy, West Burton, Milk and cream

B6160

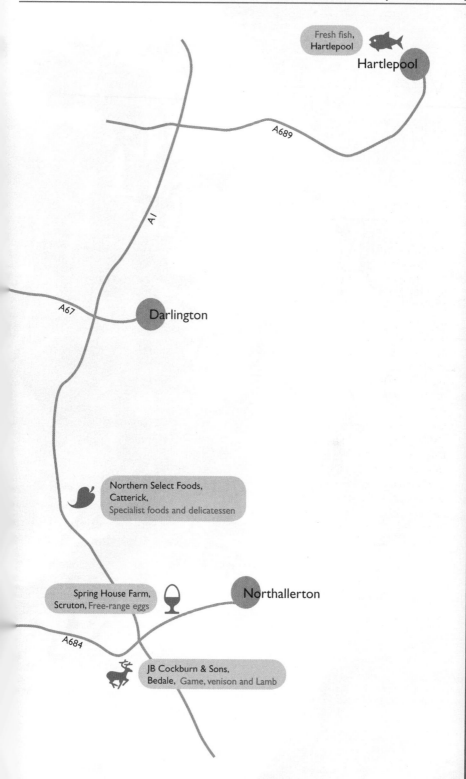

Fresh fish,
Hartlepool

Hartlepool

A689

A1

A67

Darlington

Northern Select Foods,
Catterick,
Specialist foods and delicatessen

Spring House Farm,
Scruton, Free-range eggs

Northallerton

A684

JB Cockburn & Sons,
Bedale, Game, venison and Lamb

Leyburn

The Sandpiper Inn

Market Place, Leyburn, Wensleydale,
North Yorkshire DL8 5AT
Telephone: +44(0)870 4016216
+44(0)1969 622206
hsandpiper99@aol.com

Chef-patron Jonathan Harrison has not looked back since leaving the stress of grand hotel cooking and heading north with his family to sleepy Leyburn and this 17th-century stone cottage just off the market square. In the comfortably spruced up bar a wood-burning stove, cushioned wall benches and low dark beams create an unspoilt and traditional atmosphere, while the simple, yet stylish dining area hints at Jonathan's modern approach to pub dining. Listed on a twice daily-changing blackboard, light lunchtime options may include Caesar salad with smoked salmon and Yorkshire ham with local farm eggs and fried potatoes. However, dinner reveals the true expertise in the kitchen, with a repertoire of well-balanced modern British dishes featuring the best local produce available, notably locally shot game, Swaledale lamb, Wensleydale heifer beef and home-grown herbs. Expect, perhaps, saddle of venison with braised red cabbage and port jus or cod fillet with a herb and apple crust, followed by raspberry and almond tart with clotted cream. Those in need of a comfortable bed should look no further than the two smart upstairs bedrooms or the new rooms in the cottage annexe. All are tastefully furnished and equipped with quality en suite facilities.

Rooms: 2. Double room from £65, single from £55.
Cottage Annexe (double) £85.
Prices: Main course from £10.50. House wine £11.
Last orders: Food: lunch 14.30 (Sunday 14.00);
dinner 21.00 (Friday and Saturday 21.30).
Closed: Monday.
Food: Modern British.
Real Ale: Theakston Hogshead, Black Sheep Best,
Daleside. 1 guest beer.
Other points: No-smoking area. Children welcome.
Dogs welcome in the bar. Garden/terrace. Car park.
Directions: Just off Market Square. (Map 8, D5)

Marton

The Appletree Country Inn

Marton, Pickering, North Yorkshire YO62 6RD
Telephone: +44(0)870 4016217
+44(0)1751 431457
appletreeinn@supanet.com
www.appletreeinn.co.uk

Head south along winding country lanes from the A170 at Kirkbymoorside to find sleepy Marton and the Appletree Inn, a former run-down boozer that has been transformed into one of Yorkshire's top gastropubs by young, talented licensees - chef TJ Drew and partner Melanie Thornton. Innovative monthly menus and daily creations make the most of quality local produce, including lamb, beef and pork from surrounding farms and home-grown fruit and vegetables. Arrive for dinner and follow excellent homemade breads with crab cheesecake, Parmesan crisp and red pepper salsa. Move on to beef fillet on horseradish crushed potatoes with red onion marmalade and port jus. For pudding, opt for the unusual, poached pears in blackberry soup with cinnamon biscuits, but save room for TJ's delicious petit fours with excellent coffee. First rate lunches range from seafood tartlet with caviar cream sauce to truffled wild mushroom risotto and Marton lamb stew. All are served throughout the informal and very comfortable bar/restaurant, with its deep red walls, heavy beams and open fires, neatly adorned with polished tables and hundreds of candles. In addition, expect quality wines, impeccable service, Yorkshire ales (try a pint of Double Chance), and a shop counter laden with homemade goodies.

Prices: Main course dinner from £10.50.
House wine £9.95.
Last orders: Bar: lunch 14.30 (Sunday 14.30); dinner 23.00. Food: lunch 14.00 (Sunday 15.00); dinner 21.30.
Closed: Tuesday and two weeks in January.
Food: Modern British.
Real Ale: 3 Yorkshire guest beers.
Other points: No-smoking area. Children welcome.
Garden. Car park.
Directions: From Kirkbymoorside on A170 towards Scarborough, village signposted right. (Map 8, D6)

Masham

The Black Sheep Brewery

Wellgarth, Masham, North Yorkshire HG4 4EN
Telephone: +44(0)870 4016218
+44(0)1765 689227
sue.dempsy@blacksheep.co.uk
www.blacksheep.co.uk

Set up in 1992 by Paul Theakston, a member of Masham's famous brewing family, in the former Wellgarth Maltings, Black Sheep has enjoyed continued growth. This includes brewing and bottling four award-winning real ales and developing an excellent visitor centre where you will discover how Black Sheep brew 12 million pints a year. The brewery now supplies well over 600 freehouses within an 80-mile radius of Masham. Follow a fascinating 'shepherded' tour of the brewhouse with a perfect pint and a meal in the spacious, split-level 'baa...r'-cum-bistro, with its wooden floors, bright check-clothed tables, brewery equipment and informal atmosphere. At lunchtime, tuck into wholemeal sandwiches of ham and Black Sheep chutney, say, and steak and Riggwelter pie, or one of the blackboard specials, perhaps rack of local lamb with rosemary, Black Sheep Bitter and redcurrant sauce. The more imaginative evening menu (Wednesday - Saturday) may offer honey-glazed duck confit with port sauce and fillet steak with caramelised shallots and bordelaise sauce, with homemade puddings or local Wensleydale cheese to finish. Afterwards, visit the Black Sheep shop and buy some bottled ale to take home.

Prices: Lunch main course £5.95. Evening main course from £8.95. House wine £9.95.
Last orders: Bar: lunch 14.30 (Monday, Tuesday and Sunday 17.00); dinner 23.00.
Closed: Monday, Tuesday and Sunday evening. 10 days in January.
Food: Traditional and Modern British.
Real Ale: Black Sheep Ales.
Other points: No-smoking area. Children welcome. Car park.
Directions: Masham lies midway between Ripon and Leyburn on the A6108. (Map 8, D5)

Osmotherley

The Golden Lion

6 West End, Osmotherley, Thirsk,
North Yorkshire BL6 3AA
Telephone: +44(0)870 4016219
+44(0)1609 883526

Landlord Christie Connelly presides over the bar, dispensing pints of Hambleton Bitter and Timothy Taylor Landlord and distributing menus with efficient aplomb at his old stone inn overlooking the green in pretty Osmotherley. With chef-partner Peter McCoy they have not only created a thriving food pub that appeals to well-heeled foodies in search of imaginative, good value cooking, but one that also welcomes walkers hiking the Lyke Wake Walk. Expect a lively and bustling atmosphere in the cosy, wood-panelled bar, with its whitewashed stone walls, cushioned pew bench seating, log fire, and inviting evening candlelight. Booking is advisable; essential at weekends when the upstairs dining room provides extra covers. Simple, clean and full-flavoured dishes range from fresh mussels in wine, cream and shallots, creamy lemon risotto with caramelised onion, or a deep bowl of tomato and basil soup for a light snack or starter, to warm salads, calves' liver with mash and peas, lamb casserole, or sirloin steak with peppered sauce and hand-cut chips. There are good homemade burgers and vegetarian options - goats' cheese and red pepper terrine with onion and apricot relish. Puddings may include fresh strawberry tart and very sherry trifle plus decent coffee to finish.

Prices: Restaurant main course from £6.50-£13.95. House wine from £12.
Last orders: Bar: lunch 15.30; dinner 23.00.
Food: lunch 16.00; dinner 22.00.
Closed: Rarely.
Food: Modern Pub Food.
Real Ale: Hambleton Biter, Timothy Taylor Landlord, John Smiths Cask. 1 guest beer on Bank Holidays.
Other points: No-smoking area. Children welcome.
Directions: Off the A19 north of Thirsk. (Map 8, D6)

Hambleton Stallion
at the Appletree Country Inn

Traditional handmade ale using malted barley and English hops, Hambleton Ales is a small, family run business that has flourished since its inception in 1991. Starting in a small barn under the watchful eye of the famous Hambleton White Horse it now produces 20,000 pints a week and appears in local shops and as guest beers at pubs around the country.

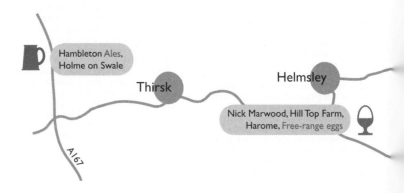

One of these pubs is the Appletree Country Inn, a recent Les Routiers Dining Pub of the Year. This stylish pub in the Yorkshire moors has bundles of atmosphere, fantastic food and, of course, quality ales from Hambleton. Brewing still employs traditional methods and they claim that the local water is particularly suited to producing top quality beer with the unique and all important Hambleton flavour. It is not just available in shops and pubs, they will also deliver to your front door, be it bottles, which can be individually named, or casks, while visits to the brewery for an afternoon of tasting is also an appetising option. With accolades such as the Champion Winter Beer of Britain at the British Beer Festival it is no surprise that pubs such as the Appletree regularly feature beers like the award winning Hambleton Nightmare and Hambleton Stallion.

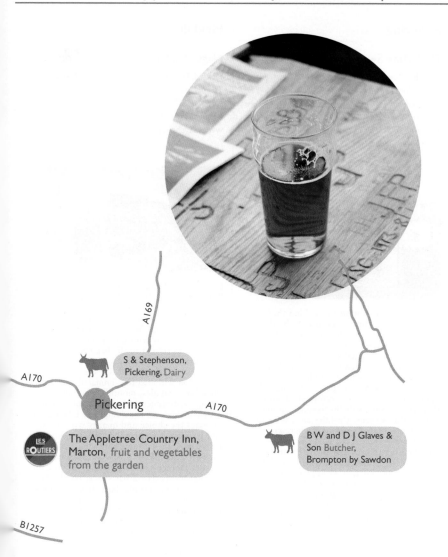

A169

A170

S & Stephenson,
Pickering, Dairy

Pickering

A170

The Appletree Country Inn,
Marton, fruit and vegetables
from the garden

LES
ROUTIERS

B W and D J Glaves &
Son Butcher,
Brompton by Sawdon

B1257

Pickering

The White Swan

Market Place, Pickering,
North Yorkshire YO18 7AA
Telephone: +44(0)870 4016220
+44(0)1751 472288
welcome@white-swan.co.uk
www.white-swan.co.uk

A charming old 'country town' inn that has been run with genuine enthusiasm by the Buchanan family for 20 years, with old-fashioned courtesy setting the style in the intimate, wood-panelled snug bar. Across the entrance passageway is a stylish lounge with deep, comfy sofas and blazing log fire. Equally impressive are the two intimate dining rooms, one recently refurbished with flagstones, tweed soft furnishings and unusual Gothic screens. Upstairs are twelve individually decorated bedrooms where you can expect brass and carved wood beds, tasteful coordinating fabrics and smart bathrooms. This level of quality and attention to detail extends to the kitchen. Using fresh Whitby fish, local meat and game, cooking is simple, contemporary, but unpretentious - Yorkshire dishes given a modern twist. Monthly lunch menus move beyond sandwiches and ploughman's to more imaginative ideas - served throughout the inn. A typical dinner may begin with potted crab with watercress salsa, then braised Ryedale lamb shank with white bean and smoked bacon casserole, with chocolate cake with local organic clotted cream to finish. The wine list includes some notable St Emilion wines. See Pub Walk on page 312.

Rooms: 12. Double/twin room from £130, single from £80, family room from £145.
Prices: Main course from £9.95. House wine from £12.50.
Last orders: Bar: lunch 15.00 (Sunday 16.00); dinner 23.00 (all day Monday, Friday, Saturday).
Food: lunch 14.00; dinner 21.00.
Closed: Never.
Food: Modern British.
Real Ale: Black Sheep Best & Special, Hambleton Goldfield, Cropton Yorkshire Moors. 1-2 guest beers.
Other points: No-smoking area. Children welcome. Dogs welcome overnight. Terrace. Car park.
Directions: Town centre, off A169. (Map 8, D7)

Pickhill

Nags Head Inn

Pickhill, Thirsk, North Yorkshire YO7 4JG
Telephone: +44(0)870 4016221
+44(0)1845 567391
enquiries@nagsheadpickhill.freeserve.co.uk
www.nagsheadpickhill.freeserve.co.uk

Ever youthful and enthusiastic publicans Raymond and Edward Boynton recently celebrated 30 years at their extended, former 17th-century coaching inn which has become synonymous with Yorkshire hospitality at its best. Popular with the racing fraternity, visitors can retreat to the beamed and comfortably furnished lounge, or the tie-adorned main bar, at any time of day for refreshment. You will also find immaculately-kept Yorkshire real ales, monthly wine selections, vintage armagnacs and an array of 40-odd malt whiskies, all the domain of Edward who oversees the choice and quality with pride and passion. Two blackboard menus show Raymond's varied repertoire which utilises the best available produce - local game in season, Doreen's black puddings, and quality butcher meats. For a bar snack, try the beef, rabbit and venison pie, large fish and chips, or a choice of sandwiches (available all day). Interesting and often adventurous main meals extend the choice to poached scallops on spinach with cheese-glazed potato and duck with lime and gin sauce, plus traditional puddings such as Yorkshire curd tart. Fifteen en suite bedrooms are split between the main building, the next-door house and a cottage. Most rooms have recently been totally refurbished to a very high standard.

Rooms: 15 plus 1 suite. Double/twin from £70, single from £45.
Prices: Main course from £7.25. House wine from £12.
Last orders: Bar: 23.00. Food: lunch 14.00; dinner 21.30.
Closed: Rarely.
Food: Modern British.
Real Ale: Black Sheep Bitter, Black Sheep Special, Hambleton Best Bitter, Theakston Old Peculier. 1 guest beer.
Other points: No smoking in the restaurant. Well behaved children welcome. Garden. Car park.
Directions: Off the A1 between Boroughbridge and Catterick, signposted Ainderby Quernhow on B6272. (Map 8, D6)

Ramsgill

Yorke Arms

Ramsgill, Harrogate, North Yorkshire HG3 5RL
Telephone: +44(0)870 4016222
+44(0)1423 755243
enquiries@yorke-arms.co.uk
www.yorke-arms.co.uk

Aysgarth Falls

Must See
- Aysgarth Falls:
spectacular falls which
rush headlong over the
River Ure for about
half a mile.
- Theakstons Brewery
- Jervaulx Abbey:
Remains of a
Cistercian monastery
founded in 1156.
- Newby Hall: Elegant
17th-century house
with interiors by
Robert Adam. Gardens
renowned for
herbaceous borders.

Newby Hall

The Atkins's rather grand and imposing, creeper-clad stone building stands in a remote hamlet deep in Nidderdale. The transition from an ecclesiastical farm building to a shooting lodge adds interest to an elegant interior of polished stone flagged floors, open log fires, antique furnishings, panelling and oak beams. Although run as a smart, yet relaxed restaurant-with-rooms rather than as an inn, Frances and Bill acknowledge the local community by running an intimate bar that serves up pints of Black Sheep Special. Yet the cooking in the restaurant draws visitors from afar with accomplished dishes that deploy a wide range of skills. While the workmanship is detailed, the wow comes from direct hits on the plate: striking combinations such as lobster ravioli with confit of fennel and tomato and shellfish broth, or Nidderdale lamb pie - faggots and braised lamb shank with horseradish lentils and Madeira sauce. Fish is a strength, whether a satisfying starter of seared tuna and red mullet with quails egg, red pepper and courgette, or a main of sea bass and langoustine with roasted fennel and champagne sauce. An enterprising wine list combines interest and value throughout. Bedrooms are well appointed; superior rooms have their own sitting area, and one spacious ground floor room comes with a carved four poster bed.

Rooms: 14. Double room from £100 per person per night, dinner, bed and breakfast.
Prices: Set Sunday lunch £29. Main course from £17.95. House wine £14.95.
Last orders: Bar: lunch 15.00; dinner 23.00.
Food: lunch 14.00; dinner 21.00.
Closed: Rarely.
Food: Modern British.
Real Ale: Black Sheep Special.
Other points: No-smoking area. Children welcome over 12 years old. Dogs welcome in the bar. Garden. Car park.
Directions: From Ripon take the B6265 to Pateley Bridge. Turn right over the River Nidd, signed to Ramsgill. (Map 8, D5)

Tourist Information Harrogate +44(0)1423 537300
Where to Shop Harrogate, Ripon, Skipton, York
Farmers Market
Ripon (3rd Sunday of month) and Harrogate
Local activities
Cycling, sailing and fishing in the area. For information
about activities on Grimworth Reservoir visit
www.grimworth.org.
Events and Festivals
Nidderdale Festival (June/July)
Nidderdale Show (Sept)

Richmond

The Hack & Spade Inn

Whashton, Richmond,
North Yorkshire DL11 7JL
Telephone: +44(0)870 4016223
+44(0)1748 823721
hackandspade@ukonline.co.uk

Jeremy Jagger and Joanna Millar have worked their magic on this 17th-century country local since taking over three years ago. Step beyond the old-fashioned stone exterior for a pleasant surprise. Here original beams, stone-flagged floors and crackling open fires blend beautifully with the warm terracotta décor, subtle lighting and modern pictures that give this old pub a contemporary, modern feel. Everything is immaculately maintained and the pub thrives as a dining pub. The menu is chalked up on boards, but there are additional printed menus, and dishes are dictated by the seasons and by whatever local farmers can supply. Thus, to start, there could be a choice of grilled black pudding on a Swaledale goat's cheese with chilli relish or potted prawns in garlic butter. Then escalopes of pork on apple mash with honey and mustard sauce or salmon fillet with tomato and pepper salsa, with whisky bread-and-butter pudding or local cheeses with homemade chutney to finish. Bar snacks take in open sandwiches, potatoes filled with the likes of gammon ham and chutney, and salads. The bin-end box on the bar displays a good selection of well-priced wines and complements the short, well-annotated and globally-ranging list from Pagendam Pratt.

Prices: Set dinner £18. Lunch from £5. Main course from £7.25. Bar snack from £4.50. House wine £9.75.
Last orders: Food: lunch 14.00; dinner 21.00.
Closed: All day Monday, Sunday evening and the first two weeks of January.
Food: Traditional/Modern British.
Real Ale: John Smiths, Theakston Ales.
Other points: No-smoking area. Children welcome. Car park.
Directions: Take the turning off the A66 signed for Kirby Hill and Ravensworth, five miles west of Scotch Corner and the A1. (Map 8, D5)

Sawley

The Sawley Arms and Cottages

Sawley, Fountains Abbey, Ripon,
North Yorkshire HG64 3EQ
Telephone: +44(0)870 4016224
+44(0)1765 620642

In a quiet village five miles south-west of Ripon stands this fine old-fashioned pub whose immaculate upkeep and enduring popularity are a tribute to the devotion of June Hawes, who has been in control here for some 35 years. She has built up an excellent reputation for good food, friendly hospitality and more recently for quality overnight accommodation in a newly built stone cottage. In a succession of alcoves and tiny rooms, each with winged armchairs, cushioned settles and attractive plates and prints, regulars find their preferred tables and order from June's varied menu and her tempting daily specials that are built around prime local materials, including smoked Nidderdale trout. Expect a good range of fresh cut sandwiches, delicious soups and snacks or starters like salmon, celeriac and herb pancake, and crab salad. In the evening one end of the pub takes on a more restaurant feel, and choice extends to steak pie with buttercrust pastry, braised lamb shank in Madeira gravy, and fresh Whitby cod. Available, on a self-catering basis, the two very comfortable cottage suites feature spacious lounges, fully equipped kitchens and spotless en suite bathrooms with power showers and bathrobes, and plenty of cosseting extras.

Rooms: 2 cottage apartments sleeping two persons each. Prices from £250. There are seasonal price variations, please call ahead.
Prices: Main course restaurant from £10.50. Main course bar from £7.70. House wine £10.50.
Last orders: Food: lunch 14.30; dinner 21.00.
Closed: Sunday and Monday evening.
Food: Traditional and Modern British.
Real Ale: Theakston Bitter and John Smiths.
Other points: Totally no smoking. Garden. Car park.
Directions: Take the B6265 from Ripon and turn at Risplith into Sawley village. (Map 8, D5)

Skipton

Whitby

The Bull at Broughton

Broughton, Skipton, North Yorkshire BD23 3AE
Telephone: +44(0)870 4016225
+44(0)1756 792065
janeneil@thebullatbroughton.co.uk
www.thebullatbroughton.co.uk

Bar 7

7 Pier Road, Whitby, North Yorkshire YO21 3PU
Telephone: +44(0)870 4016226
+44(0)1947 825346

On the A59 two miles west from Skipton, sleepy Broughton and the rambling, stone-built Bull are part of the 3,000-acre Broughton Hall Estate, and the pub's sheltered rear terrace overlooks the unspoilt parkland. Neil and Jane Butterworth arrived here two years ago from the Bull's sister pub, the highly acclaimed Shibden Mill Inn in West Yorkshire (see entry), to extend and improve the pub's reputation for honest, freshly prepared food. Using top-notch local ingredients Neil produces robust, full-flavoured dishes on a sound brasserie-style menu which has proved very popular with local diners and passers-by in search of refreshment. Bread is baked daily and Neil makes the sausages which may be served with mash and Madeira jus as a starter or main course. Dishes range from light meals like smoked haddock and gruyère quiche with mixed leaves and scambled eggs with smoked salmon, to rump of lamb on tomato and thyme flavoured beans, and chargrilled rib-eye steak with béarnaise. All served throughout several cosy little rooms, each sporting heavy beams, exposed stonework, open log fires and a mix of quarry-tiled and wooden floors. Still very much a pub, dispensing locally-brewed Bull Bitter on handpump.

Smack on the quayside opposite the fish market stands this striking, three-storey sandstone building, built in the 19th-century as a bathing and changing facility for returning fishermen. It is owned by an enthusiastic and much repected local family, the Fusco's, who have carefully refurbished the buildings, creating a popular café on the ground floor and, more recently, a modern bar on the first floor. This was once a library and it is reputed that Bram Stoker wrote some of his Dracula stories here. Today, polished wood floors, simple décor and furnishings, a modern stainless steel bar, subtle lighting and tall windows with super harbour views set the stylish scene for enjoying continental bottled beers, a mind-boggling choice of classic cocktails, and some contemporary cooking. Nibble on seasoned olives, homemade fat chips or marinated anchovies while sipping your White Russian, then try the fresh tuna steak niçoise, Fortune's kipper paté, local butcher's sausages with mash and onion relish, a bowl of Whitby crab claws with garlic mayonniase and crusty bread, or look to the chalkboard for chargrill specials and freshly landed fish from across the quay. Bar 7 challenges conventional ideas of the 'pub' and provides a welcome modern alternative in traditional Whitby.

Prices: Restaurant main course from £7.50. Main course bar from £4.20. House wine £9.90.
Last orders: Bar: 23.00 (Tuesday-Saturday, Monday lunch 14.30; dinner 22.00, Sunday 20.30). Food: lunch 14.00; dinner 21.00 (Friday and Saturday 21.30, Sunday 12.00-18.00). Open all day Bank Holiday Mondays.
Closed: Rarely.
Food: Modern British.
Real Ale: Bull Bitter. 2 guest beers.
Other points: No-smoking area. Dogs welcome. Garden. Children welcome. Car park.
Directions: On A59, 3 miles from Skipton. (Map 8, E5)

Prices: Main course bar snack from £6. House wine £9.
Last orders: Bar: 23.00
Closed: Monday to Wednesday during the Winter.
Food: Local seafood.
Other points: Children welcome until 19.00
Directions: Beside the Quay in Whitby. (Map 8, C7)

Mill Bank

The Millbank

Mill Bank, Sowerby Bridge, Halifax,
West Yorkshire HX6 3DY
Telephone: +44(0)870 4016227
+44(0)1422 825588
themillbank@yahoo.co.uk
www.themillbank.com

Chef Glen Footer bought the high-flying
Millbank gastropub off the Halsey's in late
2003. Little has changed at this stylishly
modernised old stone pub which stands on a
steep hill above Sowerby Bridge with great
views over rolling Yorkshire countryside.
The contemporary reworking of a traditional
pub interior cleverly combines log-burning
fires, flagstone floors and old wooden church
pews with chunky modern furniture, stripped
wooden floors, bold colours, abstract art, and
a smartly decked terrace that makes the most
of the pastoral view. Matching this relaxing
and cosmopolitan style is Glen's imaginative modern European menu that draws the
crowds. The emphasis is on the use of fresh
local produce simply prepared. From the
evening carte choose, perhaps, warm salad of
spiced duck confit with truffle oil, or cumin
roasted scallops with chorizo, poached egg
and pea velouté. For main course try the salt
cod with white beans, tomatoes and herbs, or
local venison with celeriac pie, green peppercorns and Madeira, and finish with chocolate
fondant cake with pistachio ice cream. Good
value fixed-price lunch and early evening
menu, plus good sandwiches and light snacks
in the bar. The wine list is usefully divided by
style, and there are 10 by the glass.

Prices: Set lunch and dinner £10.95. Main course from
£8.95. Bar meal from £4.95. House wine £10.95.
Last orders: Bar: lunch 15.00; dinner 23.00. Food: lunch
14.30 (Sunday 16.30); dinner 21.30 (Saturday 22.00).
No food Sunday evening.
Closed: All day Monday, the first week of January and
the first two weeks of October.
Food: Modern European.
Real Ale: Timothy Taylor Landlord, Tetley's Bitter.
Other points: No-smoking area. Children welcome.
Garden and decking.
Directions: J22/M62. A58 towards Sowerby Bridge,
then left at Triangle to Millbank. (Map 8, E5)

Shibden

Shibden Mill Inn

Shibden Mill Fold, Shibden, Halifax, West Yorkshire HX3 7UL
Telephone: +44(0)870 4016228
+44(0)1422 365840
shibdenmillinn@zoom.co.uk
www.shibdenmillinn.com

Keighley & Worth Valley Railway

A rambling 17th-century inn hidden in the folds of the Shibden Valley overlooking the babbling Red Beck. A surprisingly peaceful spot just minutes from the hustle and bustle of Halifax. While retaining an appealing rustic tone, sympathetic refurbishment has succeeded admirably at the difficult task of creating simultaneously a simple pubby brasserie, a restaurant with serious aspirations, and a rather fine place to stay the night. This is a class act with Adrian Jones heading the kitchen, bringing skill and finesse to the cooking. Simplicity appears to be the key to the operation, and good ingredients (much of it local). Clear, well defined flavours are to be seen in a starter of smoked duck with spiced plums and fried onion bread, in lamb shank braised with chorizo and olives, and duck leg confit with roasted beetroot and horseradish. A self-proclaimed champion of British produce, Adrian makes the best of fine materials. His take on British classics includes his version of a Cornish pasty with chips, HP sauce and pease pudding, served in the bar. Own-baked bread deserves a special mention as does the in-house shop of homemade goodies. Wines are well chosen, with a Connoisseur Collection adding weight. There are twelve bedrooms, all comfortably decorated with warmth and style and well-appointed with dressing gowns and TV videos.

Must See
- Shibden Hall: house dating from the 15th century with rooms laid out to illustrate different periods of history; craft weekends.
- Piece Hall, Halifax: unique 18th-century hall now housing an industrial museum, art galleries and shops; open market and workshops.
- Bronte Parsonage Museum, Haworth: family history of the Bronte sisters.
- Keighley & Worth Valley Railway & Museum, Haworth
- Bradford Museums & Art Gallery.
Where to Shop Halifax, Bradford, Leeds

Bradford

Rooms: 12. Double room from £72, single from £60.
Prices: Main course from £10. Main course bar meal from £8. House wine £9.95.
Last orders: Bar: lunch 15.00; dinner 23.00 (all day during the week-end). Food: lunch 14.00 (all day Sunday); dinner 21.30 (Sunday 19.30).
Closed: Rarely.
Food: Modern British.
Real Ale: John Smiths Cask, Theakston Ales, Shibden Mill Inn Bitter. 2 guest beers.
Other points: Children welcome. Garden. Car park.
Directions: Exit26/M62 on A 58; turn right into Kell Lane at Stump Cross Inn (near A6036 junction), then pub signposted. (Map 8, E5)

Tourist Information Halifax +44(0)1422 368725
Farmers Market
Halifax (3rd Sat of month), Bingley (last Sat of month)
Where to Walk
For the best walking head for the Pennine moors. North in Bronte country there are good walks around

Haworth, through Penistone Country Park, and through a remote valley to Top Withins, the original Wuthering Heights. From Hebden Bridge there are tracks along Heptonstall Craggs to the Calderdale Way; Hardcastle Crags and the Pennine Way are just a little further west.

Isle of Bute

Russian Tavern at The Port Royal Hotel

37 Marine Road, Kames Bay, Port Bannatynne,
Isle of Bute, Argyll and Bute PA20 0LW
Telephone: +44(0)870 4016258
+44(0)1700 505073
stay@butehotel.com
www.russiantavern.co.uk

The pretty village of Port Bannatyne on the beautiful Isle of Bute is the unlikely setting for what Norwegian-born landlord Dag Crawford and his wife Olga, a Russian palaeobotanist, describe as their recreation of a 'Russian Tsarist tavern'. The stone-built Georgian building stands on the waterfront in a stunning location, overlooking Kames Bay. It's an amiable place, the friendliness is genuine, and service relaxed. Dag cooks a brasserie-style menu of dishes that have a strong Russian accent having researched recipes from the Tsarist kitchen archives in St Petersburg. His beef Stroganoff is considered outstanding, but gets strong competition from blinis with marinated herring, and spicy Russian sausage served with apple, latkas, red cabbage and sauerkraut. Local produce plays a big part, notably Highland beef and game and fish and langoustines from the bay. A typical dinner of langoustine soup, halibut steak in cream and white wine sauce with new potatoes, mushrooms and artichokes, with fresh fruit, cream and ice-cream filled Russian Pavlova, is remarkable value. To drink, try one of the excellent real ales from Scottish micro-breweries, or even a glass of Imperial Russian stout. Upstairs, there are five unpretentious, good-value bedrooms.

Rooms: 5, 3 not en suite. Room from £22 per person, £26 for an en suite.
Prices: Set lunch and dinner £20. Main course £14. Bar main course from £5.50. House wine £5 per pint.
Last orders: Bar: 01.00 (Saturday 02.00).
Closed: 1-21 November.
Food: Traditional Russian.
Real Ale: Scottish micro-brewery ales.
Other points: Totally no smoking. Children welcome. Car park. 5 free yacht moorings. Beach.
Directions: Three miles north along the coast road from Rothesay (ferry). (Map 9, E3)

Isle of Whithorn

Steam Packet Hotel

Harbour Row, Newton Stewart, Isle of
Whithorn, Dumfries and Galloway DG8 8LL
Telephone: +44(0)870 4016247
+44(0)1988 500334
steampacketinn@btconnect.com
www.steampacketinn.com

Large picture windows at this friendly, family-run inn take in yachts and inshore fishing
boats, as well as the comings and goings of
folk and fishermen in what is considered one
of the prettiest natural harbours in this part
of Scotland. The Scoular family have been
here for 23 years, constantly modernising and
improving this harbourside inn that takes
its name from the paddle steamer that plied
between the Galloway coast and Liverpool
during Victorian times. The split bar, one side
with wood-burning stove, serves Theakston
XB on handpump, and has a relaxed, laid-
back atmosphere. Fish, landed on the doorstep, dictates the menu, served in the beamed,
comfortable dining room and conservatory.
Chalkboards are scrawled with the daily
catch, dishes such as langoustines with ginger,
spring onion, lime and lemongrass, complemented by seasonal game and prime Aberdeen
Angus steaks. Bar snacks take in haddock
and chips, homemade soups and filled rolls.
The well-annotated wine list tours most of
the wine-growing regions of the world. Seven
well-equipped en suite bedrooms, two of
them deluxe rooms overlooking the harbour,
are very good value for money.

Rooms: 7. Double room from £50, single from £25.
Prices: Main course from £7. Bar snack from £5.
House wine £10.50.
Last orders: Bar: 23.00 (Friday and Saturday 24.00).
Food: lunch 14.00; dinner 21.00.
Closed: Bar 14.30-18.00 from October to March.
Food: British, seafood as a speciality.
Real Ale: Theakston XB. 1 guest beer.
Other points: No-smoking area. Children welcome.
Garden.
Directions: Newton Stewart south on A714 and A746
to Whithorn, then take B7004 to Isle of Whithorn.
(Map 9, H4)

Edinburgh

A Room in the West End and Teuchters Bar

26 William Street, Edinburgh EH3 7NH
Telephone: +44(0)870 4016248
+44(0)131 226 1036
john.tindal@btconnect.com
www.aroomin.co.uk/thewestend

Go in the evening to this bar-cum-restaurant
and you will be knocked backwards by the
sheer vitality of this venture. The traditional
bar sports a large oval drinks counter, chunky
tables, and wooden floors; the basement
restaurant has candles on the wood tables,
soft spots, a massive wall mural of Scottish
characters enjoying themselves, and a breezy
informal atmosphere. Value for money is a
major part of the success of this operation,
but the inspired BYO policy adds to the popularity. However, a side order of one of over
50 malt whiskies is a popular option, and
beer is from the famous Caledonian Brewery,
including the award winning Deuchars IPA.
But there is a wine list too, and it offers a
mixed selection of mostly New World wines.
Sister restaurant to A Room in Town (18
Howe Street, New Town), the style of food
is bistro fare with a contemporary twist. At
lunch this translates to smoked mackerel
and salmon fishcakes with Thai chilli syrup
or roast chicken stuffed with black pudding
on pineapple and spring onion couscous.
Seasonal dinner menus may add seared tuna
with spinach linguini, and rack of lamb with
Lanark Blue tatties and redcurrant dressing.

Prices: Set lunch £11.95 and dinner £22.95 for parties
of 12 or more. Main course from £10.95.
House wine £10.45.
Last orders: Food: lunch 14.30; dinner 22.00 (Friday
and Saturday 22.30, Sunday 21.30).
Closed: Rarely.
Food: Modern Scottish.
Real Ale: Timothy Taylor Landlord,
Caledonian Deuchars IPA.
Other points: Children welcome.
Directions: West end of Princes Street along Shand-
wick Place. Along Shandwick Place turn down Stafford
Street and then left into William Street. (Map 10, E6)

Edinburgh

Café Royal Circle Bar and Oyster Bar Restaurant

19 West Register Street, Edinburgh EH2 2AA
Telephone: +44(0)870 4016249
+44(0)131 556 1884
caferoyale@snr.co.uk

This great Edinburgh institution was founded as a bar and restaurant in 1817 and has occupied its present location since 1862. It's a glorious example of the Victorian and Baroque, especially the elaborate plasterwork, gilding, mahogany panelling, hand painted windows depicting sporting life in the 19th century, and the famed Doulton Murals of the technological heroes of the time. Divided into two, the bar, with its dark-brown leather banquet-style seating serves a short, informal menu that delivers very good sandwiches, seafood chowder, and braised shank of lamb with rosemary and honey sauce. In the richly decorated restaurant, the emphasis is on fresh fish, shellfish and game. First courses typically include a salad in some form - perhaps grilled langoustine with a salad of marinated spring onion, young fennel and tomato vinaigrette. Variations on traditional themes might include plump, sweet, pan-seared scallops partnered with crab risotto and a light ginger and vermouth sabayon. Likewise a pairing of collops of wild Highland venison with a bitter chocolate and red wine jus is a typical example of the regularly changing carte. France is the anchor for the wine list with Italy, Spain and New World wines adding variety.

Prices: Restaurant main course from £15.50. Bar main course from £4.95. House wine £9.
Last orders: Bar: 23.00 (Thursday 24.00, Friday and Saturday 01.00). Food: lunch 14.00; dinner 22.00. Bar food: 22.00.
Closed: Rarely.
Food: Seafood and Game.
Real Ale: McEwans, Courage Directors. 1 guest beer.
Other points: Children welcome in the restaurant only.
Directions: Just off the south-east corner of St Andrew's Square, close to Princes Street. (Map 10, E6)

Kincardine

Unicorn Inn

15 Excise Street, Kincardine-on-Forth, Fife FK10 4LN
Telephone: +44(0)870 4016250
+44(0)1259 739129
info@theunicorn.co.uk
www.theunicorn.co.uk

Tony and Liz Budde's careful refurbishment of their lovely 17th-century inn, situated next to Kincardine Bridge in this historic town, successfully combines classic rural charm with the contemporary style of a modern dining pub. At ground level is a lounge that features leather sofas in soft browns and slate blues around an open fire, and the more casual of two dining areas, The Grill Room. Coffee and sandwiches or afternoon tea with warm homemade scones can be taken all day, but its greatest asset lies in the beef from the Duke of Buccleuch estate, reared by Liz's brother Robert, that scores highly for quality and flavour. Additional selections take in fresh haddock and hand-cut chips and pork and ale sausages with champ. Open on selected evenings only, you'll find the Red Room restaurant upstairs, romantically fitted out with deep red, gold-tasselled curtains and tables clothed in white linen. Nightly menus depend on the best available fresh seafood, meat and game. Start perhaps with Loch Linnhe langoustines, before sea bass baked in olive oil and crushed garlic or local venison medallions with sweetened haggis and red wine sauce. Classic puddings or Scottish and Irish cheeses round things off nicely.

Prices: Set dinner in the Red Room £26.50. Grill restaurant main course from £7.95.
House wine £11.95.
Last orders: Bar: 23.00. Food: lunch 14.00; dinner 21.00.
Closed: Monday.
Food: Scottish and Irish.
Real Ale: Schiehallion, Smithwicks Bitter and Twisted.
Other points: No-smoking area. Garden. Children welcome. Car park.
Directions: From the south, cross Kincardine Bridge, then take the first then the second left. (Map 10, E5)

St Andrews

Inn at Lathones

By Largoward, St Andrews, Fife KY9 IJE
Telephone: +44(0)870 4016154
+44(0)1334 840494
lathones@theinn.co.uk
www.theinn.co.uk

Must See
- St Andrews Cathedral & St Rules Tower: magnificent view of the town.
- Hill of Tarvit Mansion House and Garden: impressive Edwardian mansion.
- British Golf Museum, St Andrews
- St Andrews Castle & Visitor Centre
- Balmerino Abbey: ruins of Cistercian Monastery founded in 1229.

Local activities
Fife offers over 300 miles of dedicated cycle routes. Other leisure activities include sea and loch fishing, quad biking, watersports, horse riding and clay pigeon shooting,

Hill of Tarvit Mansion House and Garden

St Andrews

The ancient and modern blend perfectly at this 400-year-old former coaching inn close to St Andrews. Beautifully restored and extended by Nick and Jocelyn White, the 'Inn' has built up a sound reputation for great modern food, first-class wines and stylish bedrooms. The reception has an old-fashioned shop fronted bow-window room which houses Nick's extensive wine cellar, the large lounge has stone walls, a mix of leather and upholstered chairs, and bow windows, one facing the roadside, the other the secluded courtyard. The dining room blends elegance with informality and, with low-beamed ceilings, this part of the inn oozes a relaxed atmosphere. Here, chef Marc Guibert offers a carte built around Fife's finest produce - first-class butcher meats, fresh seafood and organic fruits and vegetables. Dinner could open with smoked haddock and salmon fishcake with lemon and chive sauce, go on to a signature dish of smoked lamb shank with garlic cream and light lamb jus, and finish with a soup of Scottish red fruits. At lunchtime, the Market menu offers a good-value soup, followed by fish and chips, say, or penne pasta with mushroom sauce. Spring 2004 saw the completion of a £200,000 refurbishment of the bedrooms. Personal comfort is paramount, so expect oak floors, goose down duvets, entertainment systems, internet access, and spanking new en suite bathrooms with fluffy robes and quality toiletries.

Prices: Set lunch £12 and dinner from £25. Main course from £14. House wine £11.50.
Last orders: Food: lunch 14.30; dinner 21.30.
Closed: Two weeks in January.
Food: Modern European.
Real Ale: Timothy Taylor Landlord.
Other points: No-smoking area. Children welcome. Garden. Car park. Licence for Civil Weddings.
Directions: On the A915 midway between St Andrews and Leven, 5 miles south of St Andrews. (Map 10, D6)

Tourist Information St Andrews +44(0)1334 472021
Where to Shop Cupar, St Andrews, Glenrothes Newport on Tay, Kirkcaldy
Farmers Market Cupar (2nd Saturday of month)
Where to Walk
A great way to blend coast and countryside is by following the 94-mile Fife Coast Walk, which explores a beautiful stretch of the Scottish coastline between

Inverkeithing, just north of the Forth Bridge, and Newburgh, near Perth. Here, you'll discover Fife's fascinating legacy of caves, castles and ancient forts.
Events and Festivals
Lammas Fair (August)
Leuchars Air Show (September)
St Andrews Week (November)

Harviestoun Schiehallion

at the Unicorn Inn

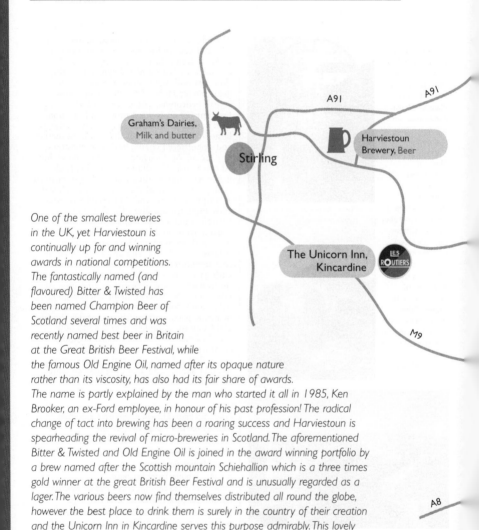

One of the smallest breweries in the UK, yet Harviestoun is continually up for and winning awards in national competitions. The fantastically named (and flavoured) Bitter & Twisted has been named Champion Beer of Scotland several times and was recently named best beer in Britain at the Great British Beer Festival, while the famous Old Engine Oil, named after its opaque nature rather than its viscosity, has also had its fair share of awards.

The name is partly explained by the man who started it all in 1985, Ken Brooker, an ex-Ford employee, in honour of his past profession! The radical change of tact into brewing has been a roaring success and Harviestoun is spearheading the revival of micro-breweries in Scotland. The aforementioned Bitter & Twisted and Old Engine Oil is joined in the award winning portfolio by a brew named after the Scottish mountain Schiehallion which is a three times gold winner at the great British Beer Festival and is unusually regarded as a lager. The various beers now find themselves distributed all round the globe, however the best place to drink them is surely in the country of their creation and the Unicorn Inn in Kincardine serves this purpose admirably. This lovely whitewashed modern dining pub is famous for its fantastic food, notably the beef which comes from the nearby estates of the Duke of Buccleuch. A glass of a Harviestoun beer could be the perfect accompaniment.

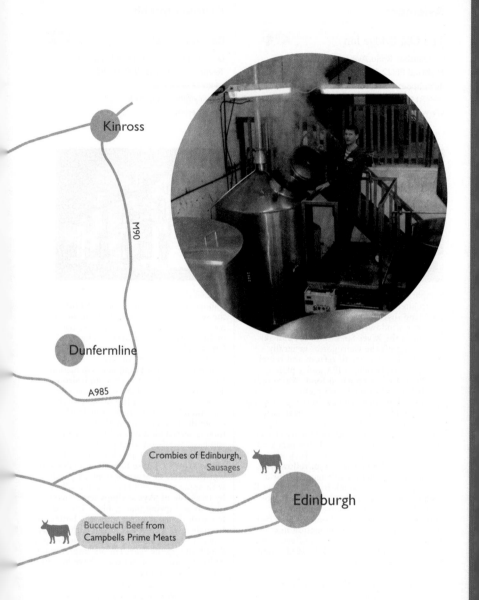

Kinross

M90

Dunfermline

A985

Crombies of Edinburgh,
Sausages

Edinburgh

Buccleuch Beef from
Campbells Prime Meats

Aviemore

The Old Bridge Inn

23 Dalfaber Road, Aviemore,
Highland PH22 1PU
Telephone: +44(0)870 4016251
+44(0)1479 811137
www.oldbridgeinn.co.uk

Sympathetically redeveloped in keeping with its architectural ancestry, that of a Scottish Highland dwelling with steep pitched roof and bow windows, the friendly Old Bridge overlooks the River Spey. Walkers and skiers coming off the Cairngorms generally head for the cosy bar to refresh and refuel with pints of Deuchers IPA and a plate of excellent, freshly prepared food. Warm red-painted walls adorned with pictures of local scenes and antique artefacts relating to winter sports, solid wood tables on a tartan carpet, and a blazing log fire set the welcoming scene. Seasonal menus and the daily chalk-board list modern Scottish dishes prepared from locally sourced produce. Tuck into a hearty carrot and lemon soup, follow with venison and ginger on celeriac mash or a 10oz Angus rib-eye steak from the chargrill, then round off with mandarin cheesecake or a platter of Scottish cheeses. Outdoor enthusiasts on a budget should book a bed in the bunk house accommodation next door. Designed to a high standard it offers good, clean and comfortable bunk-bedded rooms with en suite facilities.

Rooms: 7. Double from £29, single from £12, family room from £38.
Prices: Set lunch £12, set dinner £15. Restaurant main course from £11. Bar main course from £7. House wine £11.95.
Last orders: Bar and food: lunch 14.00; dinner 21.00 (open all day at weekends).
Closed: Rarely.
Food: Modern Scottish.
Real Ale: Caledonian Golden Promise, Batemans & Robinsons guest ales, Deuchars IPA.
Other points: No-smoking area. Garden. Children welcome. Car park.
Directions: Exit A9 for Aviemore. (Map 10, B5)

Drumnadrochit

Benleva Hotel

Drumnadrochit, Inverness, Highland IV63 6UH
Telephone: +44(0)870 4016252
+44(0)1456 450080
enquiry@benleva.co.uk
www.benleva.co.uk

Hidden down a tree-lined driveway and just a short stroll from the shores of Loch Ness, the setting of this 300-year-old former church manse is glorious. Since acquiring the hotel in 2001, hands-on owners Stephen and Allan Crossland, with James Beaton, have implemented a programme of improvements and refurbishment, including new kitchens and bar, and upgrading the en suite bedrooms. Two homely, rustic bars serve cask-conditioned ales, including Isle of Skye Brewery ales, there's a super range of malt whiskies - note the rare cask-strength one - and bar food is served all day until 9pm, with the emphasis firmly on local produce. In the evening the dinner menu kicks in, offering cullen skink, Kilmore haggis with Glen Ord whisky sauce, or Stornaway black pudding with apple sauce and berry salad, followed by fresh Isle of Skye scallops with bacon, tomato and spring onion, Black Isle lamb cutlets with thyme, lemon and garlic butter, or Lochaber venison steak served with a berry sauce. Clootie dumpling or sticky toffee pudding bring up the rear. The six unpretentious bedrooms are all en suite and have hot drinks trays, TV's and lovely views.

Rooms: 6. Double room from £20 per person, single from £25. Family room from £50.
Prices: Main course from £9. House wine £8.95.
Last orders: Bar: 24.00 (Thursday and Friday 01.00, Sunday 23.00). Food: dinner 21.00.
Closed: Rarely.
Food: Modern Scottish.
Real Ale: Isle of Skye Ales. 1 guest beer.
Other points: No-smoking area. Children welcome. Dogs welcome. Garden. Car park.
Directions: Just off the A82 on the Fort William to Inverness road. Well signposted. (Map 9, B4)

Fort Augustus

The Loch Inn

Canalside, Fort Augustus, Highland PH32 4AU
Telephone: +44(0)870 4016254
+44(0)1320 366302
www.lochinnlochness.com

On the banks of the Caledonian Canal at the heart of the village, this former bank building and Post Office dating from around 1820, was converted into a pub in 1985. It's a stylish, well-run alehouse with flagstone floors, stone walls, open fires at either end, Dutch elm tables and chairs and a popular bar where guest ales might include Nessie's Monster Mash from Tomintoul. Best Scottish traditions underpin the bar menus with fish from Mallaig, beef products approved by the Scottish Beef Guild, and Glenuig cheeses all a feature. Wild venison pâté comes with bannocks and redcurrant jelly; grilled Orkney salmon with mango and paw-paw salsa; while steak burgers and aged chargrill cuts are pure Aberdeen Angus. Mid-week summer evenings feature Scottish folk music, out on the lockside in fine weather, overlooked by the best tables in the upper Gilliegorm Restaurant. Taste of Scotland menus here might feature smoked oysters in champagne jelly, rack of hill lamb with juniper and heather honey jus and Loch Ness Mud Pie, rounded off with Highland Gaelic liqueur coffee and traditional tablet.

Prices: Set lunch £7.95 and dinner £12.50. Restaurant main course from £9. Bar snack from £5.95.
House wine £8.95.
Last orders: Bar: lunch 15.00; dinner 22.00.
Closed: Restaurant closed end of October to March.
Food: Traditional Scottish.
Real Ale: Dark Island, Nessie's Monster Mash, Sheepshagger. 2 guest beers.
Other points: No-smoking area. Totally no smoking in restaurant. Garden. Children welcome. Car park.
Directions: Take the A82 from Inverness or Fort William; situated right in the heart of the village on the banks of the Caledonian canal. (Map 9, B4)

Glencoe

The Clachaig Inn

Glencoe, Highland PH49 4HX
Telephone: +44(0)870 4016245
+44(0)1855 811252
inn@clachaig.com
www.clachaig.com

Although modernised over the years, this 300-year-old inn stands in the heart of Glencoe, against a majestic mountainous backdrop with Loch Leven not far away. A legend amongst Scottish mountaineers, with the west face of Aonach Dhu rising up from the valley floor, the inn stands close to the site of the Massacre of Glencoe (1692). Climbers and walkers and tourists exploring Glencoe feel at home amongst the marvellous collection of mountaineering photographs, and huge log fires provide a roaring welcome in the cosy, wood-floored lounge bar, and in the rustic, stone-flagged Boots Bar. In the latter, booted walkers can take refuge and seek refreshment at a bar dispensing 120 malt whiskies and six Highland micro-brewery ales. To soak up the beer and refuel weary limbs, expect traditional pub food served in generous portions, the straightforward choice ranging from filled baguettes and pasta carbonara to venison burger and char-grilled sirloin steak with hot pepper sauce. Twenty-three recently refurbished bedrooms are split between the main house and chalet-style rooms. All are decorated in contemporary style with smart pine furnishings, and equipped with modern comforts (no phones). See pub walk on page 314.

Rooms: 23. Double room from £30, prices per person.
Prices: Main course restaurant from £5.85.
House wine from £8.25.
Last orders: Bar: 23.00 (Friday 24.00, Saturday 23.30).
Food: 21.00.
Closed: Rarely.
Food: Scottish, American, Mexican.
Real Ale: Up to 8 Scottish micro-brewery beers.
Other points: No-smoking area. Dogs welcome. Garden. Children welcome. Car park. Bike shed.
Directions: Located in the heart of Glencoe just off the A82 Glasgow to Fort William road. (Map 9, C3)

Plockton

The Plockton Hotel

Harbour Street, Plockton, Highland IV52 8TN
Telephone: +44(0)870 4016255
+44(0)1599 544274
info@plocktonhotel.co.uk
www.plocktonhotel.co.uk

Commanding a beautiful waterfront location and superb views in an idyllic National Trust village, the Pearson family's unique inn occupies several converted white-washed cottages on the shores of Loch Carron. Tom and Dorothy are fully committed to caring for its guests, from fresh flowers in the lobby and hot water bottles in the beds to limited edition Hamish MacDonald prints on the walls and cosseting sofas to flop into. Day-rooms include a stone-walled leather furnished reception lounge, a non-smoking snug, two bars with crackling fires, a friendly fusion of cask ales, fine wines and finer malts, and the restaurant. Food reflects the surrounding area. Locally caught shellfish landed at the pier daily, west coast fish from Gairloch and Kinlochbervie, hill-fed lamb and Highland beef from the butcher in Dingwall and locally-made West Highland cheeses feature on comprehensive, daily-changing menus. House specialities embrace traditional fish and chips, alongside cream of smoked fish soup and the celebrated Plockton Smokies of smoked mackerel baked with cream, tomato and cheese topping. There's casserole of Highland venison with juniper berries, Highland beef steak platters, and perhaps iced cranachan parfait, among the puddings. Real food and wine, real value and real Highland hospitality make this a place that's hard to leave.

Rooms: 11 rooms in hotel and 4 in the cottage annexe. £30 per person in the cottage annexe, £45 in the hotel.
Prices: Restaurant main course from £12. Bar snack from £6.75. House wine £7.95.
Last orders: Bar: 23.00.
Closed: Never.
Food: Modern Scottish.
Real Ale: Caledonian Deuchars IPA, Sky Brewery Hebridean Gold. 1 guest beer.
Other points: No-smoking area. Children welcome. Dogs welcome in the public bar. Garden. Licence for Civil Weddings.
Directions: Seven miles north round the coast from Kyle of Lochalsh. (Map 9, B3)

Plockton

Must See
- Eilean Donan Castle: Historic 13th-century stronghold built to deter Viking raiders.
- Isle of Skye
- Duirinish Lodge: woodland garden with heathers, azaleas and rhododendrons.

Local activities
Fishing, wildlife watching, pony trekking

Nearest Golf Course Kyle of Lochalsh, Isle of Skye

Eilean Donan Castle

Tourist Information
Kyle of Lochalsh +44(0)1599 534276
Where to Shop Isle of Skye, Dornie, Plockton, Balmacara
Where to Walk
Plenty of signposted walks, including a choice at Glen Affric, immortalised by Landseer's paintings of woods, crags and tumbling waters. The glen forms part of

a long-distance trail to Kintail. Elsewhere paths and tracks reach to the heart of this awesome landscape.
Events and Festivals
Skye and Lochalse Arts and Crafts (May)
Plockton Regatta (July/August)
Highland Games, Skye (August)
Agricultural Show, Skye (August)

Shieldaig

The Shieldaig Bar

Shieldaig, Loch Torridon, Wester Ross,
Highland IV54 8XN
Telephone: +44(0)870 4016256
+44(0)1520 755251
tighaneileanhotel@shieldaig.fsnet.co.uk

Expect a warm welcome from Chris and Cathryn Field and stunning views from picture windows across Loch Torridon to the sea beyond at this popular locals' bar, connected (literally) to Tigh an Eilean Hotel and set in the heart of a charming fishing village. Built in 1800 to encourage local fishing in the area, it has stayed true to its founders' foresight for over 200 years: seafood and shellfish are as fresh as it comes with the Tigh an Eilean's custodians sourcing hand-dived scallops and clams, fish from Kinlochbervie and creel-caught crab and lobsters straight from the jetty. They also make their own bread and chips, obtain their salads and soft fruits locally and provide homemade soup and sandwiches right through the day. In addition there are daily specials such as fresh crab bisque, skate wing with black butter, Shieldaig's famous seafood stew, and perhaps heather cream cheesecake for pudding. From courtyard tables visitors can observe the herons, seals and otters out in the bay or roam the rock pools in search of crab and limpets. There are regular sessions of live-traditional music to pass the evening and, when night settles in, comfortable sleeping accommodation next door.

Prices: Bar main course from £6.25.
Last orders: Bar: lunch 15.00 (April to October open all day); dinner 23.00. Food: lunch 14.30; dinner 20.30.
Closed: Never.
Food: Scottish Seafood and dishes based on local produce.
Real Ale: Isle of Skye Red Cuillin. 1-2 guest beers.
Other points: No-smoking area. Lochside courtyard. Children welcome. Car park.
Directions: Centre of village off the A896 Lochcarron to Kinlochewe road. (Map 9, A3)

Fort William

The Grog & Gruel

66 High Street, Fort William,
Inverness PH33 6AE
Telephone: +44(0)870 4016257
+44(0)1397 705078
greatbeer@grogandgruel.co.uk
www.grogandgruel.co.uk

Active types fed up with bagging peaks and the Clachaig Inn should head for the lights of Fort William and the Clachaig's sister pub, the Grog and Gruel, for great Scottish microbrewery ales, hearty pub food and a lively atmosphere. Its tongue-in-cheek name reflects the relaxed and informal atmosphere of a traditional alehouse and restaurant. Wooden floors, tongue-and-groove walls, traditional bench seating and background rock music set the scene in which to enjoy pints of Atlas Latitude and Cairngorm Tomintoul Stag, 60 different malt whiskies, and all-day food from the printed 'alehouse' menu, served in the first-floor restaurant overlooking the High Street. From starters of 'Mucho Macho' nachos with 'hog's breath' chilli beef and smoked salmon with oakcakes and dill mayonnaise, the menu extends to homemade beef burgers, Tex-Mex chicken fajitas with sour cream and guacamole, house speciality pizzas, fresh seafood tagliatelle, traditional steak and ale pie, and freshly battered cod with a generous portion of chips. If you're not partial to a decent pint, order a litre pitcher of Tequila Sunrise to accompany your beef filled burritos. Don't miss the annual beer festivals.

Prices: Main course from £7.45.
Last orders: Bar: 23.00 (Thursday to Saturday 01.00).
Food: 22.00 Restaurant and 21.00 Bar.
Closed: Rarely.
Food: Mexican, American and Italian.
Real Ale: Isle of Skye Brewing Ales, Heather Ales, Atlas Brewery Ales, Caledonian Brewery Ales, Cairngorm Brewery Ales. Up to 10 guest beers.
Other points: No-smoking area. Dogs welcome. Garden. Children welcome in restaurant only.
Directions: Half way along Fort William's pedestrianised High Street. (Map 9, C3)

From the Isles with love
at Plockton Hotel

Skye and Lochalsh has huge potential for fresh local produce, the problem has been how to actually obtain it. A population of 12,000 people living in an area that is over 2700 sq km translates to a vastly lower population density than the national average. Limited shops and the two supermarkets getting their supplies from central depots simply add to the problem. However, Les Routiers members such as the Plockton Hotel have found the perfect solution in the Skye Food Link Van. Started in April 2000 by a group of food producers the scheme has been a huge success, winning 'Best New Food Initiative ' from the Soil Association in 2001. Any food producer based in Skye and Lochalsh is eligible to join the group, the simple aim being to make the fantastic local produce of the area available to the public, largely by selling it to restaurants and hotels. This has turned out to be more cost effective to these local establishments and the obvious benefits of it not having travelled add to the quality. The van runs once or twice a week and covers just about all of Skye and Lochalsh, delivering a mouth-watering array of goodies from blueberries, strawberries and herbs to crabs, oysters and scallops, with various cheeses, ice creams, cakes and chocolates on offer as well.

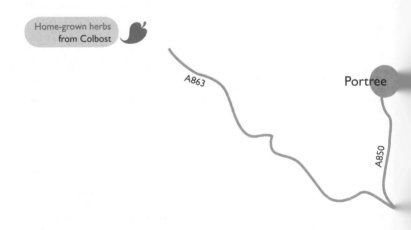

Andrew Wiseman, Aultbead
Fresh and smoked fish

A832

A896

Plockton Hotel,
Plockton

LES ROUTIERS

David Biss, West Highland Dairy,
Achmore, Cheese

A850

Mussels from
Loch Eishort

Comrie

The Royal Hotel

Melville Square, Comrie,
Perth and Kinross PH6 2DN
Telephone: +44(0)870 4016259
+44(0)1764 679200
reception@royalhotel.co.uk
www.royalhotel.co.uk

Standing back from the main square in Comrie this 18th-century coaching inn owes its present name to the days Queen Victoria stayed here. Finely restored in 1995, it exudes a country house atmosphere, with period antiques, paintings and stylish soft furnishings complemented by the Milsom family and their staff's cheerful, helpful hospitality. The cosy lounge bar, along with the wood and stone public bar, are the focus of the local community, offering an informal atmosphere and a warm welcome to all comers. Here, and in the conservatory-style brasserie, homemade venison and leek burgers, fishcakes with hot tomato sauce or haggis hash brown and whisky sauce may be washed down with a glass of Deuchar's IPA or one of 170 Highland malts. Dinner in the intimate Royal Restaurant can be a fixed-price three-course affair or taken from a seasonal carte, that makes full use of the markets' seasonal produce from fresh fish, meats and game to Tobermory cheddar, spiky tasting salad greens and luscious summer berries from the local fruit farm. The beautifully appointed bedrooms, including three four-poster suites, feature furnishings by local craftsmen and rich fabrics.

Rooms: 11. Double/twin £60 per person, single £75.
Four poster suite from £80 per person.
Prices: Set dinner £27.50. Restaurant main course from £9.95. Bar main course from £6.95. House wine £9.50.
Last orders: Bar: 23.00 (Friday and Saturday 23.45).
Food: lunch 14.00; dinner 21.00.
Closed: Rarely.
Food: Modern and Traditional English.
Real Ale: Deuchar's IPA, Bass.
Other points: Garden. Children welcome. Dogs welcome overnight. Car park.
Directions: From A9 at Greenloaning take A822 heading for Crieff; then B827 to Comrie. (Map 10, D5)

Perth

The Famous Bein Inn

Glen Farg, Perth, Perth and Kinross PH2 9PY
Telephone: +44(0)870 4016260
+44 (0)1577 830216
stay@beininn.com
www.beininn.com

Standing alone in a deep, wooded glen, five minutes' drive from the M90 (J9), this old drovers' inn is an institution and a local landmark. Since David Mundell took over five years ago the Bein has become famous for live music sessions, attracting some top recording artists. Rock music fans travel miles to experience David's Rock Bar, a museum of rock memorabilia. Décor is a tad more traditional in the MacGregor Bar, with its tartan carpet, comfortable sofas and armchairs and old local photographs, and in the more formal Balvaird Restaurant, replete with log-burning stove and large bay window. Food is honest and homecooked, the simple menus appealing to a loyal local clientele and passing travellers. From lunchtime sandwiches and light meals like the inn's classic beefburger, haggis, neeps and tatties, and pan-fried lamb's liver, to house specialities and daily dishes of tomato and roast pepper soup, grilled Shetland salmon with herb and prawn butter, and apple and sultana tart. In keeping, en suite bedrooms in the modern, two-storey extension are clean, tidy and unpretentious.

Rooms: 12. Double from £70, single from £45, family from £65. Prices include breakfast.
Prices: Set lunch £14, set dinner £18. Restaurant main course from £10.95. Bar main course from £5.95. House wine £10.50.
Last orders: Bar: lunch 14.00; dinner 23.00 (open all day at weekend). Food: lunch 14.00; dinner 21.00 (Sunday food served all day).
Closed: Rarely.
Food: Modern Scottish with some Continental dishes.
Real Ale: Inveralmond Independence.
Other points: No-smoking area. Children welcome. Car park.
Directions: Exit9/M90. Through village, Famous Bein Inn is one and a half miles into the glen. (Map 10, D6)

Pitlochry

Loch Tummel Inn

Strathtummel, By Pitlochry, Perth and Kinross PH16 5RP
Telephone: +44(0)870 4016261
+44 (0)1882 634272

Must See
- Killiecrankie: battleground and visitor centre.
- Edradour Distillery
- Blair Atholl Distillery
- Blair Castle: 13th-century castle including museum of rural artefacts.
- Queen's View Centre, Loch Tummel

Blair Castle

Local activities Cycling, fishing, horse riding, shooting, quad and mountain biking, white-water rafting

Killiecrankie

'By Tummel an', Loch Rannoch an' Lochaber I will go', and you should! Take the Kinloch Rannoch road off the A9 and keep going along the winding, narrow road into another world. Built as a coaching inn by the Dukes of Atholl, the Loch Tummel Inn enjoys breathtaking views across the loch and mountains, and landlord Michael Marsden explains that his hostelry, where mobile phones are out of range and TVs ordered on request, is a place for stopping, taking in the view, and rediscovering your forgotten childhood senses of taste, touch and smell. Even on a wet summer evening the green and burgundy colour scheme with cream walls decorated with deer antlers and maps makes the bar feel cosy. Here, against a backdrop of magnificent views of the loch, a dinner menu built around local lines of supply is served. This is good country cooking with a typical meal producing local haggis with neeps and tatties, followed by venison with red wine and redcurrant sauce, and a rhubarb and fudge crumble to die for. From the guests' sitting room furnished with comfy sofas and warmed by a log fire, a small staircase leads to six bedrooms furnished in exquisite good taste. Breakfast is served in the old hayloft and includes salmon smoked by the Marsdens in their own smokery. Fishing on the loch is free to residents.

Rooms: 6, 2 with private bathrooms. Single from £50, double from £75. Family room £100.
Prices: Main course from £10.
House wine £4.80 (half litre).
Last orders: Food: lunch 13.30; dinner 20.30.
Closed: End October - the week before Easter.
Food: Traditional Scottish.
Real Ale: Moulin Braveheart.
Other points: No-smoking area. Children welcome. Garden. Car park.
Directions: From Pitlochry take the Blair Atholl road (A9). At Garry Bridge turn left onto the B8019 for eight miles. (Map 10, C5)

Tourist Information Pitlochry +44(0)1796 472215
Where to Shop Pitlochry, Aberfeldy, Perth
Farmers Market Occasionally at Aberfeldy
Nearest Racecourse Perth
Nearest Golf Course Pitlochry
(with handicap certificate)
Where to Walk
Good walks in Tay Forest Park and close to Loch Tummel.

Best Scenic Drives
B8019 to A9 and Pitlochry, on to Aberfeldy, B846 to Tummel Bridge and return to inn
Events and Festivals
Pitlochry Festival Theatre - a different production daily
For other events and festivals contact Pitlochry Tourist Information Centre

~ **Dryburgh** ~
Post **Office.**

Auchencrow

Craw Inn

Auchencrow, Berwick-upon-Tweed,
Scottish Borders TD14 5LS
Telephone: +44(0)870 4016262
+44(0)18907 61253
info@thecrawinn.co.uk
www.thecrawinn.co.uk

A1 travellers in need of rest and refreshment
north of Berwick should look no further than
this cosy 18th-century pub. Only a 1 1/2 mile
drive from the hustle and bustle, it stands
in a peaceful hamlet surrounded by unspoilt
countryside with the Lammermuir Hills rising to the west. What's more, it offers three
comfortable, sensibly priced bedrooms, all
with private modern facilities, good food
and wines, and warm hospitality. The bar
is well stocked with real ales, a wide range
of malt whiskies and some decent wines. In
the attractive dining room, robust dishes are
built around the best local produce. With
fish sourced from Eyemouth, shellfish from
St Abbs, lamb from the Lammermuir Hills
and game from local dealers, the cooking
has a fresh, regional appeal. Expect langoustines and scallops and main dishes like
pheasant stuffed with haggis and Drambuie
sauce, roast duck with morels, an impressive
seafood platter (24 hours notice), and prime
Aberdeen Angus fillet steak with a brandy
and peppercorn sauce. For pudding try the
excellent Scottish cheeses supplied by Ian
Mellis in Edinburgh. Soups, pâtés and steak
pie are available in the bar.

Rooms: 3, 1 with private bathroom. Double/twin room
£35 per person, single £37.50. Two day breaks available.
Prices: Restaurant main course from £12.50. Bar/snack
from £3.75. House wine £9.90.
Last orders: Bar: lunch 14.30; dinner 23.00 (Saturday
24.00). Food: lunch 14.00 (Sunday 14.30); dinner 21.00.
Closed: Rarely.
Food: Scottish.
Real Ale: 2 guest beers.
Other points: No-smoking area. Children welcome.
Garden. Car park.
Directions: Off the A1 at junction with the B6437, 15
miles north of Berwick upon Tweed. (Map 10, E7)

Tweedsmuir

Crook Inn

Tweedsmuir, Scottish Borders ML12 6QN
Telephone: +44(0)870 4016263
+44(0)1899 880272
thecrookinn@btinternet.com
www.crookinn.co.uk

In 2004 Scotland's oldest licensed coaching
inn celebrated 400 years since it was first
licensed in 1604. During that time the poet
Robbie Burns wrote Willie Wastle while
staying at this famous old drovers' inn and
locally born John Buchan knew the inn well
and set many of his novels in the area - the
glorious Tweed Valley countryside. The
Crook Inn is a strange but winning amalgam
of old stone-flagged farmers' bar with open
fire and bags of character, and 1930s pure
art deco in ocean liner-style lounges. Today's
visitors are guaranteed a warm welcome from
Gordon and Susan Bell. As well as providing
comfortable accommodation in five en suite
bedrooms with lovely valley views, the inn
offers local Broughton ales on tap, a good
selection of single malts, and delicious homecooked food with supplies of beef and lamb
provided by a local farmer. Dishes range from
chicken liver pâté with plum chutney, steak
pie, Crook Pillows (cheese, mushroom and
leek parcels), Arbroath haddock and chips,
haggis with whisky cream sauce, and Borders
shepherds pie in the bar, to herb-crusted
salmon with herb butter sauce, and sirloin
steak with Drambuie cream sauce.

Rooms: 5. Double room from £60, single from £38.50.
Prices: Set dinner £15. Bar main course from £7.
House wine £10.
Last orders: Bar: 23.30.
Closed: Third week of January.
Food: Traditional Scottish.
Real Ale: Broughton Ales.
Other points: No-smoking area. Children welcome.
Dogs welcome. Garden. Car park. Licence for Civil
Weddings.
Directions: On the A701 Moffat to Edinburgh road, 16
miles north of Moffat. (Map 10, F6)

Wales

Aberaeron

Harbourmaster Hotel

Pen Cei, Aberaeron, Ceredigion SA46 0BA
Telephone: +44(0)870 4016264
+44(0)1545 570755
info@harbour-master.com
www.harbour-master.com

Built in 1811, the Grade II listed building
once controlled a thriving harbour
traffic. Carefully retained inside is the
original linen-fold panelling hung with sepia
prints of former glory days that are in stark
contrast to its total transformation into
a sparkling 21st-century small hotel and
brasserie. The seven ultra-modern, ship-shape
quarters lead off central, spiral stairs, each
with their own colour schemes in sea and
sky colours: recessed lighting, power showers and space-age radio alarms are somehow
entirely appropriate to the setting. Two new
bedrooms are in the Harbourmaster's private
cottage along the quay, also available on a
self-catering basis. Downstairs in the bar and
brasserie real ale and carefully chosen wines
stimulate spontaneous bonhomie in front of
the open fire and the erudite Anglo-Cwmreig
menus are an object lesson in what fine use
can be made of local produce. Leaving aside
Talybont preserves, Carmarthen ham, locally
reared beef and lamb, and all manner of
seafoods direct from the jetty, a memorable
dinner may comprise pork and sage faggots
with apple sauce and blackberry vinaigrette
to start, followed by pan-fried sea bass, or
vodka and fennel risotto and herb oil, with
passion fruit torte on a raspberry coulis to
finish. See page 259 for an interior shot.

Rooms: 7. Double/twin from £85, single from £55.
Prices: Restaurant main course from £9.50.
House wine £11.50.
Last orders: Bar: lunch 14.00; dinner 21.00. Food: lunch
14.00; dinner 21.00. Restaurant closed Sunday evening
and Monday lunch.
Closed: 24 December - 10 January.
Food: Modern Welsh.
Real Ale: Buckley Best, Brains.
Other points: No-smoking area. Car park.
Directions: On the A487 coastal road. (Map 3, B4)

Llandudno

Queen's Head

Glanwydden, Llandudno Junction,
Conwy LL31 9JP
Telephone: +44(0)870 4016265
+44(0)1492 546570
enquiries@queensheadglanwydden.co.uk
www.queensheadglanwydden.co.uk

Hidden down a maze of country lanes,
Glanwydden and this 18th-century former
wheelwright's cottage is best found by following the Llanrhos road from Penrhyn
Bay. The unassuming Queen's Head retains
its place at the centre of village life, with a
well-frequented locals' bar where real ale
is king and a comfortable, sectioned lounge
where food is ordered and hastily delivered
from the clearly visible, well-organised
kitchen. Chef-proprietor Robert Cureton sets
great store by careful shopping for his daily
updated chalkboard menus. They offer in
their seasons the freshest Conwy crab and
lobster, skate and sea bass from the Bay, and
summer soft fruits from farther up the Valley.
Many appetisers may double as a substantial
snack; as in crispy confit duck leg on a bed
of sticky onions, and Robert's excellent fish
soup. Alternatively there are giant open sandwiches and fresh pasta dishes. From the grill
come pork and Stilton sausages, Welsh lamb
chops, and local beef and wild mushrooms
in a short-crust pastry pie. Home-made
cheesecake effortlessly transforms an informal
evening out into a feast of indulgence.

Rooms: Storehouse cottage sleeps two. From £100-
£125 per night. Self-catering rates available.
Prices: Restaurant main course from £7.95. Bar main
course from £4.95. House wine £10.95.
Last orders: Bar: lunch 15.00; dinner 23.00. Food: lunch
14.15; dinner 21.30 (Sunday 21.00).
Closed: Rarely.
Food: Pub food.
Real Ale: Tetley's Bitter, Burton Bridge Burton Festival
Ale. 2 guest beers.
Other points: No-smoking area. Children welcome
over seven years old. Car park.
Directions: Off A470 between Conwy (A55) and
Llandudno. (Map 7, F2)

St George

The Kinmel Arms

St George, Abergele, Conwy LL22 9BP
Telephone: +44(0)870 4016266
+44(0)1745 832207
lynn@watzat.co.uk
www.thekinmelarms.co.uk

Rejuvenated after a period of closure in the 1990s, this fine village dining pub tucked away in the stunning Elwy Valley, marches on under the touch of Lynn Cunnah-Watson and Tim Watson. Amid country furniture and polished wood floors, everything operates on clean, uncluttered lines around a slate topped bar with its range of quality real ales, wines of the month and exceptional value bin ends. Meals may be taken anywhere - in the cosy lounge, a quieter segregated dining area or the sunny conservatory. From a seasonally adjusted menu, orders are taken with an enthusiasm and confidence matched by the prodigious kitchen output of award-winning chef Weston Holmes. His signature dish of Welsh beef fillet with stuffed courgette, caramelised leeks, sautéed root vegetables and roast garlic and shallot jus is exemplary. Alongside a range of sandwiches and snacks, smoked chicken and bacon salad with honey and mustard dressing, or 'boat sinking battered cod' with tartare sauce make for a more than adequate lunch, with perhaps braised ham hock with creamy mash and white wine and herb sauce as a mainstay of a full-blown evening feast. Look out for market fresh and local meats on the boards. Four bedrooms are available from November 2004.

Prices: Set lunch on Sunday £11.95. Restaurant main course from £9. Main course bar from £4. House wine £9.95.
Last orders: Bar: lunch 15.00 (Sunday 17.30); dinner 23.00. Food: lunch 14.00; dinner 21.30.
Closed: Monday.
Food: Traditional British.
Real Ale: Tetley's Bitter, Castle Eden, Everards Tiger.
Other points: No-smoking area. Children welcome before 21.00. Patio. Car park.
Directions: Exit 16/M56. A5517 and A550 to A55; St George is 2 miles south east of Abergele. (Map 7, G3)

Aberdyfi

Penhelig Arms Hotel

Aberdyfi, Gwynedd LL35 OLT
Telephone: +44(0)870 4016267
+44(0)1654 767215
info@penheligarms.com
www.penheligarms.com

To sit on the sea wall, drink in hand, or on a balcony of one of the rear bedrooms with a magnificent sunset looking out over the bay, surely ranks amongst life's purest pleasures. So said our inspector following a stay at Robert and Sally Hughes's wonderful 18th-century inn, which enjoys superb views across the Dyfi estuary. In the Fisherman's Bar, locals and visitors alike congregate to enjoy traditional ales, first-class wines, and imaginative bar food. This is a true 'local' also, in that fresh fish, meats, fruit, vegetables and bakery goods all arrive at the door from local suppliers, featuring within minutes, it seems, on the daily changing menus that provide such excellent value for money. Diners are charged simply by the amount they eat from a host of choices: smoked haddock chowder, seared tuna salad niçoise, Welsh black sirloin steak with peppercorn sauce, and apricot frangipane tart, being typical temptations to indulgence. The Penhelig Arms just gets better and better: in addition to 14 spacious and beautifully appointed bedrooms, new for 2004 is a stylish loft-style apartment with its own private terrace. A splendid Welsh breakfast will set you up for the day's sightseeing or just lazing around which lies ahead.

Cader Idris

Rooms: 14. Double/twin room from £118 with dinner.
Prices: Set lunch, 2 course from £10.95 and dinner £26.
Restaurant main course from £8.95. Bar snack from £4.95. House wine £10.
Last orders: Bar: lunch 15.30; dinner 23.00. Food: lunch 14.30; dinner 21.30.
Closed: Rarely.
Food: Welsh and Seafood.
Real Ale: Adnams Broadside, Hancock's HB, Greene King Abbot Ale, Felinfoel Double Dragon Ale.
2 guest beers.
Other points: No smoking in restaurant or bedrooms. Dogs welcome. Children welcome. Garden. Car park.
Directions: A493 to Aberdyfi from the A487 in Machynlleth. (Map 7, H2)

Where to Walk
Hilly walks abound, particularly up the friendly slopes of Cader Idris and the hills and valleys near Llanfihangel. South of the estuary: easy beach & nature reserve walk from Ynyslas; excellent rambles through Vale of Rheidol close to Devil's Bridge. Long distance trail - Dyfi Valley Way - 108 miles circular trail to Bala Lake from Aberdyfi.

Where to Shop
Machynlleth
Aberystwyth

MACHYNLLETH

Tourist Information Machynlleth +44(0)1654 702401
Must See
- Ynyshir Bird Reserve: Birdwatching on Dovey Estuary.
- Celtica, Machynlleth: history and legend of the Celts.
- Centre for Alternative Technology, Machynlleth.
- Tal-y-Llyn Railway: glorious journey to old slate mine at Abergynolwyn.
- Aberystwyth: Vale of Rheidol Railway & Devil's Bridge.

Farmers Market Machynlleth (every 2nd Wednesday)
Nearest Golf Course Aberdyfi (good links gourse)
Nearest Racecourse Bangor
Local Activities Birdwatching, boat trips, sea & river fishing, swimming (good beaches)
Events & Festivals
Aberystwyth International Music Festival (July), Welsh International Film Festival, Aberystwyth (November)

Bettws Newydd

The Black Bear Inn

Bettws Newydd, Usk,
Monmouthshire NP15 1JN
Telephone: +44(0)870 4016268
+44(0)1873 880701

Hidden down narrow lanes amid rolling
countryside, and dedicated for over a decade
to 'Food by Molyneux', the black and white
timbered Black Bear has the outward appearance of a Dickensian inn that time forgot.
Indeed it is 'the food and the man' that draws
a steadfast band of regular diners here to
enjoy his touches of eccentricity, produce
drawn exclusively from the day's shopping
and unexpected food combinations and flavours that are the mark of a man who lives
for his passion; somewhat quirky, always
inventive and often genuinely surprising.
Everything Stephen Molyneux finds locally he
uses to good effect, and when it runs out he'll
substitute a handy alternative; the best illus-
tration of this being his inclusive 'whatever
comes out of the kitchen' tasting menu that
might include a pheasant terrine, Usk salmon,
whole Dover sole with lime jelly glaze and
beef medallions in Madeira sauce. Now after
a hearty feed and pints of London Pride you
can sleep fitfully in one of three simply furnished en suite bedrooms. You will be one of
the family and made to feel totally at home
- dogs, muddy boots and all - for there is
simply no standing on ceremony here.

Rooms: 3. Double/twin from £50, single from £30.
Prices: Sunday lunch £12.95. Set dinner £23. Restaurant
main course from £12. Bar snack from £5.
House wine £12.
Last orders: Food: lunch 14.00; dinner 21.30.
Closed: Closed Monday lunch.
Food: Modern British.
Real Ale: Bass, Fuller's London Pride, Tomos Watkin
Ales. 2 guest beers.
Other points: No-smoking area. Dogs welcome
overnight. Garden. Children welcome. Car park.
Directions: Exit24/M4. A449 to Usk, then B4595
towards Abergavenny; village signposted in two miles.
(Map 4, C6)

Raglan

The Beaufort Arms Coaching Inn and Restaurant

High Street, Raglan, Monmouthshire NP15 2DY
Telephone: +44(0)870 4016269
+44(0)1291 690412
thebeauforthotel@hotmail.com
www.beaufortraglan.co.uk

The Lewis family have brought a fresh new
look to this proper 16th-century
coaching inn. While outstanding period
features include a huge fireplace taken from
nearby Raglan Castle, Welsh slate floors and
an impressive heavily carved oak bar in the
lounge, renovation has introduced a modern
feel, best summed up in the restaurant where
contemporary colours complement heavy
beams. However, open fires and a warm welcoming atmosphere are a traditional reflec-
tion of a vibrant, acclaimed inn that is very
much at the heart of things in this commu-
nity-minded village. A team of talented chefs
are committed to using first-class local ingredients. Bar menus comprise simple things
such as rustic sandwiches of Welsh ham and
green salad alongside inventive modern dishes
listed on the daily specials board; overall
quality and presentation is well above average for an inn. In the restaurant, imaginative
cooking produces highlights such as lemon-
infused smoked salmon, and seared, marinated lamb with fine green beans, warm basil
and mint oil on a red wine deglaze. All 15
en suite bedrooms have been stylishly refurbished and kitted out with modern comforts.

Rooms: 15. Double/twin room from £55,
single from £50.
Prices: Restaurant main course from £10.95. Bar main
course from £5.75. House wine £8.95.
Last orders: Bar: 23.00. Food: lunch in the lounge bar
served daily. Dinner: 21.00 (20.30 Sunday).
Closed: Never.
Food: Modern British.
Real Ale: Brains Rev James, Fuller's London Pride.
Other points: No-smoking area. Terrace garden.
Children welcome. Car park.
Directions: Just off junction with A40 from Aberga-
venny and the A449 to Monmouth. (Map 4, C6)

Smoked Barbarie Duck

at the Greyhound Inn

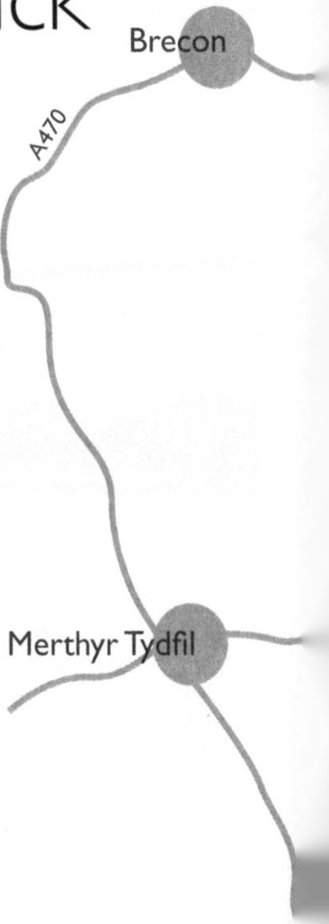

Brecon

A470

Merthyr Tydfil

At the Greyhound Inn, Usk warm smoked duck might arrive at your table accompanied by crispy pancetta, garlic croutons and a citrus dressing. The duck is from Minola Smokery, a traditional, whilst also being one of the most progressive, smokeries in the land. From Oak Smoked Barbarie duck to Oak Smoked Scottish salmon, fish, game, more poultry and cheeses this is a unique place and well worth the awards and accolades that frequently come knocking. They have been produced from Filkins near the source of the Thames in the Cotswolds for the last sixteen years and, to meet the increasing demand for its smoked delicacies, Minola has bought a factory in Abergavenny in Monmouthshire, just north of the Greyhound. What sets this smokery apart from most of its competitors is the use of whole and split Welsh oak logs fired in iron smoke pots, which are housed in ten smoke houses. There is a pride in the fact that no humidifiers, electric or gas equipment are used in the smoking process, only natural convection.

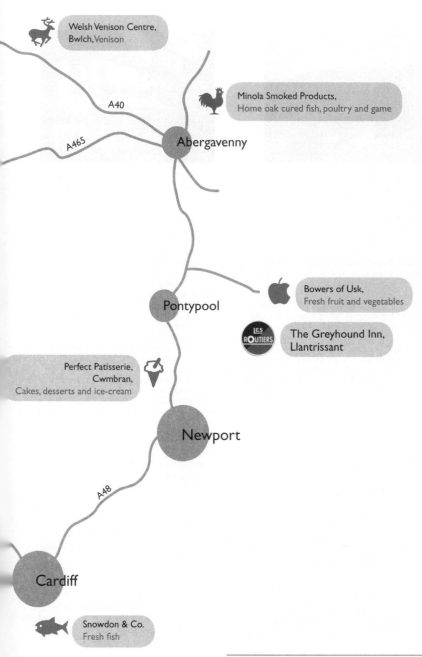

Welsh Venison Centre,
Bwlch, Venison

A40

A465

Abergavenny

Minola Smoked Products,
Home oak cured fish, poultry and game

Pontypool

Bowers of Usk,
Fresh fruit and vegetables

The Greyhound Inn,
Llantrissant

Perfect Patisserie,
Cwmbran,
Cakes, desserts and ice-cream

Newport

A48

Cardiff

Snowdon & Co.
Fresh fish

Skenfrith

The Bell at Skenfrith

Skenfrith, Abergavenny,
Monmouthshire NP7 8UH
Telephone: +44(0)870 4016270
+44(0)1600 750235
enquiries@skenfrith.co.uk
www.skenfrith.co.uk

Janet and William Hutchings's handsome 17th-century coaching inn stands by a bridge spanning the River Monnow, just a stone's throw from the imposing ruins of Skenfrith Castle. Beautifully restored to its former glory in 2000, the Bell oozes sophisticated charm with Welsh slate floors, old settles and fireside easy chairs in the stylish open-plan bar and dining area, and eight luxuriously appointed, en suite bedrooms. A commitment to local produce is a strong point in the kitchen, with fish from Abergavenny, Welsh black beef and lamb and regional Welsh cheeses. Bar lunches bring Gloucester Old Spot pork open sandwiches or venison steak with red onion marmalade and cranberry jus, followed by apple tart with caramel sauce. In the dining room, the set dinner menu is noted for interesting combinations of, say, tiger prawns and seared scallops, chorizo, pickled mango and rocket with blueberry maple vinaigrette, and roast fillet of turbot served with fennel and artichoke risotto cake. There are impressive wines selected by William, local Broome Farm cider, and tip-top ales from Freeminer. See Pub Walk on page 316.

Rooms: 8. Double/twin from £90. Single from £75, family room from £140.
Prices: Restaurant main course from £10.20. Bar main course from £5.50. House wine from £10.
Last orders: Bar: 23.00. Food: lunch 14.30; dinner 21.30.
Closed: Two weeks end of January and early February. Mondays from November to March.
Food: Modern British.
Real Ale: Hook Norton Best. Freeminer Best Bitter, Timothy Taylor Landlord.
Other points: No-smoking in restaurant/bedrooms. Dogs welcome. Garden. Children welcome. Car park.
Directions: From A40 at Monmouth take A49 towards Hereford. After 5 miles turn left onto the B4521 towards Abergavenny, the inn is 2 miles on. (Map 4, C6)

Usk

Greyhound Inn

Llantrissant, Usk, Monmouthshire NP15 1LE
Telephone: +44(0)870 4016271
+44(0)1291 672505
enquiry@greyhound-inn.com
www.greyhound-inn.com

Originally a traditional 17th-century Welsh longhouse and later a staging post for coaches travelling between Wales and England, the spick-and-span Greyhound Inn stands surrounded by woodland and pasture in the beautiful Usk Valley. Noted for open fires and a comfortable atmosphere, visitors will find a printed bar menu detailing traditional pub favourites alongside interesting homecooked specials listed on a daily-changing chalkboard. Using fresh produce from well-sourced suppliers, including locally-grown fruit and vegetables, venison from the Welsh Venison Centre, game and fish from Vin Sullivan in Abergavenny, and smoked products from Minola Smokery at nearby Triley Mill, typical choices may feature Usk salmon, venison and ale pie, lamb shank with red wine and rosemary, and fish pie. Conversion of the former stables has produced ten spacious en suite bedrooms, all decorated in a cottage style that suits both the building's nature and rural location. Ground floor rooms open on to private patios in a garden setting and all rooms are well equipped with modern comforts. Summer al fresco drinking is a real treat among the colourful flower borders and hanging baskets of the Greyhound's award-winning garden, a regular Wales in Bloom Gold Award winner.

Rooms: 10. Double room from £70, single from £51.
Prices: Bar main course from £6.50. House wine £11.
Last orders: Food: lunch 14.15; dinner 22.30.
Closed: Sunday evening (bar open 19.00-22.30).
Food: Traditional Welsh.
Real Ale: Bass, Flowers Original, Greene King Abbot Ale. 1 guest beer.
Other points: No-smoking area. Children welcome. Dogs welcome in the bar. Garden. Car park.
Directions: Exit 24/M4. Usk town square, second left, follow signs to Llantrissant for 2.5 miles. (Map 4, C6)

Wolfscastle

The Wolfe Inn

Wolfscastle, Haverfordwest, Pembrokeshire SA62 5LS
Telephone: +44(0)870 4016272
+44(0)1437 741662
eat@the-wolfe.co.uk
www.thewolfe.info

Ever-ebullient chef-patron Gianni di Lorenzo is a leading light in the Pembrokeshire Food Growers' Association, and his sourcing of local produce and suppliers is a feature of daily-updated menus at his unpretentious stone-built coaching inn beside the A40. Throughout the inter-linked dining areas away from the road a sensible 'as-you-like-it' policy offers an intimate Victorian parlour, the joviality of the hunting room or simple relaxation in a leafy conservatory. Typical brasserie lunch and supper dishes include Welsh lamb faggots with mint and leeks, 'cawl cymraeg' with Llangloffan cheese and yes, tagliatelli Putanesca with charcuterie and juicy black olives. From the carte at night, diners might go for toasted goats' cheese on brioche with homemade pesto and pine nut dressing, followed by locally reared beef sirloin with brandy and peppercorn sauce, or locally landed fish and seafood, perhaps St Brides Bay scallops with hollandaise. Cheeses on display are pure Welsh; best value wines are true Italian from a list that includes a 50-bin personal collection. Draught ales and a simple snack in the front-facing bar are 'simply no problem' with low calorie, vegetarian and children's choices available. Take note of the diary of theme nights or events that take in a Daddy's Day Luncheon, lively Spanish evenings with paella and sangria and a summer fish week in early July.

Must See
- Fishguard Lower Town: the 1971 movie 'Under Milk Wood' with Richard Burton and Peter O'Toole was filmed here.
- St David's: the ruined Bishops Palace next to the town's impressive Cathedral.
- Carreg Sampson: ancient burial chamber on the coast at Abercastle.
- Pentreifan, Newport: ancient burial chamber.

Nearest Golf Course
Letterston, Haverfordwest, Newport

Prices: Set Sunday lunch £12.95. Restaurant main course from £12.50. Bar main course from £5.95. House wine £10.50.
Last orders: Bar: lunch 15.00; dinner 23.00 (open all day 9 April - 4 September). Food: lunch 14.30; dinner 21.30 (Sunday 21.00).
Closed: Rarely.
Food: Modern British.
Real Ale: Worthington's Draught, Hartley's.
Other points: No-smoking area. Children welcome. Dogs welcome overnight. Garden. Car park.
Directions: Exit29/M4. Beside A40 mid-way between Haverfordwest and Fishguard. (Map 3, C3)

Tourist Information Fishguard +44(0)1348 873484
Where to Shop Fishguard, Haverfordwest, St David's
Farmers Market Fishguard (1st and 3rd Sat of month)
Where to Walk
Pembrokeshire Coast National Park offers unlimited potential for walking and exploring on foot. The Pembrokeshire Coast Path extends for 186 miles and includes quiet beaches, historic landmarks and

dramatic cliffs. The trail is rich in bird life too, and the views are magnificent.
Best Scenic Drives
Unclassified roads to B4313, then B4329 and A487 to Aberaeron, A482 and B4342 to Tregaron. B4343 to ancient monastery at Strata Florida, then head southwest to Lampeter and A475 to Newcastle Emlyn. Take B4332 and A487 to Fishguard, then the A40 back.

Brecon

The Felin Fach Griffin

Felin Fach, Brecon, Powys LD3 0UB
Telephone: +44(0)870 4016273
+44(0)1874 620111
enquiries@eatdrinksleep.ltd.uk
www.eatdrinksleep.ltd.uk

Charles Inkin's smart ochre-coloured inn is unmissable beside the main Builth Wells road. It shines like a beacon in the Brecons and ranks among the new-breed of classy Welsh pubs offering innovative modern food and stylish, individually designed bedrooms. Inside, the building has been opened out to form inter-linked dining areas around a single, central bar. Look for flagstone floors, open fireplaces, stripped pine beams and doors, and particularly the Aga cooker retained in an inglenook. With assorted dining and refectory tables, a glorious assortment of antique chairs and walls spotted with black and white photographs and pastoral memorabilia, anticipation of exciting dining is raised. The ethos in the kitchen is to use fresh local ingredients and keep it simple to maintain freshness and flavours. Daily updated chalkboard menus may list pan-fried scallops with asparagus and black pepper butter and terrine of foie gras for starters, followed by rump of Carmarthen lamb with lentils, chorizo and colcannon. Dark chocolate mousse or exemplary Welsh cheeses to finish. Extensions and modifications have led to the addition of bedrooms that exhibit a similar flair for interior design with bright, eye-catching colours and a contemporary feel.

Rooms: 7. Double room from £92.50, single from £67.50. Four poster room £115.
Prices: Main course from £10. Starters from £4.50. House wine £10.75.
Last orders: Bar: lunch 15.00; dinner 23.00. Food: lunch 14.30; dinner 21.30 (Sunday 21.00).
Closed: Monday lunch.
Food: Modern British.
Real Ale: Crow Valley Crwr Taff, Tomos Watkin Ales.
Other points: No-smoking area. Children welcome. Dogs welcome overnight (£10 fee). Garden. Car park.
Directions: North of Brecon on the A470. (Map 4, B5)

Crickhowell

Bear Hotel

High Street, Crickhowell, Powys NP8 1BW
Telephone: +44(0)870 4016274
+44(0)1873 810408
bearhotel@aol.com
www.bearhotel.co.uk

One of the original coaching inns on the London to Aberystwyth route, the Bear today bristles with personality and honest endeavour due to the enthusiasm and commitment of the Hindmarsh family. It stays abreast of the best trends and traditions of good innkeeping and continual improvements have seen expansion deep into its 15th-century fabric, unearthing along the way ever more beams and fireplaces, stone-faced walls, nooks and crannies. Front bars are resplendent with oak panelling, ornamental sideboards and blazing log fires - a perfect location for light lunches featuring salmon fishcakes and daily specials such as oxtails braised in red wine with roast beetroot. More extensive menus in the separate, more formal dining rooms display solid reliance on local suppliers for Brecon lamb and venison, market-fresh fish and Welsh cheeses. A sample meal may take in confit duck leg with steamed pak choi, followed by sea bass with crab and ginger risotto, or Welsh Black beef with leek and gruyère spring roll, with poached pear and lemon delice for pudding. Former stables have been converted into a courtyard of up-to-date bedrooms.

Rooms: 35. Double room from £75, single from £57. Family room from £102.
Prices: Main course from £15. Bar meal from £7. House wine £10.50.
Last orders: Bar: lunch 15.00; dinner 23.00. Food: lunch 14.00; dinner 21.30.
Closed: Rarely.
Food: Modern/eclectic.
Real Ale: Hancock's HB, Bass, Greene King Old Speckled Hen, Reverend James.
Other points: No-smoking area. Children welcome. Dogs welcome overnight. Garden. Car park.
Directions: On A40 in town centre. (Map 4, C6)

Harbourmaster Hotel, Aberaeron, Ceredigion

Welsh Venison

at the Felin Fach Griffin

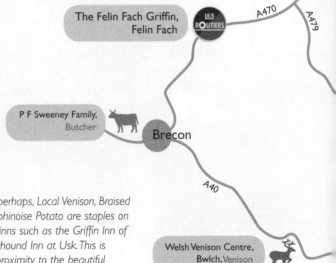

The Felin Fach Griffin, Felin Fach

P F Sweeney Family, Butcher

Brecon

Welsh Venison Centre, Bwlch, Venison

A470

A479

A40

Venison and Ale Pie or, perhaps, Local Venison, Braised Red Cabbage and Dauphinoise Potato are staples on menus in classic Welsh inns such as the Griffin Inn of Felin Fach and the Greyhound Inn at Usk. This is possible down to their proximity to the beautiful Brecon Beacons National Park and the existence of the fantastic Welsh Venison Centre, a family run business established in 1985 by the Morgan family. With the farmed deer raised in the beautiful surroundings of the national park and the guarantee of superb animal husbandry, animal welfare is of the highest order as is taste. Venison here is as tender as other red meats with a mild yet distinctive and succulent flavour, not at all like the tough gamey reputation venison often has, usually attributed to wild deer. Usually a contradiction in terms, this is also a delicious but low-fat meat. Venison is naturally lean and lower in fat and cholesterol than chicken with higher iron level than red meats, plus it is packed full of vitamins and protein. We cannot see any better reason not to give it a go!

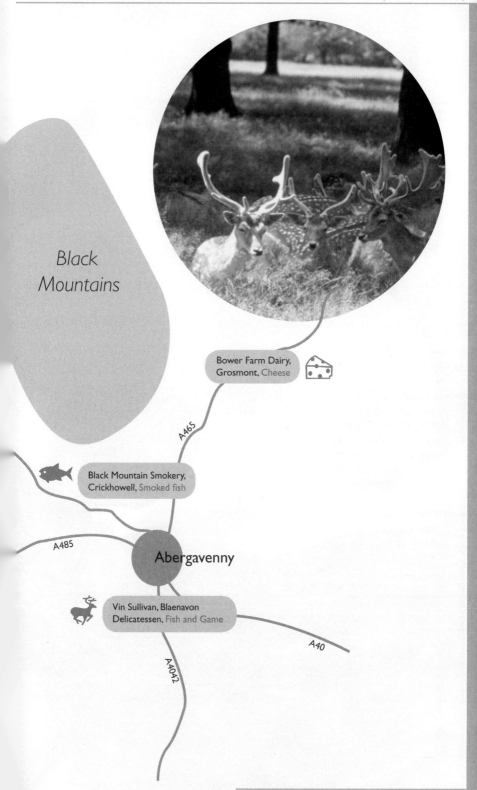

Black
Mountains

Bower Farm Dairy,
Grosmont, Cheese

A465

Black Mountain Smokery,
Crickhowell, Smoked fish

A485

Abergavenny

Vin Sullivan, Blaenavon
Delicatessen, Fish and Game

A40

A4042

Llanrhidian

Welcome To Town Country Bistro & Bar

Llanrhidian, Gower, Swansea SA3 1EH
Telephone: +44(0)870 4016275
+44(0)1792 390015
www.thewelcometotown.co.uk

The 300-year-old whitewashed country inn-cum-bistro is situated on the Gower Peninsula overlooking the Penclawdd Cockle beds. Noted for friendly service and a relaxed atmosphere, fresh produce is essential to the kitchen's aspirations, and in this part of Wales, nature's larder is a particularly handy resource: locally grown asparagus, cockles from Penclawdd, seasonal lobsters, laver bread, salt-marsh lamb, Welsh Black beef, cheeses from Swansea market. As an example of what all this bounty adds up to on the plate, look no further than pan-fried local sewin with braised samphire and laver bread sauce. Seafood can turn up in a starter of mackerel escabeche, or again in a main course of pan-fried wild sea bass with creamed potatoes and garden peas. A roast saddle of Welsh lamb may be simply served by some niçoise vegetables, and a fillet of Welsh Black beef with buttered spinach and fondant potato. Everything stays on an even keel, right through to desserts, such as fresh fruit vacharin with passion fruit sorbet, or a smooth, delicate vanilla panna cotta with local strawberries. Bread, baked on the premises, is delicious, and the same attention to detail extends to homemade ice creams and sorbets. The well-chosen house wine is especially good value.

Prices: Set lunch £14.95. Restaurant main course from £11. Bar main course from £6.50. House wine £11.

Aberthaw

The Blue Anchor

East Aberthaw, Vale of Glamorgan CF62 3DD
Telephone: +44(0)870 4016276
+44(0)1446 750329
www.blueanchoraberthaw.com

The famous Blue Anchor closed its doors to customers for the first time in living memory on 20th February 2004 following a serious fire which destroyed the whole roof and upper floor of this unique thatched building. This much loved pub was due to re-open in early autumn 2004. Until now it had an unbroken history as a pub back to 1380, with stories of pirates and contraband and evidence of ancient tunnelling down to the nearby shore-line. Thankfully untouched by the fire are the warren of inter-linked rooms with tiny doorways, narrow passages and stairs that lead nowhere, stone fireplaces under vast oak lintels and a central bar that attracts swarms of real ale buffs. Family-owned and run for over 40 years, the property includes a three-acre kitchen garden and owns the private shoot that provides winter game. When normal service resumes expect to find the likes of lamb and leek casserole, spicy beef curry and pheasant breast in apple and cider cream sauce supplementing lunch-time sandwiches, jacket potatoes, assorted regional cheeses and things for kids and vegetarians. At dinner the menu choice extends to poached Wye salmon with fresh asparagus, rack of Welsh lamb with grain mustard crusting and chicken supreme in coconut and tar-

The Five Arrows Hotel, Waddesdon

The Delights of Waddesdon Manor

Make a day of it visiting the palatial home of a famous banking family and then enjoy this attractive walk through its extensive parkland.

Start. With your back to the inn turn left, then left again by the war memorial into High Street. Walk along to some beautifully decorated gates, the public entrance to Waddesdon Manor, and continue on the drive. When it emerges from the trees, look for a waymark and follow the grassy path ahead, keeping a hedge and pavilion on the right and the snaking main drive over to the left.

Start

2 Cross the drive further on and follow the bridleway signposted to Windmill Hill Farm. Cut between fields and bursts of woodland and follow the drive as it bends right over a cattle-grid.

3 On the horizon now is the awesome façade of Waddesdon Manor, a jumble of exuberant architectural styles. The drive swings left at the next cattle-grid and cuts through a copse. Keep on the bridleway to Windmill Hill Farm and follow the track between the outbuildings.

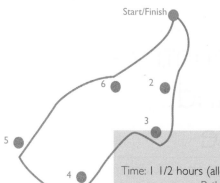

Start/Finish

6   2

3

5

4

Look out for

The Five Arrows: Mayer Amschel Rothschild founded the famous banking dynasty in the 18th-century. The family coat of arms focuses on a red shield and includes a fist holding five arrows. The arrows represent his five sons, four of whom left Frankfurt to establish banking houses in Europe's other financial centres.
Waddesdon Manor is one of England's grandest country houses. It is a French Renaissance-style chateau built by Ferdinand de Rothschild in the late 19th century.

4 Continue between fields to a gate and along the field edge to the next gate. Turn right and keep the hedge on the right. Keep ahead in the next field and on reaching the boundary, cross it and then turn immediately right over a stile and footbridge.

5 Keep along the right-hand boundary, cross the stile in the field corner and continue to two stiles and a footbridge in the right fence. Go diagonally left in the field and head up the slope towards trees. Head for a gap and follow the path up the bank to the main drive to Waddesdon Manor.

6 Turn right and when you reach a waymark for the Tramway Trail, branch off half left across the grassy slopes. Make for a wrought iron kissing gate and follow the path ahead towards trees. Go through a gate on the far side of the field, cut through woodland and cross a drive to reach some lock-up garages. Ahead now are the war memorial and the Five Arrows.
For pub entry see page 57

Five Arrows Hotel

The Pheasant Inn, Chester

Sandstone Country - Burwardsley and Beeston Castle

Follow the scenic Sandstone Trail on this pretty walk, discovering a delightfully unspoiled rural corner of the north-west with glorious views across the Cheshire Plain.

The Pheasant Inn

Start. On leaving the pub turn right and follow the lane with good views on the left. Pass a cottage opposite the car park entrance, followed by a footpath on the left. Continue on the lane, passing a row of cottages. On reaching the entrance to Spring House on the left, keep ahead on the track, following it through the woods.

2 Climb steadily, following the waymarks and signs for Beeston Castle. Further on, there are glimpses of the castle between the trees. At the road turn right and pass Moathouse Farm. Avoid two rights of way immediately beyond it and continue to the next left path, part of the Sandstone Trail.

3 Take the path, following it down the field boundary to a footbridge and some steps. Cross the field to the road, turn left to Tabernacle Cottage and then swing right to follow the next section of the Sandstone Trail. Follow the path up through the trees and alongside a stone wall.

4 Go straight ahead for a few paces at the next road to reach the entrance to Beeston Castle. Retrace your steps along the road, round the left bend and into Beeston village. Turn left at the T junction, then left again at the next junction by a telephone box.

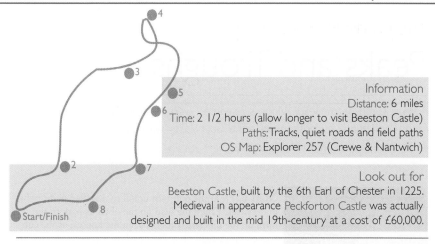

Information
Distance: 6 miles
Time: 2 1/2 hours (allow longer to visit Beeston Castle)
Paths: Tracks, quiet roads and field paths
OS Map: Explorer 257 (Crewe & Nantwich)

2

7

Look out for
Beeston Castle, built by the 6th Earl of Chester in 1225.
Medieval in appearance Peckforton Castle was actually
designed and built in the mid 19th-century at a cost of £60,000.

Start/Finish

8

5 Follow the road for 120 yards, then swing right at the turning for Bunbury. Pass a farm and cottage and when the road bends left, veer right at a track signposted Peckforton. Cross two stiles and then aim half left in the field, heading for a curtain of woodland. There are good views here of Beeston Castle and Peckforton Castle. Pass a pond and make for the trees.

6 Go straight ahead through the wood, avoiding the path on the right. Emerge from the trees at the next stile and cross the field to a stile in the far right corner. Opposite is the entrance to Peckforton Castle. Turn left and follow the road to some steps and a path signposted Burwardsley.

7 Cross two stiles and then head diagonally across the field towards woodland. Make for a stile in the top corner, followed shortly by a second and third stile, then cut between trees and fence to reach a track. Turn left for several paces, then right to cross the Peckforton Hills.

8 Merge with another track and pass under a bridge. Cut between trees and fields and briefly rejoin the Sandstone Trail. When it turns right continue on a tarmac lane, passing Rockhouse Farm. Turn right at the junction and right again for the Pheasant.
For pub entry see page 62

The Oddfellows Arms, Mellor

Peaks and Troughs

A short climb onto Mellor Moor is rewarded with spectacular views across the Dark Peak, then you descend into the Goyt Valley with its wildflower-rich woodlands and fascinating industrial heritage.

Oddfellows Arms

Start. From the pub turn uphill to a walled path, right, in 40 yards. Climb the field up the obvious path to the farm on the hillcrest. Pass between the houses; as the cobbles end fork right on a short path to a concreted track and turn left to a crossroads.

2 Go straight over into the rough Primrose Lane. Remain with this across Mellor Moor, eventually bending left to reach a wooded corner and cross-lanes beyond a farm. Turn right on Castle Edge Road to a golf clubhouse. Turn right along the rough lane immediately before this, keep left at the fork and drop to a road. Turn right to Brook Bottom.

3 Just before The Fox Inn turn left down the Goyt Way (GW). Pass under Strines Station bridge and down the cobbled road. As the cobbles become tarmac, turn right along the lane (GW).

4 At Greenclough Farm bend right, cross the bridge and turn left (GW). Keep on the upper path to leave the woods. At a fork keep left on a gravel track to Richmond Farm, then go under the railway. The track joins the river Goyt (look left opposite a cottage for the sublime Roman Bridge packhorse bridge); remain with this beneath the viaduct and past old mill lodges known as Roman Lakes. At the junction past the lake turn right to Bottoms Hall. Fork right (signed for Cobden Edge) and trace the rough lane through Linnet Clough Woods.

Start/Finish

Information
Distance: 6 miles
Time: 3 hours
Paths: Old moorland roads, field paths and lanes
OS Map: Explorer OL1 (The Peak District, Dark Peak Area)

Look out for
Mellor Moor is criss-crossed by old walled lanes dating from the 18th-century. St Thomas's Church dates back nearly 1000 years and houses a medieval wooden pulpit. There is alternative parking at Mellor Church (Point 6) should the pub car park be unavailable. Access is via Church Road, left off Longhurst Lane, 1/2 mile before the pub.

5 Turn left into the scouting complex. Near the far end (fingerpost for Mellor) turn left at climbing frames to find a waymark post at the back-right of the grassy area. Cross the brook and take the left gateway a short way beyond, aiming in-line towards distant Mellor Church. Several stiles bring you to an isolated house; take the drive to the road. Take the narrow path opposite, dropping steeply to and across a stream. Climb the bank and turn right up the lane. Turn right in the farmyard to walk to Mellor Church.

6 Turn down the lane beyond the churchyard. At the right-bend pass left of the entrance to Lower Hall along a wide old track. Take the left hand gate and keep a wall on your right. In 250 yards, slip through the walker's gate and trace the path through to The Oddfellows Arms.

For pub entry see page 63

The Rose and Crown at Romaldkirk

Romaldkirk and Teesdale

An invigorating ramble through the heart of Teesdale, exploring rough hillside pastures dotted with isolated farmsteads, and the sheltered wooded valley beside the swiftly flowing River Tees.

Start. Turn left on leaving the inn and follow the dead-end lane ahead to the left of the green. Take the arrowed path left opposite Klein Cottage and follow the walled path down to a footbridge and stile. Continue ahead across pasture behind the cemetery and bear right alongside the wall, heading uphill to a stile. Head across the field to a stile and follow the wall on your right, high above the River Tees with views of Eggleston Hall, to reach a gate beyond a stone building.

2 Turn right along the road, cross the bridge and climb the stile right to follow the Teesdale Way along a metalled drive. Just before a gate, cross the stile on the left and ascend steps through trees, the path eventually reaching a stile and field. Continue ahead beside the wall to a stile and follow the path uphill towards farm buildings. Beyond a stile, keep right along the wall and pass to the rear of the farmhouse.

3 Follow the arrow (on telegraph pole) to a gate and bear slightly right, following the path through rough pasture to cross a beck, then a wall stile. Head gently downhill to a stile and bear slightly left with waymarker across the field to a visible stone stile. Bear left then right with the arrow, cross a stile and proceed ahead beside the wall above Shipley Wood.

4 Beyond the next stile, at the edge of the trees, bear right to reach the Perry Myre Rock viewpoint. Alternatively, keep to the path ahead and bear left down a track. Cross a beck and the stile immediately on your right. Cross a further stile and follow the defined path downhill towards Cotherstone and walk across a static caravan park to a gate.

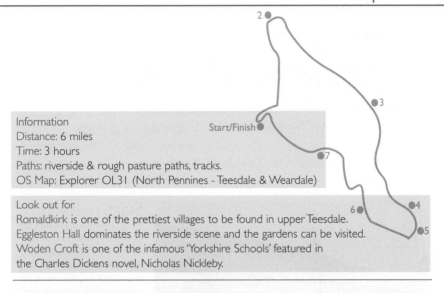

Information
Distance: 6 miles
Time: 3 hours
Paths: riverside & rough pasture paths, tracks.
OS Map: Explorer OL31 (North Pennines - Teesdale & Weardale)

Look out for
Romaldkirk is one of the prettiest villages to be found in upper Teesdale.
Eggleston Hall dominates the riverside scene and the gardens can be visited.
Woden Croft is one of the infamous 'Yorkshire Schools' featured in
the Charles Dickens novel, Nicholas Nickleby.

5 Head downhill along the track, bearing right at the bottom to cross the footbridge over the River Tees. Follow the Teesdale Way right along the bank, then uphill to a stile. Keep parallel with the river, cross a stile and bear left down stone steps to cross a beck via stepping stones. Climb the next stile and follow the path uphill to a gate to the right of a stone building. Go through the gate ahead and pass in front of Woden Croft.

6 Cross the drive, pass in front of cottages and keep right of a corrugated barn to a stile. Beyond the next stile ahead bear immediately right downhill into woodland beside the River Tees. Follow the undulating woodland path (narrow and slippery in places) close to the river. Eventually leave the river, cross a stile and keep to the right-hand field edge to pass a derelict cottage.

7 Go through a gate and follow the grassy track left uphill. Bear off right to a tiny gate and head across the field to a further gate. Maintain direction and soon bear slightly right through trees to a gate. Join a narrow path and follow this back into Romaldkirk.
For pub entry see page 65

The Dukes Head, Armathwaite

Stepping into Eden

Unspoilt. Undiscovered. The Eden Valley really does live up to these billings. Peaceful paths, spectacular scenery, dramatic views; all these are part of this superb, easy walk in the foothills of The Pennines.

The Dukes Head Inn

Start. From the inn, walk down to and cross the bridge over the river Eden. At the far end take the steps left, and loop back beneath the bridge to join a widening path through fine oak, beech and pine woods. Through the trees are glimpses to the imposing Pele tower or castle.

2 At a waymark post above an old weir turn back-left, walk 50 paces to another way-marked post and turn right along a woodland path beside a fence. Shortly, climb a stile and keep ahead up the wide track rising gently into Coombs Wood. At one point a narrow path diverges right to a spectacular viewpoint up the Eden Valley (BEWARE - this is unfenced and slippery). At any major forks keep left, eventually leaving the woods at a parking area and Forest Enterprise board.

3 Turn left and walk to the phone box and sign for Longdales. Turn right along this lane, rising past cottages. As the tarred lane fades turn left along a track signposted 'To Bridleway'. Passing beside a cottage, this rough lane rises gradually to a summit. At this point turn right through a gate along the signposted bridleway to Bascodyke. Cross to the left of the hedgerow and follow it to a gate into a farm lane. Follow this to Bascodyke Head Farm.

Start/Finish

5

2

4

3

Information
Distance: 5 1/2 miles
Time: 2 1/2 - 3 hours
Paths: Woodland and field paths and quiet by-roads.
OS Map: Explorer OL5 (The English Lakes North-eastern Area)

Look out for
Armathwaite is a sleepy little village beside an ancient crossing of the River Eden. The church has two colourful windows including one by Sir Edward Byrne-Jones. Longdales is a veneer of cottages beside a no-through-road. Marvellous views up and down the Pennines unfold with every step along the lane.

4 Bear left to the farmyard; take the track, right, just past the first barn and walk to the very top of the complex, above the front farmyard. Turn left and follow the farm lane. This soon develops as a tarred lane; follow this past farms up to a minor road. Turn left to drop to Ainstable. The way is straight over the crossroads, soon passing a mill. About 300 yards past this, turn left up the lane signed for Ainstable Church. Take the gate beside the churchyard wall and bend right to another kissing gate. Go through and turn left, dropping through a series of stiles to reach a lane.

5 Go up the entrance virtually opposite, enter the pasture and shadow the wall, right, to reach a waymarked stile. Continue along the right-hand edge of the next few pastures to reach a stile into a green lane. Turn left, signed for Oatlands Cottage. At the road turn left to reach a bridge over a brook. Take the footpath signed right here, joining a riverside path that returns you to the bridge at Armathwaite. Re-cross this to return to the Dukes Head.
For pub entry see page 72

The Burnmoor Inn, Eskdale

Burnmoor Tarn and Miterdale

Here's a walk with a steep climb. Your reward is to stand beside a remote tarn in the shadows of England's highest peaks, with views to die for and a return leg through a sublime valley and tarn-speckled moors.

Start. From the inn, walk up to the old packhorse bridge beside the watermill. Go through the gate beyond this and turn right. In about 100 yards go through the bridle-gate on your right. The track rises gradually through a series of gates beside oakwoods high above the lively Whillan Beck, finally passing through a last wall to continue across gently sloping moorland.

2 At the first fork keep ahead-right along the lesser path, walking in line towards the towering Scafell. Keep right at the next fork, passing well above the footbridge at Lambford. Occasional cairns mark the route. Eventually, the remote Burnmoor Tarn is revealed. To your right, Scafell scrapes the sky; ahead are the stunning peaks clustering at Wasdale Head. (An additional 2 miles [return] walk to the low horizon beyond Burnmoor Tarn reveals this wonderful panorama).

3 Above the near shoreline, turn left to walk to Burnmoor Lodge. Pass just left of this and take a narrow path to the right, this soon crests a gentle rise to reveal hidden Miterdale. Pick a way down to the bank of the infant River Mite and trace a path along either side of the water. You'll ultimately need to be on the left bank to take a ladder stile near to fir woods. Walk ahead to find a stile beside a tree. Don't take this; rather turn uphill to follow the wall around to a gate at the edge of woods. Stay on this old stony lane as the woods peel away.

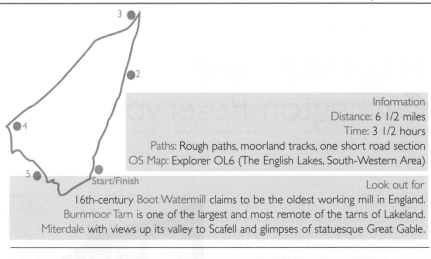

Information
Distance: 6 1/2 miles
Time: 3 1/2 hours
Paths: Rough paths, moorland tracks, one short road section
OS Map: Explorer OL6 (The English Lakes, South-Western Area)

Look out for
16th-century Boot Watermill claims to be the oldest working mill in England.
Burnmoor Tarn is one of the largest and most remote of the tarns of Lakeland.
Miterdale with views up its valley to Scafell and glimpses of statuesque Great Gable.

4 Continue along this to a gate; keep ahead to a second gate. Don't go through this; instead turn left up alongside the wall, commencing a lengthy and potentially boggy climb up to a forestry road at a woodland gate. Remain outside the woods to the point where the trees and wall turn away right. Here, bear left along an indistinct path which circles to the left of a knoll. Fork right in 200 yards through a dip in the low ridge and walk ahead to a lone rowan tree. A more obvious path now passes left of reedy Siney Tarn and crests a rise to reveal lovely Blea Tarn.

5 Pass right of the tarn and pick up a path which passes to the right of the snout of the knoll beyond the tarn. This bends left to start a series of lazy zig-zags down into Eskdale. At the bottom, go through a gate and cross the railway to Beckfoot Station. Turn left along the road, pass Dalegarth Station to find the turn for Boot beside Brook House Inn.

For pub entry see page 75

The Red Lion Inn, Ashbourne

Hognaston and Carsington Reservoir

Discover how a secluded reservoir has transformed a quiet Derbyshire valley on this delightfully varied walk in the spectacular Peak District.

Start. From the inn car park turn left and walk along to the church. Swing left here and briefly follow the lane. Turn right at the footpath sign and cross the field. Make for a gap stile in the boundary and continue ahead with a holly hedge on the left. Look for two stiles in the corner and go straight on in the next field, making for a stile and some steps leading down to a track.

Red Lion Inn

2 Turn right on the bend, go up the slope and on reaching a crossing path, turn left at a gap stile. Follow the clear path across several pastures and on reaching a stile, keep right. Make for the next stile and then cut between trees and banks of vegetation. On reaching the next field, keep ahead towards a track.

3 Turn right and walk along to a gate, followed by a ford and bridge. Cross a tarmac drive and follow the waymarked track up the slope. Look to your right as you approach the road and you'll see a memorial to John Jepson - one of the key figures in the construction of the reservoir.

3

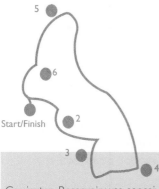

4 Cross the road, go up the grassy bank to a path and turn left. Pass alongside the reservoir to the yacht marina and a turning for the visitor centre. Turn left at a footpath sign and head up the bank to two stiles with the road in between.

5 Cross into the field and walk ahead, following the boundary to a stile. Go diagonally right in the pasture and pass into the next field by some ancient stones. Keep left and walk along to the next pasture. Turn right and make for a gap stile and gate.

6 Turn left and follow the track until you see a little gate on the right, bearing the sign 'dogs to be kept on lead.' Follow the path out across the field, avoiding the stile on the right. Pass to the right of a stone cottage, cut through the garden to a track and turn right. Climb quite steeply between trees, turn right at the church and return to the pub.
For pub entry see page 83

The Fox Inn, Corscombe

Corscombe to Hardy's Evershot

An undulating and very scenic walk taking in the beautiful church at West Chelborough and the unspoilt village of Evershot, Evershead in Hardy's Tess of the D'Urbervilles.

Start. From the Fox turn right along lane, then right by the post box. Take the footpath right beside Norwood Cottage to a gate. Proceed through the wood to a gate and continue across pasture to enter a copse. Cross the footbridge, go through a gate, cross a further field and pass through another wood to a gate.

The Fox Inn

2 Follow the yellow arrow right uphill across pasture (farm on the left). Bear left along the fence to a gate in the field corner. Go through the gate immediately right, bear left and ignore the path left down to a gate. Keep ahead and proceed towards the houses. Bear left along the fence (blue arrow), pass behind barns to a gate, then right in front of a farmhouse. Turn left along drive to West Chelborough church.

3 Take the track to the left of the churchyard, then the footpath (yellow arrow) through a gate and right around the field edge down into the valley. Go through the second gate on the right, cross the footbridge to a gate, then head uphill across the field. Pass beneath telegraph wires, enter the next field and continue parallel with the poles, uphill to a track. Bear left through Manor Farm to a lane.

4 Cross over and pass beside a workshop (not signed). Head downhill along the field edge, then across the field to a stile in the left corner. Cross the stream, ascend to a gate and head across a large field, uphill towards a farm. Pass between the barns, bear right to a gate and join the track at Girt Farm.

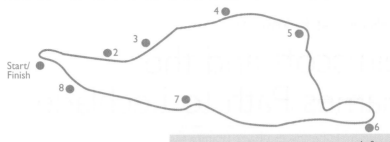

Information
Distance: 7 miles
Time: 4 hours
Paths: field paths, tracks, metalled lanes
OS Map: Explorer 117 (Cerne Abbas & Bere Regis)

Look out for
West Chelborough Church commands beautiful rural views and is noted for its 17th century stone effigy tomb of a mother and child and a 12th-century font. Evershot is a sleepy village of mellow-stone houses set among the hills south of the beautiful Melbury Park Estate.

5 Follow the metalled track right and climb steeply. As it levels look for a stile in the left hedge. Follow the field edge ahead, go through the left-hand gate in the corner and cross the field to a stile. Cross the stile opposite and bear half right to a stile hidden behind the barn. Pass between the houses to a lane, turn left, then right and enter the car park behind the Acorn Inn.

6 Turn right along the village street, pass the church and leave the village for a mile. Take the second lane right, signed Chelborough. Cross over staggered crossroads, signed West Chelborough, then at a sharp right bend take the track left.

7 Immediately bear off right steeply uphill to a gate. Keep to the right-hand field edge onto Chelborough Hill. Enter the next field and bear slightly left to a gate. Beyond the next gate walk along the field edge towards a barn. Join the track, go through a gate and keep to the high level track (two gates), eventually reaching a crossing of paths.

8 Go through the gate ahead and take the right-hand path to a stile in the corner. Pass through the trees to a gate and keep ahead to a futher gate. Head towards the house and bear left to enter the next field. Follow the path to a stile, pass through the trees to a stile and pass through the narrow field to a gate and the Fox Inn. For pub entry see page 94

The Plough at Kelmscott

Kelmscott and the Thames Path to Lechlade

This easy ramble beside the River Thames takes in St Mary's Church at Buscot, historic Lechlade and Kelmscott Manor, once the home of William Morris, founder of the Arts and Crafts Movement.

Start. From the inn turn right along the lane beside the inn and walk through the village to a T junction. Turn right towards Kelmscott Manor, pass the entrance and continue along the track to the River Thames. Go through the gate on your right to join the Thames Path. Walk beside the river for 11/2 miles and cross the second footbridge over the river. Follow the path around the field edge and cross a stile to reach Buscot Lock.

2 To view Buscot Weir, church and Old Parsonage (NT), cross the lock gates on your left and follow the path over the weir. Pass Lock Cottage and take the footpath right to visit the church and adjacent Old Parsonage. Return across the weir and lock and keep ahead across the second lock to a stile. Turn left along the field edge and rejoin the Thames Path.

3 Continue around the meanders to a further footbridge. Ignore the alternative Thames Path right across the footbridge. Shortly, pass beneath the A417 to reach St John's Lock. With excellent views of Lechlade church, continue for a further 1/2 mile to Ha'penny Bridge and the A361. Leave the Thames Path and cross the bridge to enter Lechlade.

4 Turn right at the T junction in the town centre, then bear off right to the church. Take the paved path through the churchyard (Shelley's Walk) to a lane. Cross and pass through two gates, then cross a meadow to a kissing gate. Follow the raised, tree-lined path ahead to a lane opposite a caravan park.

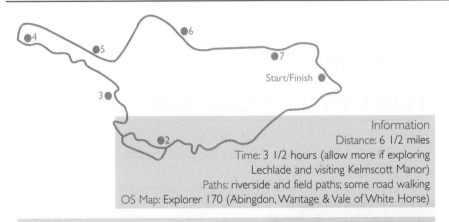

5 Take the lane ahead beside the Trout Inn. Follow the waymarked path left just before a house and stream. Skirt the house, then follow the path across fields close to the River Leech and pass behind a house to reach Mill Lane. Turn right, cross the river and pass Lechlade Mill. Continue along the narrow lane to a T junction.

6 Turn right, then left with the footpath sign (Willow Walk) and bear diagonally left across pasture to a stile. Keep left along the field edge to a stile in the field corner and maintain direction. Cross a footbridge and proceed across the field ahead on worn path to a lane.

7 Turn right and follow the road into Kelmscott. Pass the church and turn right, signed to the Plough Inn.
For pub entry see page 103

The Plough Inn

The White Hart Inn, Winchcombe

To Belas Knap from Winchcombe

Follow the Windrush Way past magnificent Sudeley Castle and climb the Cotswold scarp for spectacular views across Gloucestershire to one of the great burial mounds of ancient Britain.

Start

Start. Turn left downhill from the pub car park. At Sudeley Country Cottages, take the arrowed path right (Windrush Way) through a kissing gate into parkland. Follow the path across pasture, crossing a track, soon to pass through a further gate in the field corner by woods. Turn left, cross the entrance drive to Sudeley Castle and go through a gate to the left of double gates, following half green & white marker of the Windrush Way (WW).

2 Continue across parkland, with Sudeley Castle visible left, keeping left through further gateway. Here, at fork of ways, bear half right and keep to markers posts on a defined grassy path, gently descending to cross a brook. Go through a swing gate, bear right across the river and turn left (WW) to a stile beside a gate.

3 Bear half right uphill through pasture (right of telegraph pole) to a stile. Keep ahead to a stile, walk beside woodland to a stile and descend to a stile by a brook. Continue across a meadow to a track. Leave the WW and turn right along 'road used as public path'. Soon reach a gate and New Meadow Farm.

4 Beyond the gate take the waymarked path left through a green gate. Head uphill on a track between fields to a further gate. Continue uphill and turn right through double gates at woodland. Follow the path to a T-junction of tracks by Humblebee Cottages.

3

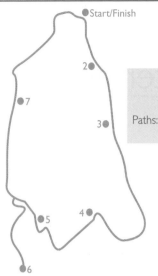

Start/Finish
2
7
3
5 4
6

Information
Distance: 5 miles
Time: 3 hours
Paths: field paths, defined tracks, the Cotswold Way; quiet lanes
OS Map: Explorer OL 45 (The Cotswolds)

Look out for
Winchcombe has a considerable history. Visit the huge
'wool church' and its two interesting museums -
Folk Museum and the Railway Museum.
Visit Sudeley Castle to see its ruined banqueting
hall and the ornate, immaculate gardens.
Belas Knap dates to around 2500BC
and is an impressive burial mound.

5 Turn left uphill along the Cotswold Way to a metalled lane. Turn right for 1/4 mile to reach a sign for Belas Knap. Climb the stile on your left, head uphill through trees to a kissing gate and follow the field edge left, soon to follow it right steeply uphill to a gate in the field corner (superb views). Keep left to reach Belas Knap.

6 Retrace steps back to the road and turn left. Where the road bends sharp right, take the arrowed path ahead up to a stone stile, signed Winchcombe. Head downhill across pasture following marker posts to reach a stile. Turn right along a metalled track, passing the cricket pitch. to a gate and road.

7 Turn left, then just beyond houses on your left, take arrowed path right, through the first kissing gate. Follow field edge path to a gate and continue along the narrow path to another gate. Cross pasture to a metal gate and turn left, crossing the river, then at village road turn right back ot the inn. For pub entry see page 109

Wykeham Arms, Winchester

Historic Winchester and the Itchen Valley

A gentle stroll through Winchester's historic streets and through the beautiful Itchen Valley.

Start. From the Wykeham's front door walk towards Kingsgate Arch and turn right along College Street and, shortly to pass the entrance to Winchester College. Beyond the road barrier, bear right along College Walk, then turn right at the end of the wall, along a track. Go left through a gate by a private entrance to the College. Follow the path beside the River Itchen for 1/2 mile to a gate and road.

Start

2 Cross straight over and follow the gravel path alongside a tributary to a gate and cross the open meadow towards the Hosptial of St Cross. Keep left alongside the wall and through an avenue of trees to a stile. Proceed ahead along the gravel path to two further stiles and join a farm track leading to a road. Turn left and walk the length of the now gated road (traffic-free), crossing the River Itchen to reach a junction of paths by the M3.

3 Turn left along a metalled path. For a great view across Winchester, go through the gate on your right and ascend the wooden steps up St Catherine's Hill. Return to the metalled path. Keep left at a fork and drop down to follow a narrow path beside the Itchen Navigation. Go through the car park to the road.

4 Turn left across the bridge and take the footpath immediately right. Keep to path beside the water, disregarding the path left (College nature reserve). Soon cross the bridge by rowing sheds to join a metalled track.

5a

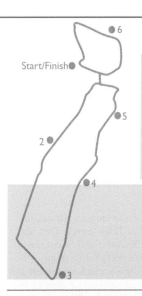

Start/Finish●

● 6

● 5

2 ●

● 4

● 3

Information
Distance: 3 1/2 miles
Time: 2 hours (longer if visiting the city sights)
Paths: Riverside paths through water-meadows, city streets
Map: OS Explorer 132 (Winchester)
Parking: Difficult in the vicinity of the pub; you may have to use the city centre car parks and start the walk from King Alfred's statue or the Cathedral (point 6).

Look out for
Winchester College
Hospital of St Cross
St Catherine's Hill
Winchester Cathedral
Other City Sights - Great Hall

5b

6a

6b

5 Turn left, then left again at the road. Follow the road right along College Walk, then bear right at the end and soon follow the Riverside Walk beside the River Itchen. Ascend steps and turn left to reach The Broadway and King Alfred's statue.

6 Walk towards the city centre, passing the Guildhall on your left. Join the pedestrianised High Street, then in 100yards, turn left along Market Street. Continue ahead into the Cathedral Close to pass the cathedral main door. Turn left down a cloister, then right through The Close, signed to Wolvesey Castle, to Cheyney Court and exit via Prior's Gate. Turn left though Kingsgate, with the tiny Church of St Swithun above, to return to the Wykeham Arms.

For pub entry see page 114

The Stagg Inn, Kington

Titley and Mortimer Trail

This glorious figure-of-eight walk takes the walker right to the heart of the Welsh Marches, a wonderfully quiet and unspoilt rural district, following the Mortimer Trail, one of its loveliest upland routes.

Start/Finish

Start. From the inn turn left and follow the road to Titley church. Turn left immediately beyond it and follow the Mortimer Trail (MT) beside farm outbuildings. Avoid a path on the left and head up through the fields, following the frequent trail waymarks. When the path curves left in line with the field boundary, look for a gap in the hedgerow and take the MT across pastures to Green Lane Farm.

2 Pass to the right of the outbuildings and keep to the MT, following the track beside a large corrugated barn. Cross several stiles to reach the remains of an old byre. To return to Titley go to point 6; to complete the full walk keep ahead on the MT.

3 Skirt the pasture, keeping woodland on the left, and make for the field corner. Enter bluebell woodlands and follow the trail through the trees to a stile on the right. Cross a field and look for a stile in the top boundary. Join an enclosed path and follow it for some time to a stile. Cut through a pine forest and drop down some steps to reach a waymark.

4 Turn sharp right here, leaving the MT, and descend steeply, bending to the left. Keep dropping, avoiding any turnings to the left and right and eventually you reach a T junction with a track. Turn right and walk along to a ford and some cottages. Turn right before the water, avoid a turning on the right and follow the cycle trail between trees and hedges to reach Little Brampton.

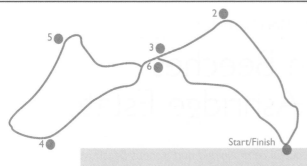

Information
Distance: 7 1/2 miles (or 4 miles for the first loop and 3 1/2 the second)
Time: 4 hours for the full walk
Paths: Field and woodland paths and tracks, sections of the Mortimer Trail.
The full route is quite an adventurous walk, particularly the second loop.
OS Map: Explorer 201 (Knighton and Presteigne)

Look out for
The evocative 30-mile Mortimer Trail, running from Ludlow to Kington,
takes walkers through a land of lush pastures, wooded valleys and rolling hills.
Titley church is mainly a Victorian restoration. In the churchyard is the grave of
Lazar Meszarios, an Hungarian general who became ill and died while visiting the area.

5 Turn right at the footpath sign, following the track to a field. Keep ahead towards the wooded escarpment and head for a stile. Swing left and climb through the trees. This is a lengthy pull. Cross the edge of a tree-ringed field to two stiles with a path in between and turn left along the field.

6 Look for the path signposted to Titley (1 1/2 miles) and follow the clear waymarks. The path eventually makes for the foot of the wooded escarpment and a line of coniferous trees. Cross the fields and continue on a track. Go through a gate and pass some outbuildings and a house. Turn right at the lane and return to the Stagg.
For pub entry see page 115

The Alford Arms, Berkhamsted

Frithsden Beeches and the Ashridge Estate

A charming blend of peaceful commonland and glorious beech woodland forms the scenic backdrop of this very varied walk through the beautiful Ashridge Estate.

Start. From the front of the pub cross the road and take the path opposite, following it uphill through trees and bluebell woods. Keep to the wide path, cross a drive and continue alongside hedging. Enter woodland and bend right, keeping right after a few paces to pass alongside trees and private gardens.

2 Soon you reach the fairways of a golf club. Skirt the fairways, following the path through the trees to the road. Cross over, following the Hertfordshire Way across more fairways. Cut between trees and further on you reach a waymarked crossroads.

3 Turn right, following the bridleway down into a dip at Frithsden Beeches and ascend the other side. Join a tarmac drive and when it bends right, keep ahead along the field edge and then down through the undergrowth to reach the road.

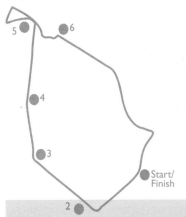

Information

Distance: 6 3/4 miles

Time: 3 1/2 hours

Paths: Common paths and bridleways, parkland paths and drives, field paths

OS Map: Explorer 181 (Chiltern Hills North)

Look out for

The 5,000-acre Ashridge Estate is characterised by sprawling woodland, farmland and open downland now in the care of the National Trust. The vastness of Ashridge House quite literally takes the breath away. It was built in 1276 and restored by James Wyatt in 1808.

4 Cross over and take the path signposted to Little Gaddesden. Pass the entrance to a house called Rodinghead and then follow the path ahead between fences and across rolling parkland. Keep to the left and head down to a large dead tree and two beech trees. Cross the next stile to a track and veer left.

5 Swing left after 120 yards and take the path up the slope to Ashridge House. Turn right at the corner of the building and follow the drive to a left bend. Turn right here by a NT bridleway sign and follow the track through the trees and across parkland. Enter woodland and as the track loops dramatically to the left, look for a path running up the bank to an adventure playground. Cross it diagonally to the right corner and turn left at a path T junction to reach the road.

6 Cross over to a field path and follow it down through a grassy valley. Cross a track and continue through the fields, passing a solitary tree before reaching Nettleden. Join the road, pass a waymarked path to St Margaret's and turn right a few steps beyond it by Pightle Cottage. Follow the lane and further up the slope take the woodland path parallel to it on the left. Rejoin the lane and return to the Alford Arms. For pub entry see page 115

Inn at Whitewell

Stepping Stones
to Bowland

*Over the stepping stones from a famous inn for a circuit amongst the
Forest of Bowland's little-known limestone scenery.*

Start. From the front of the inn, pass
the church on the right and walk down
into the car park. Go through the gateway
and turn right towards the river. The riverbank path drops down to the left below the
garden wall and leads to the stepping stones.
Cross the River Hodder and follow the
waymarks on the opposite side to a gate at
New Launds Farm.

Inn at Whitewell

2 Go through the gate and turn left through another gate on a track steeply up the bank.
The track peters out but the line is clear, with woods dropping down to the river on the left
and open pastureland ahead and right. Continue up through the field to a gateway. Continue
over the shoulder and bear slightly right before dropping down to a stile. Follow the fence on
the right then bear right, up to a gate and stile. Through these, turn left and join the track to
Fair Oak. Descend through a gateway, cross a brook and walk up the ramp into a hamlet.

3 Bear left then turn right,
opposite the barn, into a
yard. Pass the cowshed on
the left and locate a handgate
by the barn wall in the far
corner. Follow the path to a
stile into a field. Walk across
the field, aiming to intercept
the fence on the left-hand
side at the far end. Cross a
stile then cut off the field
corner to a stile leading to
the road. Turn right and follow the road for 200 yards
to a crossroads.

4 Go straight ahead, over the cattle grid. Follow the track over another cattle grid and then
around a bend. It becomes surfaced and crosses another cattle grid, heading for sheds on the
left. Go through a gateway by the buildings and continue, as the track swings left to descend
to Dinkling Green Farm. Over another cattle grid, cross bridge over Dinkling Green Brook
and bear left into farmyard.

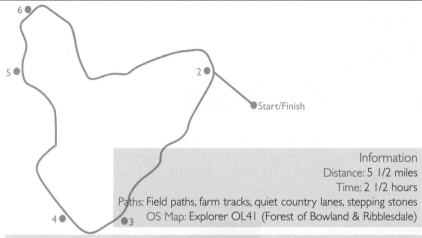

6 ●

5 ●

2 ●

● Start/Finish

Information
Distance: 5 1/2 miles
Time: 2 1/2 hours
Paths: Field paths, farm tracks, quiet country lanes, stepping stones
OS Map: Explorer OL41 (Forest of Bowland & Ribblesdale)

4 ●   ● 3

Look out for
Forest of Bowland: Not a forest in the sense that it was wooded, but open moorland that was a hunting domain owned by the Duchy of Lancaster.

5 From a courtyard, turn right to a gate between a wooden shed and garden wall. Follow the snicket to a stile then cross the field ahead, maintaining direction to a stile in the fence to the left of the gate. Cross the stile and bear half right to another stile. Cross into the paddock and turn left towards the chicken sheds. Beyond these cross the wooden bridge over the brook. Go through the gate and up a track into the farmyard.

stepping stones

6 Go through the gate on the the other side, continue up the access track, bearing right at the fork. Follow the track over the saddle then right, over the cattle grid and past Tunstall Ing. After a left turn, emerge at a minor road by a cattle grid. Turn left for 200 yards to a gate on the right. Go through and aim for the base of a round hillock. The contouring trod leads round the foot of the hill to two gates. Take the left-hand gate and walk down the field with the fence on the right. At the bottom take the right-hand gate to join the track that skirts the base of the escarpment. Through the next gate turn right into New Launds Farm. Walk up through the yard, descend to a gate then retrace your steps back to the stepping stones and return to the Inn. For pub entry see page 132

The Victoria at Holkham

Around the Holkham Estate

Choose from three very different and very beautiful walks in and around Holkham Hall, taking in magnificent parkland, a wildlife rich nature reserve and a huge sandy beach and, on the longer walk, tidal creeks and Nelson's home village of Burnham Thorpe.

Start. From the Victoria turn right up the estate drive and pass beneath the gatehouse into Holkham Park. Continue ahead on or beside the metalled drive to pass in front of Holkham Hall. Bear left with the drive by the lake and turn right, signed to the Nursery.

2 With the ice house on your left, bear off right and go through a gateway at the end of the lake. Follow the defined path across the park towards and pass St Withburga's Church. At the crossing of paths by Church Lodge turn right (for longer walks see point 3). Drop down through trees, pass round the top of the lake and keep to the main track. With monument right, bear left and follow the track back to the gatehouse. Turn left back to the inn.

3 Keep ahead at Church Lodge, go through the gate and cross the A149. Cross a stile and walk down the track into the Nature Reserve. At a junction, keep straight on towards woodland. Follow the track left, then right through the trees (hide left), and keep ahead at a crossing of paths.

4 Keep to the undulating path (becomes sandy) through pine trees and soon reach Holkham Dunes & Beach. At the top of the beach turn right (for longer walk - see point 5) and keep to the top of the beach until reaching Holkham Gap, a significant V-shaped break in the corner of the woods. Climb steps and head inland on duckboard path, then follow Lady Ann's Drive back to the inn.

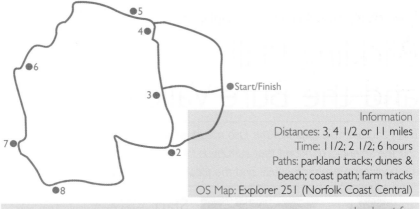

Information
Distances: 3, 4 1/2 or 11 miles
Time: 1 1/2; 2 1/2; 6 hours
Paths: parkland tracks; dunes &
beach; coast path; farm tracks
OS Map: Explorer 251 (Norfolk Coast Central)

Look out for
Holkham Hall is a classic 18th-century Palladian-style mansion set in
3,000 acres of parkland. Attractions include a Bygones Museum,
History of Farming, a pottery and fine food centre.
Holkham Beach is one of the most unspoilt and beautiful stretches of sand in the
country. The Nature Reserve is home to many rare species of flora and fauna.

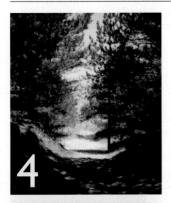

5 Turn left along the top of beach (for 400 yards a naturist beach), round the dune headland and lookout for the Coast Path marker (acorn symbol). Head inland here across the dunes and duckboards, then follow the raised dyke inland beside Overy Creek to Burnham Overy Staithe.

6 Go through a gate and soon turn left to reach the A149 opposite the Hero pub. Cross straight over into Gong Lane. Where the lane ends, proceed ahead along the track and follow this to cottages and the B1155. Turn right, cross over and take the waymarked footpath by the parish notice board.

7 Walk along edge of two fields to reach a raised embankment path (old railway) and turn left. In 50 yards, turn right through a gate and follow the defined path across a watermeadow (possibly boggy in winter). Cross a footbridge and keep left to a gate and lane. Turn right to visit Burnham Thorpe church.

8 Turn left up a gravel track and cross a metalled lane onto a signed bridleway. Pass a flint barn, keeping ahead at the crossing of paths. At a T junction of paths, turn left alongside the wall. On reaching a gate house (West Gate), turn right and follow the metalled drive through Holkham Estate, passing the Nursery back to Holkham Hall. Retrace steps back to the Victoria.
For pub entry see page 147

The Walpole Arms, Itteringham

Blickling Hall and the Bure Valley

This gentle ramble explores the lush meadows in the peaceful Bure Valley and the splendid parkland that surrounds Blickling Hall, a magnificent Jacobean house and the focal point of the walk.

The Walpole Arms

Start. From the Walpole Arms pub car park turn left, then right at the T-junction and cross the River Bure into Itteringham. Take the lane right (signed village stores) and turn immediately right along a track beside Manor Farm. Continue to a gate, bear slightly right to a stile and follow the field edge uphill. Bear right into the adjacent field and keep left along the field edge.

2 Follow the track past White House Farm and with good views of Wolterton Hall (left) soon turn left along the metalled access lane. Pass a cottage on your left, then at a sharp right bend take the arrowed path ahead along a track.

3 Soon bear left with yellow arrow along the left-hand field edge and cross the second stile right. Bear left across a meadow and walk alongside woodland to reach a footbridge across the River Bure. Bear slightly left across pasture (can be wet or flooded if river high) to a footbridge and follow the path to a metalled lane.

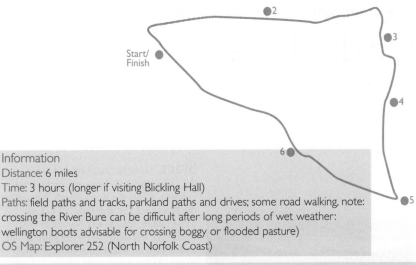

Information
Distance: 6 miles
Time: 3 hours (longer if visiting Blickling Hall)
Paths: field paths and tracks, parkland paths and drives; some road walking, note: crossing the River Bure can be difficult after long periods of wet weather: wellington boots advisable for crossing boggy or flooded pasture)
OS Map: Explorer 252 (North Norfolk Coast)

Look out for
Wolterton Hall was built in the 1720's for Horatio Walpole, younger brother of Britain's first Prime Minister - Sir Robert Walpole.
Blickling Hall is one of the finest Jacobean houses remaining in England.

4 Turn right, then left in front of Moorgate Cottages, and follow the path left around the field edge. Continue to a junction with the Weaver's Way by a tree seat. Follow the track ahead across Blickling Park, with lake left and the house soon visible ahead, to the main park gates.

5 Exit the park and follow the lane left to visit Blickling Hall. Retrace steps to the park gates and take the track left across the park. Keep ahead at a fork and soon walk beside the Great Wood (Mausoleum), disregarding estate walk markers.

6 Pass beside a gate and walk through trees to a metalled lane by a cottage. Turn left and keep to this quiet road through Itteringham Common back to the Walpole Arms.
For pub entry see page 147

Itteringham Church

The Pheasant Inn, Kielder Water

Kielder Forest

Forest roads and bridlepaths take this walk to clearings high in the forest to reveal airy views across the wild Northumbrian countryside. The return route follows peaceful lakeside paths beside Kielder Water.

Start. From the inn, turn left along the main road and then right, signposted Falstone. Cross the River North Tyne, pass the Blackcock Inn and turn left having passed under the railway bridge. In 100 yards fork left onto the former railway line and remain on this, signed Reivers Cycle Route. At a junction keep ahead to reach a cross-tracks above a farm. Turn right and ascend the track left of a house to pass through a wall.

2 In 50 yards fork left off the track along a grassy forestry road. Gently climb towards the woods, the track eventually emerging from the trees to reveal some excellent views across the southern end of Kielder Water. The trees gather once again before parting to allow distant views north across Kielder Forest to The Cheviot Hills. Walk down to the wide forestry road.

3 Turn left and walk downhill (800 yards) to the second white post bearing the legend 'Wave Chamber', and a cycle route waymarker. Fork right onto a sandy track though the trees, then turn right in 100 yards along a waymarked path, dropping to cross a marshy isthmus. Keep right at a fork, tracing the circular path out onto the Belling Peninsula and savour superb views across the lake from rocky promontories.

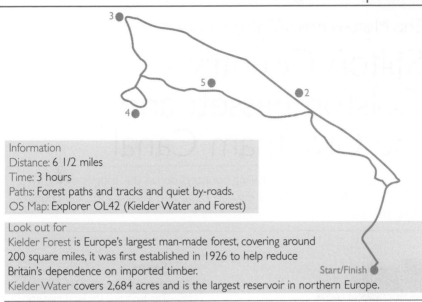

Information
Distance: 6 1/2 miles
Time: 3 hours
Paths: Forest paths and tracks and quiet by-roads.
OS Map: Explorer OL42 (Kielder Water and Forest)

Look out for
Kielder Forest is Europe's largest man-made forest, covering around
200 square miles, it was first established in 1926 to help reduce
Britain's dependence on imported timber.
Kielder Water covers 2,684 acres and is the largest reservoir in northern Europe.

Start/Finish

4 Remain on the path, marked by occasional orange waymarks, to reach a white post signed 'Belvedere'. Turn right along a gravelly path through trees, in 100 yards gaining a wider track along which turn right. This narrows to a delightful path around rocky inlets and bays before reaching the remains of Gordon's Walls Castle. Just beyond this the path leaves the shoreline at some rail fencing, soon reaching a wide forestry road. Turn right along this.

5 Remain on this roadway, passing behind the Hawkhope car park, sited at the north end of the reservoir dam close to the immense valve tower. Don't take the road to the dam, instead take the road signed 'Forestry Vehicles only'. At Hawkhope Farm, passed earlier in the walk, turn right at the cross-tracks, pass beside the farm and take the gate on the left, joining a gated road to Falstone. At the junction by the Blackcock Inn turn right and retrace outward steps back to The Pheasant Inn. For pub entry see page 154

The Martins Arms, Colston Bassett

Stilton Country - Colston Bassett and the Grantham Canal

Explore the peaceful, gently rolling countryside on the fringes of the Vale of Belvoir on foot, following a disused canal, and visiting a ruined church along the way.

Start. From the pub turn right and walk along the lane, passing The Barn and the local primary school. Look for a stile just beyond the last house on the right and go diagonally across the field. Make for a pair of galvanised gates and a bridge over the River Smite.

2 Go forward, avoiding a waymark on the left, and head up the field to a gate. Continue ahead on a clear track running between fields to the road. Turn left and follow it for about half a mile. On reaching the Grantham Canal, turn right and join the towpath.

3 Walk along to the next road, cross over and rejoin the towpath, avoiding the waymarked footpath to Cropwell Bishop. Make for the next road, cross over and continue with the disused canal now on your right. Follow the towpath to the next road where the buildings of Cropwell Bishop can be seen on the right. To extend the walk, follow point 4, otherwise go to point 5.

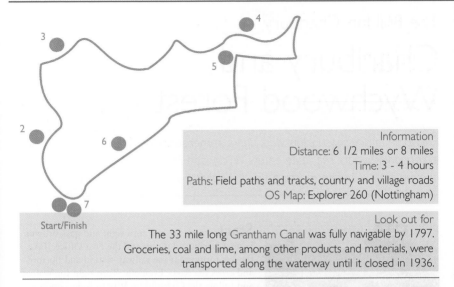

Information
Distance: 6 1/2 miles or 8 miles
Time: 3 - 4 hours
Paths: Field paths and tracks, country and village roads
OS Map: Explorer 260 (Nottingham)

Start/Finish

Look out for
The 33 mile long Grantham Canal was fully navigable by 1797.
Groceries, coal and lime, among other products and materials, were
transported along the waterway until it closed in 1936.

4 Cross over and continue on the path to a bridge (number 20). Cross it and keep right, following an enclosed path alongside trees. Enter the woodland and follow the path to the far side. Cut between hedge and fence, down to a junction. Swing right, follow a gated bridleway to the road at Cropwell Bishop and turn left.

5 Walk through Cropwell Bishop, following the road towards Barnstone. Go up the hill and turn right by Manor Farm to follow a bridleway. Cut between hedgerows and at the end of the track, turn half left across the field. Pass through a gate and keep along the left boundary. Go through a gateway and alongside a farm.

6 Cross a track, pass through a gate and join a farm road on a bend. Keep ahead and cross over at the next junction. Pass to the left of the ruined church and drop down the slope to the cricket pavilion. Keep it on your left and follow the line of the fence and trees. Look for the spire of the church at Colston Bassett and keep to the clear path.

Martin's Arms Inn

7 Recross the Smite at a concrete bridge and then go up the slope through the trees. On reaching the road, turn right and pass the church. Keep ahead and return to the pub. For pub entry see page 155

The Bull Inn, Charlbury

Charlbury and Wychwood Forest

Enjoyable in any season, this walk offers immense variety and exceptional beauty. The route enters Wychwood Forest, once a royal hunting ground, before reaching classic English parkland at Cornbury.

Bull Inn

Start. From the pub turn right and pass Browns Lane, Charlbury Library and the Post Office. Take the left turning for the railway station and Burford and cross the River Evenlode. Turn right for Walcot and follow the Oxfordshire Way to some cottages. When the track swings right go straight on at the bridleway sign for Chilson. Pass a dilapidated stone barn and continue to the road.

2 Turn left and climb gently to the B4437. Cross it and take the turning for Leafield. Keep right at the next road junction, passing Ranger's Lodge. Follow the road through the woodland, pass a large tree-ringed field and then look for a stile on the left by a galvanised gate. Opposite is the drive to Waterman's Lodge Farm.

3 Take the path (signposted Finstock) and swing right after several paces at the next way-mark. Cut through the wood and keep left at the fork. Follow the path as it climbs gently through the trees and avoid a turning on the right. The path widens to a broad grassy ride, running down to Vista Gate.

4 Turn right and follow the track, keeping to the right of the outbuildings, drop down beside a fence to a lake and turn left. Keep right at the next fork, where the left track can be seen running up a steep slope. Climb through the trees, keep left at the next fork and soon fields are visible. Continue ahead towards the houses of Finstock, crossing an undulating patchwork of fields.

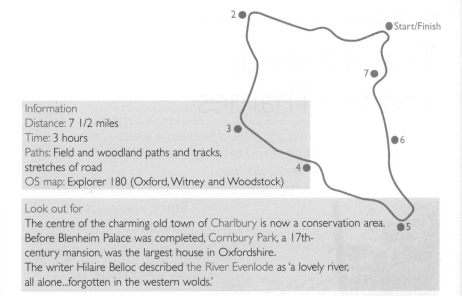

Information
Distance: 7 1/2 miles
Time: 3 hours
Paths: Field and woodland paths and tracks,
stretches of road
OS map: Explorer 180 (Oxford, Witney and Woodstock)

Look out for
The centre of the charming old town of Charlbury is now a conservation area.
Before Blenheim Palace was completed, Cornbury Park, a 17th-
century mansion, was the largest house in Oxfordshire.
The writer Hilaire Belloc described the River Evenlode as 'a lovely river,
all alone...forgotten in the western wolds.'

5 Turn left at the road, pass School Road on the right and then turn left after about 70 yards, at the footpath sign for Charlbury. Go diagonally right across the garden of a large house to a gate in the corner, avoiding the one on the right leading to the car park of a converted barn. Follow the path ahead, down the slope and round to the right. Keep to the left boundary in the next field and make for a junction with a track.

6 Turn right and then swing left at an avenue of trees. Follow the path down to the edge of a lake and join a tarmac drive leading to Cornbury House. Cross the dam and then keep right at a lodge and cattle-grid. Take the path up the slope to a stile and then follow the path alongside the deer fence.

7 On reaching a gate at North Lodge, look to the left for a glimpse of Cornbury House. Turn right and follow the wide drive over the Evenlode and the railway. Turn left at the road and walk back into Charlbury. The Bull is facing you as you reach the T junction.
For pub entry see page 161

The Perch & Pike Inn, South Stoke

The Ridgeway and the Thames

Join the meandering Thames and follow a picturesque stretch of the Ridgeway upstream to North Stoke before exploring spectacular downland country to the east of the river.

Start. From the pub turn right and walk along the village street, passing the church. On reaching the junction, veer left at the Ridgeway sign. Keep left at the next Ridgeway sign and make for the Thames.

2 Turn right and head upstream with the river on your left. Pass under Brunel's railway bridge and continue on the Ridgeway to a picturesque Georgian house with shutters and a cottage nearby. Follow the waymarks, keeping the river over to your left, and head for the church at North Stoke.

3 Go through the churchyard, passing Dame Clara Butt's grave on the right by the church, and take the lane to the T junction. Turn right, pass North Stoke Farm and follow the road round to the left, crossing over at the junction into White House Road. Walk along to the A4074 and take the lane opposite for Ipsden. Avoid a concrete farm track on the left and turn right immediately beyond Larkstoke Farm.

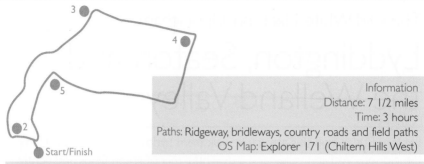

Information
Distance: 7 1/2 miles
Time: 3 hours
Paths: Ridgeway, bridleways, country roads and field paths
OS Map: Explorer 171 (Chiltern Hills West)

Look out for
The 85-mile Ridgeway national trail follows the route of Britain's oldest road, extending from Ivinghoe Beacon in Buckinghamshire to Avebury in Wiltshire. The churchyard at North Stoke contains the grave of Dame Clara Butt (1873-1936), the concert and operatic contralto who performed the works of Edward Elgar.

4 Follow the bridleway (Swan's Way) down to the next road, cross over and continue ahead between fields. Recross the A4074 and follow the obvious path between fields. Turn right at a waymarked T junction and follow the path across open downland country. Pass Middle Barn, then a wood, and head for the road. Cross over and take the road signposted Littlestoke.

5 On reaching the manor, swing left by the entrance at a sign for South Stoke (1 mile). Cross the field to a stile and footbridge and continue on the grassy path towards the railway line. Go through the pedestrian tunnel and cross the field, keeping woodland on the right. Exit the pasture, pass some houses and turn right at the road. Swing left and return to the pub.

For pub entry see page 166

Perch and Pike Inn

The Old White Hart Inn, Uppingham

Lyddington, Seaton and the Welland Valley

Explore Rutland on this attractive walk from Lyddington to Seaton. Glimpse the glorious Welland valley and a delightful mix of green fields and gently rolling hills forms a constant scenic backdrop.

Start A. (To avoid Lyddington's Main Street, go to point B). From the pub turn left and follow Main Street through Lyddington, following the sign for Uppingham. Head out of the village, avoid a footpath on the left and right and when the road bends left, keep ahead towards Bisbrooke and Seaton.

Start/Finish

Start B. For the off-road alternative, turn left out of the pub, then right at the sign for Chapel Lane Farm and follow the footpath to a junction of paths. Turn left and follow the footpath across the fields to the road. Turn right and rejoin the main walk.

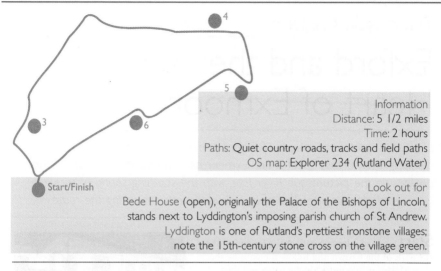

Information
Distance: 5 1/2 miles
Time: 2 hours
Paths: Quiet country roads, tracks and field paths
OS map: Explorer 234 (Rutland Water)

Look out for
Bede House (open), originally the Palace of the Bishops of Lincoln,
stands next to Lyddington's imposing parish church of St Andrew.
Lyddington is one of Rutland's prettiest ironstone villages;
note the 15th-century stone cross on the village green.

3 Walk uphill, with lovely views of the Welland valley over to the right. Pass a turning to Breach Farm on the left and one to Southfield Lodge on the right, following the road down to a junction. Turn right, pass some farm outbuildings and when the road curves right, join a track and keep ahead.

4 Eventually go through a gate and keep to the left of the hedge, maintaining the same easterly direction. Pass into the next field and when you reach a waymark in the corner, turn right to join a footpath. Head south across the fields towards Seaton, cross into the next pasture and walk ahead to the road.

5 To visit the churchyard turn left, to continue the walk turn right. Swing left at the sign for Grange Farm and go down the track. Cross two stiles by farm outbuildings and when the track sweeps round to the left, go straight on at the waymark. Follow the track as it curves to the right, passing alongside trees and a stream.

6 Turn left at the next waymark, keeping the ditch on your right, and pass beneath pylon cables. Turn right, then left at waymarks and look for the spire of Lyddington church on the horizon. Make for the field corner, cross a stile and follow the grassy ride between woodland, fencing and hedgerows. Cross another stile and keep ahead on the woodland path. On reaching the road, turn left and return to the pub.

For pub entry see page 171

The Crown, Exford

Exford and the Heart of Exmoor

Leave the sights and sounds of Exford behind you and follow this stunning walk across spectacular Exmoor hills. The middle and latter stages are beside the picturesque River Exe, with the soothing sound of trickling water and glorious stretches of tree-shaded path enhancing the route.

Start. Go to a kissing gate at the far end of the car park of the Crown and follow the path by the Exe. Make for two more kissing gates and then turn right across the river to the small settlement of North Court.

The Crown

2 Turn left by Rowan Cottage and Mountain Ash Cottage and follow the bridleway. As the drive bends right, go straight on through a gate and follow the track uphill and then down alongside Court Copse. Pass through several gates, climbing steeply to a junction.

3 Avoid the 'permissive' path on the left and turn right towards Road Hill. Follow the path along the right-hand edge of several fields and when you reach a fork, keep left and head for the next waymark.

4 Keep left here, following the sign for Winsford. When the track dwindles to a grassy path continue ahead, avoiding a gate over in the right-hand boundary hedge. Begin to descend steeply into a tranquil valley, keep the Exe on your left and look for a gate and footpath in the right boundary.

5 Follow the 'permissive' path alongside the river until you reach a concrete bridge spanning it. Follow the track round to the left, passing the buildings of East Nethercote and avoiding a track on the right. Keep ahead to neighbouring West Nethercote.

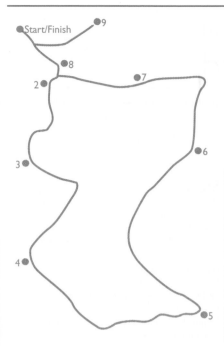

Start/Finish

9
8
2
7
3
6
4
5

Information
Distance: 6 1/2 miles
Time: 3 hours
Paths: Moorland bridleways, riverside and
field paths and tracks. Some climbing.
OS Map: Explorer OL9 (Exmoor)

Look out for
Exford with its prominent church, triangular
green and clusters of pretty cottages.
Exmoor: Hidden valleys, vast expanses of
heather moorland and wild ponies.

6 Follow the track through a series of gates, using the parallel field path on the right if conditions underfoot are wet. On reaching a fork, keep right and follow the path as it climbs above the river. Pass the buildings of Lyncombe and go through a gate just beyond them.

7 Turn left after about 20 yards and follow the obvious path through the field, sweeping round and across the middle of it. Make for a stile by the riverbank, continue to two more stiles and keep ahead across the pasture. Look for some gorse bushes and cut across the lower slopes of the hill.

8 Go through a gate and keep the field boundary on the right. Look for a stile in the top corner, head up the field slope and cross a stile by a sign for Higher Combe. Go forward down the track towards North Court and then turn right at the footpath sign for the church.

9 Cross the field to a farm and follow the drive to the road. Cross over and keep to the right of Exford church. Head for two gates with a stile between them. Bear left into the field, keeping to the left edge to a stile. Continue ahead, passing to the right of houses, and look for a stile on the left. Follow the path to the road, turn right and return to Exford. For pub entry see page 173

The Crown and Castle, Orford

Historic Orford

Combine a gentle walk beside the Ore estuary and along green lanes to Sudbourne Church with a visit to Orford's well preserved Norman castle keep for the view over this once thriving medieval port.

Start

Start. Turn right on leaving the inn, pass through the square and turn right at the T-junction opposite the church. Walk through the village and pass the Jolly Sailor to reach Orford Quay. Take the footpath (Suffolk Heath & Coast Path) on your right close to the water's edge and pass in front of Quay House. Shortly, join the raised embankment and keep to this path beside the River Ore. Go round Chantry Point, with Havergate Island (bird sanctuary) opposite and continue for 1/2 mile.

2 At a waymarker post, bear off right to a stile and gate and head inland along a grassy track. Bear right, then left around a copse and soon reach a lane. Turn right and soon take the arrowed path left up a sandy track. Ignore the path on your right and keep to the track which soon passes beside coniferous woodland (Gedgrave Broom). In 1/4 mile pass cottages and keep ahead at a crossing of tracks by Orford Lodge to reach a road.

3 Cross straight over to join a narrow wooded path beside a house called Hillside. Stay on this path through trees and along field edges towards Sudbourne church. Cross a lane and continue to the church.

3

4 Take the arrowed path right before the road and walk beside the churchyard wall (access to church at far end). Keep to the field edge, soon to bear slightly right across the field to a road. Cross the road and maintain direction across two fields to a waymarked crossing of paths.

4
5
3 6
Start/Finish
2

Information

Distance: 6 miles

Time: 3 hours

Paths: raised path beside estuary, field paths, sandy tracks, metalled road

OS Map: Explorer 212 (Woodbridge & Saxmundham)

Look out for

Orford was once a thriving port when Henry II had a castle built here in 1165, although it declined as the shingle spit of Orford Beach grew and cut it off from the sea. Orford Ness is the largest vegetated shingle spit in Europe, an important location for breeding and passage birds as well as shingle flora. Havergate Island is home to Britain's largest colony of avocets, also breeding terns and many wading birds in spring and autumn. Accessible by boat with permit from warden.

5 Turn right and follow the bridleway along the field edge to a track. Cross the track and the field corner and bear right along the field edge. Follow the bridleway below Lodge Farm, keeping to the field edge and then through the centre of a field to reach a lane.

6 Turn left and follow the lane towards Orford. Pass the 30mph sign and soon take the footpath left across the corner of a field towards houses. Pass between fences to a road, then cross over to follow the enclosed path to the churchyard. Walk through the churchyard, pass the church entrance and continue to road and the village square by the Kings Head. Retrace steps back to the Crown & Castle.

For pub entry see page 185

Orford Church

The White Swan, Pickering

On the Right Track in Newtondale

Begin this moorland ramble with a ride on a steam railway, then explore the splendour of Newtondale, and Levisham village. Superb views across the Vale of Pickering.

Start. Alight at Levisham Station, cross to the signal box and walk the lane to cross a cattle grid. Take the signed footpath, right, for Levisham, a steep path through woods emerging into a pasture. Stick with the wall, left, to cross a stile at the head of the field and turn right to a path junction. Take the steepest path, signed 'Village', rising up the side of Newtondale. The path becomes a ledged track before reaching another stile. Walk the left side of two fields to reach a lane; go ahead into Levisham.

Start

2 Follow the single street down to a bend and take the signed path left. Keep right at the fork past a bench and shortly bend left. Within a few paces take a steep path right, dropping back to the road. Turn left to find a rough lane on the right, signed 'Link'. Drop into the valley of Levisham Beck to reach the ruined St Mary's Church. Cross the footbridge beyond and rise to a wide field road and turn right. Continue through pastures and woodland; just beyond the woods keep right to reach the farm and tearooms at Farwath.

North Yorkshire Moors Railway

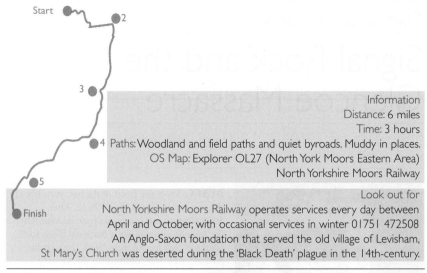

Start
2
3
4
5
Finish

Information
Distance: 6 miles
Time: 3 hours
Paths: Woodland and field paths and quiet byroads. Muddy in places.
OS Map: Explorer OL27 (North York Moors Eastern Area)
North Yorkshire Moors Railway

Look out for
North Yorkshire Moors Railway operates services every day between
April and October, with occasional services in winter 01751 472508
An Anglo-Saxon foundation that served the old village of Levisham,
St Mary's Church was deserted during the 'Black Death' plague in the 14th-century.

3 Cross the railway and then the footbridge across Pickering Beck. Turn immediately left and head uphill along the dirt path. At a cross-track bear left to a fork and take the steeper option to the right. Climb steadily through the woods, eventually emerging into a field and head diagonally across to the ruined barn. Beside this is a field gate (the right-hand one of two visible), take this and turn left, tracing the field road (signed Newtondale Horse Trail) to a farm.

4 Join the farm drive, pass a second farm complex and keep right at a fork at an artificial pond, the farm road eventually losing itself in fields. Keep left of the isolated barn to a gate into woods. Descend the track through the trees to a rough lane. Turn right and remain on it past a railway depot. Turn left along the main road and cross both the railway and Pickering Beck.

5 100 yards past the beck turn right to cross a footbridge. Walk past the cottages, re-cross the line and pass a terrace to find a footpath on the left along a field track. Cross the tops of meadows to and past a cottage and then along a rough lane to a sharp right bend. Take the field gate on the left, and then follow path to a walled corner beside the beck. Cross step stile to access a waterside path, remaining on this to cross a level crossing. Turn right along the road to Pickering Station.

For pub entry see page 222

Clachaig Inn, Glencoe

Signal Rock and the Glencoe Massacre

A short forest walk reveals some surprising views of this great mountain valley.

Clachaig Inn

Start. From the front of the inn, turn left up the road towards Glencoe village. After 50 yards turn left into a car parking area. On the far side you will see a National Trust for Scotland sign for An Torr. Walk through the parking area and continue up the forestry track to a gate in the deer fence. Go through the gate and continue along the forest track. After 110 yards take the path ascending on the right, signposted 'An Torr'.

2 Follow the narrow footpath as it climbs up through woods to the highpoint of An Torr. There are views behind you into Clachaig Gully. From the rocky outcrop there are views across Achnacon towards Meall Mor. From the summit retrace your steps back to the larger forestry track and turn right. Continue as it winds past an area of clear felled woodland and swings left down to a junction.

Glencoe

3 Turn right here, following the sign for Signal Rock. The track swings round to the left past another area of clear felled woodland. Ignore turnings to the left and right and continue up the muddy bank. Over the brow of a rise, continue to a gate in a deer fence and an NTS sign explaining access rights to Signal Rock.

4 Go through a deer gate and follow the track. It leads over a little shoulder and down some rocky steps. As it levels out in a clearing, ignore paths right and left and continue up the bank opposite with wood and earth steps cut into it.

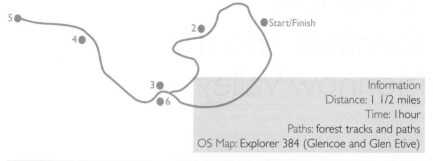

5

4

2 ● Start/Finish

3
6

Information
Distance: 1 1/2 miles
Time: 1 hour
Paths: forest tracks and paths
OS Map: Explorer 384 (Glencoe and Glen Etive)

Look out for
Glencoe provides walkers and climbers with a formidable range of mountains to clamber all over. The glen achieved its principal notoriety in 1692, when 38 members of the MacDonald clan were murdered here by Government troops. Signal Rock is believed to be the point from which the Government troopers gave the signal to move on the MacDonald clansmen.

Glencoe

River Coe

5 At the top of the hill, Signal Rock comes into view. A short scramble leads up to the summit, or you can slip round on a path to the right of the rock and ascend by the series of steps on far side. Now retrace your steps to the junction passed on your outward journey with signs to Signal Rock and Clachaig Inn.

6 Bear right and carry on the good track down to the kissing gate in deer fence. Descend to the river. The bridge here over the River Coe used to give access to the old visitor centre, before its site was levelled. Don't cross the bridge but turn left along the riverside path to some stepping stones. Cross over and turn left again now following the tributary upstream with the fence on the right. Follow the little path as it crosses another tributary and eventually emerges on a back road to Glencoe village. Turn left to return to the inn.

For pub entry see page 237

The Bell at Skenfrith

Skenfrith and the Monnow Valley

A delightful riverside walk through the peaceful Monnow Valley with a final sharp ascent to the top of Coedanghred Hill for glorious views across Skenfrith and the upper Monnow Valley to the Black Mountains.

The Bell at Skenfrith

Start. Cross the river bridge on leaving the pub and take the path right, signed 'Tregate Bridge 6.5km'. Follow the path beside the River Monnow and pass in front of Sand House. Walk through a copse to a stile and bear right around the field beside the river. Bear left in the corner and follow the arrowed path right into the adjacent field. Bear slightly left towards farm buildings and silos, cross a stile and continue up the slope to a gate.

2 Walk through the farm (Llanrothal) and follow the access lane to cottages. Cross the stream and take the footpath right and soon follow the path left to reach St John the Baptist Church. Exit the churchyard via a stile and turn left around the field edge. Follow the river for nearly a mile to a stile and turn right across Tregate Bridge.

3 Cross the stile on your right and bear diagonally left across the field towards a farm. Pass through a gate and continue behind the farm to a gate and poplar plantation.

Short Walk:

Follow the path ahead and walk through the plantation, crossing a stream and eventually exiting the woodland on reaching the riverbank. Bear left across the field, soon to rejoin the riverbank and keep beside the river through more woodland, soon to join the road by a house. Turn left steeply uphill, bearing right at the top (join long walk at directions 8).

Long walk:

4 Turn left to a stile on the plantation edge and left again along the field edge to a stile. Bear right to the farm drive and walk uphill to the road. Turn right, then as you begin to descend cross the stile on the left and follow the narrow path beside fencing downhill towards a house. Pass in front of a garage, drop down steps and continue downhill (can be overgrown) to cross the stream and the stile ahead.

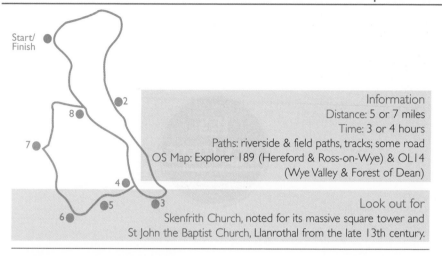

Information
Distance: 5 or 7 miles
Time: 3 or 4 hours
Paths: riverside & field paths, tracks; some road
OS Map: Explorer 189 (Hereford & Ross-on-Wye) & OL14
(Wye Valley & Forest of Dean)

Look out for
Skenfrith Church, noted for its massive square tower and
St John the Baptist Church, Llanrothal from the late 13th century.

Start

5 Keep ahead along the field edge, cross a stile and footbridge on your right and walk in front of a derelict cottage to a stile. Proceed across the field, ignore the stile on the boundary and turn left up the field edge to a stile. Climb the stile immediately to your right and bear half-left to pass to the right of a barn to a stile. Bear left and enter St Maughans churchyard.

6 At the road turn right, pass a farm, then at a fork of drives bear right towards Little Coxstone. Descend steeply, then follow the hedged track to the left of the property uphill, then descend to a stream. Climb up the sunken path (can be very wet), the path soon becoming a track leading to a metalled drive opposite a bungalow.

7 Turn right, pass to the left of the farmhouse, then at a track turn left downhill to a junction of paths. Bear right, then left and ascend beside woodland towards a house on the hill. Follow the field edge left, pass below White House to reach the drive. Turn right, then turn left at the T-junction at the top of a steep hill.

8 At a fork, keep left up the drive, pass to the left of the property and continue across the side of Coedanghred Hill. Soon steeply ascend and pass beside a house to reach a stile on the summit. Descend steeply through fields to reach a lane. Turn left back to the inn.
For pub entry see page 256

Les Routiers Guide - De bons restaurants pas chers et pour tous was originally written for truck drivers who were looking for fairly priced hotels and restaurants. It soon became popular with travelling salesmen, French and foreign tourists.

Today, the red and blue Les Routiers sign has become a cult symbol, standing alongside the Gitannes pack and the Ricard logo as the essence of French style, and the Routiers' original concept of a warm homely welcome and affordable good value is as strong today as when it was first conceived in the 1930s.

Les Routiers Guide - De bons restaurants pas chers et pour tous is a boon for travellers in France, listing simple, inexpensive roadside restaurants and hotels for both truck drivers and motorists.

To obtain a copy visit:

www.routiers.com

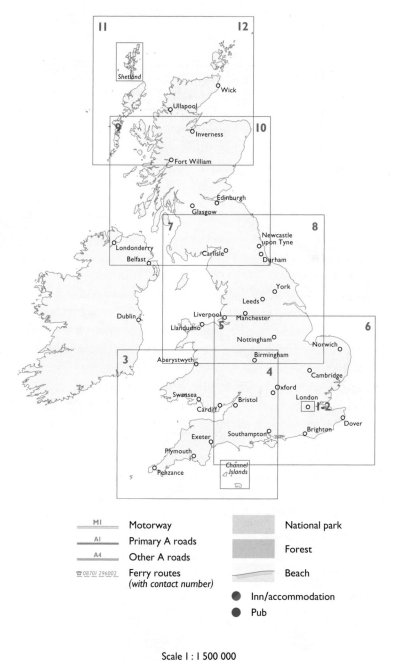

11		12	

Shetland

Wick

Ullapool

9

Inverness

10

Fort William

Edinburgh

Glasgow

7

8

Newcastle upon Tyne

Londonderry

Carlisle

Durham

Belfast

York

Leeds

Liverpool

Manchester

6

Dublin

Llandudno

5

Nottingham

Norwich

Aberystwyth

3

Birmingham

4

Cambridge

Swansea

Oxford

London

1-2

Cardiff

Bristol

Dover

Exeter

Southampton

Brighton

Plymouth

Penzance

Channel Islands

M1 — Motorway	▦ National park
A1 — Primary A roads	▦ Forest
A4 — Other A roads	≈ Beach
☎ 08701 296002 Ferry routes *(with contact number)*	● Inn/accommodation
	● Pub

Scale 1 : 1 500 000

```
0        10        20        30        40        50 miles
0   10   20   30   40   50   60   70 km
```

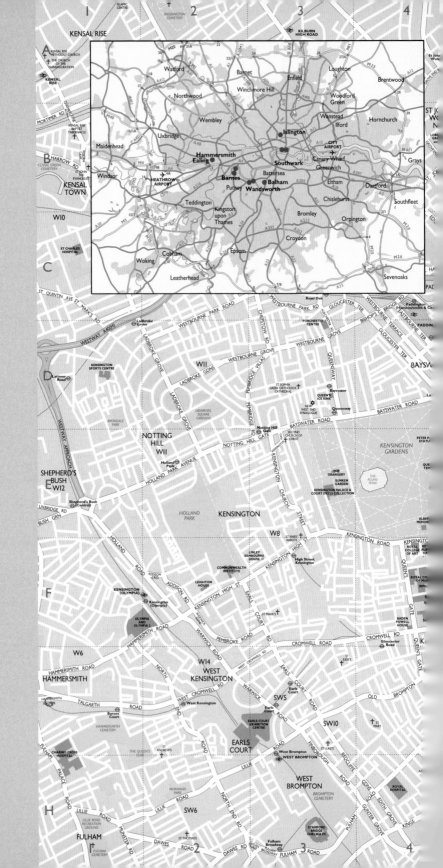

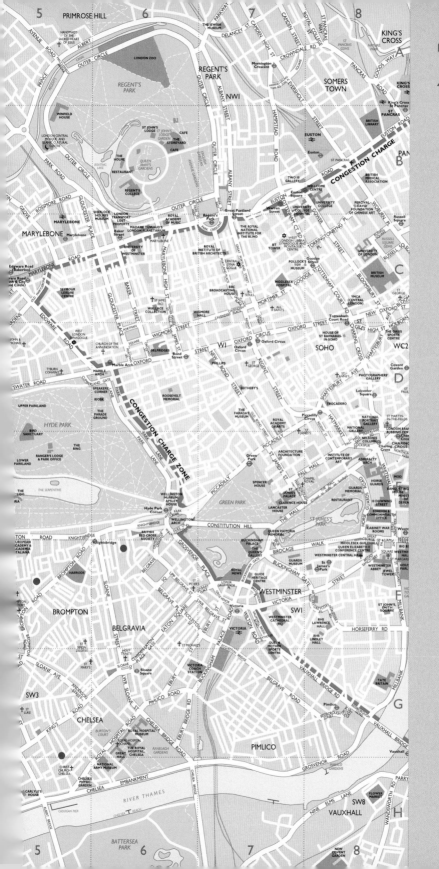

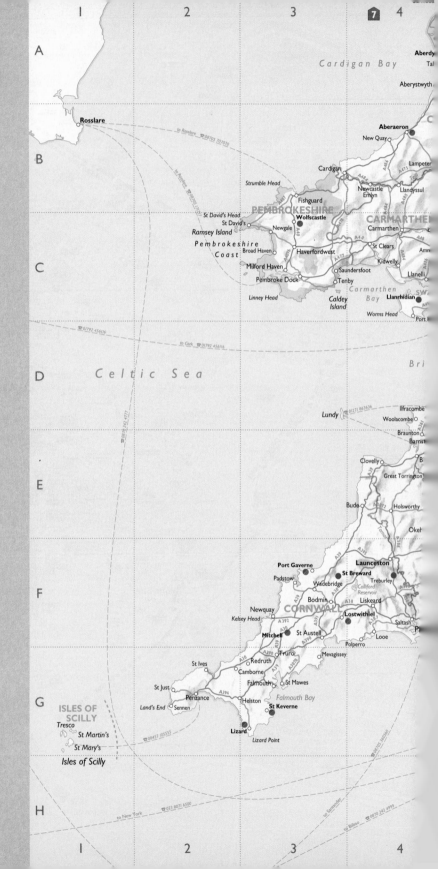

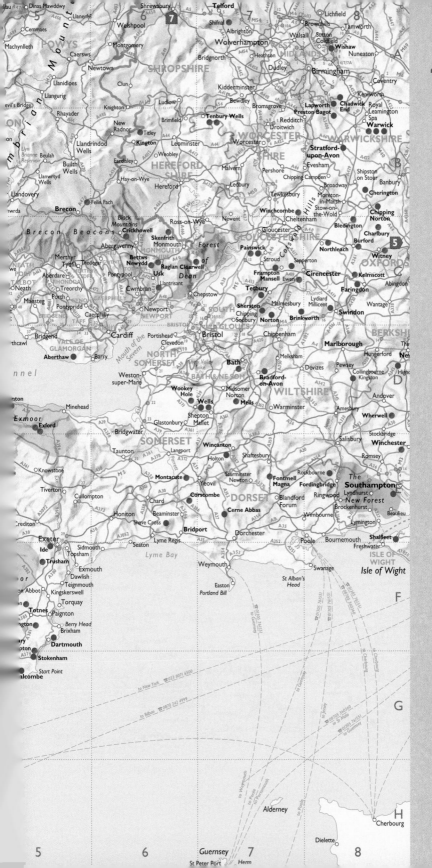

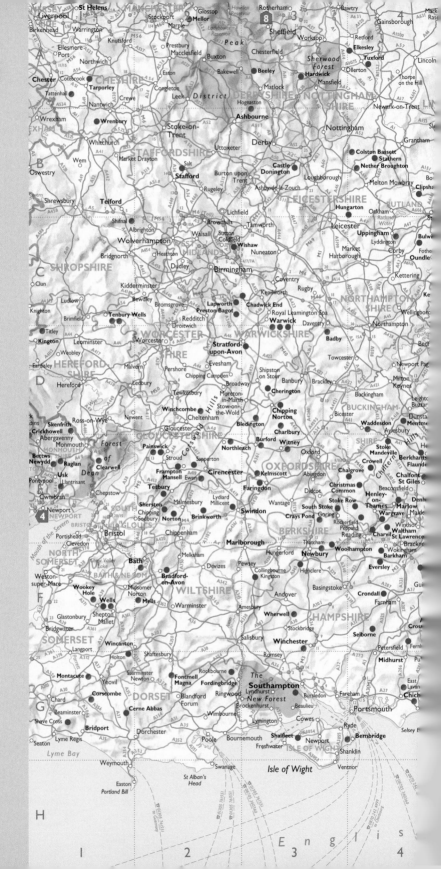

5

8

A

B

C

D

E

F

G

H

1   2   3   4

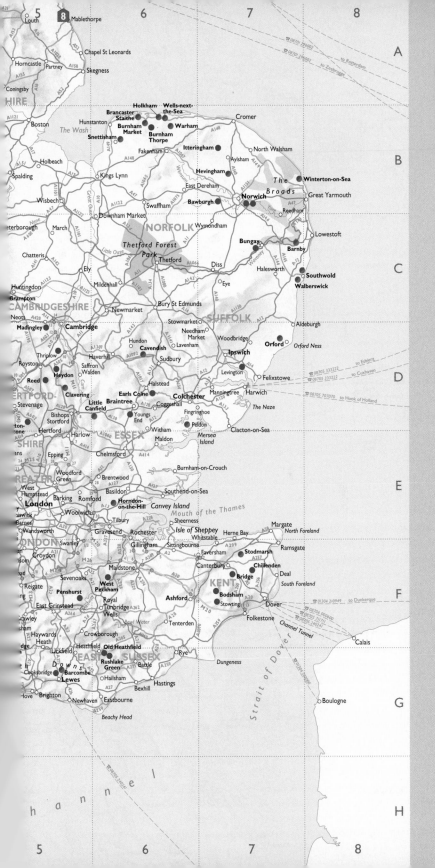

2 · LANARKSHIRE · 3 · SCOTTISH BORDERS · 4

Ardrossan · Kilmarnock · Peebles · Galashiels · Melrose · Colds
Irvine · Biggar · **10** · Selkirk · Kelso
Troon · EAST · A76 · A708 · Hawick · Jedburgh
Ayr · AYRSHIRE · **Tweedsmuir** · The Cheviot Hi · Ne
Cumnock
A · Patna · New · Sanquhar · Moffat · Kielder
Maybole · Cumnock · Dalmellington · Beattock · Water · Stannerst
Girvan · SOUTH · Kielder
AYRSHIRE · Loch Doon · DUMFRIES AND GALLOWAY · Forest
Ballantrae · Galloway · Langholm · Park
Forest · New · Dumfries
B · Cairnryan · Park · Galloway · Gretna · Longtown · Brampton
Newton · Castle Douglas · Dumfries · South Tyne
Glenluce · Stewart · A75 · Wigton · Carlisle · Alston
Loch · Kirkcudbright · M6 · Armathwaite
Drummore · Whithorn · Ken · Abbey · Solway Firth · Great Salkeld · Melmerby
Mull of · Burrow · **Isle of** · Head · Maryport · CUMBRIA · **Penrith** · Applet
Galloway · Head · **Whithorn** · Cockermouth · Ullswater · Tirril · Westn
C · Workington · Bassenthwaite · Keswick · Lake
Whitehaven · Buttermere · Lake District · Kendal · Sedbergh
St Bees Head · **Ennerdale** · Grasmere · York
Bridge · **Wasdale** · **Ambleside** · Troutbeck · Appleby
Egremont · **Head** · **Hawkshead** · **Windermere** · Kirkby
Seascale · Boot · **Coniston** · Milnthorpe · Lonsdale
D · Isle of Man · Ramsey · **Eskdale** · Hornby
Maughold Head · **Broughton-** · Cartmel · Grange- · Carnforth
Peel · Laxey · **in-Furness** · over-Sands
Contrary Head · Douglas · Barrow-in-Furness · Morecambe · Lancaster
Castletown · Isle of Walney · Bay · Morecambe
Spanish · Heysham
Head · LANCASH
E · Fleetwood · **Whitewell** · Down
Clitheroe
Blackpool · Poulton-le-Fylde · **Kirkham** · Bla
Irish Sea · Lytham · Preston
St Anne's · Leyland · Ramsb
Southport · Mawdesley · Wrightington
F · Ormskirk · Bar
Amlwch · **Wigan**
ISLE OF · Crank
ANGLESEY · Wallasey · Liverpool · **St Helens**
Holyhead · Great Ormes · Birkenhead · Warrington · Knu
Anglesey · Head · **Llandudno** · Prestatyn
Holy Island · Llangefni · Conwy · Colwyn · Rhyl · Mostyn · Ellesmere
Rhosneigr · Bangor · Bay · St George · Holywell · Port · Northwich
G · Caernarfon · Llanrwst · Asaph · Denbigh · **Chester** · CHES
Capel · Betws-y-coed · Mold · Tattenhall · Cotebrook · **Tarporley**
Caernarfon · Curig · Ruthin · Nantwich
Bay · Beddgelert · Blaenau · Cerrigydrudion · Wrexham · **Wren**
Nefyn · Criccieth · Ffestiniog · Llangollen · Whitchur
Pwllheli · Porthmadog · Bala · Wem
H · Abersoch · Snowdonia · Oswestry · **Telfo**
Bardsey Island · Llanbedr · Lake · Llanfyllin
Barmouth · Dolgellau · Dinas Mawddwy · Llanerfyl · Shrewsbury
Cemmaes · POWYS · Welshpool · S
Aberdyfi · Machynlleth · **4** · Caersws · Montgomery · Bridg
Cardigan Bay · Talybont · Newtown · SHROPSHIRE
Llanidloes · 3 · 4

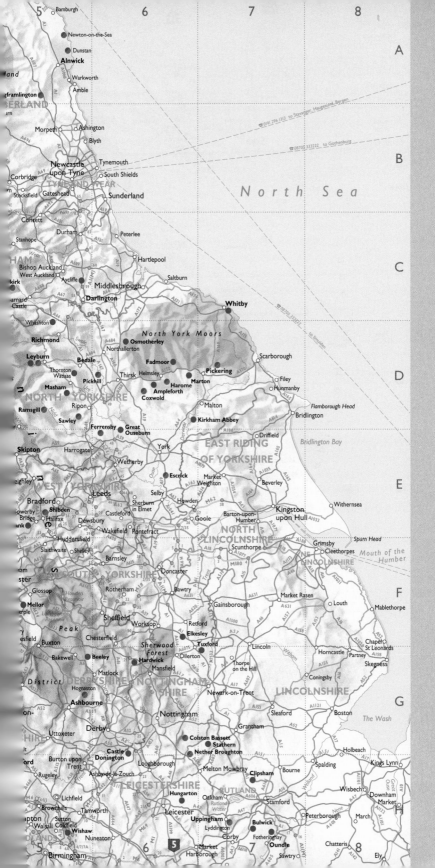

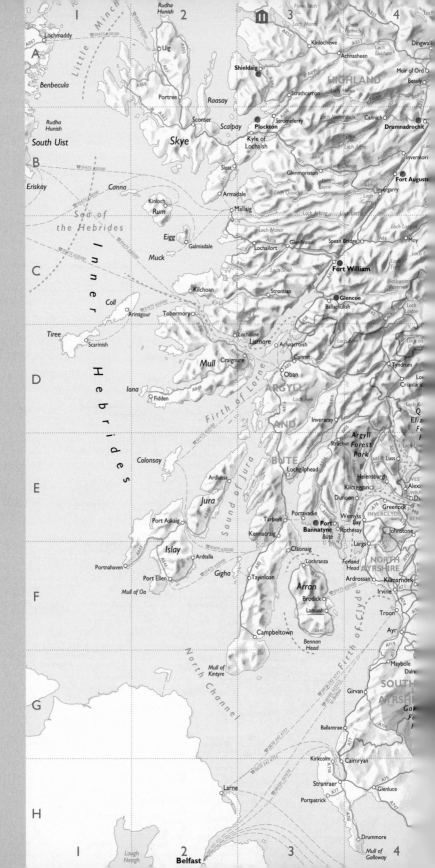

9

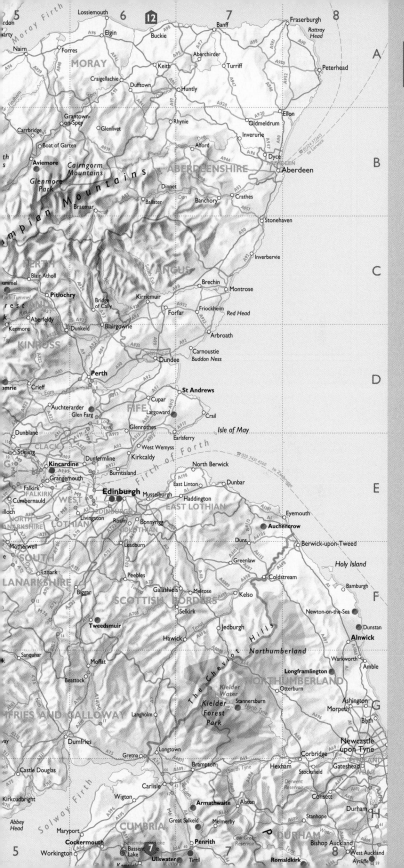

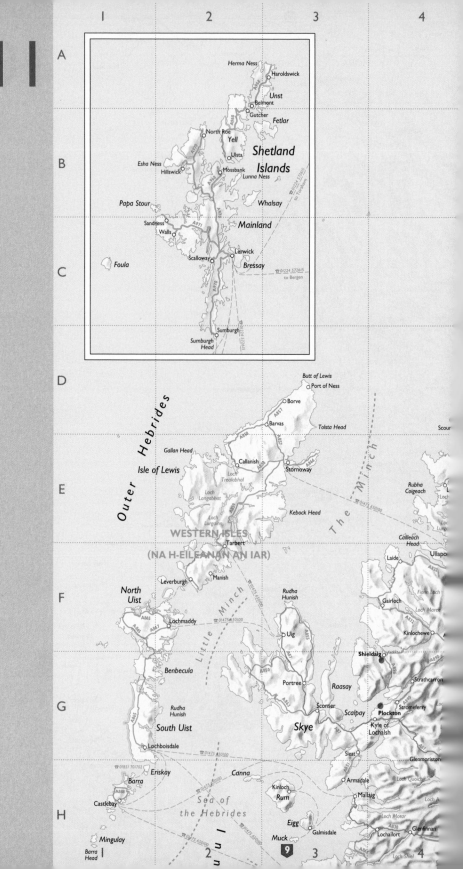

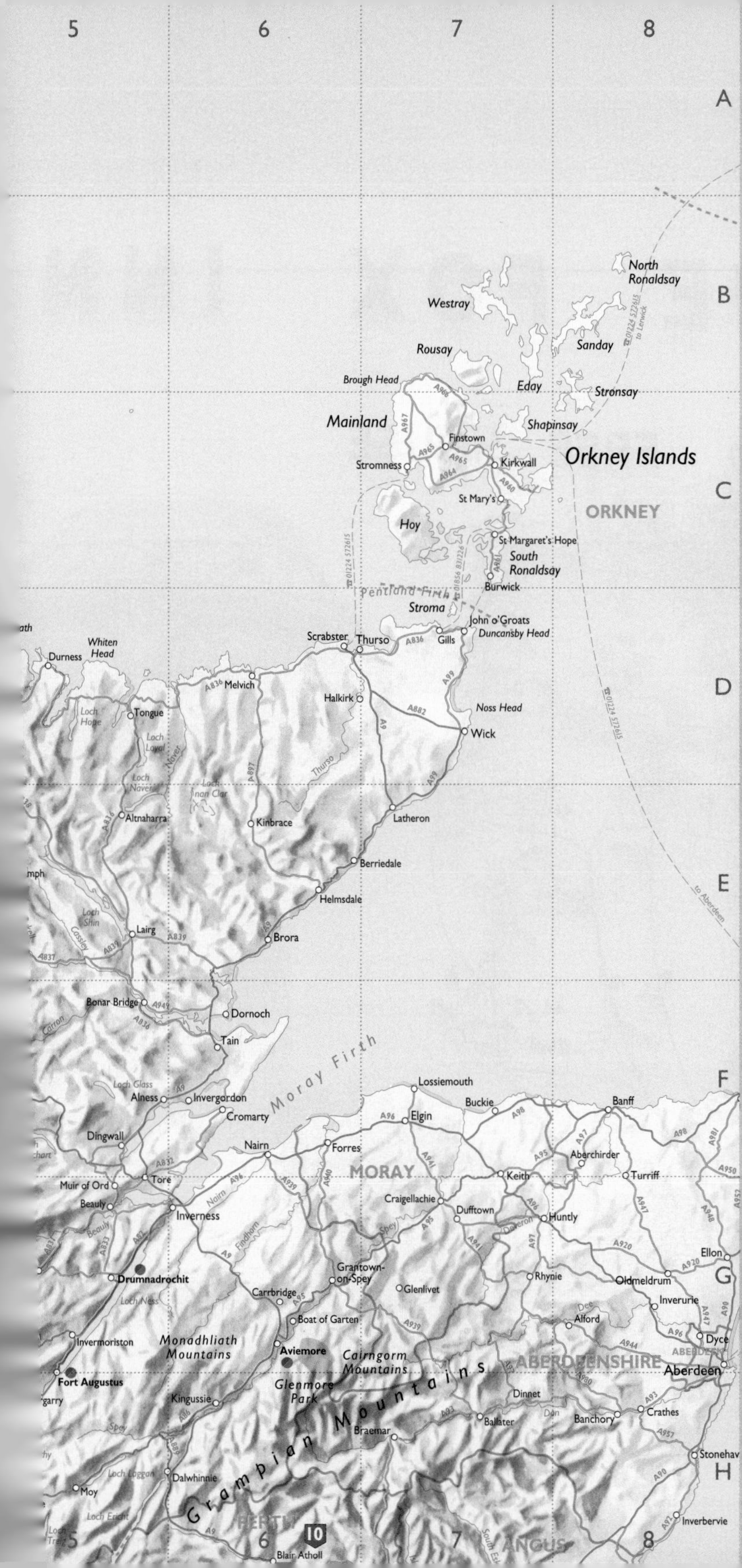
5
6
7
8
A
B
C
D
E
F
G
H
North Ronaldsay
Westray
Sanday
Rousay
Brough Head
Eday
Stronsay
Mainland
Shapinsay
Finstown
Orkney Islands
Stromness
Kirkwall
ORKNEY
St Mary's
Hoy
St Margaret's Hope
South Ronaldsay
Burwick
Pentland Firth
Stroma
John o'Groats
Duncansby Head
Scrabster
Thurso
Gills
Whiten Head
Durness
Melvich
Halkirk
Noss Head
Wick
Tongue
Loch Hope
Loch Loyal
Loch Naver
Loch nan Clar
Thurso
Altnaharra
Kinbrace
Latheron
Berriedale
Helmsdale
Loch Shin
Lairg
Brora
Bonar Bridge
Dornoch
Tain
Moray Firth
Loch Glass
Alness
Invergordon
Cromarty
Lossiemouth
Buckie
Banff
Elgin
Dingwall
Nairn
Forres
Aberchirder
MORAY
Keith
Turriff
Muir of Ord
Tore
Beauly
Inverness
Craigellachie
Dufftown
Huntly
Ellon
Drumnadrochit
Loch Ness
Grantown-on-Spey
Rhynie
Oldmeldrum
Carrbridge
Glenlivet
Inverurie
Boat of Garten
Alford
Dyce
Invermoriston
Monadhliath Mountains
Aviemore
Cairngorm Mountains
ABERDEENSHIRE
Aberdeen
Fort Augustus
Glenmore Park
Dinnet
Kingussie
Grampian Mountains
Ballater
Banchory
Crathes
Braemar
Stonehav
Loch Laggan
Dalwhinnie
Moy
Loch Ericht
PERTH
10
ANGUS
Inverbervie
Blair Atholl
to Lerwick
to Aberdeen

The Fox Inn, Corscombe, Dorset

A-Z by Establishment Name

A Room in the West End and
  Teuchters Bar, Edinburgh, 231
Abbey Inn, Coxwold, North Yorkshire 209
Alfold Barn, Alfold Crossways, Surrey 189
Alford Arms, Berkhamsted, Hertfordshire 115
Alma Tavern, South West London 42
Anchor Inn, Barcombe, East Sussex 191
Anglers Arms, Longframlington,
  Northumberland 155
Appletree Country Inn, Marton,
  North Yorkshire 218
Assheton Arms, Downham, Lancashire 130
Bar 7, Whitby, North Yorkshire 225
Barleycorn Inn, Marlborough, Wiltshire 203
Bear Hotel, Crickhowell, Powys 258
Beaufort Arms Coaching Inn
  and Restaurant, Raglan, Monmouthshire 253
Bell at Sapperton, Cirencester,
  Gloucestershire 99
Bell at Skenfrith, Skenfrith, Monmouthshire 256
Bell Inn, Walberswick, Suffolk 188
Bell Inn & Hill House, Horndon-on-the-Hill,
  Essex 98
Benleva Hotel, Drumnadrochit, Highland 236
Black Bear Inn, Bettws Newydd,
  Monmouthshire 253
Black Boy Inn, Hungarton, Leicestershire 133
Black Bull, Coniston, Cumbria 74
Black Bull Inn, Escrick, North Yorkshire 210
Black Sheep Brewery, Masham, North Yorkshire 219
Blacksmiths Arms, Broughton in Furness,
  Cumbria 73
Blue Anchor, Aberthaw, Vale of Glamorgan 263
Boot Inn, Lapworth, Warwickshire 196
Brackenrigg Inn, Ullswater, Cumbria 79
Bricklayers Arms, Flaunden, Hertfordshire 116
Bridge Pub and Dining Rooms,
  South West London 42
Bryce's, Ockley, Surrey 189
Buck Inn, Bedale, North Yorkshire 209
Bull at Broughton, Skipton, North Yorkshire 225
Bull Inn, Barkham, Berkshire 48
Bull Inn, Charlbury, Oxfordshire 161
Bull's Head and Stables Bistro,
  South West London 43
Bunk Inn, Newbury, Berkshire 49
Burnmoor Inn, Eskdale, Cumbria 75
Butchers Arms, Painswick, Gloucestershire 107
Cabinet, Reed, Hertfordshire 116
Cadgwith Cove Inn, The Lizard, Cornwall 70
Café Royal Circle Bar and Oyster Bar Restaurant,
  Edinburgh 232
California Country Inn, Modbury, Devon 88
Carpenters Arms, Sherston, Wiltshire 204
Carved Angel, Earls Colne, Essex 97

Castle Hotel, Hornby, Lancashire 130
Chequers, Chipping Norton, Oxfordshire 161
Cherington Arms, Cherington, Warwickshire 196
Clachaig Inn, Glencoe, Highland 237
Cock Inn, Wishaw, Birmingham 201
Coopers Arms, South West London 43
Cottage Inn, Alnwick, Northumberland 153
County, Darlington, Co Durham 64
Crab & Lobster Inn, Benbridge, Isle of Wight 121
Crabmill, Preston Bagot, Warwickshire 197
Craw Inn, Auchencrow, Scottish Borders 247
Cricketers, Clavering, Essex 96
Cridford Inn, Trusham, Devon 90
Crook Inn, Tweedsmuir, Scottish Borders 274
Crooked Billet, Stoke Row, Oxfordshire 167
Crown, Great Ouseburn, North Yorkshire 211
Crown, Southwold, Suffolk 188
Crown and Castle, Orford, Suffolk 185
Crown at Wells and Anton's Bistrot, Wells,
  Somerset 175
Crown & Coach House, Fontmell Magna, Dorset 95
Crown Hotel, Exford, Somerset 173
Crown Hotel, Wells-next-to-Sea, Norfolk 151
Dalesman Country Inn, Sedbergh, Cumbria 79
Devonshire Arms, Beeley, Derbyshire 83
Drapers Arms, North London 39
Drunken Duck Inn, Ambleside, Cumbria 71
Duke of Cumberland, Midhurst, West Sussex 195
Duke of York, North West London 39
Dukes Head, Armathwaite, Cumbria 72
Durham Ox, Warwick, Warwickshire 199
Dusty Miller, Wrenbury, Cheshire 64
Exmoor White Horse Inn, Exford, Somerset 174
Falcon Inn, Oundle, Northamptonshire 153
Falcon Inn, Painswick, Gloucestershire 108
Famous Bein Inn, Perth, Perth & Kinross 244
Felin Fach Griffin, Brecon, Powys 258
Fisherman's Return, Winterton-on-Sea, Norfolk 151
Five Arrows Hotel, Waddesdon, Buckinghamshire 57
Fleece, Witney, Oxfordshire 167
Floating Bridge Inn, Dartmouth, Devon 86
Fountain Inn, Tenbury Wells, Worcestershire 205
Fountain Inn and Boxer's Restaurant, Wells,
  Somerset 176
Fox and Barrel, Tarporley, Cheshire 63
Fox and Hounds, Christmas Common,
  Oxfordshire 162
Fox Inn, Corscombe, Dorset 94
Friar's Head at Akebar, Leyburn, North Yorkshire 213
Froggies at the Timber Batts, Bodsham, Kent 123
General Tarleton Inn, Ferrensby, North Yorkshire 211
George, Cavendish, Suffolk 183
George and the Dragon, Watton-at-Stone,
  Hertfordshire 117
George & Dragon, Chichester, West Sussex 193

Golden Lion, Osmotherley, North Yorkshire	219
Golden Pot, Eversley, Hampshire	110
Grange Hotel, Brampton, Cambridgeshire	58
Green Dragon, Braintree, Essex	95
Green Man, Cambridge, Cambridgeshire	58
Green Man, Partridge Green, West Sussex	195
Greyhound, Henley-on-Thames, Oxfordshire	166
Greyhound Inn, Chalfont St Peter, Buckinghamshire	52
Greyhound Inn Hotel, Usk, Monmouthshire	256
Griffins Head, Chillenden, Kent	126
Grog & Gruel, Fort William, Inverness	239
Grove, South West London	44
Hack & Spade Inn, Richmond, North Yorkshire	224
Hampshire Arms, Crondall, Hampshire	110
Harbourmaster Hotel, Aberaeron, Ceredigion	250
Hardwick Inn, Hardwick, Derbyshire	84
Highland Drove Inn, Penrith, Cumbria	78
Holly Bush, Stafford, Staffordshire	177
Horse and Groom, Rushlake Green, East Sussex	192
Hoste Arms, Burnham Market, Norfolk	142
Hundred House Hotel, Telford, Shropshire	172
Hunters Rest Inn, Bath	48
Inn at Lathones, St Andrews, Fife	233
Inn at Whitewell, Whitewell, Lancashire	132
Inn @ West End, West End, Surrey	190
Ivy House, Chalfont St Giles, Buckinghamshire	52
King William IV, Heydon, Cambridgeshire	59
Kings Arms, Bradford-on-Avon, Wiltshire	202
Kings Arms Inn, Montacute, Somerset	175
Kings Head, Bawburgh, Norfolk	139
Kings Head Inn, Bledington, Oxfordshire	157
Kinmel Arms, St George, Conwy	251
Lamb Inn, Burford, Oxfordshire	160
Land's End, Charvil, Berkshire	49
Last Wine Bar and Restaurant, Norwich, Norfolk	148
Lay and Wheeler in Leadenhall Market, Central London	36
Lay & Wheeler on Cornhill, Central London	36
Lion and Lamb, Little Canfield, Essex	98
Loch Inn, Fort Augustus, Highland	237
Loch Tummel Inn, Pitlochry, Perth & Kinross	245
Lord Nelson, Burnham Thorpe, Norfolk	143
Marsham Arms Inn, Hevingham, Norfolk	143
Martins Arms Inn, Colston Bassett, Nottinghamshire	155
Millbank, Mill Bank, West Yorkshire	226
Mulberry Tree, Wigan, Lancashire	133
Mussel and Crab, Tuxford, Nottinghamshire	156
Nag's Head, Central London	37
Nags Head Inn, Castle Donington, Derbyshire	84
Nags Head Inn, Pickhill, North Yorkshire	222
New Inn, Shalfleet, Isle of Wight	122
Oddfellows Arms, Mellor, Cheshire	63
Old Bridge Inn, Aviemore, Highland	236
Old Inn, St Breward, Cornwall	68
Old Inn, Wincanton, Somerset	176
Old White Hart Inn, Uppingham, Rutland	171
Olive Branch, Clipsham, Rutland	171
One Elm, Stratford-upon-Avon, Warwickshire	197
Orange Tree, Chadwick End, West Midlands	200
Peacock Inn, Tenbury Wells, Worcestershire	205
Peldon Rose Inn, Colchester, Essex	97
Penhelig Arms Hotel, Aberdyfi, Gwynedd	252
Perch & Pike Inn, South Stoke, Oxfordshire	166
Pheasant, Cockermouth, Cumbria	73
Pheasant Inn, Chester, Cheshire	62
Pheasant Inn, Keyston, Cambridgeshire	59
Pheasant Inn, Kielder Water, Northumberland	154
Plockton Hotel, Plockton, Highland	238
Plough at Kelmscott, Kelmscott, Gloucestershire	103
Plough Inn, Fadmoor, North Yorkshire	210
Plume of Feathers, Mitchell, Cornwall	67
Port Gaverne Hotel, Port Gaverne, Cornwall	68
Queen's Head, Bulwick, Northamptonshire	152
Queen's Head, Llandudno, Conwy	250
Queen's Head Hotel, Hawkshead, Cumbria	75
Queen's Head Inn , Penrith, Cumbria	78
Queens Head, Windermere, Cumbria	82
Rainbow Inn, Lewes, East Sussex	191
Red Cat, St Helens, Merseyside	138
Red House, Nether Broughton, Leicestershire	135
Red Lion, South West London	45
Red Lion, Mawdesley, Lancashire	131
Red Lion, Stodmarsh, Kent	127
Red Lion Inn, Ashbourne, Derbyshire	83
Red Lion Inn, Chalgrove, Oxfordshire	160
Red Lion Inn, Stathern, Leicestershire	138
Robin Hood Inn, Elkesley, Nottinghamshire	156
Rose and Crown, Snettisham, Norfolk	149
Rose and Crown, Warwick, Warwickshire	199
Rose and Crown at Romaldkirk, Romaldkirk, Co Durham	65
Rose and Thistle, Fordingbridge, Hampshire	111
Royal Hotel, Comrie, Perth & Kinross	244
Royal Oak, Cerne Abbas, Dorset	91
Royal Oak, Chichester, West Sussex	194
Royal Oak, Lostwithiel, Cornwall	66
Royal Oak, Marlow, Buckinghamshire	53
Russian Tavern at The Port Royal Hotel, Isle of Bute, Argyll & Bute	230
Sandpiper Inn, Leyburn, North Yorkshire	218
Sawley Arms and Cottages, Sawley, North Yorkshire	224
Saxon Mill, Warwick, Warwickshire	200
Sea Trout Inn, Totnes, Devon	90
Selborne Arms, Selborne, Hampshire	111
Shave Cross Inn, Bridport, Dorset	91
Shepherd's Arms Hotel, Ennerdale, Cumbria	74
Shepherd's Crook, Crowell, Oxfordshire	163
Shibden Mill Inn, Shibden, West Yorkshire	227
Shieldaig Bar, Shieldaig, Highland	239
Ship Inn, Alnwick, Northumberland	154
Ship Inn, Ipswich, Suffolk	184

Ship Inn, South West London	45
Snooty Fox Inn, Faringdon, Oxfordshire	163
Spotted Dog, Penshurst, Kent	126
Springer Spaniel, Launceston, Cornwall	66
St George & Dragon, Wargrave, Berkshire	51
St Peter's Hall, Bungay, Suffolk	182
Stag, Mentmore, Buckinghamshire	56
Stagg Inn & Restaurant, Kington, Herefordshire	115
Staghunters Hotel, Lynton, Devon	87
Star Inn, Harome, North Yorkshire	212
Star Inn, Old Heathfield, East Sussex	192
Star Inn, Waltham-St-Lawrence, Berkshire	51
Steam Packet Hotel, Isle of Whithorn, Dumfries and Galloway	231
Stone Trough Inn, Kirkham Abbey, North Yorkshire	213
Sun Inn, Swindon, Wiltshire	204
Swag and Tails, Central London	37
Swan Inn, Barnby, Suffolk	182
Swan Inn, Denham, Buckinghamshire	53
Swan on the Green, West Peckham, Kent	127
Talbot 15th Century Coaching Inn, Mells, Somerset	174
Three Crowns, Brinkworth, Wiltshire	202
Three Horseshoes, Madingley, Cambridgeshire	61
Three Horseshoes, Warham, Norfolk	149
Tiger Inn, Ashford, Kent	122
Tower Inn, Slapton, Devon	89
Tradesmans Arms, Stokenham, Devon	89
Trouble House, Tetbury, Gloucestershire	108
Tufton Arms Hotel, Appleby-in-Westmorland, Cumbria	72
Twisted Oak, Exeter, Devon	87
Unicorn Inn, Kincardine, Fife	232
Victoria at Holkham, Holkham, Norfolk	147
Victoria Inn, Salcombe, Devon	88
Villa Country House Hotel, Kirkham, Lancashire	131
Vine Tree, Norton, Wiltshire	203
Walpole Arms, Itteringham, Norfolk	147
Wasdale Head Inn, Wasdale, Cumbria	82
Waterfall Hotel, Peel, Isle of Man	117
Waterman's Arms, Ashprington, Devon	86
Welcome To Town Country Bistro & Bar, Llanrhidian, Swansea	263
Wheatsheaf Hotel, Milnthorpe, Cumbria	77
Wheatsheaf Inn, Northleach, Gloucestershire	103
White Hart Hotel, St Keverne, Cornwall	70
White Hart Inn, Winchcombe, Gloucestershire	109
White Horse, Brancaster Staithe, Norfolk	139
White Horse, Frampton Mansell, Gloucestershire	102
White Horse Inn, Bridge, Kent	123
White Lion, Crays Pond, Oxfordshire	162
White Lion, Wherwell, Hampshire	113
White Star Tavern & Dining Rooms, Southampton, Hampshire	113
White Swan, Ampleforth, North Yorkshire	208
White Swan, Pickering, North Yorkshire	222
Wig and Pen, Norwich, Norfolk	148
Wild Duck Inn, Cirencester, Gloucestershire	99
Windmill at Badby, Badby, Northamptonshire	152
Wolfe Inn, Wolfscastle, Pembrokeshire	257
Wookey Hole Inn, Wookey Hole, Somerset	177
Woolpack, Stoke Mandeville, Buckinghamshire	56
Wykeham Arms, Winchester, Hampshire	114
Wyndham Arms, Clearwell, Gloucestershire	102
Yew Tree Inn, Newbury, Berkshire	50
Yorke Arms, Ramsgill, North Yorkshire	223

A-Z by Listing Town

Aberaeron, Ceredigion	250
Aberdyfi, Gwynedd	252
Aberthaw, Vale of Glamorgan	263
Alfold Crossways, Surrey	189
Alnwick, Northumberland	153
Ambleside, Cumbria	71
Ampleforth, North Yorkshire	208
Appleby-in-Westmorland, Cumbria	72
Armathwaite, Cumbria	72
Ashbourne, Derbyshire	83
Ashford, Kent	122
Ashprington, Devon	86
Auchencrow, Scottish Borders	247
Aviemore, Highland	236
Badby, Northamptonshire	152
Barcombe, East Sussex	191
Barkham, Berkshire	48
Barnby, Suffolk	182
Bath	48
Bawburgh, Norfolk	139
Bedale, North Yorkshire	209
Beeley, Derbyshire	83
Benbridge, Isle of Wight	121
Berkhamsted, Hertfordshire	115
Bettws Newydd, Monmouthshire	253
Bledington, Oxfordshire	157
Bodsham, Kent	123
Bradford-on-Avon, Wiltshire	202
Braintree, Essex	95
Brampton, Cambridgeshire	58
Brancaster Staithe, Norfolk	139
Brecon, Powys	258
Bridge, Kent	123
Bridport, Dorset	91
Brinkworth, Wiltshire	202
Broughton in Furness, Cumbria	73
Bulwick, Northamptonshire	152
Bungay, Suffolk	182
Burford, Oxfordshire	160
Burnham Market, Norfolk	142
Burnham Thorpe, Norfolk	143
Cambridge, Cambridgeshire	58
Castle Donington, Derbyshire	84
Cavendish, Suffolk	183

A-Z Index

Cerne Abbas, Dorset	91	Hevingham, Norfolk	143
Chadwick End, West Midlands	200	Heydon, Cambridgeshire	59
Chalfont St Giles, Buckinghamshire	52	Holkham, Norfolk	147
Chalfont St Peter, Buckinghamshire	52	Hornby, Lancashire	130
Chalgrove, Oxfordshire	160	Horndon-on-the-Hill, Essex	98
Charlbury, Oxfordshire	161	Hungarton, Leicestershire	133
Charvil, Berkshire	49	Ipswich, Suffolk	184
Cherington, Warwickshire	196	Isle of Bute, Argyll & Bute	230
Chester, Cheshire	62	Isle of Whithorn, Dumfries and Galloway	231
Chichester, West Sussex	193	Itteringham, Norfolk	147
Chillenden, Kent	126	Kelmscott, Gloucestershire	103
Chipping Norton, Oxfordshire	161	Keyston, Cambridgeshire	59
Christmas Common, Oxfordshire	162	Kielder Water, Northumberland	154
Cirencester, Gloucestershire	99	Kincardine, Fife	232
Cirencester, Gloucestershire	96	Kington, Herefordshire	115
Clavering, Essex	96	Kirkham, Lancashire	131
Clearwell, Gloucestershire	102	Kirkham Abbey, North Yorkshire	213
Clipsham, Rutland	171	Lapworth, Warwickshire	196
Cockermouth, Cumbria	73	Launceston, Cornwall	66
Colchester, Essex	97	Lewes, East Sussex	191
Colston Bassett, Nottinghamshire	155	Leyburn, North Yorkshire	213
Comrie, Perth & Kinross	244	Little Canfield, Essex	98
Coniston, Cumbria	74	Llandudno, Conwy	250
Corscombe, Dorset	94	Llanrhidian, Swansea	263
Coxwold, North Yorkshire	209	London	36
Crays Pond, Oxfordshire	162	Longframlington, Northumberland	155
Crickhowell, Powys	255	Lostwithiel, Cornwall	66
Crondall, Hampshire	110	Lynton, Devon	87
Crowell, Oxfordshire	163	Madingley, Cambridgeshire	61
Darlington, Co Durham	64	Marlborough, Wiltshire	203
Dartmouth, Devon	86	Marlow, Buckinghamshire	53
Denham, Buckinghamshire	53	Marton, North Yorkshire	218
Downham, Lancashire	130	Masham, North Yorkshire	219
Drumnadrochit, Highland	236	Mawdesley, Lancashire	131
Earls Colne, Essex	97	Mellor, Cheshire	63
Edinburgh	231	Mells, Somerset	174
Elkesley, Nottinghamshire	156	Mentmore, Buckinghamshire	56
Ennerdale, Cumbria	74	Midhurst, West Sussex	195
Escrick, North Yorkshire	210	Mill Bank, West Yorkshire	226
Eskdale, Cumbria	75	Milnthorpe, Cumbria	77
Eversley, Hampshire	110	Mitchell, Cornwall	67
Exeter, Devon	87	Modbury, Devon	88
Exford, Somerset	173	Montacute, Somerset	175
Fadmoor, North Yorkshire	210	Nether Broughton, Leicestershire	135
Faringdon, Oxfordshire	163	Newbury, Berkshire	49
Ferrensby, North Yorkshire	211	Northleach, Gloucestershire	103
Flaunden, Hertfordshire	116	Norton, Wiltshire	203
Fontmell Magna, Dorset	95	Norwich, Norfolk	148
Fordingbridge, Hampshire	111	Ockley, Surrey	189
Fort Augustus, Highland	237	Old Heathfield, East Sussex	192
Fort William, Inverness	239	Orford, Suffolk	185
Frampton Mansell, Gloucestershire	102	Osmotherley, North Yorkshire	219
Glencoe, Highland	237	Oundle, Northamptonshire	153
Great Ouseburn, North Yorkshire	211	Painswick, Gloucestershire	107
Hardwick, Derbyshire	84	Partridge Green, West Sussex	195
Harome, North Yorkshire	212	Peel, Isle of Man	117
Hawkshead, Cumbria	75	Penrith, Cumbria	78
Henley-on-Thames, Oxfordshire	166	Penshurst, Kent	126

Perth, Perth & Kinross	244
Pickering, North Yorkshire	222
Pickhill, North Yorkshire	122
Pitlochry, Perth & Kinross	245
Plockton, Highland	238
Port Gaverne, Cornwall	68
Preston Bagot, Warwickshire	197
Raglan, Monmouthshire	253
Ramsgill, North Yorkshire	223
Reed, Hertfordshire	116
Richmond, North Yorkshire	224
Romaldkirk, Co Durham	65
Rushlake Green, East Sussex	192
Salcombe, Devon	88
Sawley, North Yorkshire	224
Sedbergh, Cumbria	79
Selborne, Hampshire	111
Shalfleet, Isle of Wight	122
Sherston, Wiltshire	204
Shibden, West Yorkshire	227
Shieldaig, Highland	239
Skenfrith, Monmouthshire	256
Skipton, North Yorkshire	225
Slapton, Devon	89
Snettisham, Norfolk	149
South Stoke, Oxfordshire	166
Southampton, Hampshire	113
Southwold, Suffolk	188
St Andrews, Fife	233
St Breward, Cornwall	68
St George, Conwy	251
St Helens, Merseyside	138
St Keverne, Cornwall	70
Stafford, Staffordshire	177
Stathern, Leicestershire	138
Stodmarsh, Kent	127
Stoke Mandeville, Buckinghamshire	56
Stoke Row, Oxfordshire	167
Stokenham, Devon	89
Stratford-upon-Avon, Warwickshire	197
Swindon, Wiltshire	204
Tarporley, Cheshire	63
Telford, Shropshire	172
Tenbury Wells, Worcestershire	205
Tetbury, Gloucestershire	108
The Lizard, Cornwall	70
Totnes, Devon	90
Trusham, Devon	90
Tuxford, Nottinghamshire	156
Tweedsmuir, Scottish Borders	274
Ullswater, Cumbria	79
Uppingham, Rutland	171
Usk, Monmouthshire	256
Waddesdon, Buckinghamshire	57
Walberswick, Suffolk	188
Waltham-St-Lawrence, Berkshire	51
Wargrave, Berkshire	51
Warham, Norfolk	149
Warwick, Warwickshire	199
Wasdale, Cumbria	82
Watton-at-Stone, Hertfordshire	117
Wells, Somerset	175
Wells-next-to-Sea, Norfolk	151
West End, Surrey	190
West Peckham, Kent	127
Wherwell, Hampshire	113
Whitby, North Yorkshire	225
Whitewell, Lancashire	132
Wigan, Lancashire	133
Wincanton, Somerset	176
Winchcombe, Gloucestershire	109
Winchester, Hampshire	114
Windermere, Cumbria	82
Winterton-on-Sea, Norfolk	151
Wishaw, Birmingham	201
Witney, Oxfordshire	167
Wolfscastle, Pembrokeshire	257
Wookey Hole, Somerset	177
Wrenbury, Cheshire	64

Les Routiers Guides 2006
Report Form

☐ From my personal experience the following establishment should be
a member of Les Routiers.

☐ From my personal experience the following establishment should not
be a member of Les Routiers.

Establishment .... PLEASE PRINT IN BLOCK CAPITALS

Address ....

....

....

I had ☐ lunch ☐ dinner ☐ stayed there on (date) ....

Details ....

....

....

....

....

....

....

Reports received up to the end of June 2005 will be used in the research of the
2006 edition.

☐ I am not connected in any way with management or proprietors.

Name ....

Address ....

....

....

As a result of your sending Les Routiers this report form, we may send you information on Les Routiers in the future.
If you would prefer not to receive such information, please tick this box ☐

To send your report...
Fax: Complete this form and fax it to 020 7370 4528
Post: Complete this form and mail it to
The Editor, FREEPOST, Les Routiers, 190 Earl's Court Road, London, SW5 9QG
E-mail: info@routiers.co.uk

Les Routiers Guides 2006
Report Form

☐ From my personal experience the following establishment should be
a member of Les Routiers.

☐ From my personal experience the following establishment should not
be a member of Les Routiers.

Establishment
.... PLEASE PRINT IN BLOCK CAPITALS

Address
....
....

I had ☐ lunch ☐ dinner ☐ stayed there on (date)
....

Details
....
....
....
....
....
....
....

Reports received up to the end of June 2005 will be used in the research of the
2006 edition.

☐ I am not connected in any way with management or proprietors.

Name
....

Address
....
....
....

As a result of your sending Les Routiers this report form, we may send you information on Les Routiers in the future.
If you would prefer not to receive such information, please tick this box ☐

To send your report...
Fax: Complete this form and fax it to 020 7370 4528
Post: Complete this form and mail it to
The Editor, FREEPOST, Les Routiers, 190 Earl's Court Road, London, SW5 9QG
E-mail: info@routiers.co.uk

Les Routiers Guides 2006
Report Form

From my personal experience, the following establishment should be a member of Les Routiers.

From my personal experience, the following establishment should not be a member of Les Routiers.

Establishment:

Address:

Food	Wine	Service	Value	Overall impression

Details:

Reports received up to the end of June 2005 will be used in the Routiers of the 2006 edition.

I am not connected in any way with management or proprietor.

Name:

Address:

If I wish to complain about a badly run establishment even if they are not a member of Les Routiers, please tick here and follow the instructions below.

To send your report:

Fax: Complete the form and fax it to 020 7371 9529

Post: Complete the form and mail it to
The Editor, FREEPOST, Les Routiers, 199 Kings Court Road, London, SW3 5QG

E-mail: info@routiers.co.uk

Les Routiers Guides 2006
Report Form

☐ From my personal experience the following establishment should be a member of Les Routiers.

☐ From my personal experience the following establishment should not be a member of Les Routiers.

Establishment ....

PLEASE PRINT IN BLOCK CAPITALS

Address ....

....

....

I had ☐ lunch ☐ dinner ☐ stayed there on (date) ....

Details ....

....

....

....

....

....

....

....

Reports received up to the end of June 2005 will be used in the research of the 2006 edition.

☐ I am not connected in any way with management or proprietors.

Name ....

Address ....

....

....

As a result of your sending Les Routiers this report form, we may send you information on Les Routiers in the future. If you would prefer not to receive such information, please tick this box ☐

To send your report...
Fax: Complete this form and fax it to 020 7370 4528
Post: Complete this form and mail it to
The Editor, FREEPOST, Les Routiers, 190 Earl's Court Road, London, SW5 9QG
E-mail: info@routiers.co.uk

Les Routiers Guides 2006
Report Form

Les Routiers Guides 2006
Report Form

☐ From my personal experience the following establishment should be
a member of Les Routiers.

☐ From my personal experience the following establishment should not
be a member of Les Routiers.

Establishment .... PLEASE PRINT IN BLOCK CAPITALS

Address ....

....

....

I had ☐ lunch ☐ dinner ☐ stayed there on (date) ....

Details ....

....

....

....

....

....

....

Reports received up to the end of June 2005 will be used in the research of the
2006 edition.

☐ I am not connected in any way with management or proprietors.

Name ....

Address ....

....

....

As a result of your sending Les Routiers this report form, we may send you information on Les Routiers in the future.
If you would prefer not to receive such information, please tick this box ☐

To send your report...
Fax: Complete this form and fax it to 020 7370 4528
Post: Complete this form and mail it to
The Editor, FREEPOST, Les Routiers, 190 Earl's Court Road, London, SW5 9QG
E-mail: info@routiers.co.uk

Les Routiers Guides 2006
Report Form

From my personal experience the following establishment should be a member of Les Routiers:

From my personal experience the following establishment should not be a member of Les Routiers:

Establishment:

Address:

☐ Had   ☐ lunch   ☐ dinner   ☐ stayed there (in total)

Date:

Reports received up to the end of June 2005 will be used in the research of the 2006 edition.

I am not connected in any way with management or proprietors.

Name:

Address:

To send your reports:
Fax: Complete this form and fax it to 020 7370 5338
Post: Complete this form and mail it to
The Editor FREEPOST, Les Routiers, 130 Earls Court Road, London SW5 9QG
E-mail: info@routiers.co.uk

Les Routiers Pubs and Inns invite you to join them for a complimentary glass of wine

Les Routiers would like to offer all its readers the opportunity to have a complimentary glass of wine on us. Thanks to the generosity of a number of our establishments across the country, we are inviting you to go in and enjoy a free glass of wine at one of the participating Les Routiers establishments.

To take up this offer, simply look for the wine symbol 🍷 alongside the individual establishments name. Only those with wine symbols will be participating in this 'free glass of wine' offer. Then, cut out one of the vouchers from below, and take it into the establishment, ordering your free glass of wine at the same time as presenting your voucher.

Terms and Conditions

1. The offer will be valid during the individual bar opening hours of each establishment.
2. Offer valid until 1 September 2005.
3. The free glass of wine, made available for this offer, will be chosen at the discretion of the establishment.
4. Voucher holders are entitled to upgrade on the glass of wine offered and pay the difference.
5. One voucher entitles the bearer to one glass of wine only.
6. Only one voucher is valid per person.
7. The vouchers may only be used once, and must be given up upon redemption.
8. A maximum of two vouchers are valid per group/visit.
9. This offer cannot be used in conjunction with any other offer.
10. Les Routiers accepts no responsibility financial or otherwise for the misuse of this voucher.
11. All participating establishments reserve the right to refuse admission.
12. The vouchers have no monetary value and are non-transferable.
13. Photocopies of the vouchers will not be accepted.

Les Routiers
Free glass of wine
ucher is valid until Sept 1st 2005
to availability 1 voucher per person

Les Routiers
Free glass of wine
This voucher is valid until Sept 1st 2005
Subject to availability 1 voucher per person

Les Routiers
Free glass of wine
This voucher is valid until Sept 1st 2005
Subject to availability 1 voucher per person

Les Routiers
Free glass of wine
cher is valid until Sept 1st 2005
o availability 1 voucher per person

Les Routiers
Free glass of wine
This voucher is valid until Sept 1st 2005
Subject to availability 1 voucher per person

Les Routiers
Free glass of wine
This voucher is valid until Sept 1st 2005
Subject to availability 1 voucher per person

Les Routiers
Free glass of wine
her is valid until Sept 1st 2005
availability 1 voucher per person

Les Routiers
Free glass of wine
This voucher is valid until Sept 1st 2005
Subject to availability 1 voucher per person

Les Routiers
Free glass of wine
This voucher is valid until Sept 1st 2005
Subject to availability 1 voucher per person